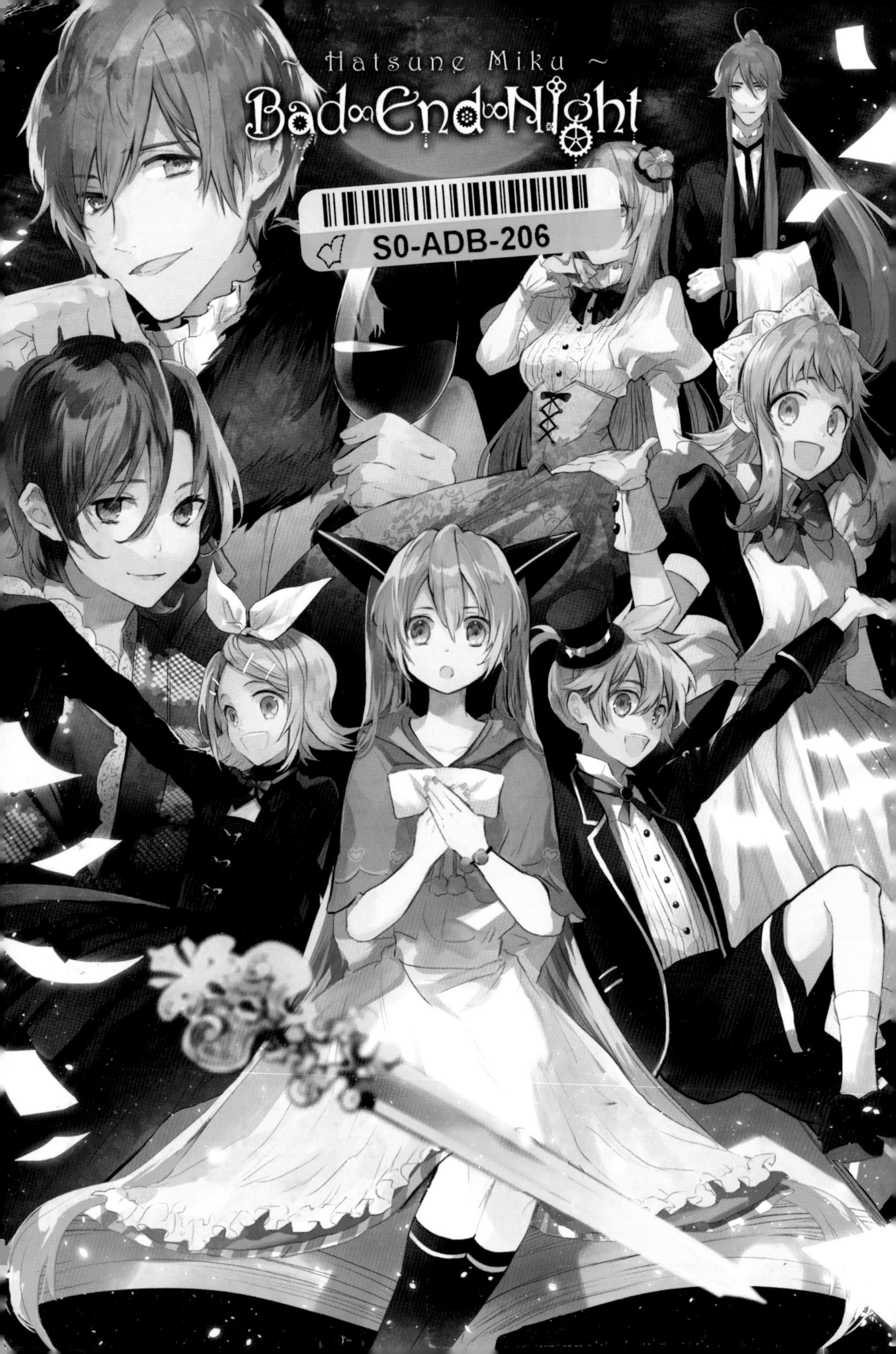
~ Hatsune Miku ~
Bad∞End∞Night

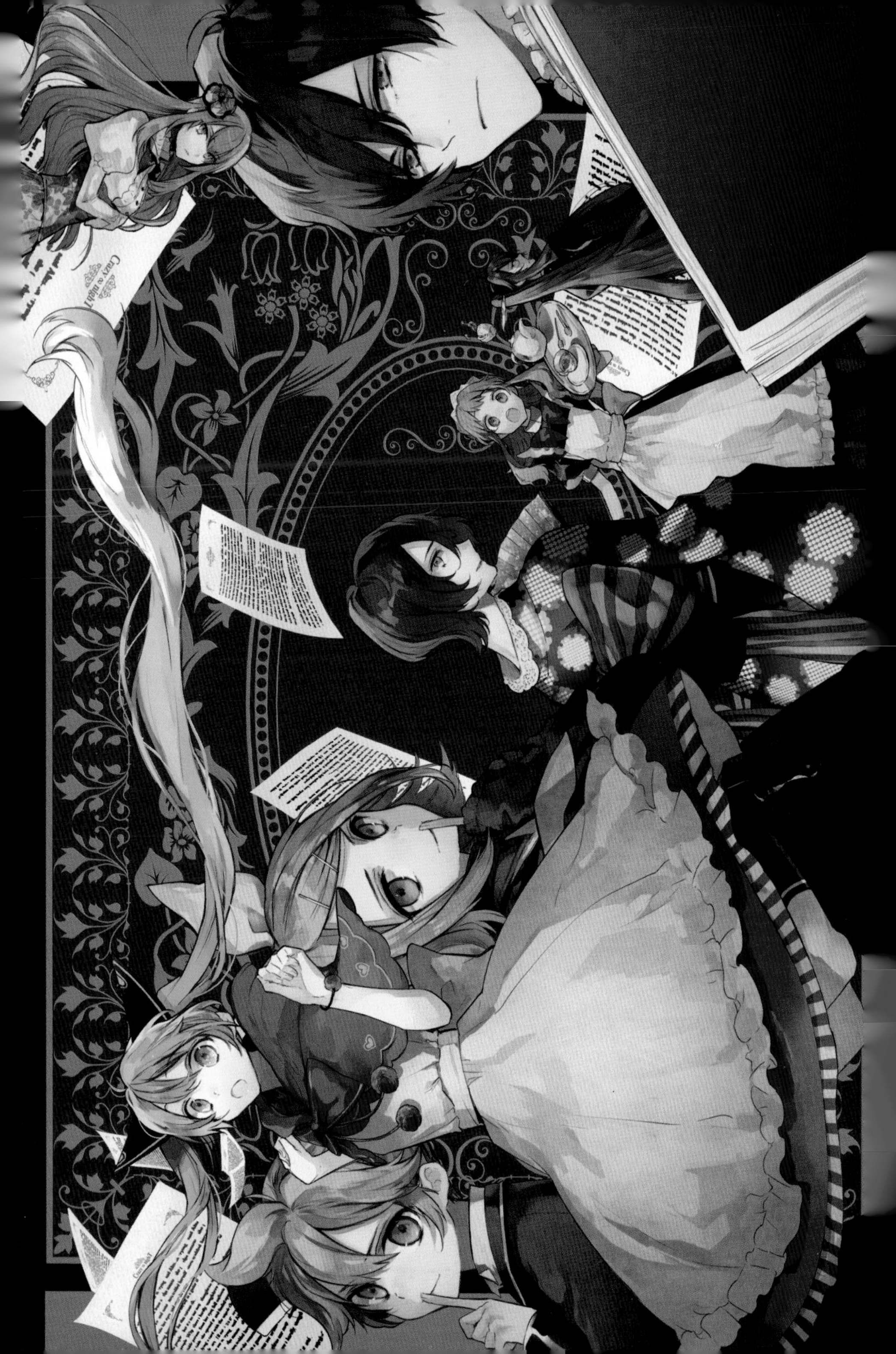

Act 1: The Curtain Rises

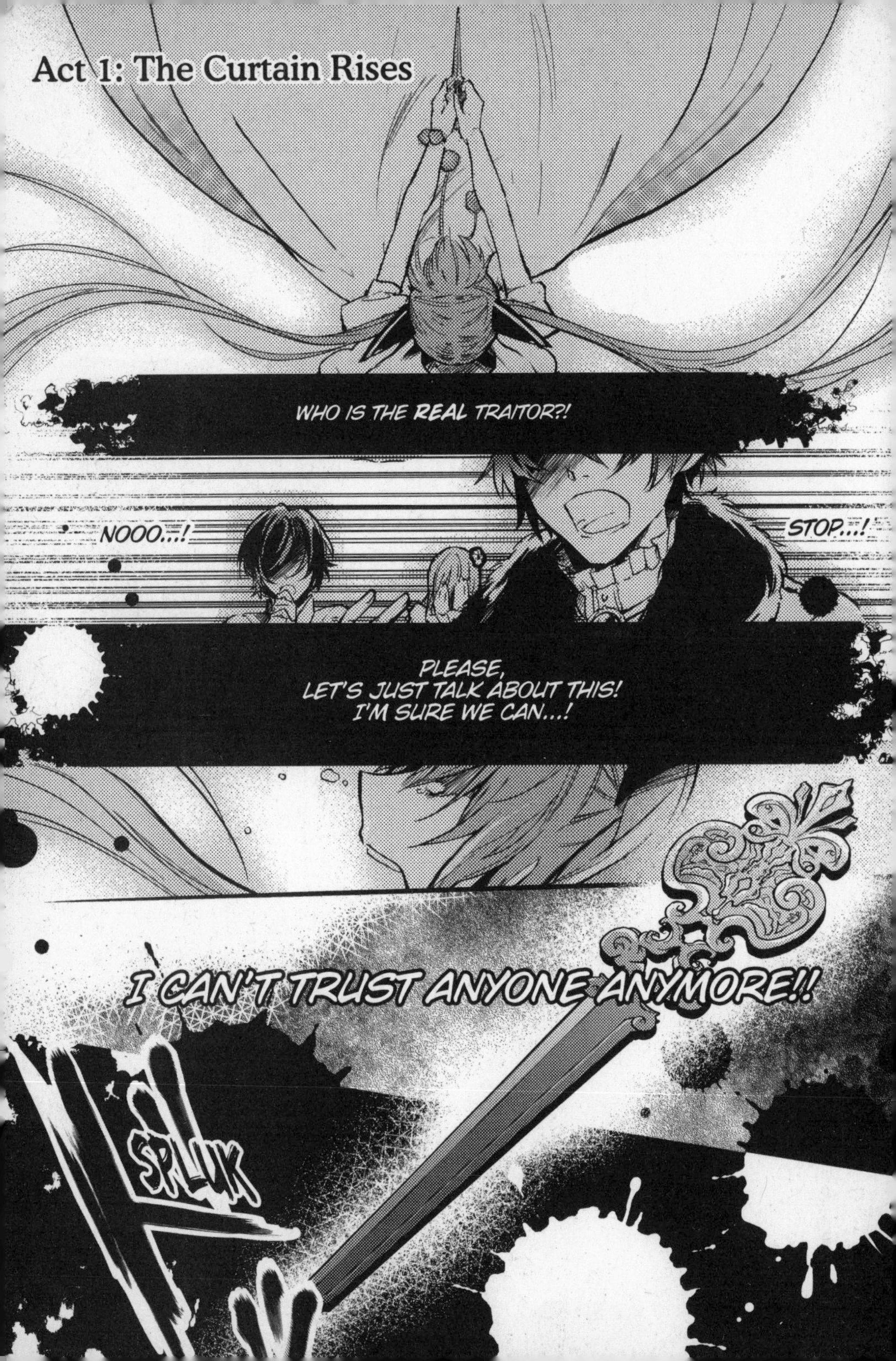
WHO IS THE REAL TRAITOR?!
STOP...!
NOOO...!
PLEASE, LET'S JUST TALK ABOUT THIS! I'M SURE WE CAN...!
I CAN'T TRUST ANYONE ANYMORE!!
SPLUK

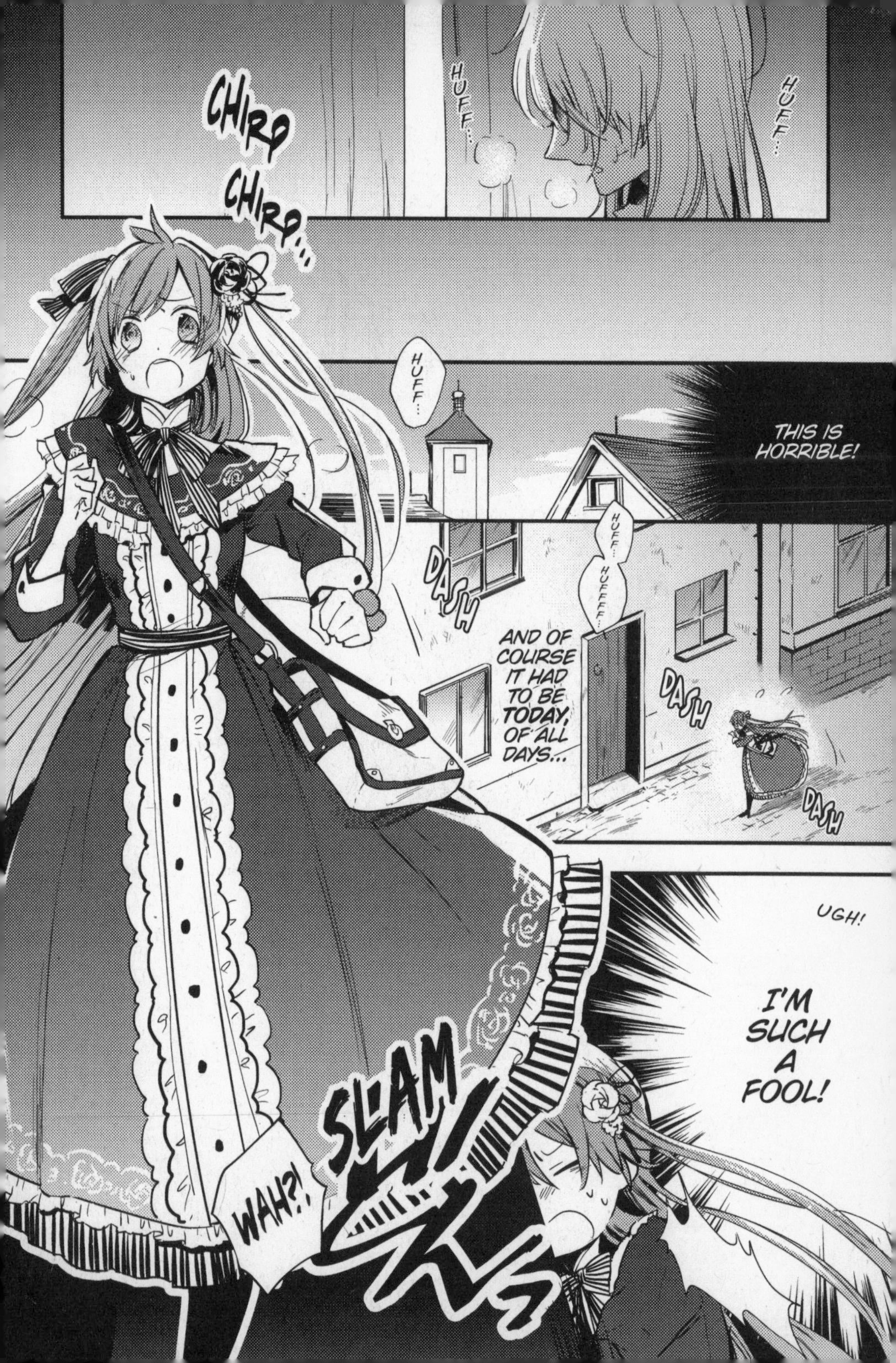
HUFF...
HUFF...
CHIRP CHIRP...
THIS IS HORRIBLE!
HUFF...
HUFF... HUFFFF...
DASH
AND OF COURSE IT HAD TO BE TODAY, OF ALL DAYS...
DASH
DASH
UGH!
I'M SUCH A FOOL!
SLAM
WAH?!

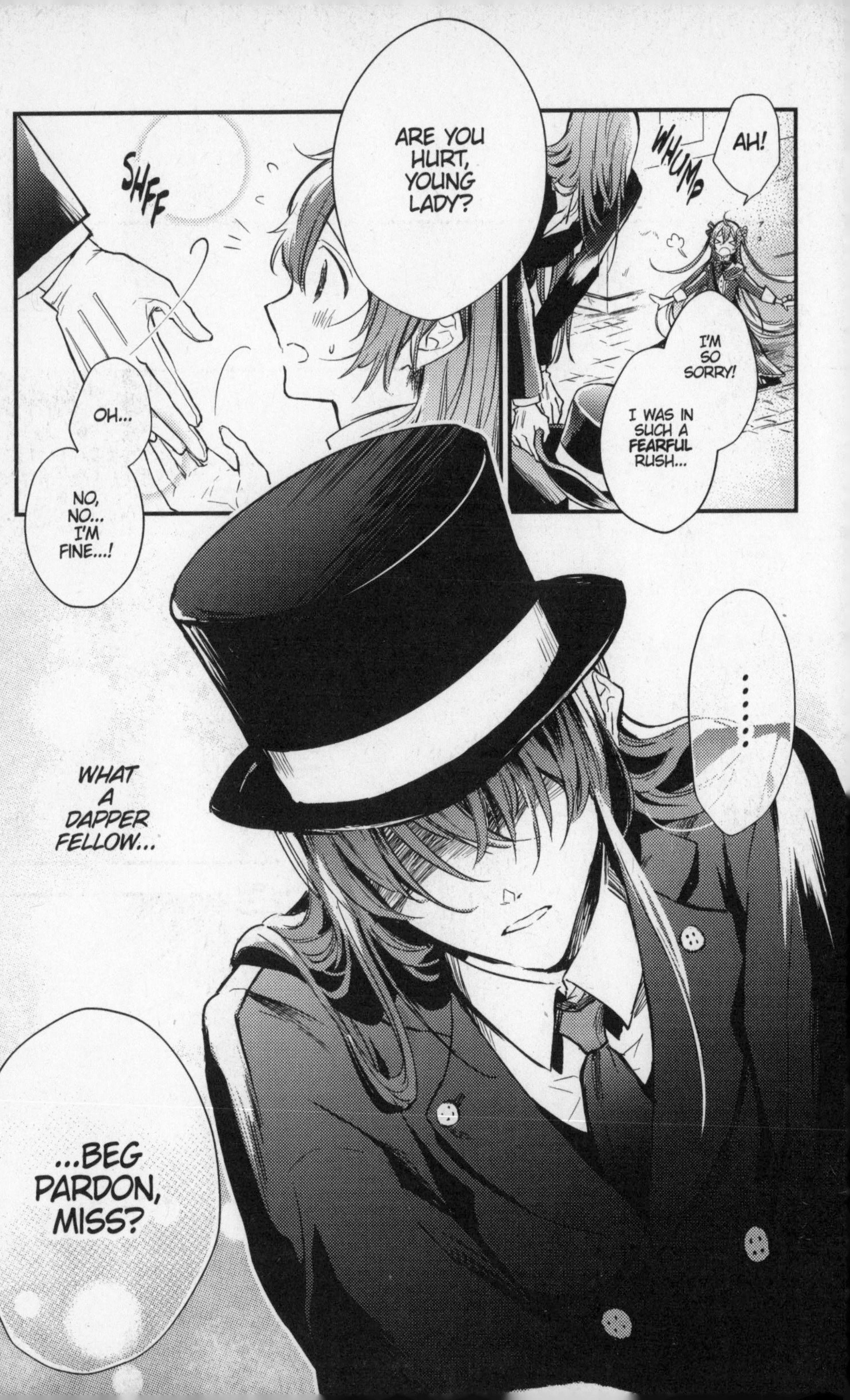
AH!
WHUMP
I'M SO SORRY!
I WAS IN SUCH A FEARFUL RUSH...
ARE YOU HURT, YOUNG LADY?
SHFF
OH...
NO, NO... I'M FINE...!
......
WHAT A DAPPER FELLOW...
...BEG PARDON, MISS?

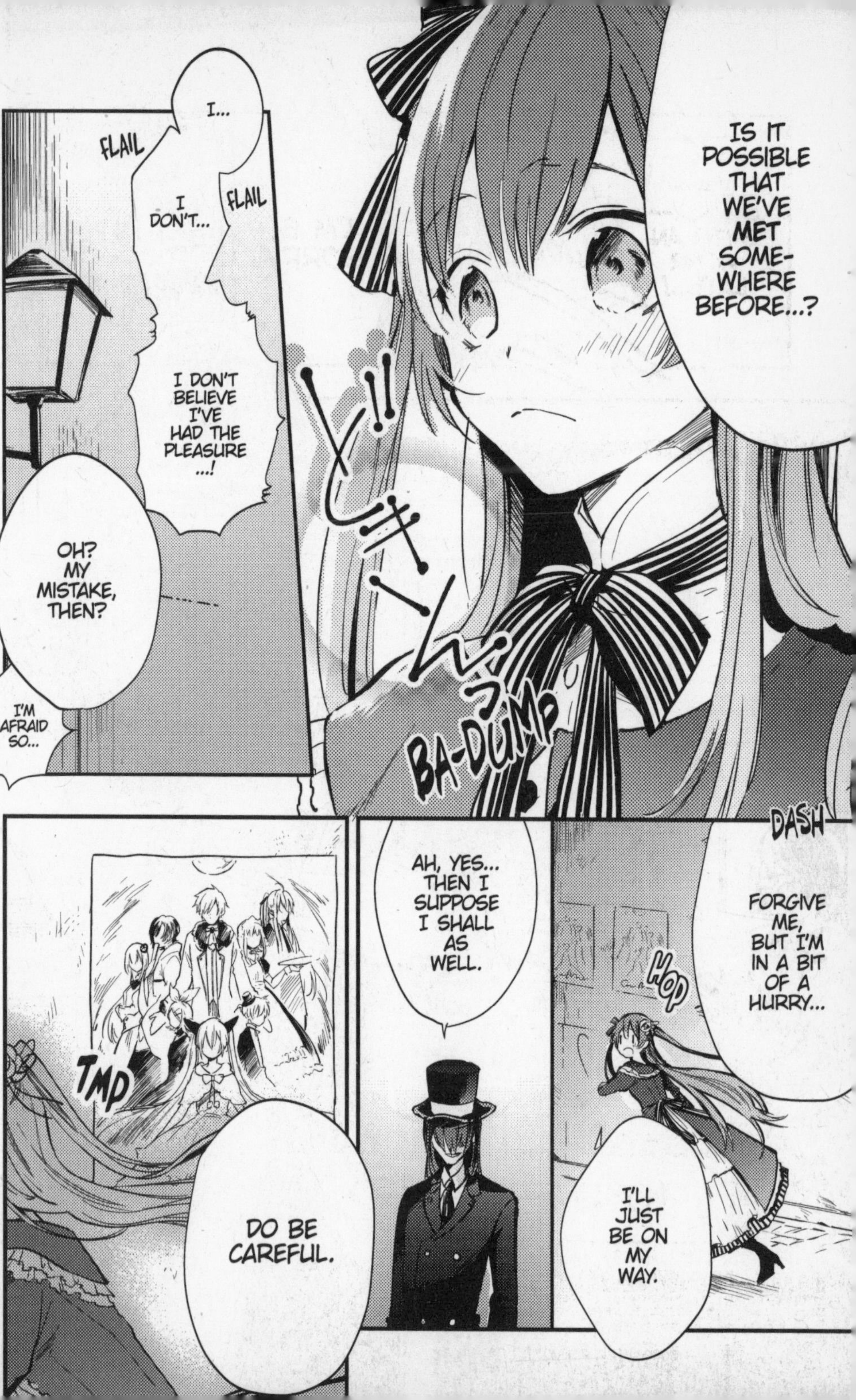
IS IT POSSIBLE THAT WE'VE MET SOME-WHERE BEFORE...?
BA-DUMP
I...
FLAIL
I DON'T...
FLAIL
I DON'T BELIEVE I'VE HAD THE PLEASURE ...!
OH? MY MISTAKE, THEN?
I'M AFRAID SO...
DASH
FORGIVE ME, BUT I'M IN A BIT OF A HURRY...
HOP
I'LL JUST BE ON MY WAY.
AH, YES... THEN I SUPPOSE I SHALL AS WELL.
TMP
DO BE CAREFUL.

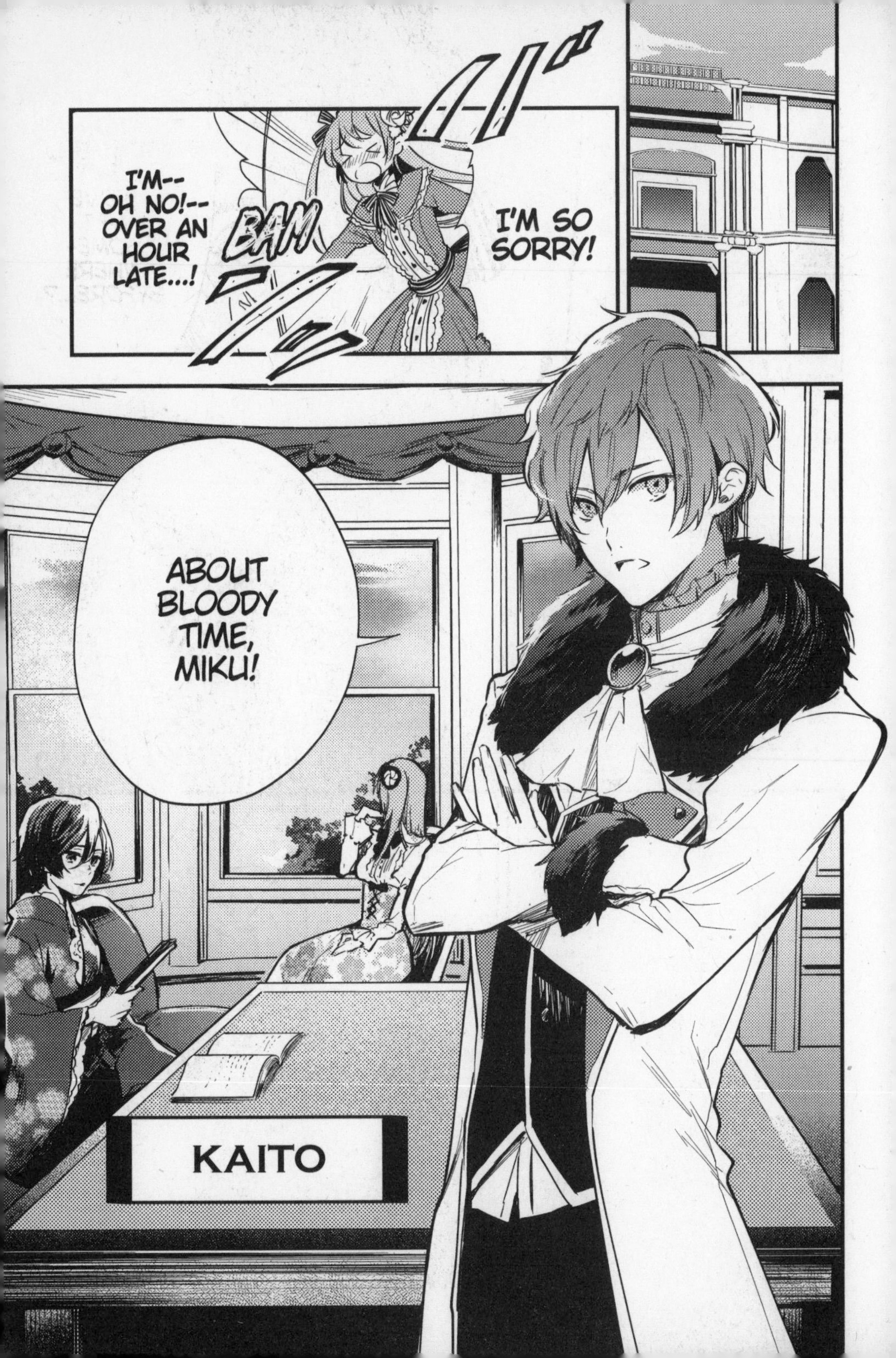
I'M SO SORRY!
BAM
I'M-- OH NO!-- OVER AN HOUR LATE...!
ABOUT BLOODY TIME, MIKU!
KAITO

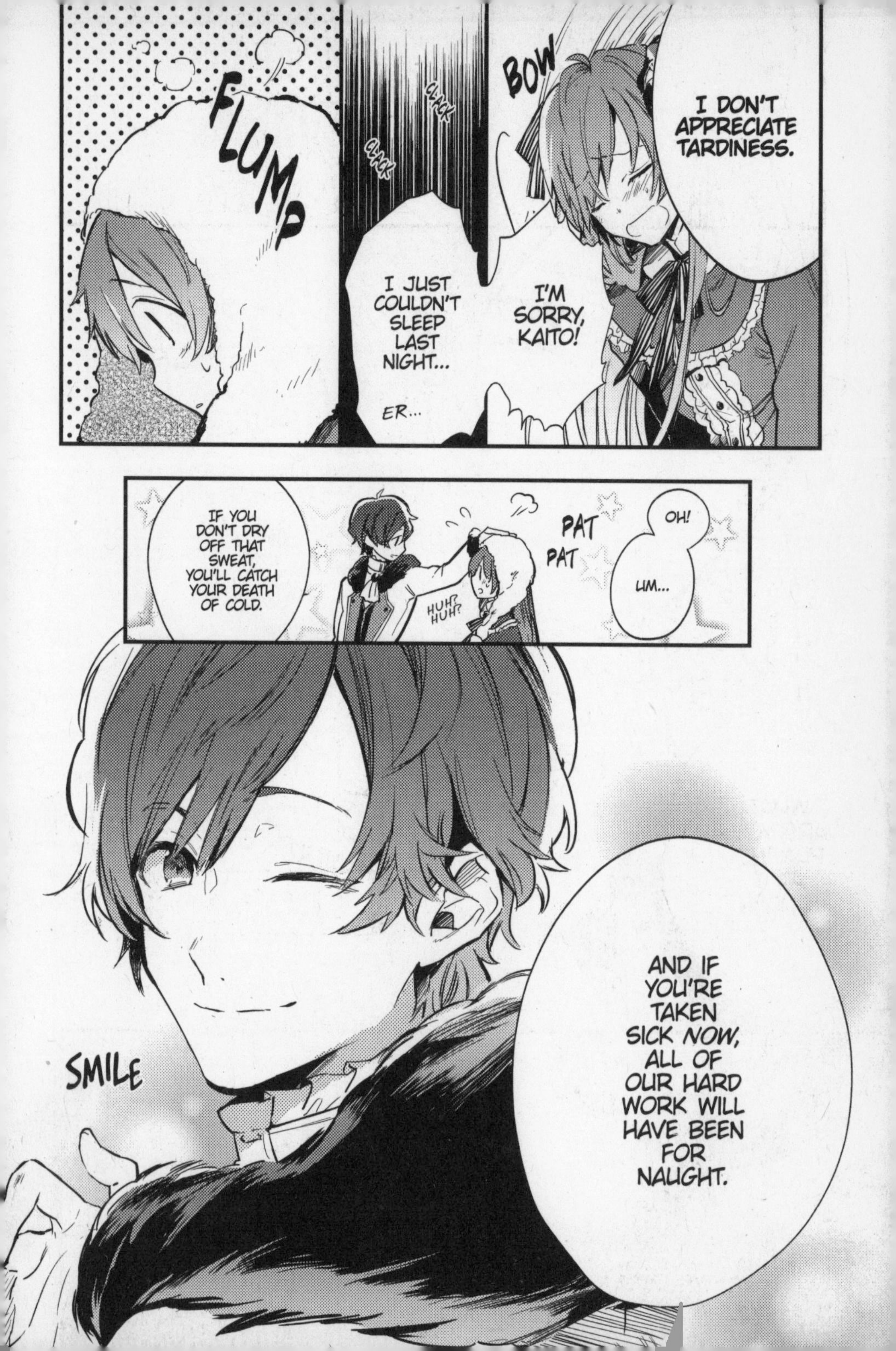
BOW
I DON'T APPRECIATE TARDINESS.
I'M SORRY, KAITO!
CLACK
CLACK
I JUST COULDN'T SLEEP LAST NIGHT...
ER...
FLUMP
OH!
UM...
PAT
PAT
HUH? HUH?
IF YOU DON'T DRY OFF THAT SWEAT, YOU'LL CATCH YOUR DEATH OF COLD.
AND IF YOU'RE TAKEN SICK *NOW*, ALL OF OUR HARD WORK WILL HAVE BEEN FOR NAUGHT.
SMILE

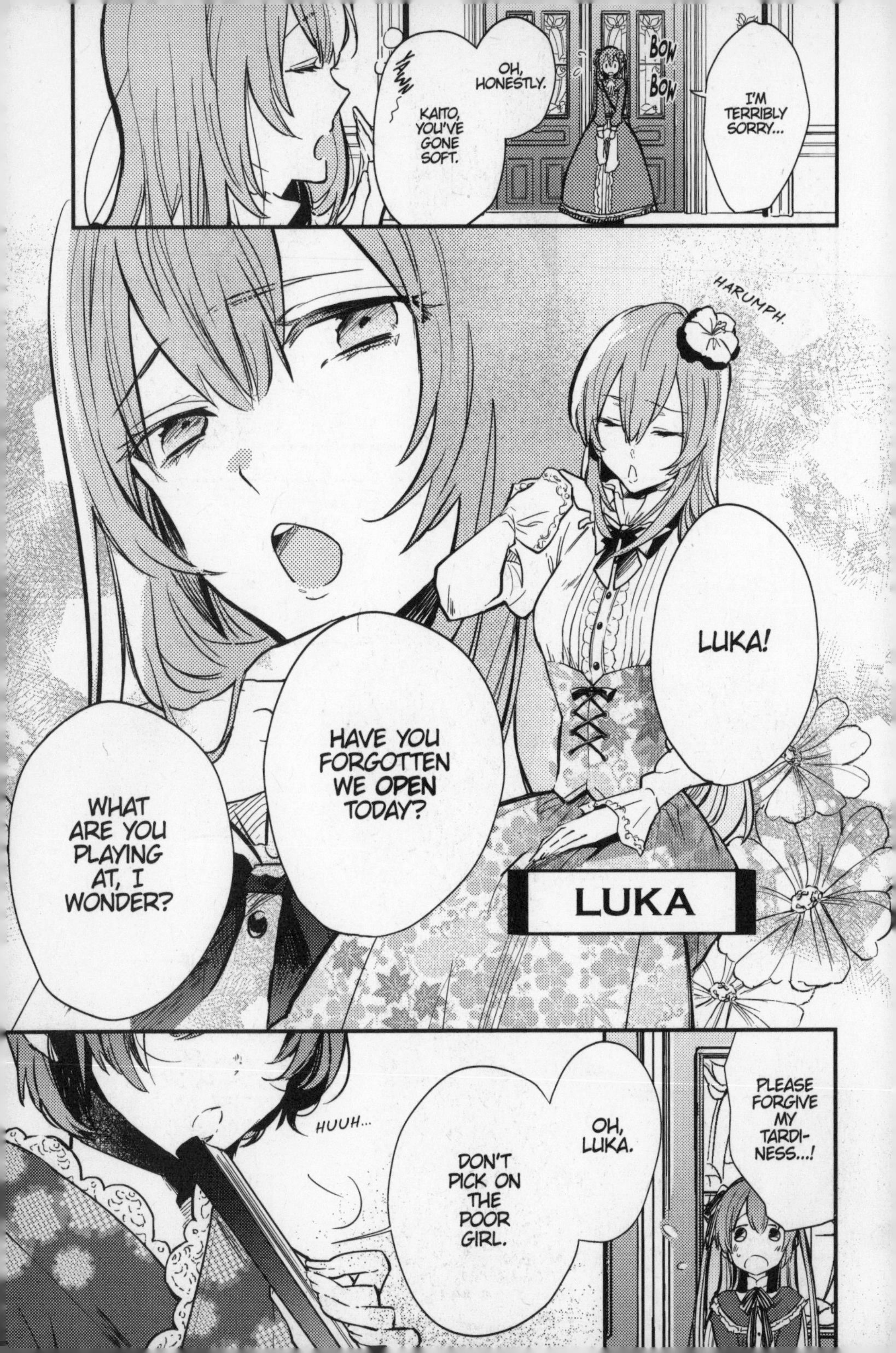

I'M TERRIBLY SORRY...
BOW BOW
OH, HONESTLY.
KAITO, YOU'VE GONE SOFT.
YAWN
HARUMPH.
LUKA!
HAVE YOU FORGOTTEN WE OPEN TODAY?
WHAT ARE YOU PLAYING AT, I WONDER?
LUKA
PLEASE FORGIVE MY TARDINESS...!
OH, LUKA.
DON'T PICK ON THE POOR GIRL.
HUUH...

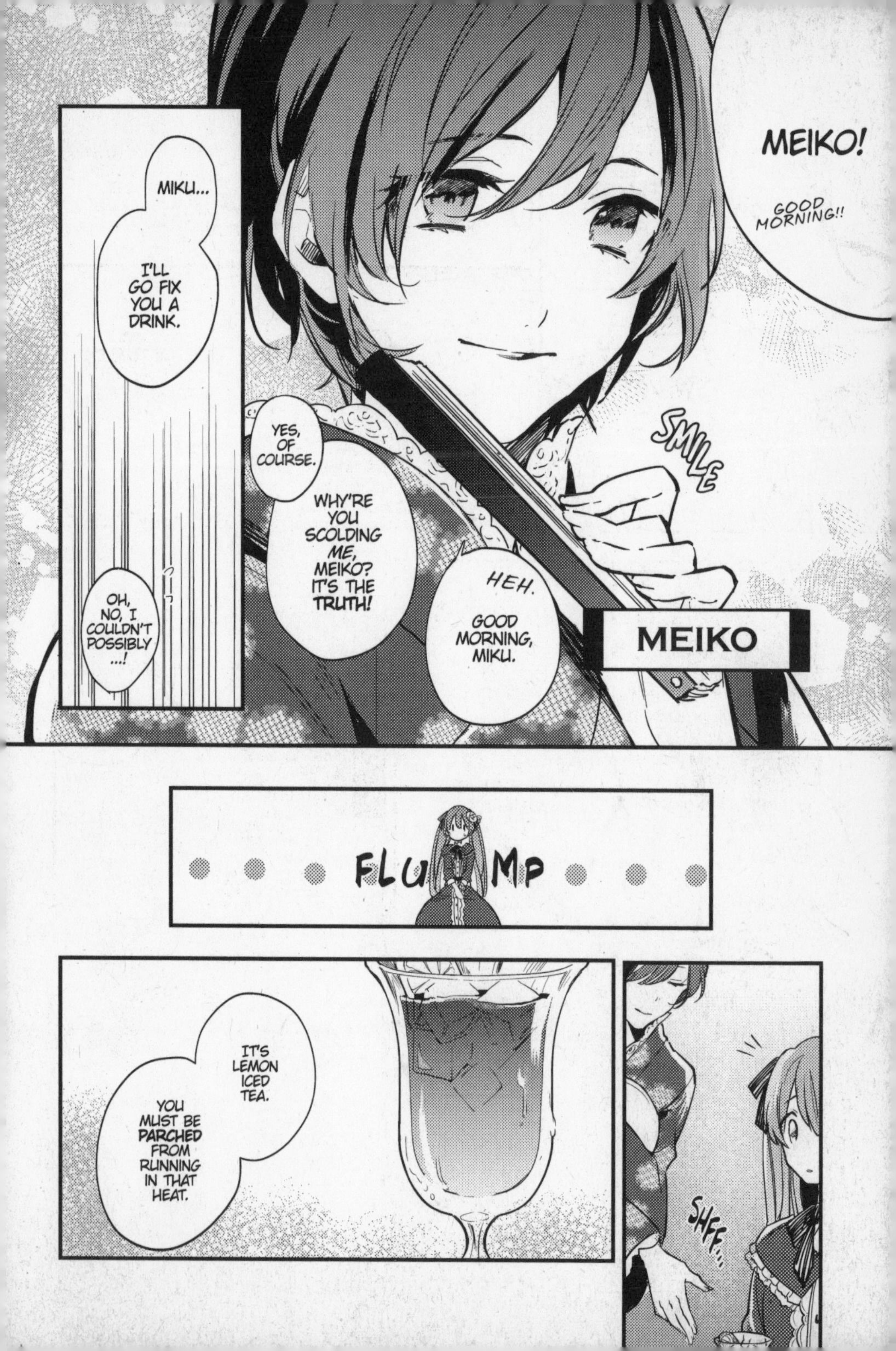
MEIKO!
GOOD MORNING!!
SMILE
MEIKO
HEH.
GOOD MORNING, MIKU.
WHY'RE YOU SCOLDING *ME*, MEIKO? IT'S THE **TRUTH**!
YES, OF COURSE.
MIKU...
I'LL GO FIX YOU A DRINK.
OH, NO, I COULDN'T POSSIBLY ...!
FLUMP
SHFF...
IT'S LEMON ICED TEA.
YOU MUST BE **PARCHED** FROM RUNNING IN THAT HEAT.

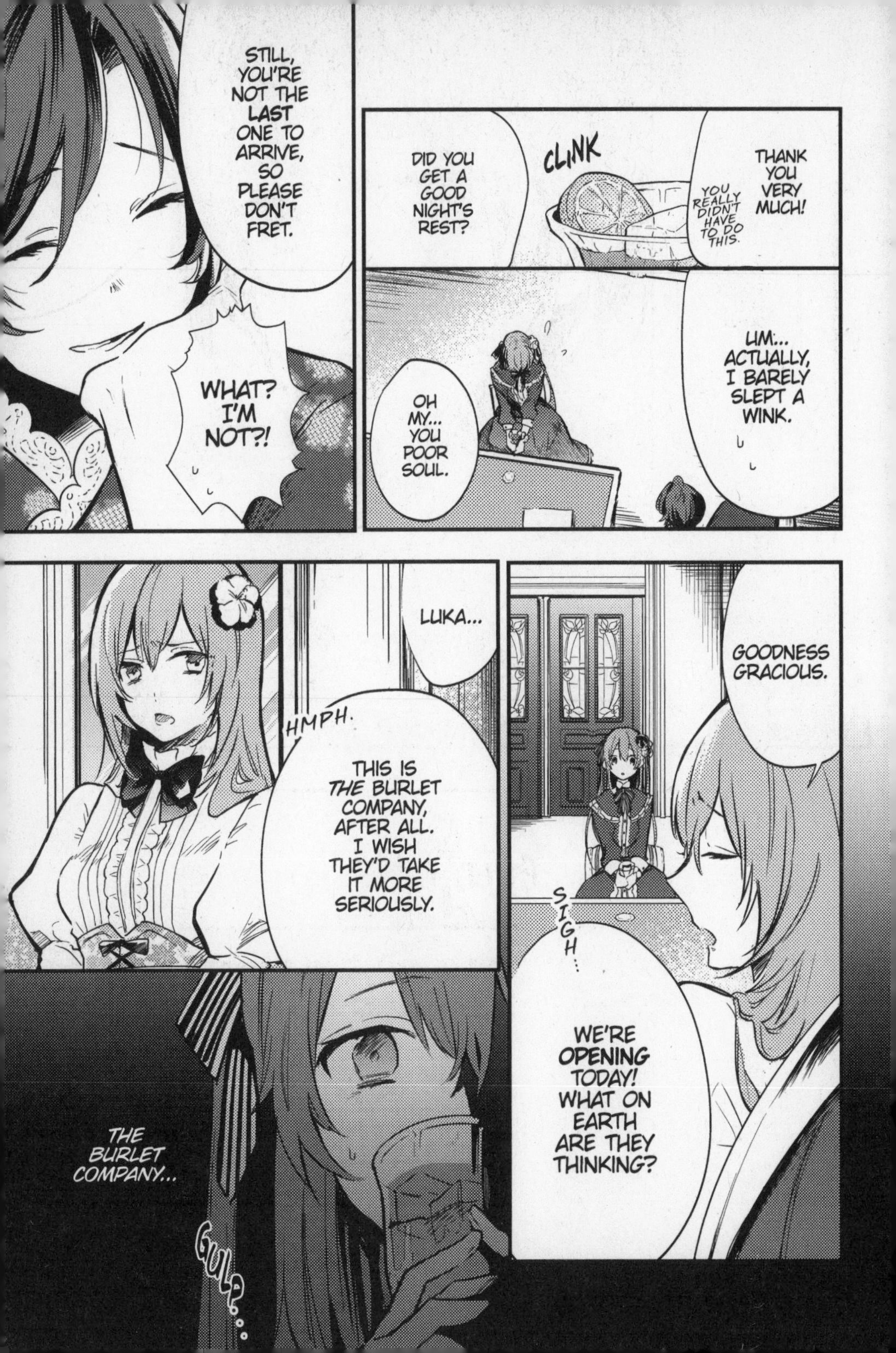
THANK YOU VERY MUCH!
YOU REALLY DIDN'T HAVE TO DO THIS.
CLINK
DID YOU GET A GOOD NIGHT'S REST?
UM... ACTUALLY, I BARELY SLEPT A WINK.
OH MY... YOU POOR SOUL.
STILL, YOU'RE NOT THE **LAST** ONE TO ARRIVE, SO PLEASE DON'T FRET.
WHAT? I'M NOT?!
GOODNESS GRACIOUS.
SIGH...
WE'RE **OPENING** TODAY! WHAT ON EARTH ARE THEY THINKING?
LUKA...
HMPH.
THIS IS *THE* BURLET COMPANY, AFTER ALL. I WISH THEY'D TAKE IT MORE SERIOUSLY.
THE BURLET COMPANY...
GULP...

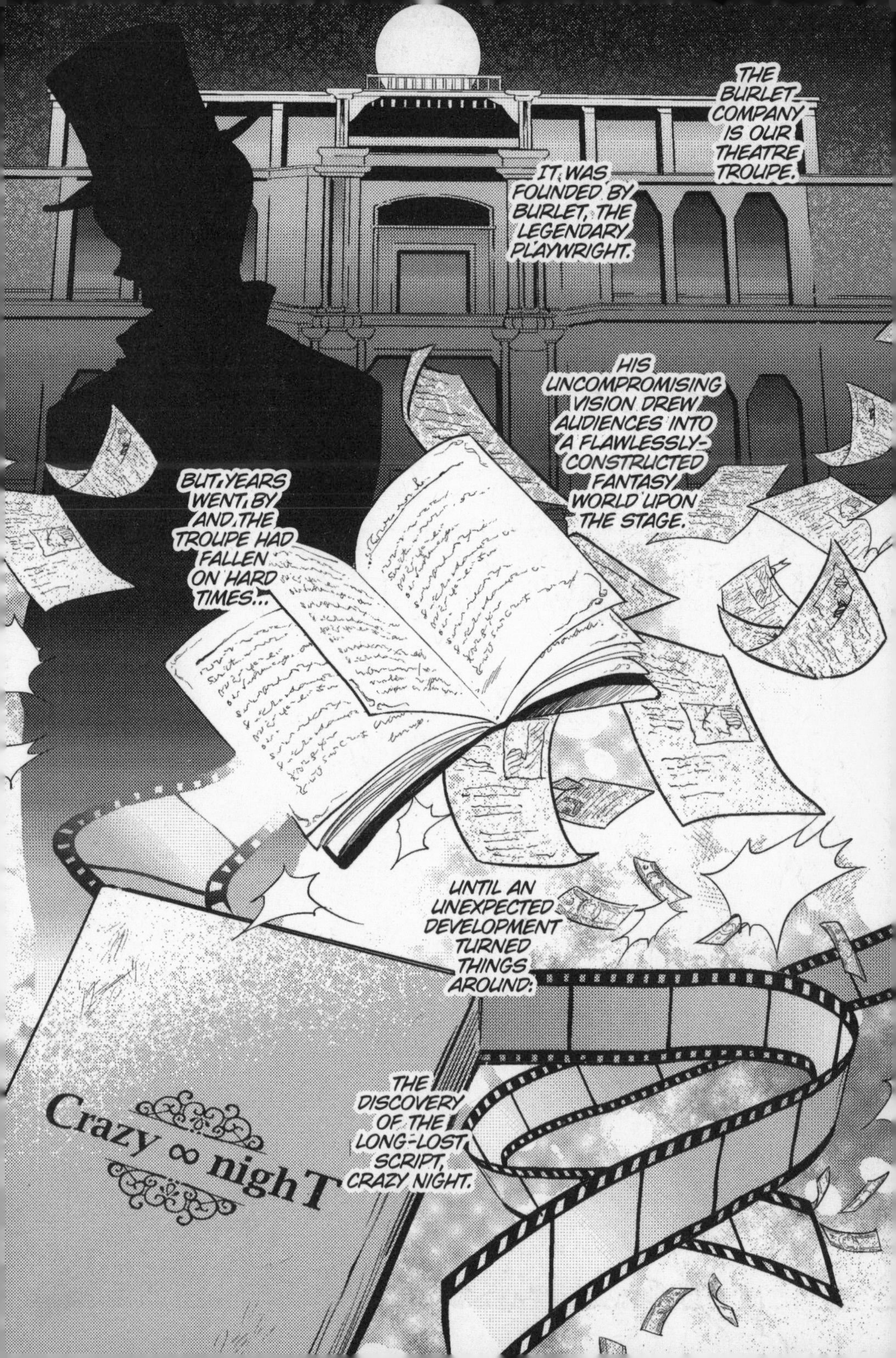
THE BURLET COMPANY IS OUR THEATRE TROUPE.
IT WAS FOUNDED BY BURLET, THE LEGENDARY PLAYWRIGHT.
HIS UNCOMPROMISING VISION DREW AUDIENCES INTO A FLAWLESSLY-CONSTRUCTED FANTASY WORLD UPON THE STAGE.
BUT YEARS WENT BY AND THE TROUPE HAD FALLEN ON HARD TIMES...
UNTIL AN UNEXPECTED DEVELOPMENT TURNED THINGS AROUND:
THE DISCOVERY OF THE LONG-LOST SCRIPT, CRAZY NIGHT.
Crazy ∞ nighT

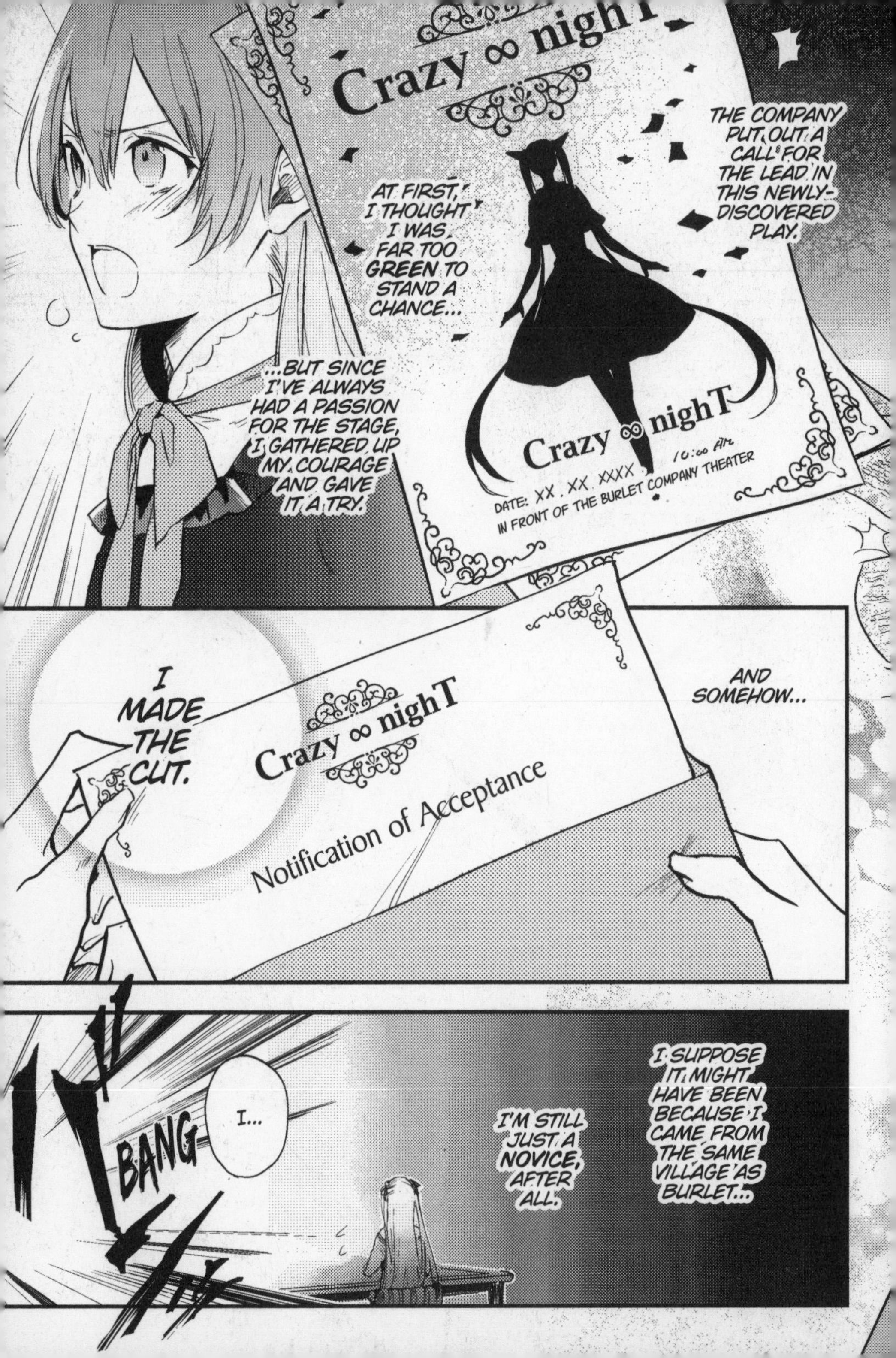
Crazy ∞ nighT
THE COMPANY PUT OUT A CALL FOR THE LEAD IN THIS NEWLY-DISCOVERED PLAY.
AT FIRST, I THOUGHT I WAS FAR TOO GREEN TO STAND A CHANCE...
Crazy ∞ nighT
DATE: XX . XX . XXXX 10:00 AM
IN FRONT OF THE BURLET COMPANY THEATER
...BUT SINCE I'VE ALWAYS HAD A PASSION FOR THE STAGE, I GATHERED UP MY COURAGE AND GAVE IT A TRY.
AND SOMEHOW...
Crazy ∞ nighT
Notification of Acceptance
I MADE THE CUT.
I SUPPOSE IT MIGHT HAVE BEEN BECAUSE I CAME FROM THE SAME VILLAGE AS BURLET...
I'M STILL JUST A NOVICE, AFTER ALL.
I...
BANG

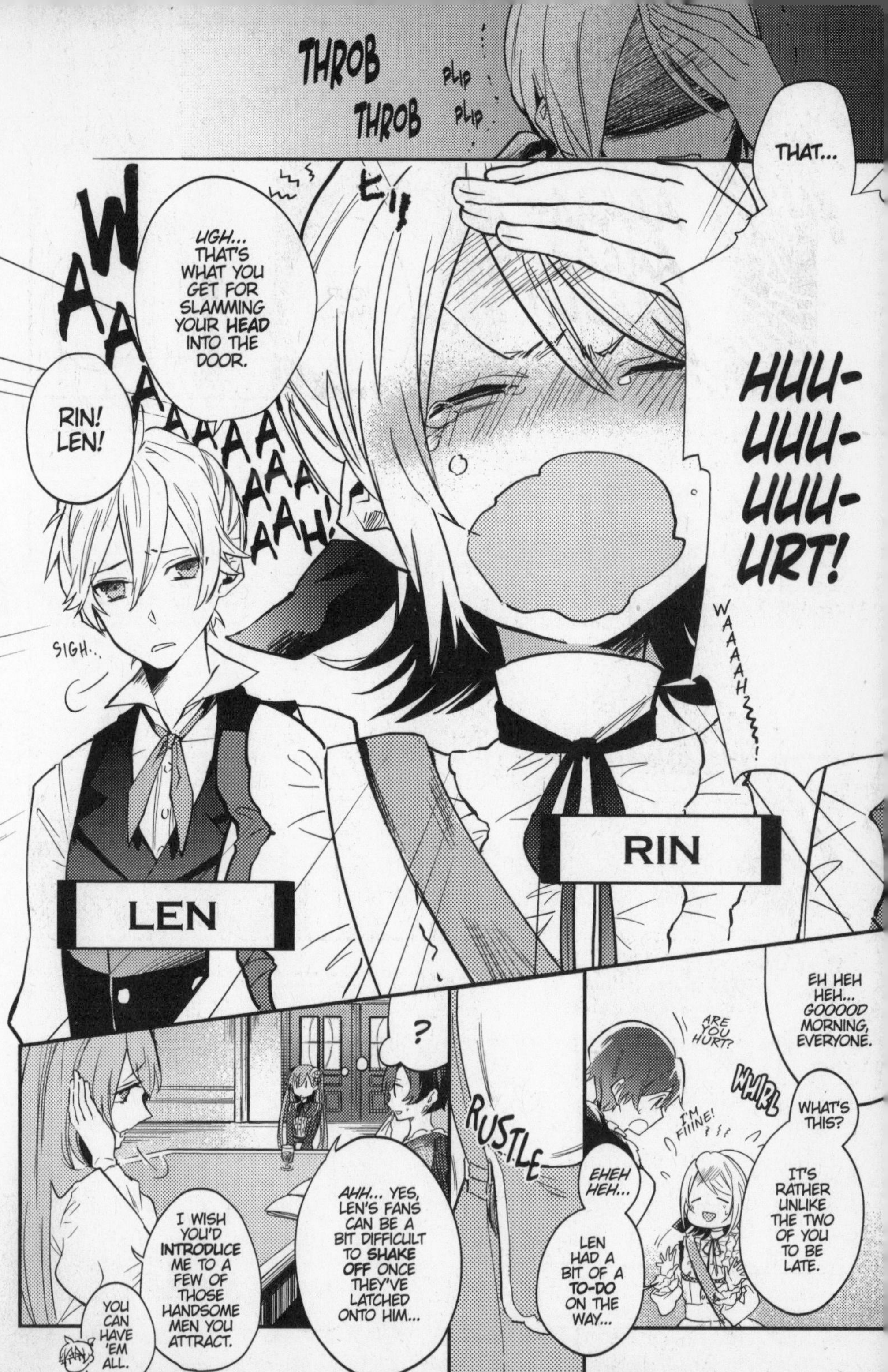
THAT...
PLIP PLIP
THROB THROB
HUUUUUUUUUURT!
WAAAAAH!
RIN
WAAAAAAAAAAAAH!
UGH... THAT'S WHAT YOU GET FOR SLAMMING YOUR HEAD INTO THE DOOR.
RIN! LEN!
SIGH...
LEN
EH HEH HEH... GOOOOD MORNING, EVERYONE.
ARE YOU HURT?
WHIRL
WHAT'S THIS?
IT'S RATHER UNLIKE THE TWO OF YOU TO BE LATE.
I'M FIIINE!
EHEH HEH...
LEN HAD A BIT OF A TO-DO ON THE WAY...
RUSTLE
?
AHH... YES, LEN'S FANS CAN BE A BIT DIFFICULT TO SHAKE OFF ONCE THEY'VE LATCHED ONTO HIM...
I WISH YOU'D INTRODUCE ME TO A FEW OF THOSE HANDSOME MEN YOU ATTRACT.
YOU CAN HAVE 'EM ALL.

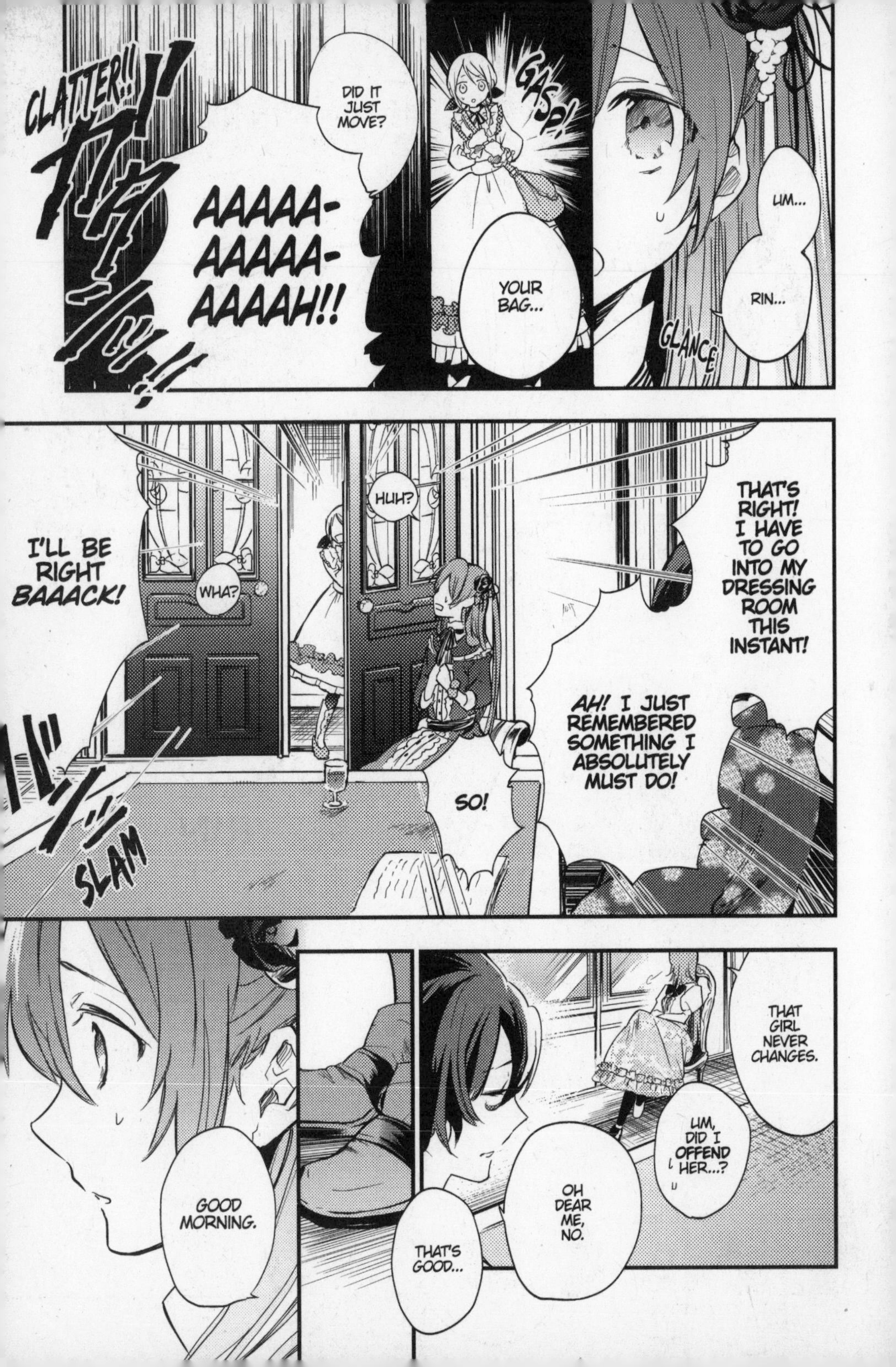
UM...
RIN...
GLANCE
GASP!
YOUR BAG...
DID IT JUST MOVE?
AAAAA-AAAAA-AAAAH!!
CLATTER!!
THAT'S RIGHT! I HAVE TO GO INTO MY DRESSING ROOM THIS INSTANT!
AH! I JUST REMEMBERED SOMETHING I ABSOLUTELY MUST DO!
SO!
HUH?
WHA?
I'LL BE RIGHT BAAACK!
SLAM
THAT GIRL NEVER CHANGES.
UM, DID I OFFEND HER...?
OH DEAR ME, NO.
THAT'S GOOD...
GOOD MORNING.

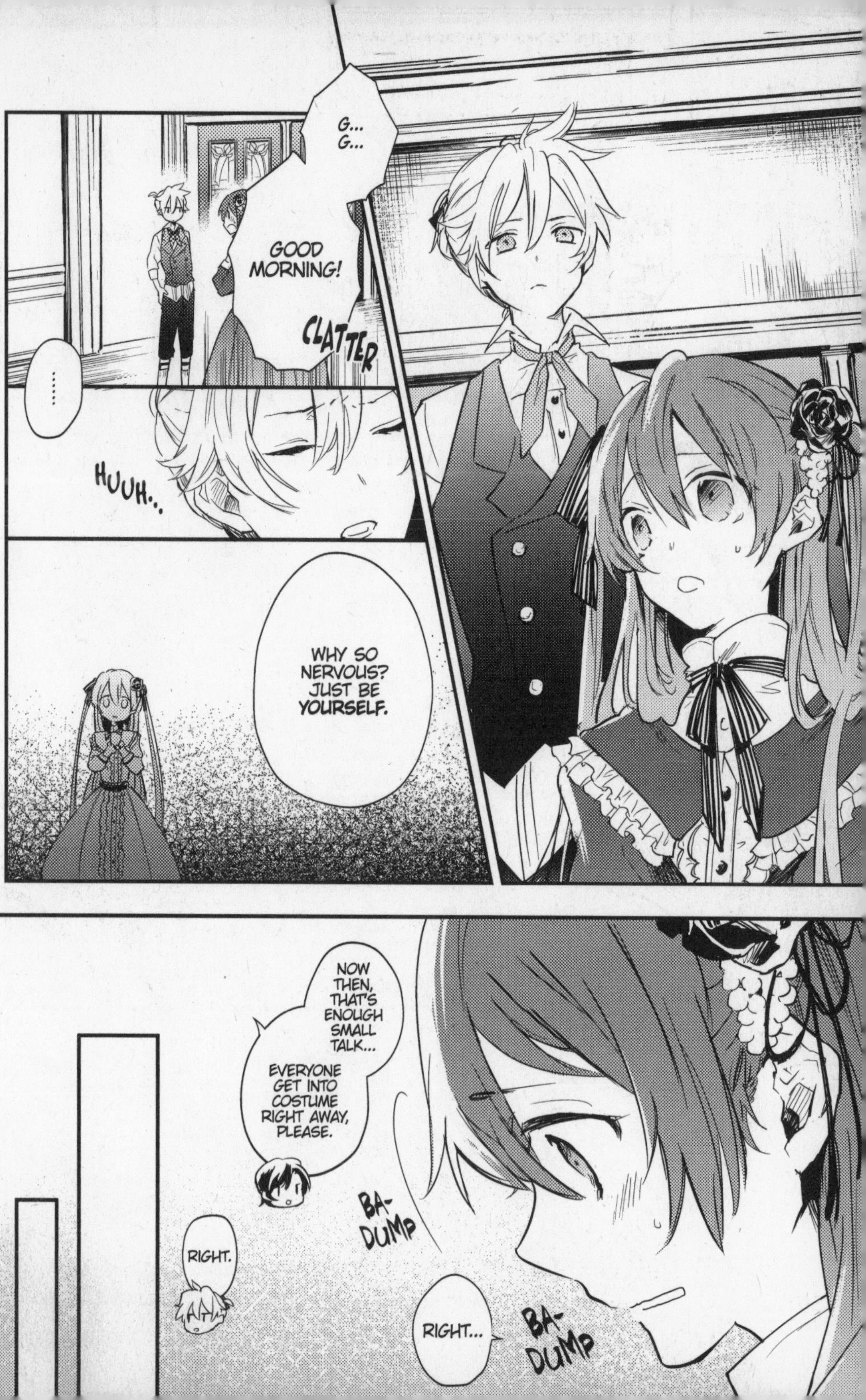
G... G...
GOOD MORNING!
CLATTER
......
HUUH...
WHY SO NERVOUS? JUST BE YOURSELF.
NOW THEN, THAT'S ENOUGH SMALL TALK...
EVERYONE GET INTO COSTUME RIGHT AWAY, PLEASE.
BA-DUMP
RIGHT.
BA-DUMP
RIGHT...

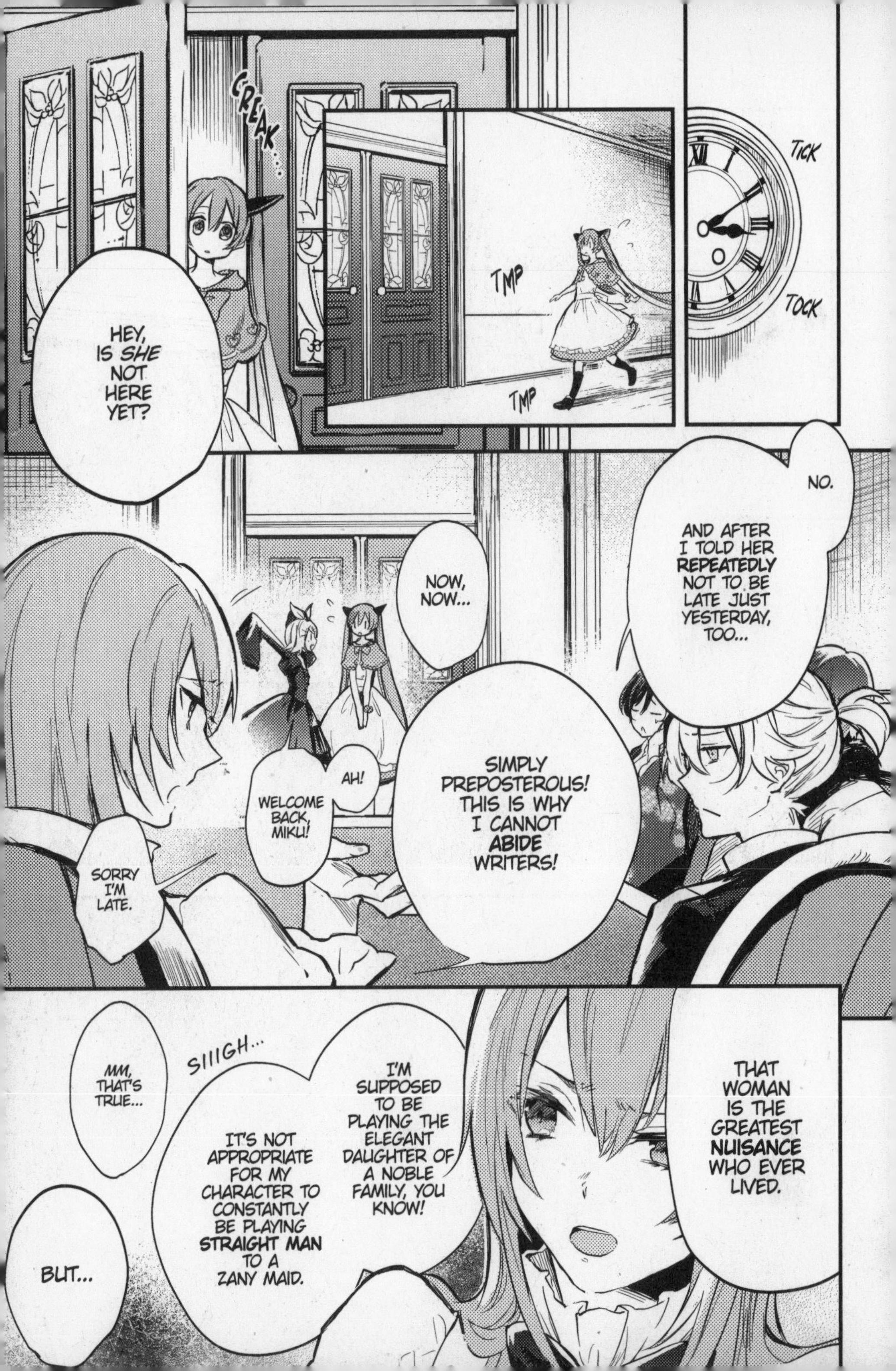
TICK
TOCK
TMP
TMP
CREAK...
HEY, IS *SHE* NOT HERE YET?
NO.
AND AFTER I TOLD HER **REPEATEDLY** NOT TO BE LATE JUST YESTERDAY, TOO...
NOW, NOW...
SIMPLY PREPOSTEROUS! THIS IS WHY I CANNOT **ABIDE** WRITERS!
AH!
WELCOME BACK, MIKU!
SORRY I'M LATE.
THAT WOMAN IS THE GREATEST **NUISANCE** WHO EVER LIVED.
I'M SUPPOSED TO BE PLAYING THE ELEGANT DAUGHTER OF A NOBLE FAMILY, YOU KNOW!
IT'S NOT APPROPRIATE FOR MY CHARACTER TO CONSTANTLY BE PLAYING **STRAIGHT MAN** TO A ZANY MAID.
SIIIGH...
MM, THAT'S TRUE...
BUT...

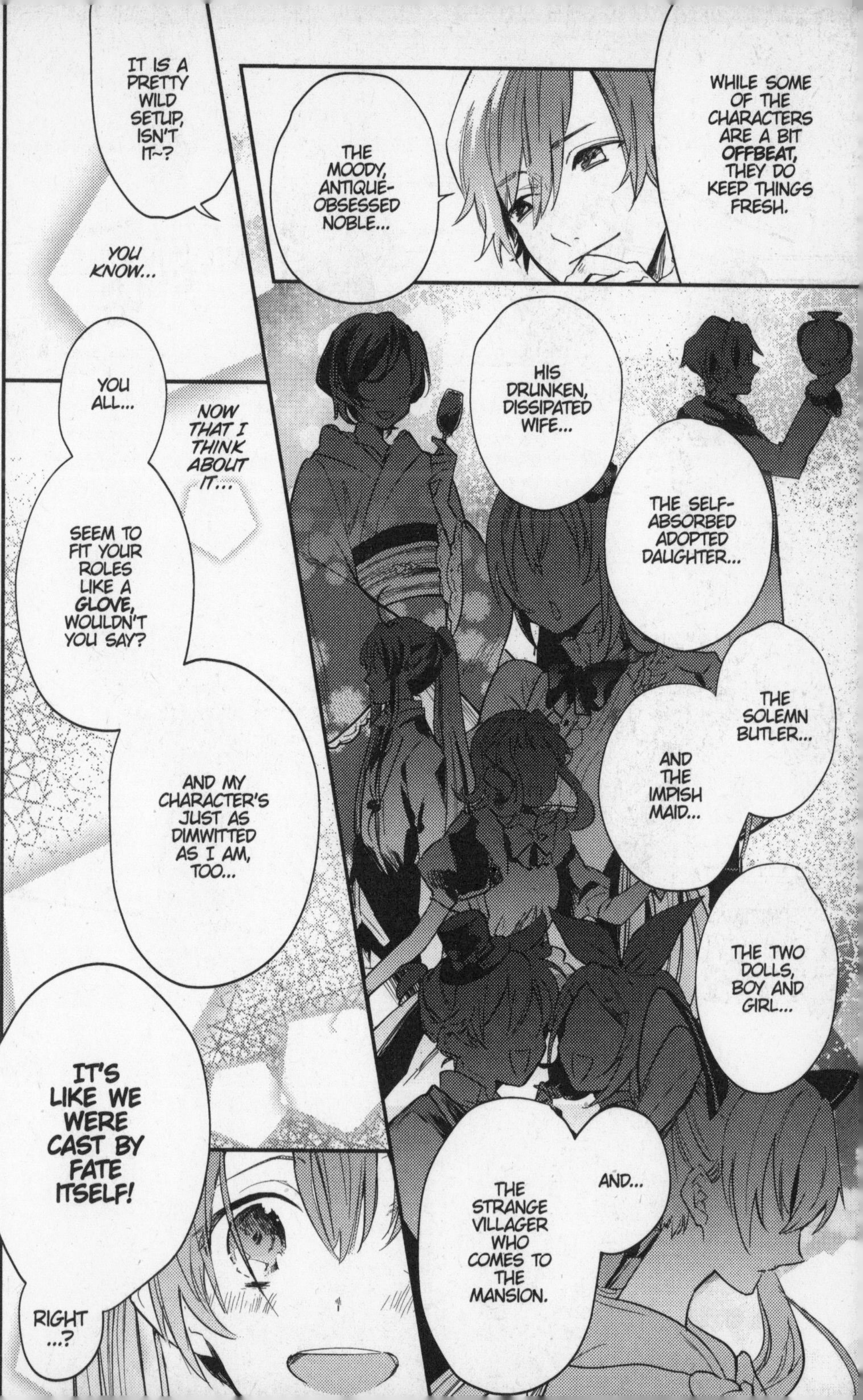
WHILE SOME OF THE CHARACTERS ARE A BIT **OFFBEAT**, THEY DO KEEP THINGS FRESH.
THE MOODY, ANTIQUE-OBSESSED NOBLE...
IT IS A PRETTY WILD SETUP, ISN'T IT~?
YOU KNOW...
HIS DRUNKEN, DISSIPATED WIFE...
THE SELF-ABSORBED ADOPTED DAUGHTER...
THE SOLEMN BUTLER...
AND THE IMPISH MAID...
THE TWO DOLLS, BOY AND GIRL...
AND...
THE STRANGE VILLAGER WHO COMES TO THE MANSION.
NOW THAT I THINK ABOUT IT...
YOU ALL...
SEEM TO FIT YOUR ROLES LIKE A **GLOVE**, WOULDN'T YOU SAY?
AND MY CHARACTER'S JUST AS DIMWITTED AS I AM, TOO...
IT'S LIKE WE WERE CAST BY FATE ITSELF!
RIGHT ...?

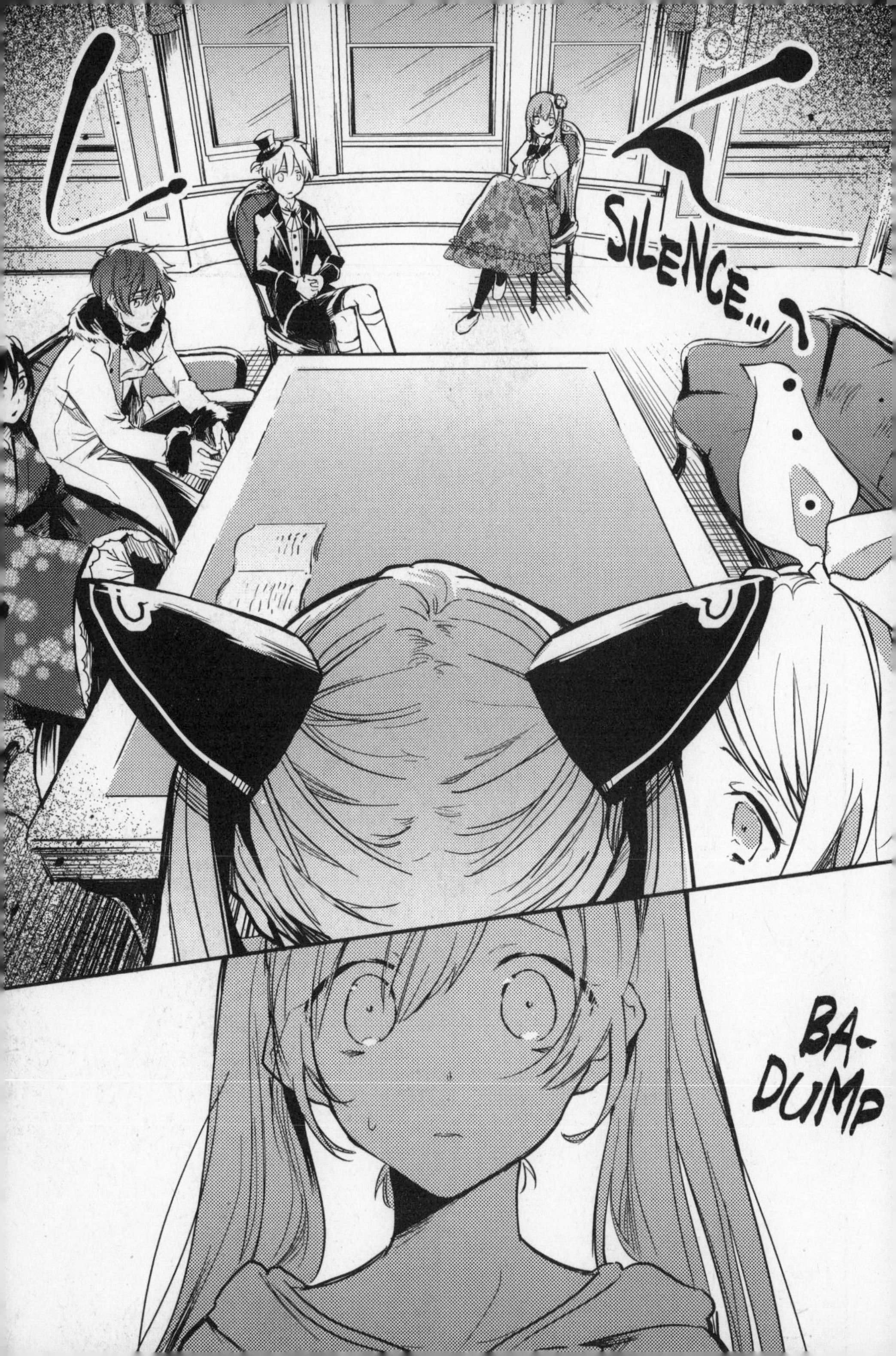
SILENCE...
BA-
DUMP

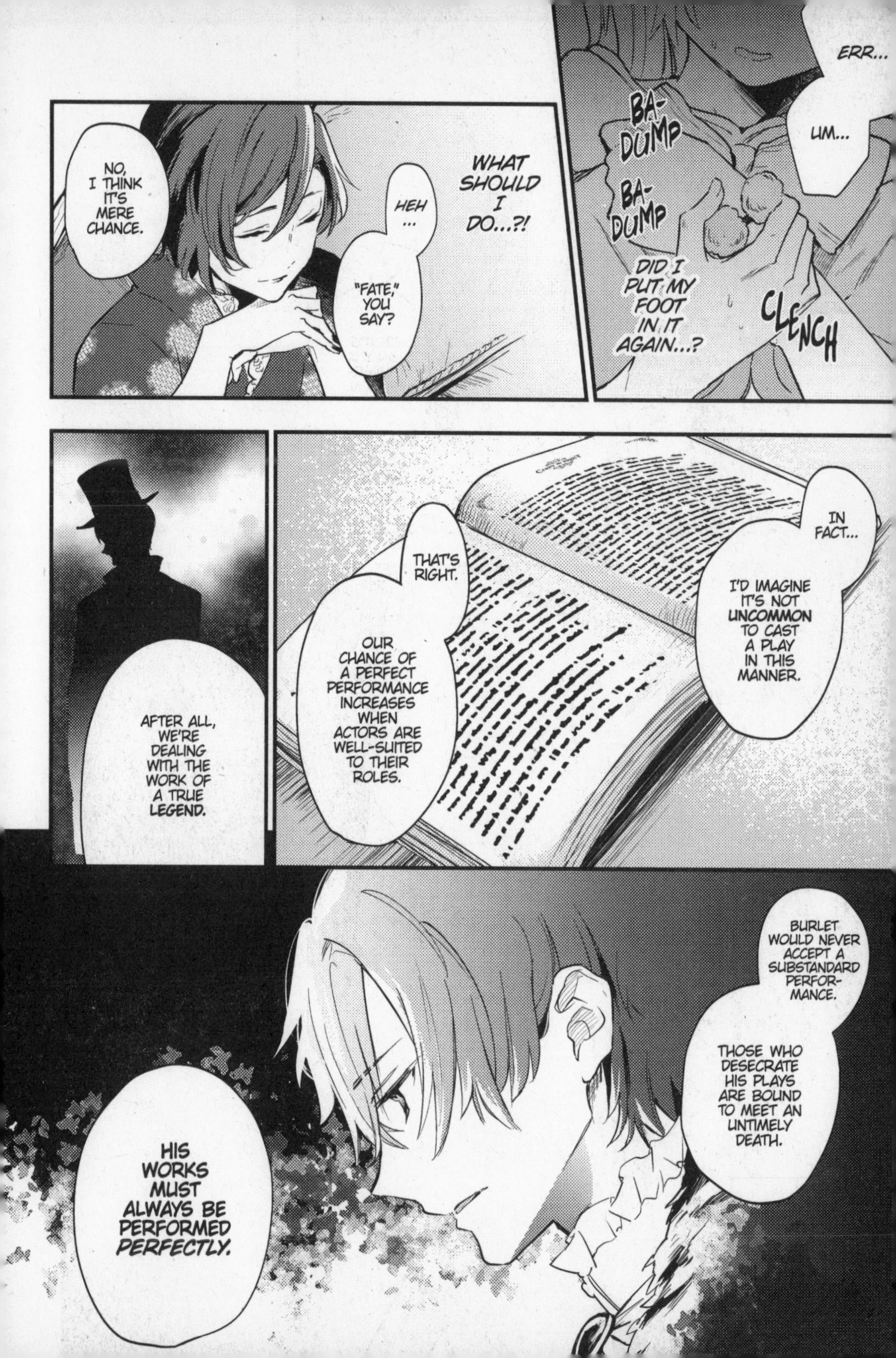
ERR...
UM...
BA-DUMP
BA-DUMP
DID I PUT MY FOOT IN IT AGAIN...?
CLENCH
WHAT SHOULD I DO...?!
HEH...
"FATE," YOU SAY?
NO, I THINK IT'S MERE CHANCE.
IN FACT...
I'D IMAGINE IT'S NOT **UNCOMMON** TO CAST A PLAY IN THIS MANNER.
THAT'S RIGHT.
OUR CHANCE OF A PERFECT PERFORMANCE INCREASES WHEN ACTORS ARE WELL-SUITED TO THEIR ROLES.
AFTER ALL, WE'RE DEALING WITH THE WORK OF A TRUE LEGEND.
BURLET WOULD NEVER ACCEPT A SUBSTANDARD PERFOR-MANCE.
THOSE WHO DESECRATE HIS PLAYS ARE BOUND TO MEET AN UNTIMELY DEATH.
HIS WORKS MUST ALWAYS BE PERFORMED PERFECTLY.

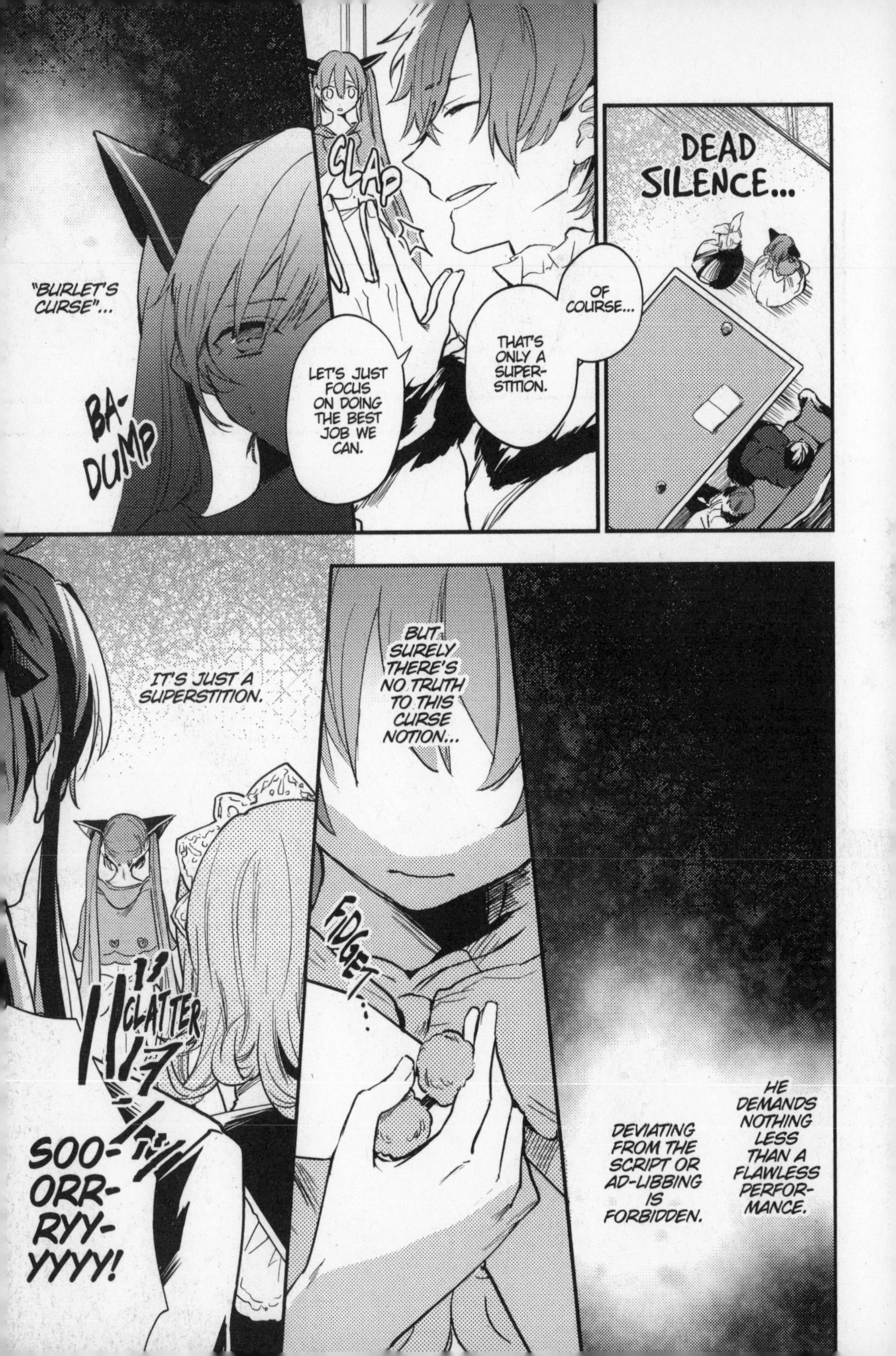
DEAD SILENCE...
OF COURSE...
THAT'S ONLY A SUPER-STITION.
CLAP
LET'S JUST FOCUS ON DOING THE BEST JOB WE CAN.
"BURLET'S CURSE"...
BA-DUMP
BUT SURELY THERE'S NO TRUTH TO THIS CURSE NOTION...
FIDGET...
HE DEMANDS NOTHING LESS THAN A FLAWLESS PERFOR-MANCE.
DEVIATING FROM THE SCRIPT OR AD-LIBBING IS FORBIDDEN.
IT'S JUST A SUPERSTITION.
CLATTER
SOO-ORR-RYY-YYYY!

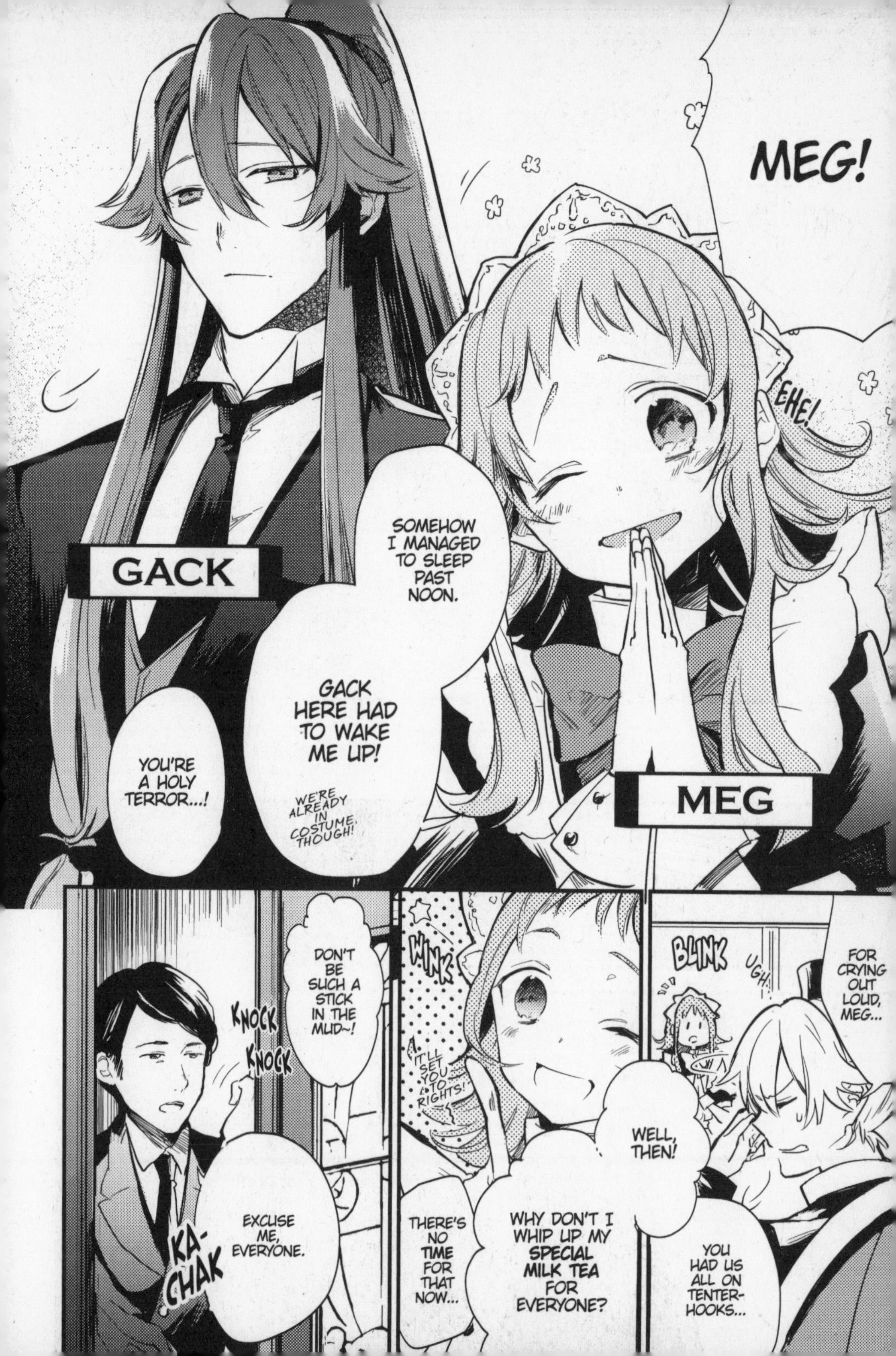
MEG!
MEG
EHE!
SOMEHOW I MANAGED TO SLEEP PAST NOON.
GACK HERE HAD TO WAKE ME UP!
WE'RE ALREADY IN COSTUME, THOUGH!
GACK
YOU'RE A HOLY TERROR...!
BLINK
UGH.
FOR CRYING OUT LOUD, MEG...
YOU HAD US ALL ON TENTER-HOOKS...
WINK
WELL, THEN!
WHY DON'T I WHIP UP MY SPECIAL MILK TEA FOR EVERYONE?
IT'LL SET YOU TO RIGHTS!
THERE'S NO TIME FOR THAT NOW...
DON'T BE SUCH A STICK IN THE MUD~!
KNOCK KNOCK
KA-CHAK
EXCUSE ME, EVERYONE.

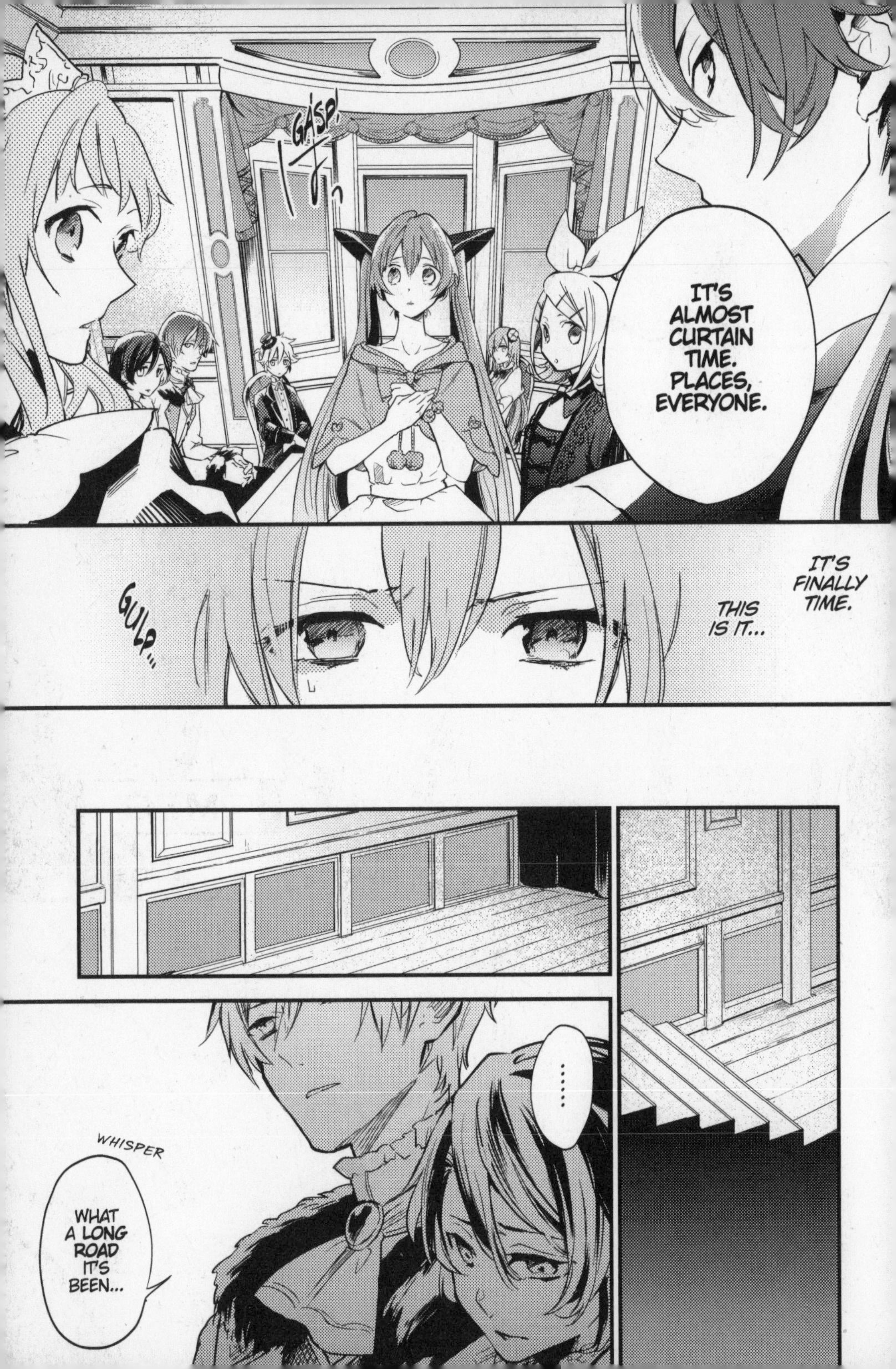
IT'S ALMOST CURTAIN TIME. PLACES, EVERYONE.
GASP!
IT'S FINALLY TIME.
THIS IS IT...
GULP...
......
WHISPER
WHAT A LONG ROAD IT'S BEEN...

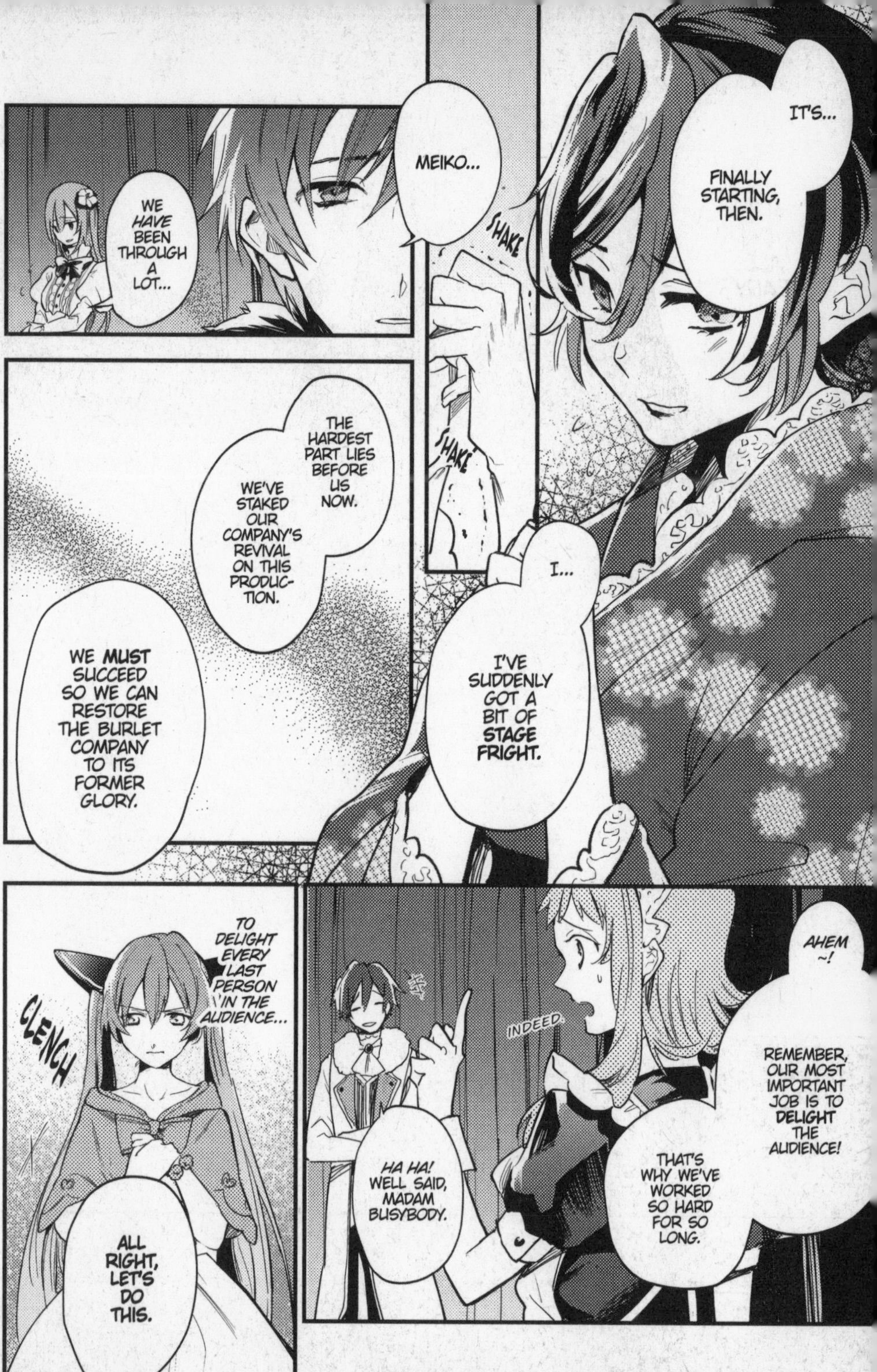
IT'S...
FINALLY STARTING, THEN.
I...
I'VE SUDDENLY GOT A BIT OF STAGE FRIGHT.
SHAKE
SHAKE
MEIKO...
WE HAVE BEEN THROUGH A LOT...
THE HARDEST PART LIES BEFORE US NOW.
WE'VE STAKED OUR COMPANY'S REVIVAL ON THIS PRODUCTION.
WE MUST SUCCEED SO WE CAN RESTORE THE BURLET COMPANY TO ITS FORMER GLORY.
AHEM ~!
REMEMBER, OUR MOST IMPORTANT JOB IS TO DELIGHT THE AUDIENCE!
THAT'S WHY WE'VE WORKED SO HARD FOR SO LONG.
INDEED.
HA HA! WELL SAID, MADAM BUSYBODY.
TO DELIGHT EVERY LAST PERSON IN THE AUDIENCE...
CLENCH
ALL RIGHT, LET'S DO THIS.

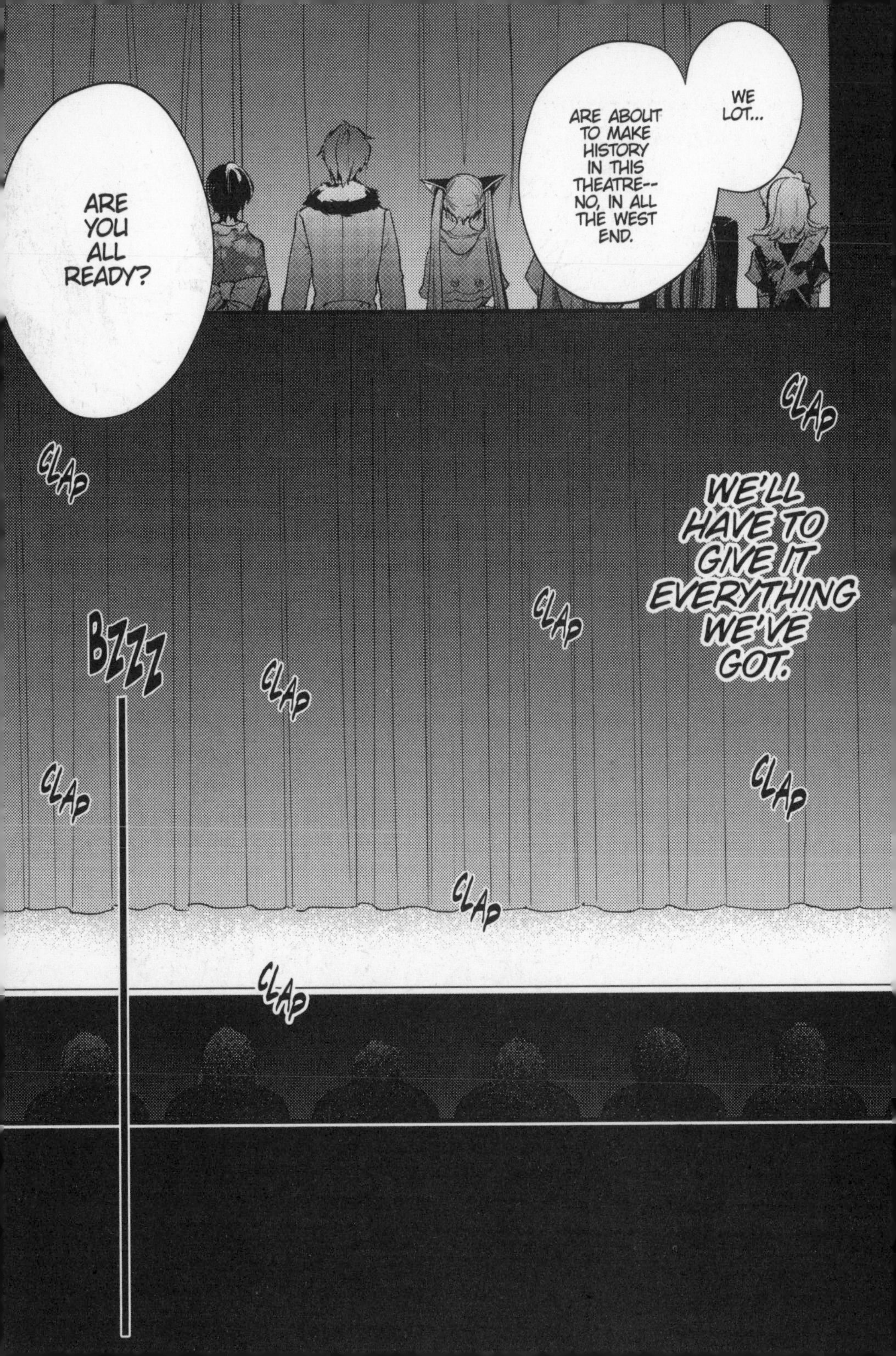
WE LOT...
ARE ABOUT TO MAKE HISTORY IN THIS THEATRE-- NO, IN ALL THE WEST END.
ARE YOU ALL READY?
CLAP
CLAP
WE'LL HAVE TO GIVE IT EVERYTHING WE'VE GOT.
CLAP
CLAP
BZZZ
CLAP
CLAP
CLAP
CLAP

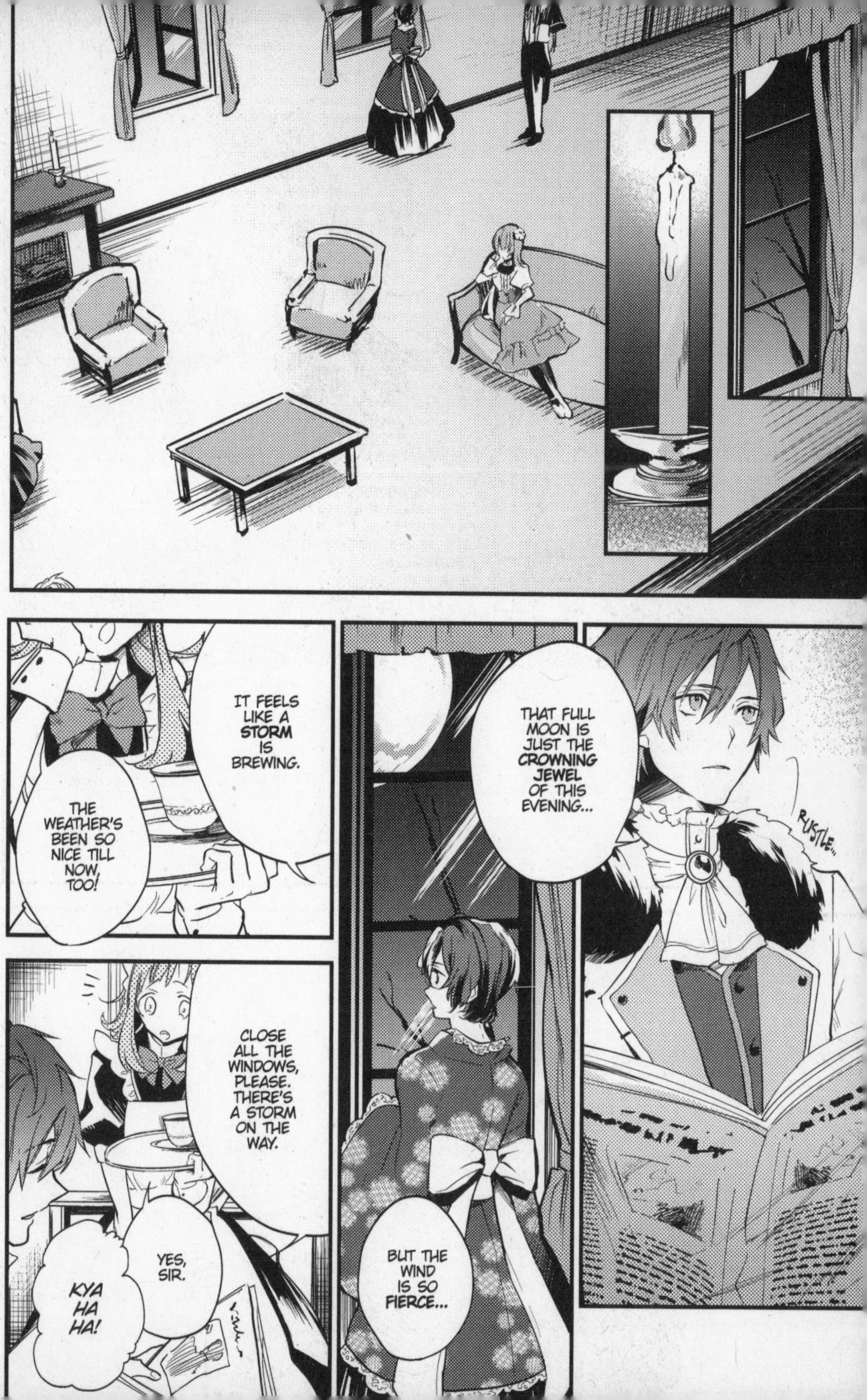
THAT FULL MOON IS JUST THE CROWNING JEWEL OF THIS EVENING...
RUSTLE...
BUT THE WIND IS SO FIERCE...
IT FEELS LIKE A STORM IS BREWING.
THE WEATHER'S BEEN SO NICE TILL NOW, TOO!
CLOSE ALL THE WINDOWS, PLEASE. THERE'S A STORM ON THE WAY.
YES, SIR.
KYA HA HA!

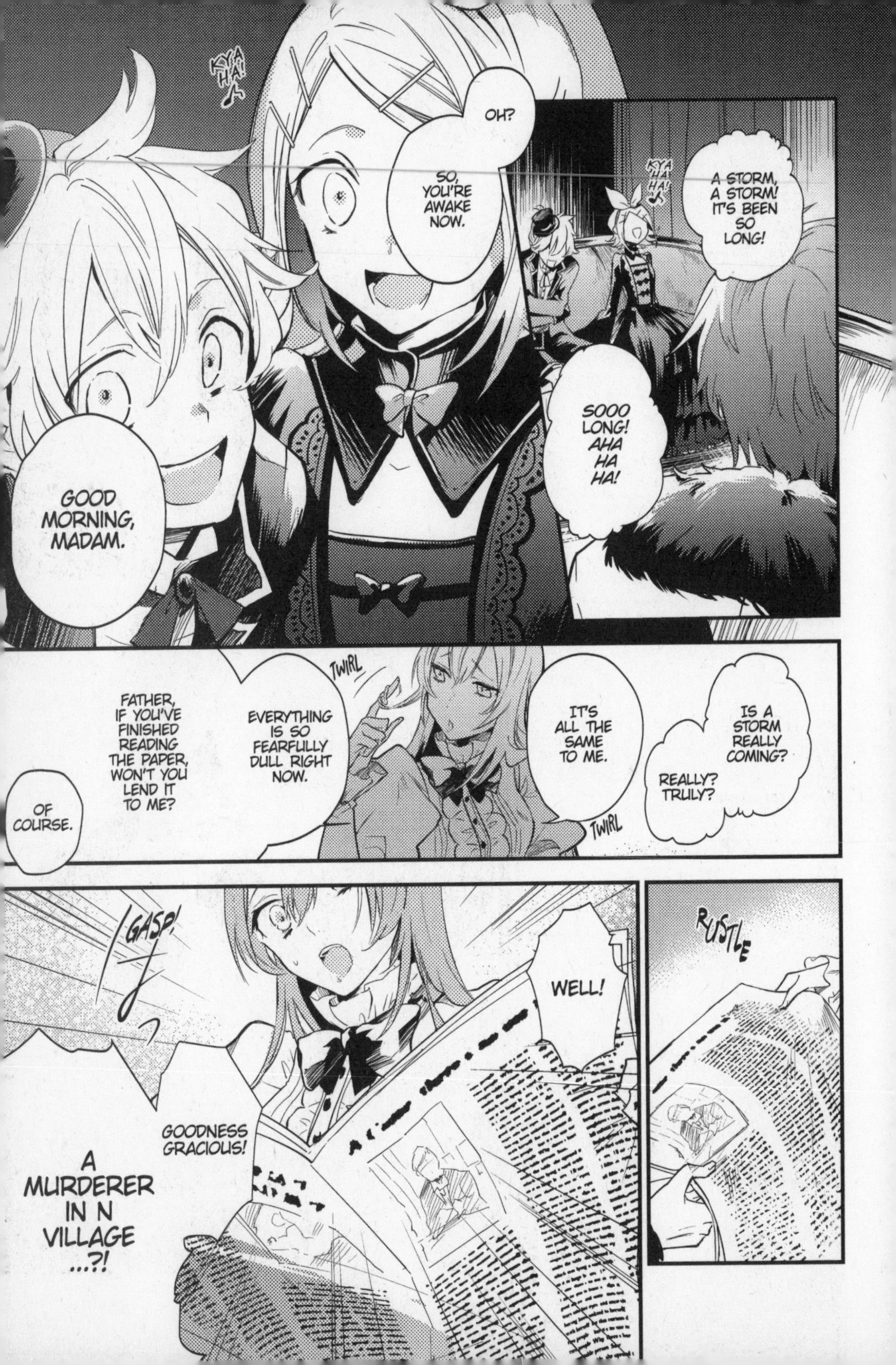
A STORM, A STORM! IT'S BEEN SO LONG!
KYA HA HA! ♪
SOOO LONG! AHA HA HA!
OH?
SO, YOU'RE AWAKE NOW.
KYA HA HA! ♪
GOOD MORNING, MADAM.
IS A STORM REALLY COMING?
REALLY? TRULY?
IT'S ALL THE SAME TO ME.
TWIRL
TWIRL
EVERYTHING IS SO FEARFULLY DULL RIGHT NOW.
FATHER, IF YOU'VE FINISHED READING THE PAPER, WON'T YOU LEND IT TO ME?
OF COURSE.
RUSTLE
WELL!
GASP!
GOODNESS GRACIOUS!
A MURDERER IN N VILLAGE ...?!

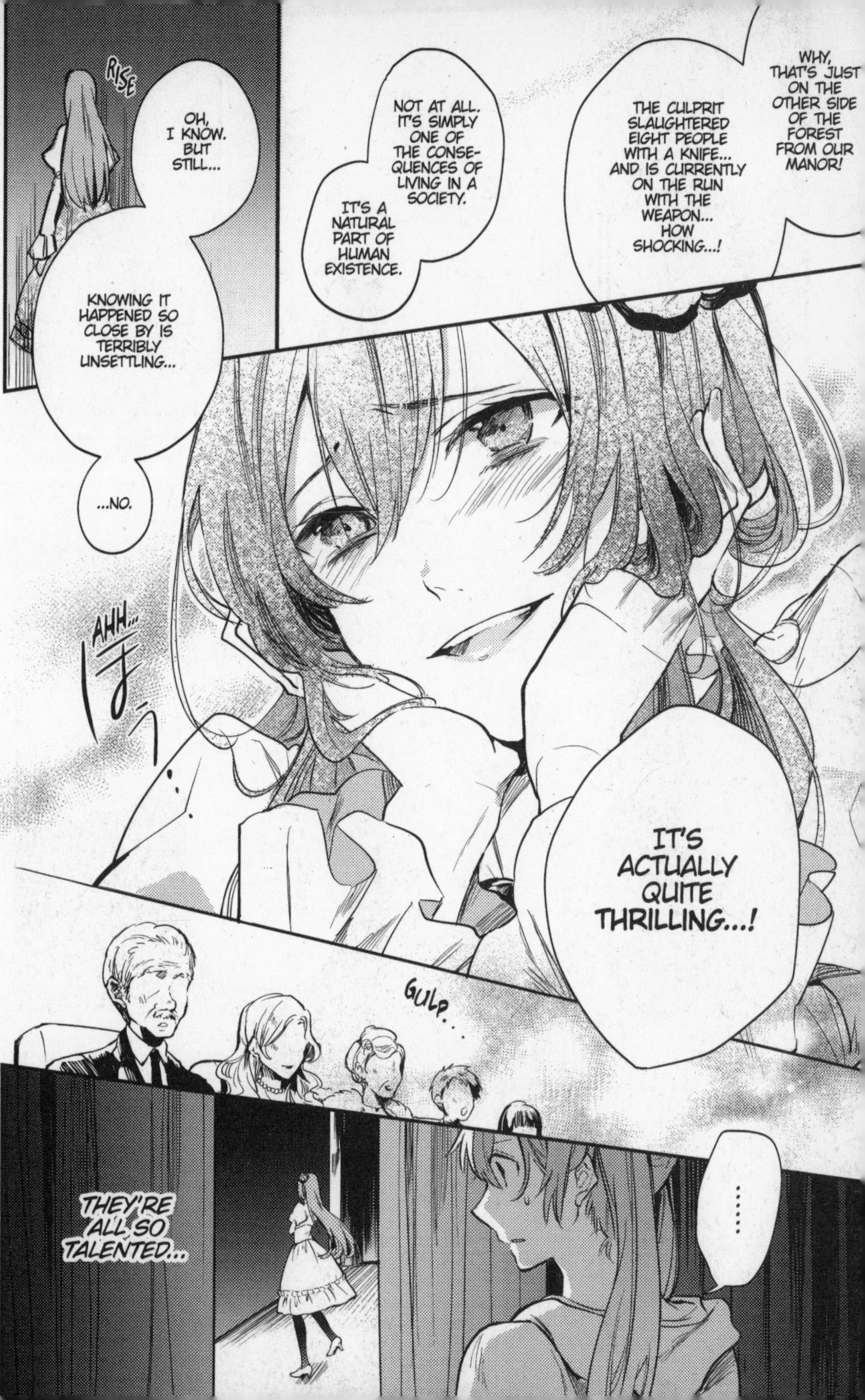
WHY, THAT'S JUST ON THE OTHER SIDE OF THE FOREST FROM OUR MANOR!
THE CULPRIT SLAUGHTERED EIGHT PEOPLE WITH A KNIFE... AND IS CURRENTLY ON THE RUN WITH THE WEAPON... HOW SHOCKING...!
NOT AT ALL. IT'S SIMPLY ONE OF THE CONSE-QUENCES OF LIVING IN A SOCIETY.
IT'S A NATURAL PART OF HUMAN EXISTENCE.
RISE
OH, I KNOW. BUT STILL...
KNOWING IT HAPPENED SO CLOSE BY IS TERRIBLY UNSETTLING...
...NO.
AHH...
IT'S ACTUALLY QUITE THRILLING...!
GULP...
......
THEY'RE ALL SO TALENTED...

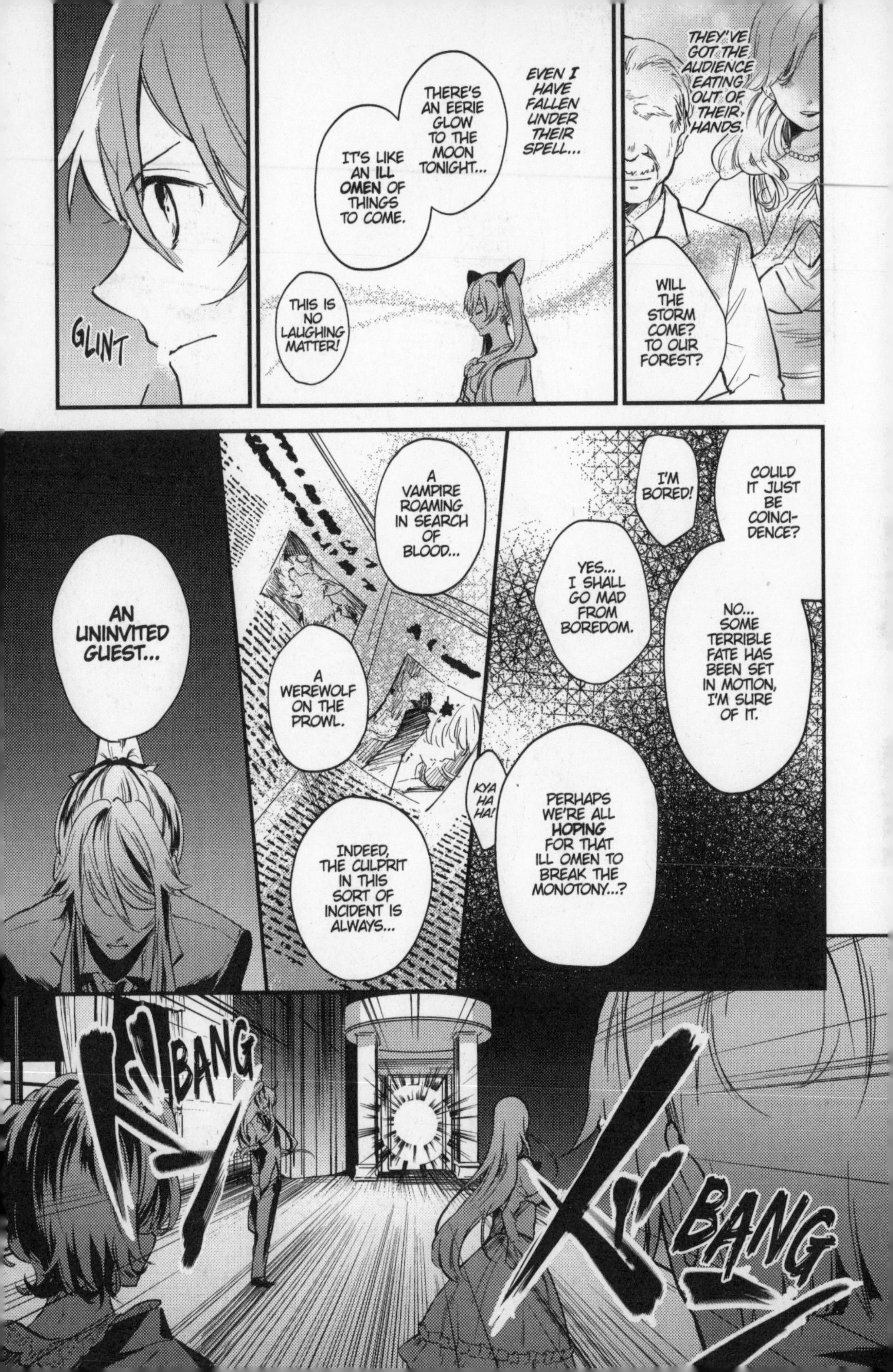
THEY'VE GOT THE AUDIENCE EATING OUT OF THEIR HANDS.
WILL THE STORM COME? TO OUR FOREST?
EVEN I HAVE FALLEN UNDER THEIR SPELL...
THERE'S AN EERIE GLOW TO THE MOON TONIGHT...
IT'S LIKE AN ILL OMEN OF THINGS TO COME.
THIS IS NO LAUGHING MATTER!
GLINT
COULD IT JUST BE COINCIDENCE?
I'M BORED!
YES... I SHALL GO MAD FROM BOREDOM.
NO... SOME TERRIBLE FATE HAS BEEN SET IN MOTION, I'M SURE OF IT.
PERHAPS WE'RE ALL HOPING FOR THAT ILL OMEN TO BREAK THE MONOTONY...?
KYA HA HA!
A VAMPIRE ROAMING IN SEARCH OF BLOOD...
A WEREWOLF ON THE PROWL.
INDEED, THE CULPRIT IN THIS SORT OF INCIDENT IS ALWAYS...
AN UNINVITED GUEST...
BANG
BANG

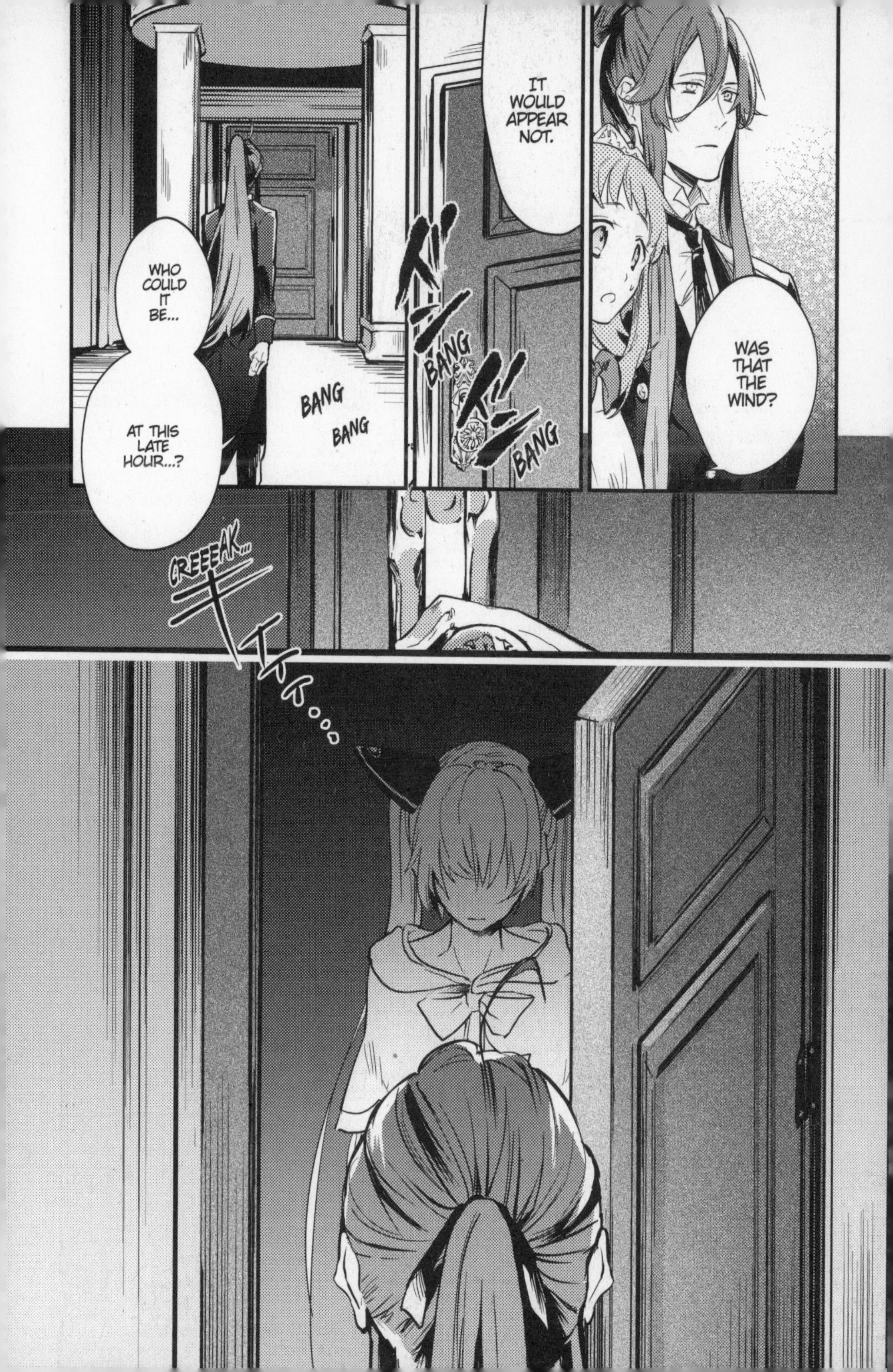
WAS THAT THE WIND?
IT WOULD APPEAR NOT.
BANG
BANG
WHO COULD IT BE...
AT THIS LATE HOUR...?
BANG
BANG
CREEEAK...

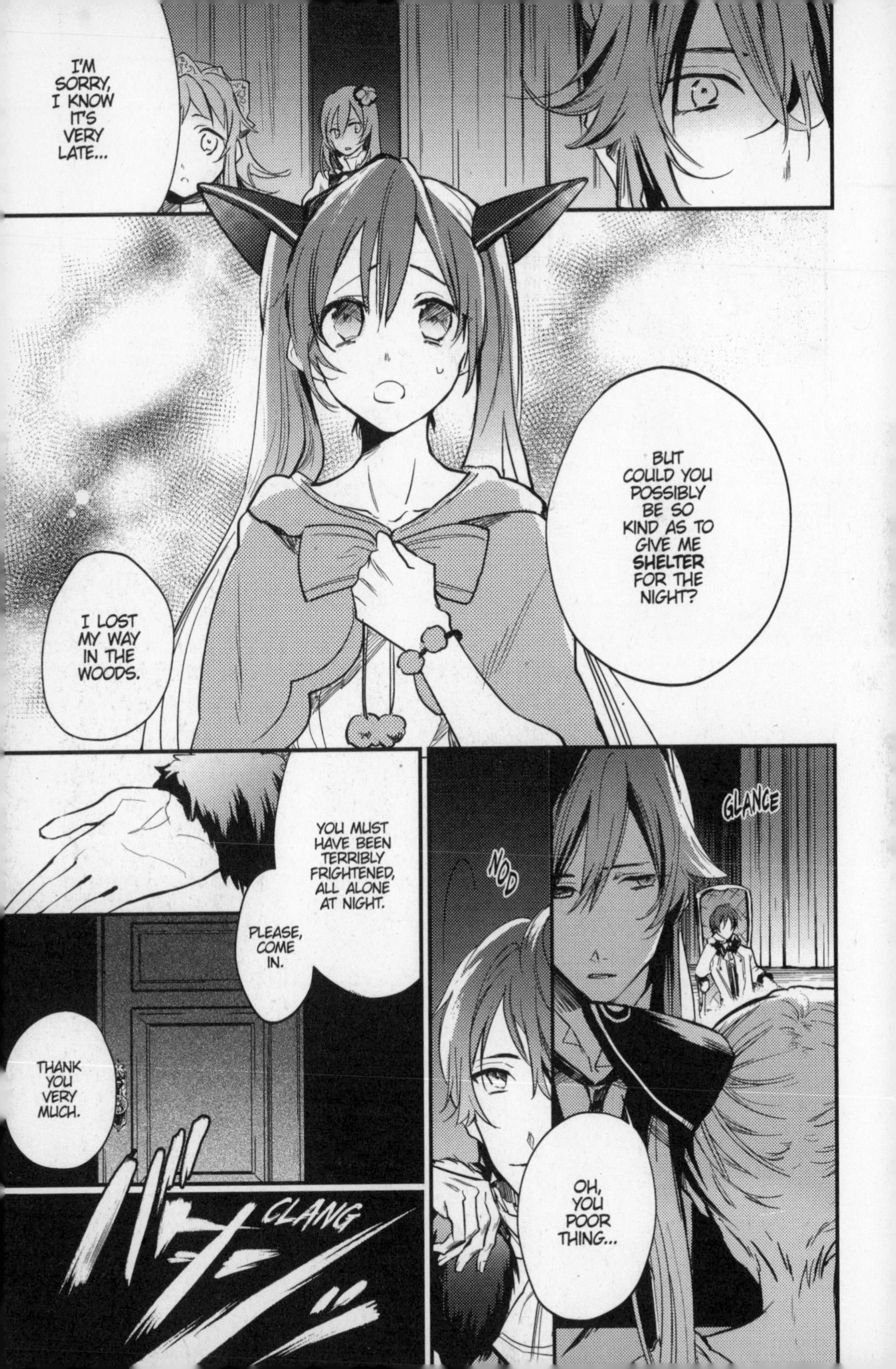

I'M SORRY, I KNOW IT'S VERY LATE...
BUT COULD YOU POSSIBLY BE SO KIND AS TO GIVE ME **SHELTER** FOR THE NIGHT?
I LOST MY WAY IN THE WOODS.
GLANCE
NOD
OH, YOU POOR THING...
YOU MUST HAVE BEEN TERRIBLY FRIGHTENED, ALL ALONE AT NIGHT.
PLEASE, COME IN.
THANK YOU VERY MUCH.
CLANG

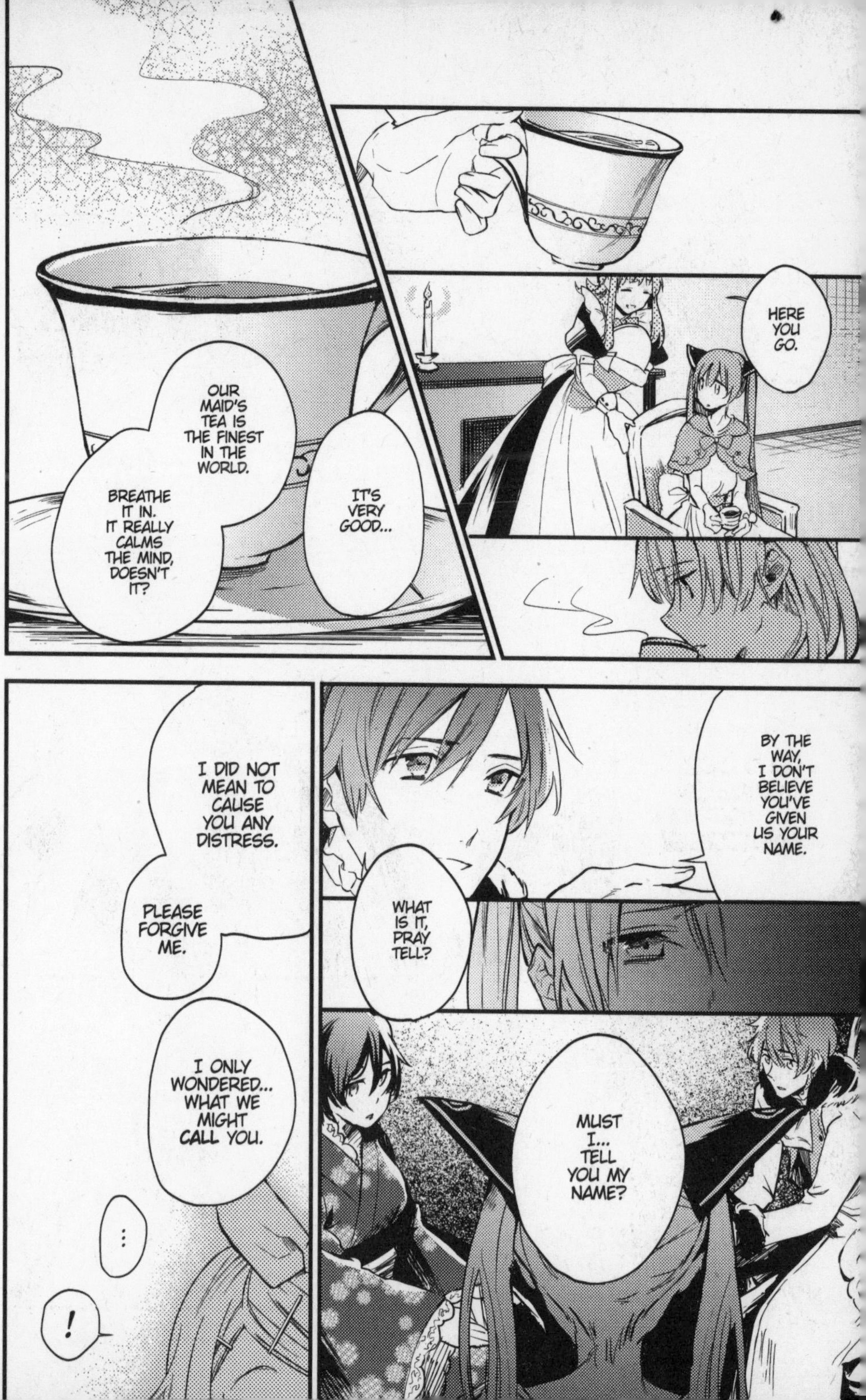
HERE YOU GO.
OUR MAID'S TEA IS THE FINEST IN THE WORLD.
IT'S VERY GOOD...
BREATHE IT IN. IT REALLY CALMS THE MIND, DOESN'T IT?
BY THE WAY, I DON'T BELIEVE YOU'VE GIVEN US YOUR NAME.
WHAT IS IT, PRAY TELL?
MUST I... TELL YOU MY NAME?
I DID NOT MEAN TO CAUSE YOU ANY DISTRESS.
PLEASE FORGIVE ME.
I ONLY WONDERED... WHAT WE MIGHT CALL YOU.
...
!

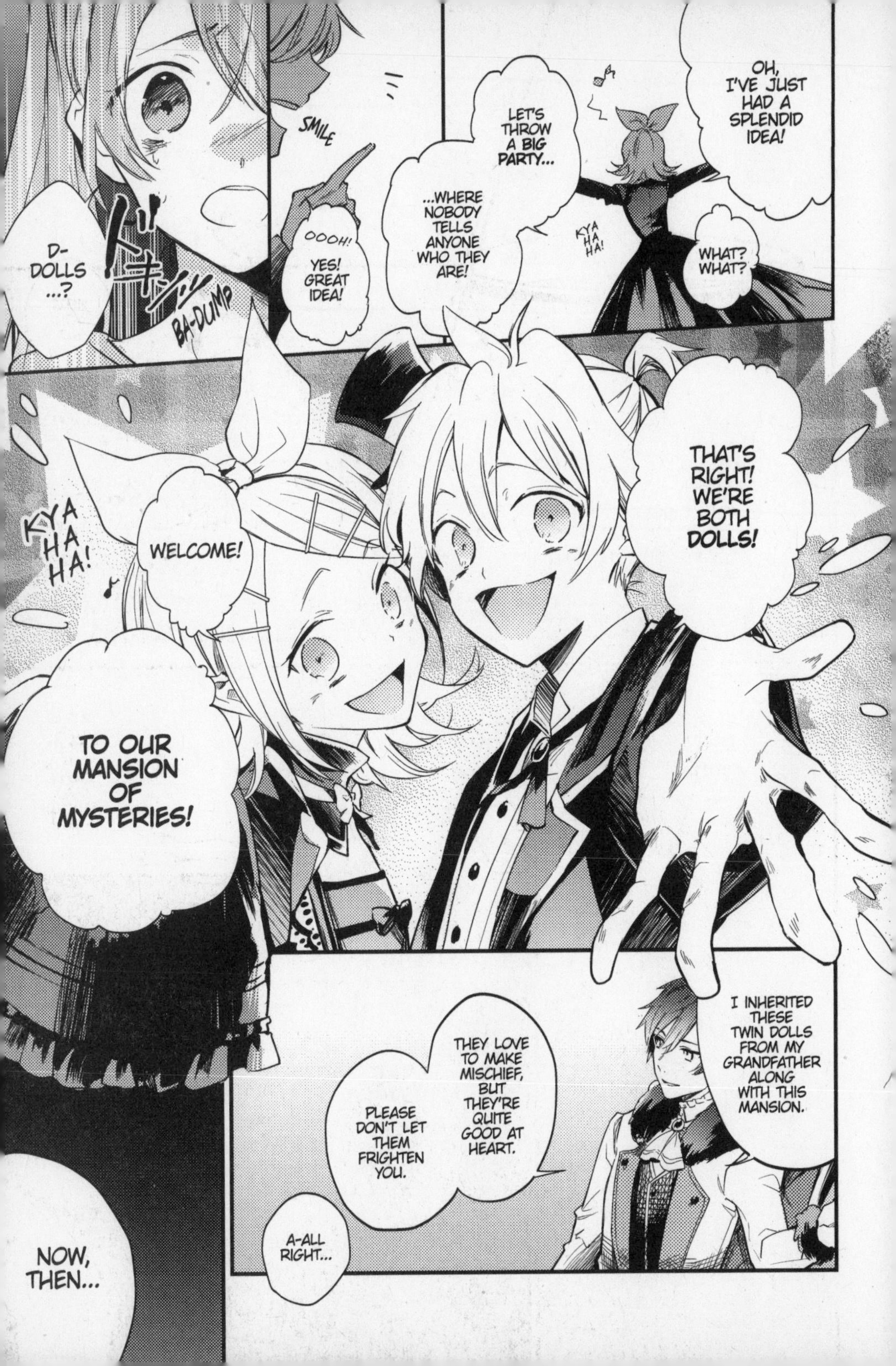
OH, I'VE JUST HAD A SPLENDID IDEA!
WHAT? WHAT?
KYA HA HA!
LET'S THROW A BIG PARTY...
...WHERE NOBODY TELLS ANYONE WHO THEY ARE!
SMILE
OOOH! YES! GREAT IDEA!
D-DOLLS ...?
BA-DUMP
THAT'S RIGHT! WE'RE BOTH DOLLS!
WELCOME!
KYA HA HA!
TO OUR MANSION OF MYSTERIES!
I INHERITED THESE TWIN DOLLS FROM MY GRANDFATHER ALONG WITH THIS MANSION.
THEY LOVE TO MAKE MISCHIEF, BUT THEY'RE QUITE GOOD AT HEART.
PLEASE DON'T LET THEM FRIGHTEN YOU.
A-ALL RIGHT...
NOW, THEN...

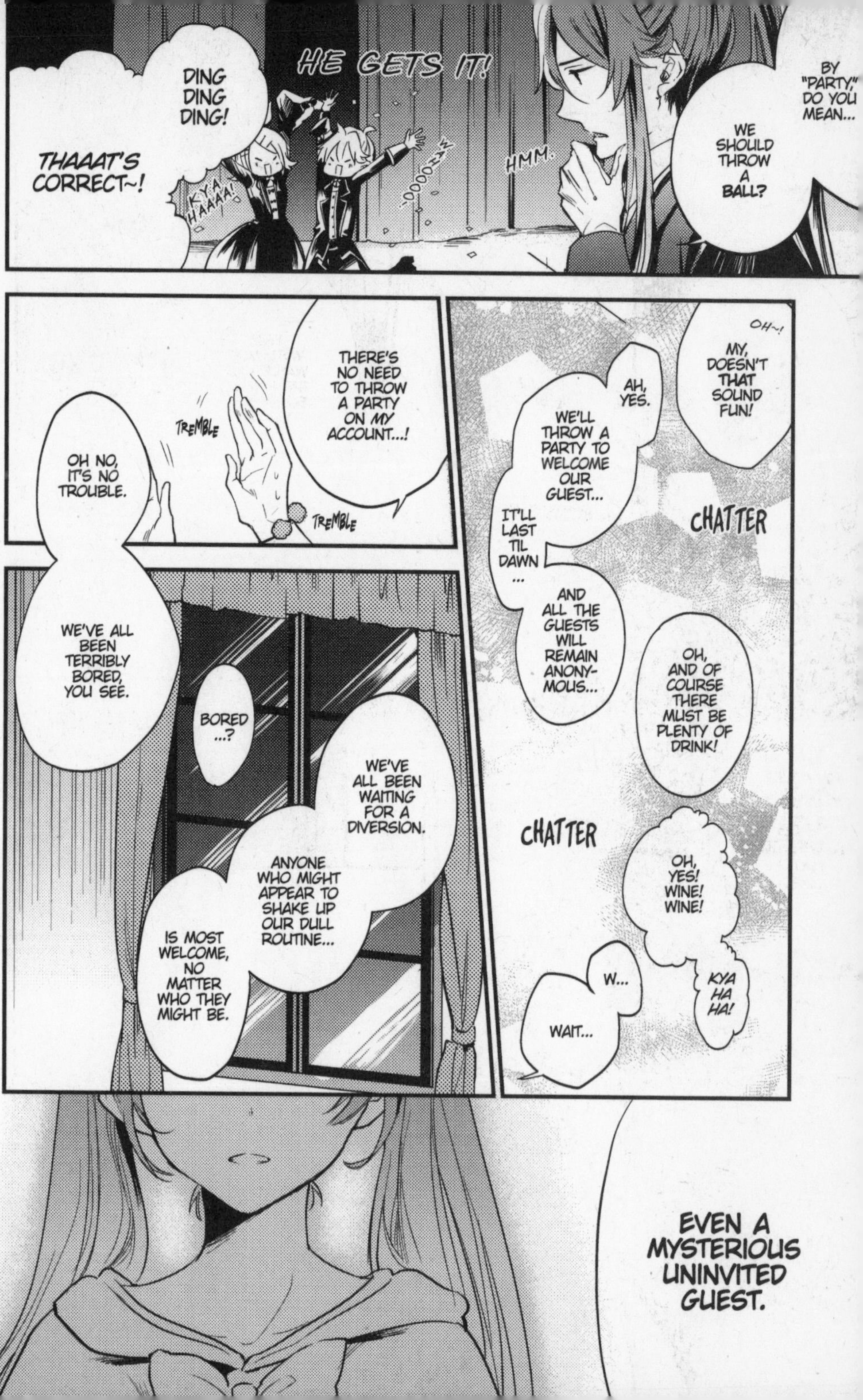
BY "PARTY," DO YOU MEAN...
WE SHOULD THROW A BALL?
HMM.
HE GETS IT!
WAHOOOOO!
DING DING DING!
KYA HAAAA!
THAAAT'S CORRECT~!
OH~!
MY, DOESN'T THAT SOUND FUN!
AH, YES.
WE'LL THROW A PARTY TO WELCOME OUR GUEST...
IT'LL LAST TIL DAWN...
AND ALL THE GUESTS WILL REMAIN ANONY-MOUS...
CHATTER
OH, AND OF COURSE THERE MUST BE PLENTY OF DRINK!
CHATTER
OH, YES! WINE! WINE!
KYA HA HA!
W...
WAIT...
THERE'S NO NEED TO THROW A PARTY ON MY ACCOUNT...!
TREMBLE
TREMBLE
OH NO, IT'S NO TROUBLE.
WE'VE ALL BEEN TERRIBLY BORED, YOU SEE.
BORED...?
WE'VE ALL BEEN WAITING FOR A DIVERSION.
ANYONE WHO MIGHT APPEAR TO SHAKE UP OUR DULL ROUTINE...
IS MOST WELCOME, NO MATTER WHO THEY MIGHT BE.
EVEN A MYSTERIOUS UNINVITED GUEST.

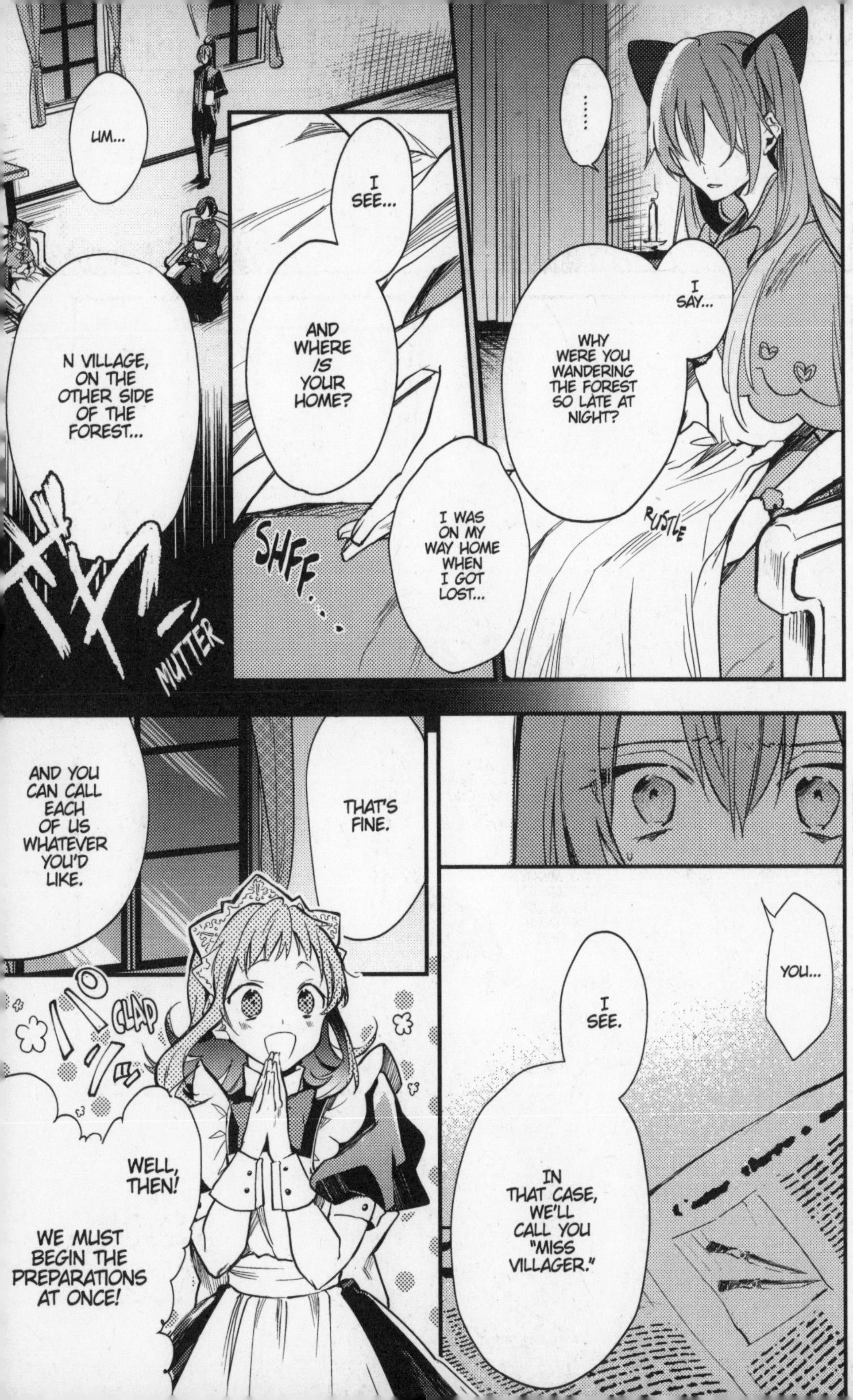
......
I SAY...
WHY WERE YOU WANDERING THE FOREST SO LATE AT NIGHT?
RUSTLE
I WAS ON MY WAY HOME WHEN I GOT LOST...
SHFF...
I SEE...
AND WHERE IS YOUR HOME?
UM...
N VILLAGE, ON THE OTHER SIDE OF THE FOREST...
MUTTER
YOU...
I SEE.
IN THAT CASE, WE'LL CALL YOU "MISS VILLAGER."
THAT'S FINE.
AND YOU CAN CALL EACH OF US WHATEVER YOU'D LIKE.
CLAP
WELL, THEN!
WE MUST BEGIN THE PREPARATIONS AT ONCE!

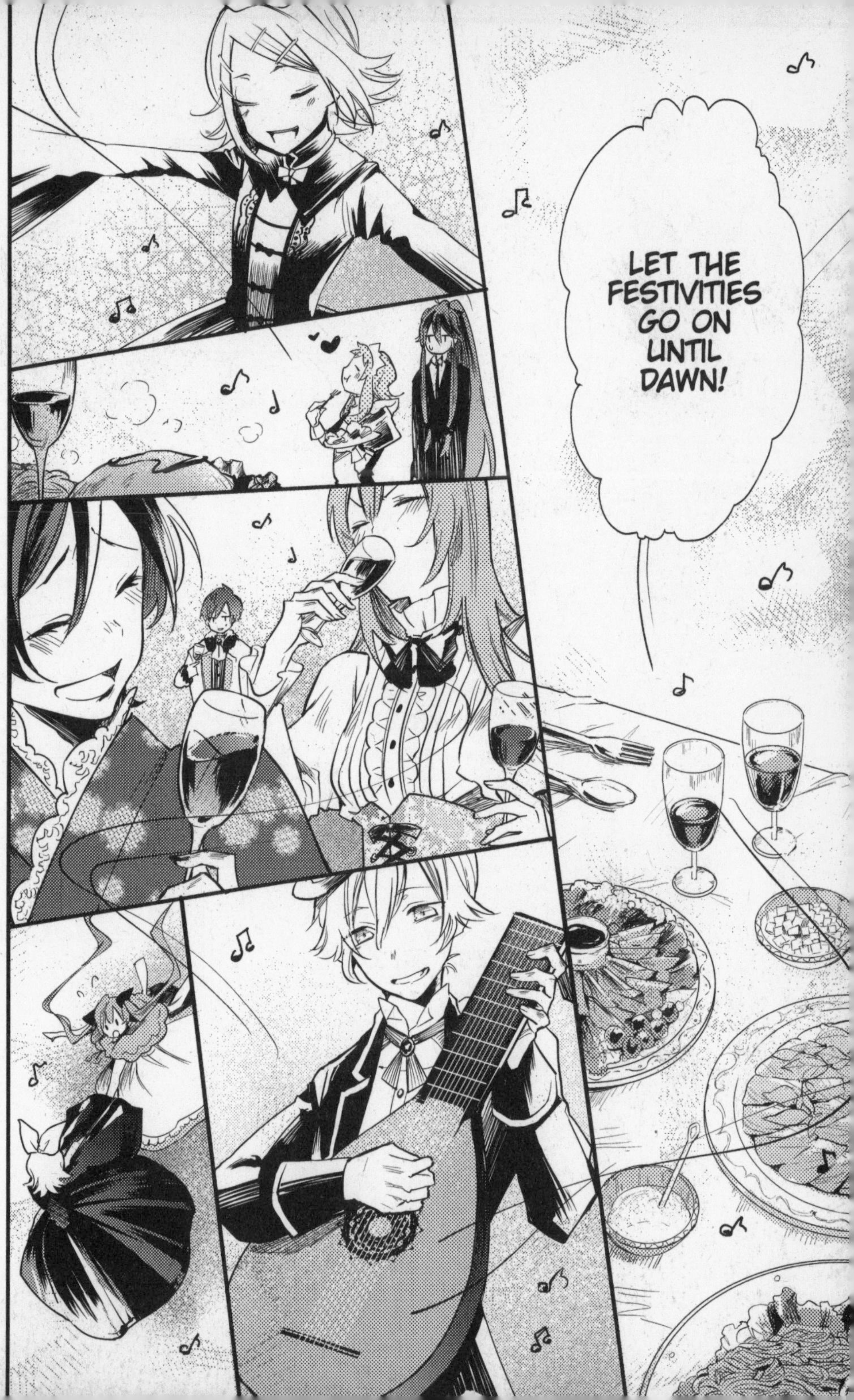
LET THE FESTIVITIES GO ON UNTIL DAWN!

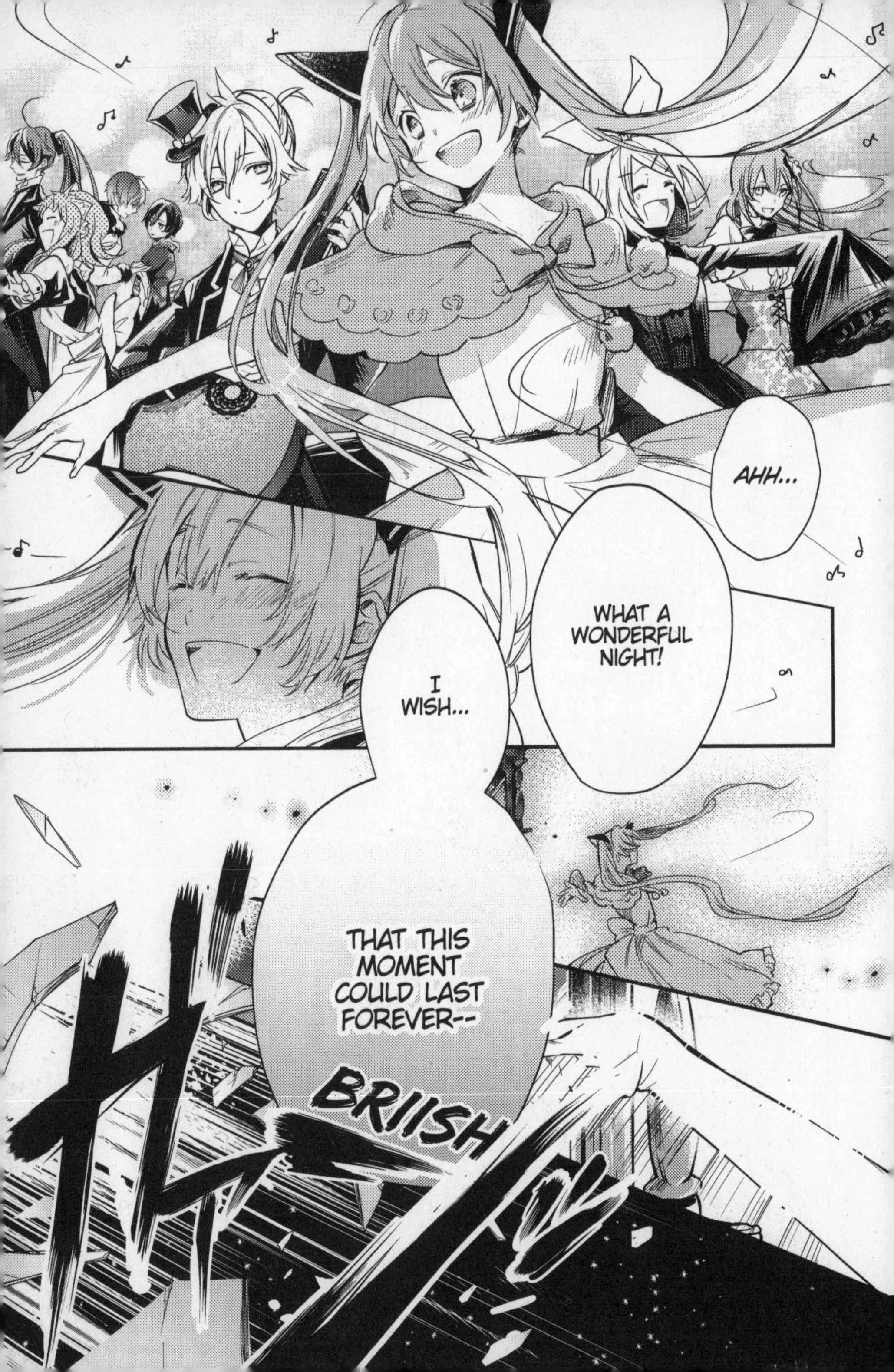
AHH...
WHAT A WONDERFUL NIGHT!
I WISH...
THAT THIS MOMENT COULD LAST FOREVER--
BRIISH

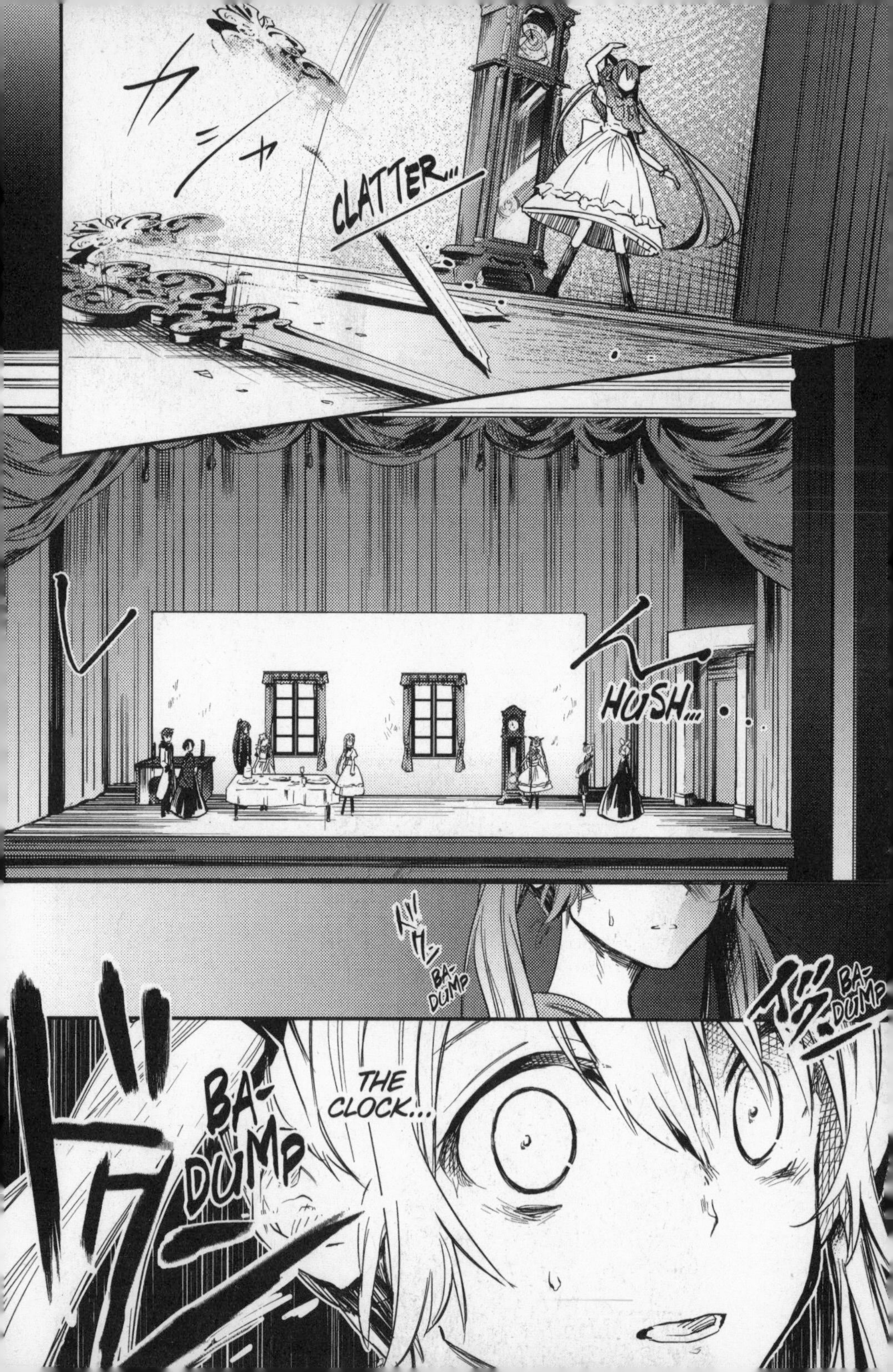
CLATTER...
HUSH...
BA-DUMP
BA-DUMP
THE CLOCK...
BA-DUMP

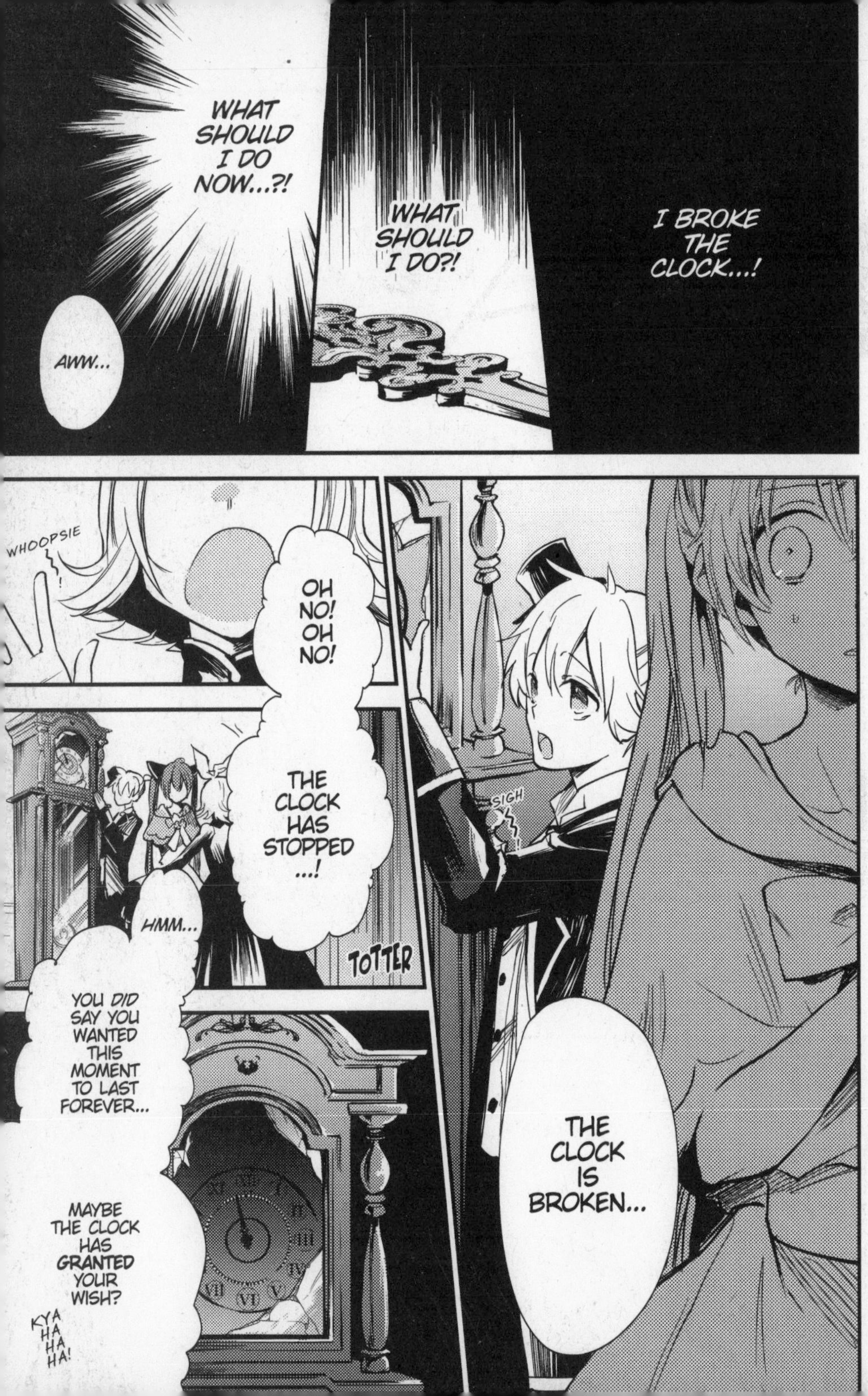
I BROKE THE CLOCK...!
WHAT SHOULD I DO?!
WHAT SHOULD I DO NOW...?!
AWW...
THE CLOCK IS BROKEN...
SIGH
OH NO! OH NO!
WHOOPSIE
THE CLOCK HAS STOPPED ...!
TOTTER
HMM...
YOU *DID* SAY YOU WANTED THIS MOMENT TO LAST FOREVER...
MAYBE THE CLOCK HAS GRANTED YOUR WISH?
KYA HA HA HA HA!

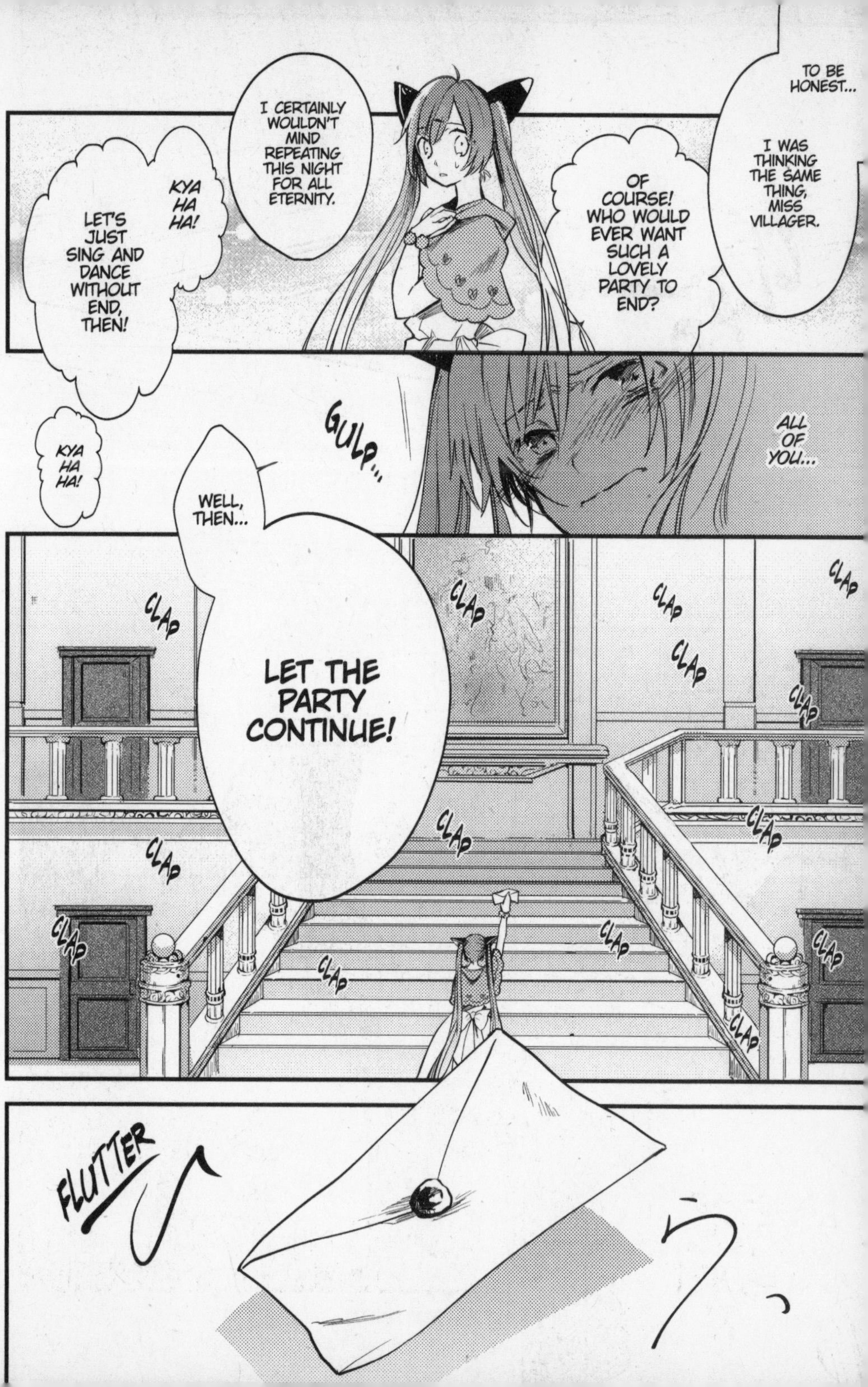

TO BE HONEST...
I WAS THINKING THE SAME THING, MISS VILLAGER.
OF COURSE! WHO WOULD EVER WANT SUCH A LOVELY PARTY TO END?
I CERTAINLY WOULDN'T MIND REPEATING THIS NIGHT FOR ALL ETERNITY.
KYA HA HA!
LET'S JUST SING AND DANCE WITHOUT END, THEN!
ALL OF YOU...
GULP...
KYA HA HA!
WELL, THEN...
CLAP
CLAP
CLAP
CLAP
CLAP
CLAP
CLAP
CLAP
CLAP
CLAP
CLAP
CLAP
CLAP
LET THE PARTY CONTINUE!
FLUTTER

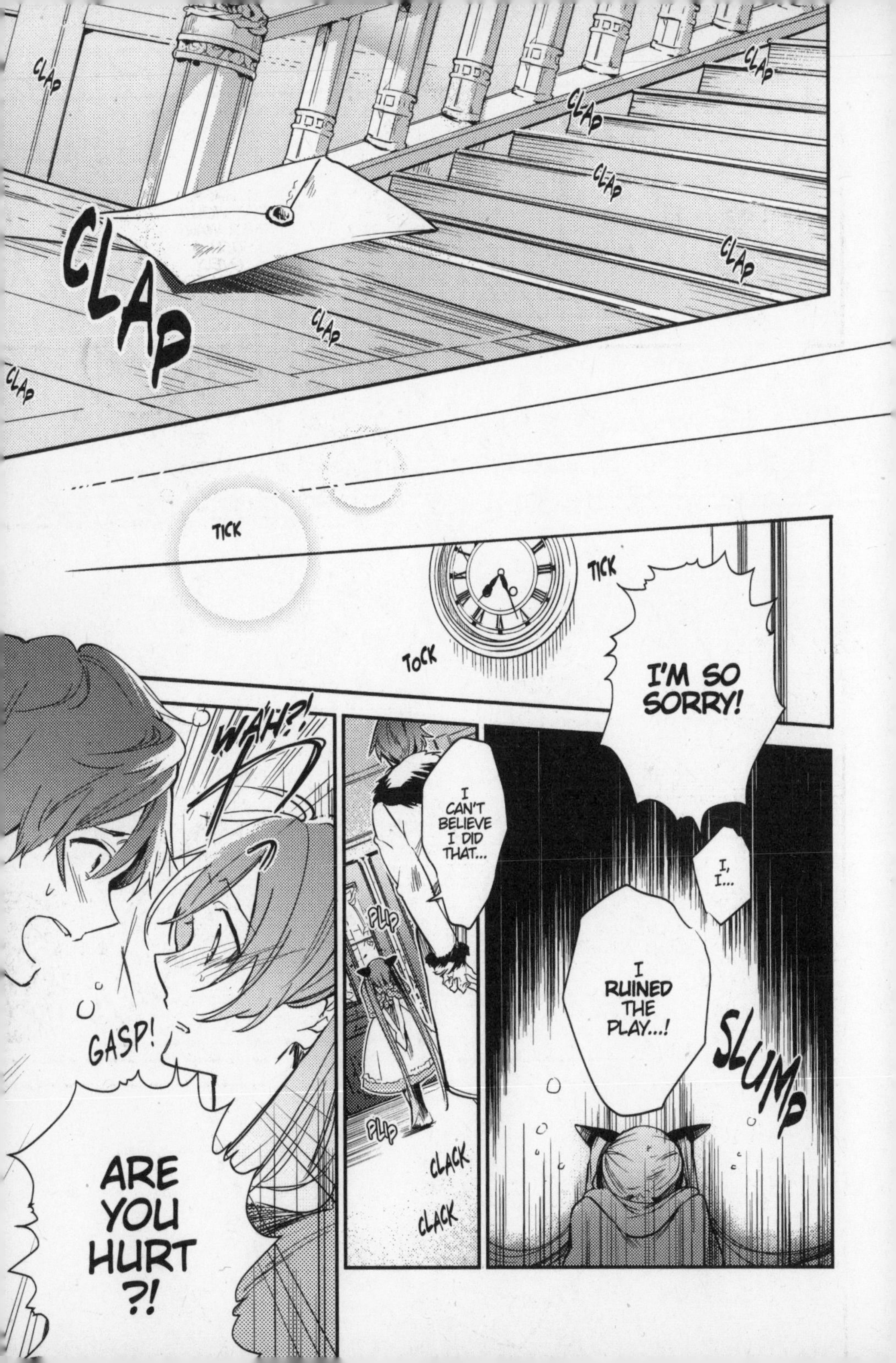
CLAP
CLAP
CLAP
CLAP
CLAP
CLAP
CLAP
CLAP
TICK
I'M SO SORRY!
TICK
TOCK
I, I...
I RUINED THE PLAY...!
SLUMP
I CAN'T BELIEVE I DID THAT...
PLIP
PLIP
CLACK
CLACK
WAH?!
GASP!
ARE YOU HURT?!

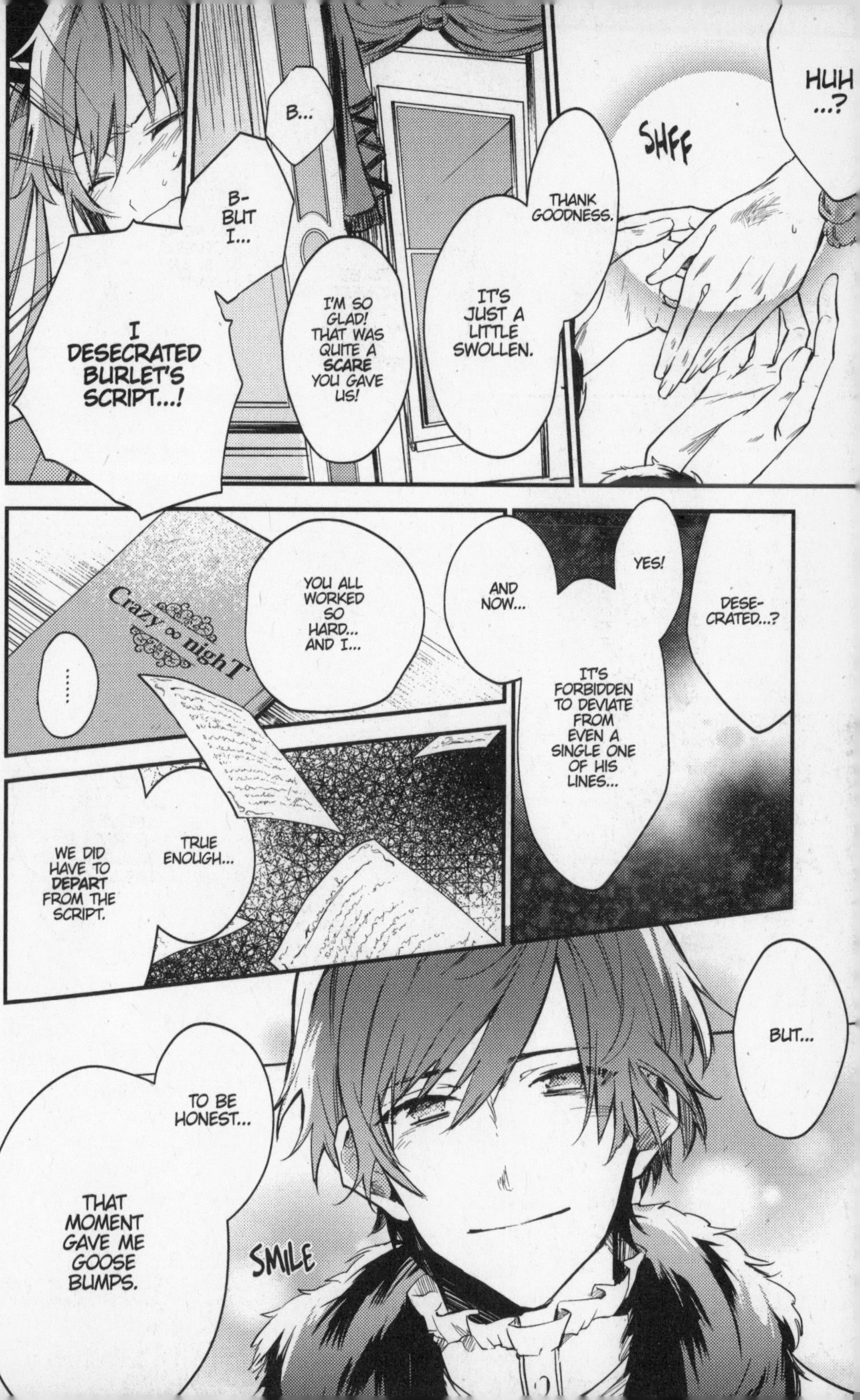
HUH ...?
SHFF
THANK GOODNESS.
IT'S JUST A LITTLE SWOLLEN.
I'M SO GLAD! THAT WAS QUITE A SCARE YOU GAVE US!
B...
B-BUT I...
I DESECRATED BURLET'S SCRIPT...!
DESE-CRATED...?
YES!
AND NOW...
IT'S FORBIDDEN TO DEVIATE FROM EVEN A SINGLE ONE OF HIS LINES...
YOU ALL WORKED SO HARD... AND I...
Crazy ∞ nighT
......
TRUE ENOUGH...
WE DID HAVE TO DEPART FROM THE SCRIPT.
BUT...
TO BE HONEST...
THAT MOMENT GAVE ME GOOSE BUMPS.
SMILE

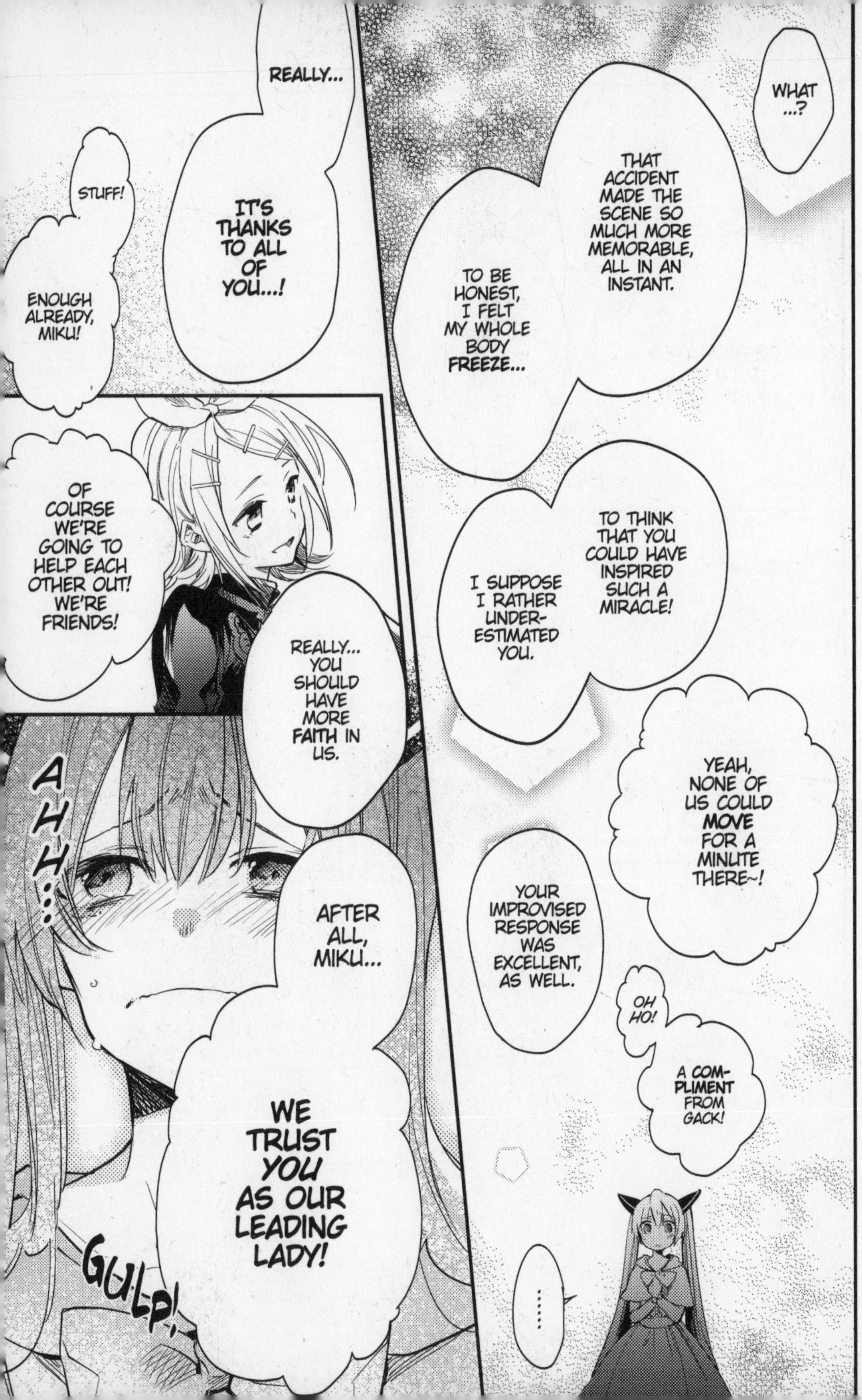
WHAT ...?
THAT ACCIDENT MADE THE SCENE SO MUCH MORE MEMORABLE, ALL IN AN INSTANT.
TO BE HONEST, I FELT MY WHOLE BODY FREEZE...
TO THINK THAT YOU COULD HAVE INSPIRED SUCH A MIRACLE!
I SUPPOSE I RATHER UNDER-ESTIMATED YOU.
YEAH, NONE OF US COULD MOVE FOR A MINUTE THERE~!
YOUR IMPROVISED RESPONSE WAS EXCELLENT, AS WELL.
OH HO!
A COM-PLIMENT FROM GACK!
......
REALLY...
IT'S THANKS TO ALL OF YOU...!
STUFF!
ENOUGH ALREADY, MIKU!
REALLY... YOU SHOULD HAVE MORE FAITH IN US.
OF COURSE WE'RE GOING TO HELP EACH OTHER OUT! WE'RE FRIENDS!
AFTER ALL, MIKU...
WE TRUST YOU AS OUR LEADING LADY!
AHH...
GULP!

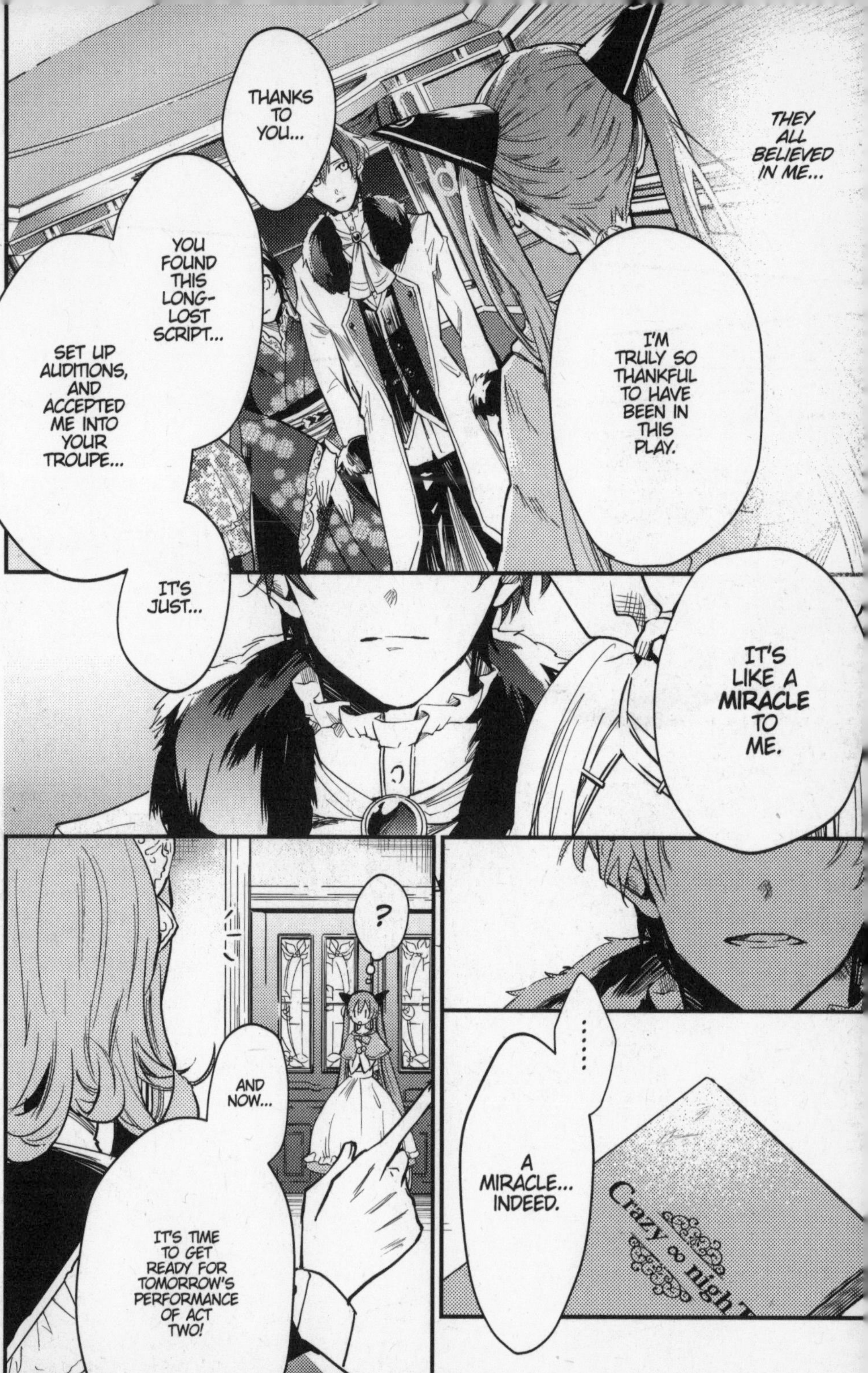

THEY ALL BELIEVED IN ME...
THANKS TO YOU...
I'M TRULY SO THANKFUL TO HAVE BEEN IN THIS PLAY.
YOU FOUND THIS LONG-LOST SCRIPT...
SET UP AUDITIONS, AND ACCEPTED ME INTO YOUR TROUPE...
IT'S JUST...
IT'S LIKE A MIRACLE TO ME.
......
A MIRACLE... INDEED.
Crazy ∞ nigh
?
AND NOW...
IT'S TIME TO GET READY FOR TOMORROW'S PERFORMANCE OF ACT TWO!

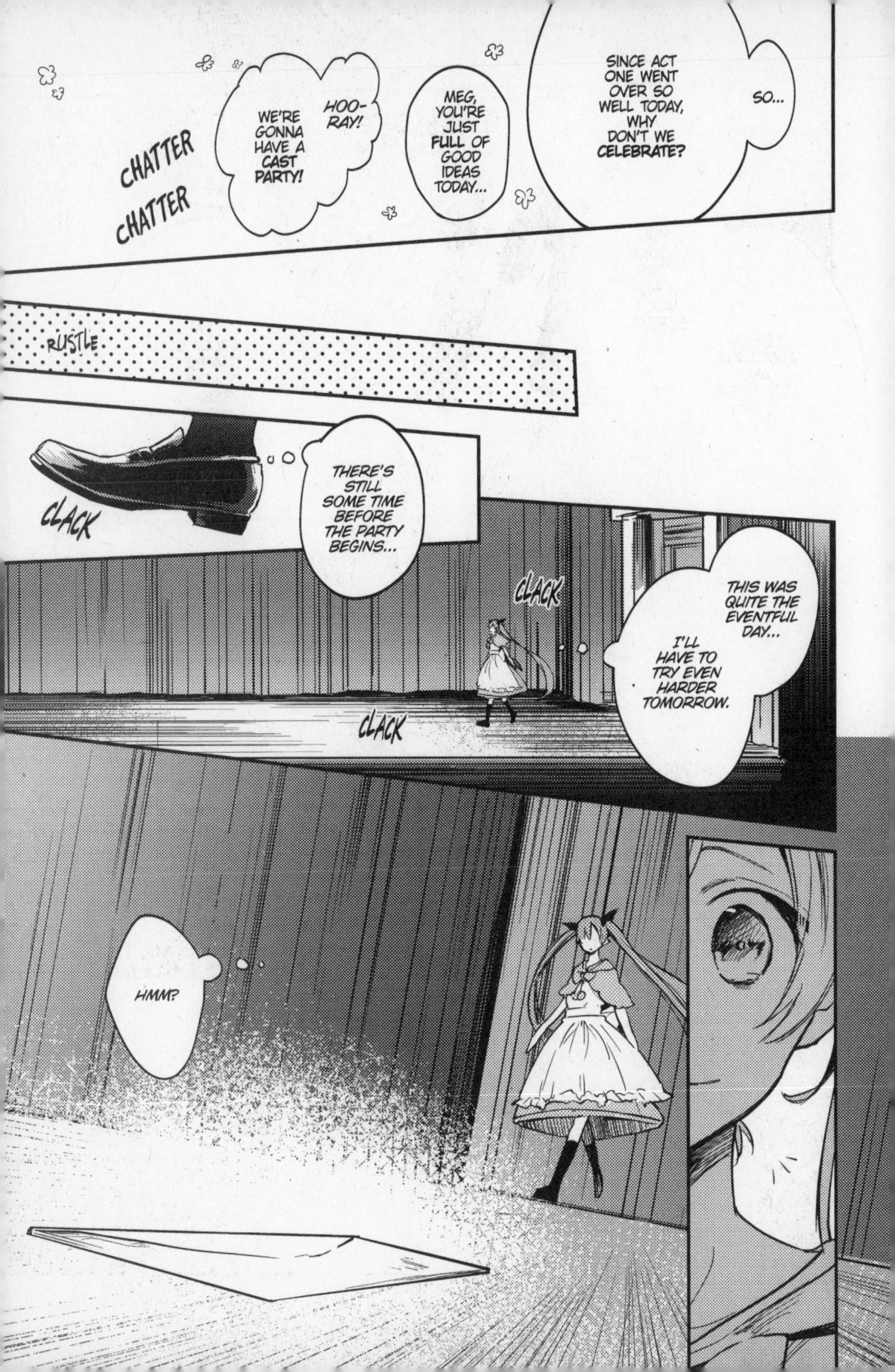
SO...
SINCE ACT ONE WENT OVER SO WELL TODAY, WHY DON'T WE CELEBRATE?
MEG, YOU'RE JUST FULL OF GOOD IDEAS TODAY...
HOO-RAY!
WE'RE GONNA HAVE A CAST PARTY!
CHATTER
CHATTER
RUSTLE
THERE'S STILL SOME TIME BEFORE THE PARTY BEGINS...
CLACK
THIS WAS QUITE THE EVENTFUL DAY...
I'LL HAVE TO TRY EVEN HARDER TOMORROW.
CLACK
CLACK
HMM?

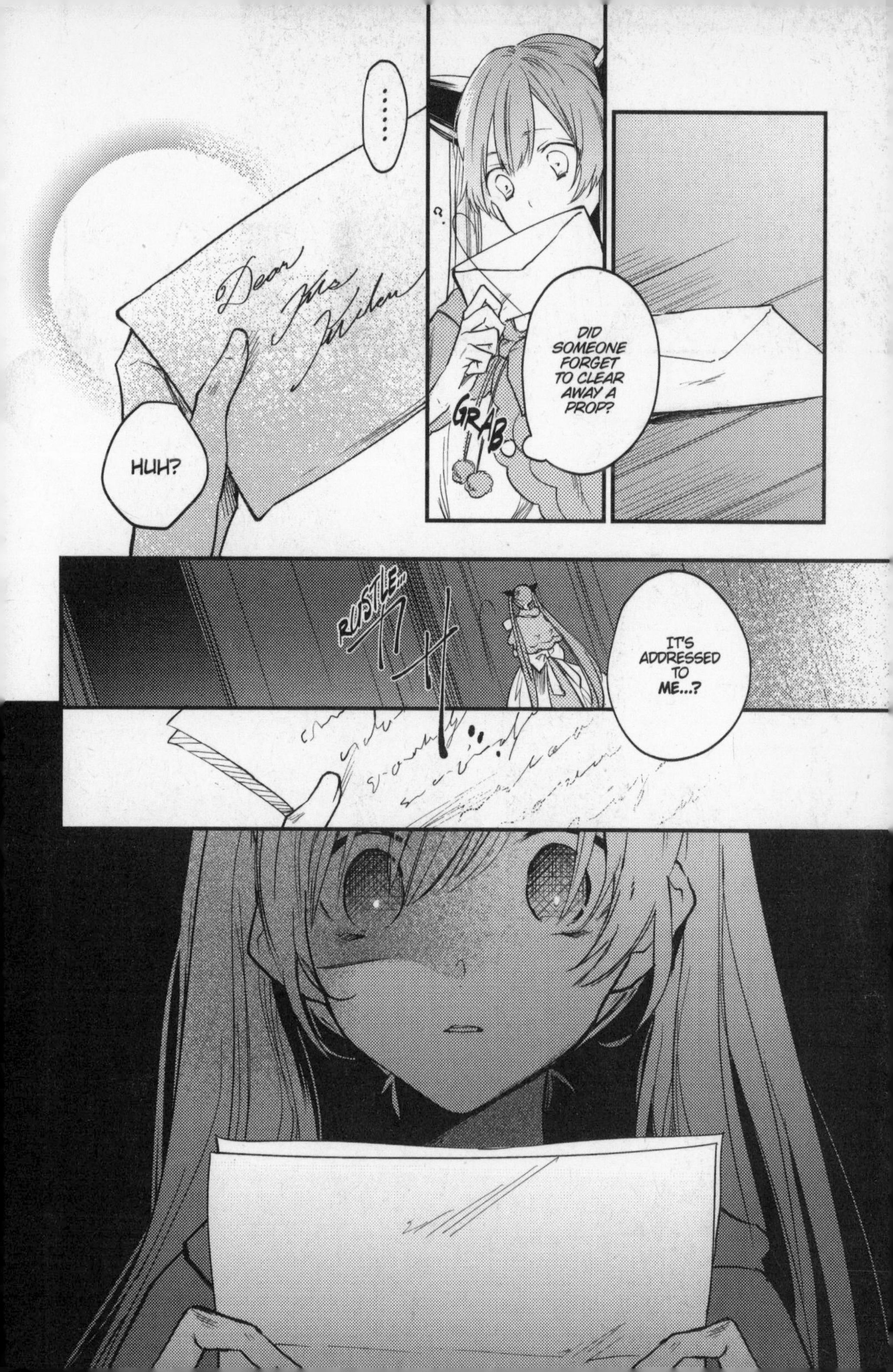
?
GRAB
DID SOMEONE FORGET TO CLEAR AWAY A PROP?
......
HUH?
IT'S ADDRESSED TO ME...?
RUSTLE...

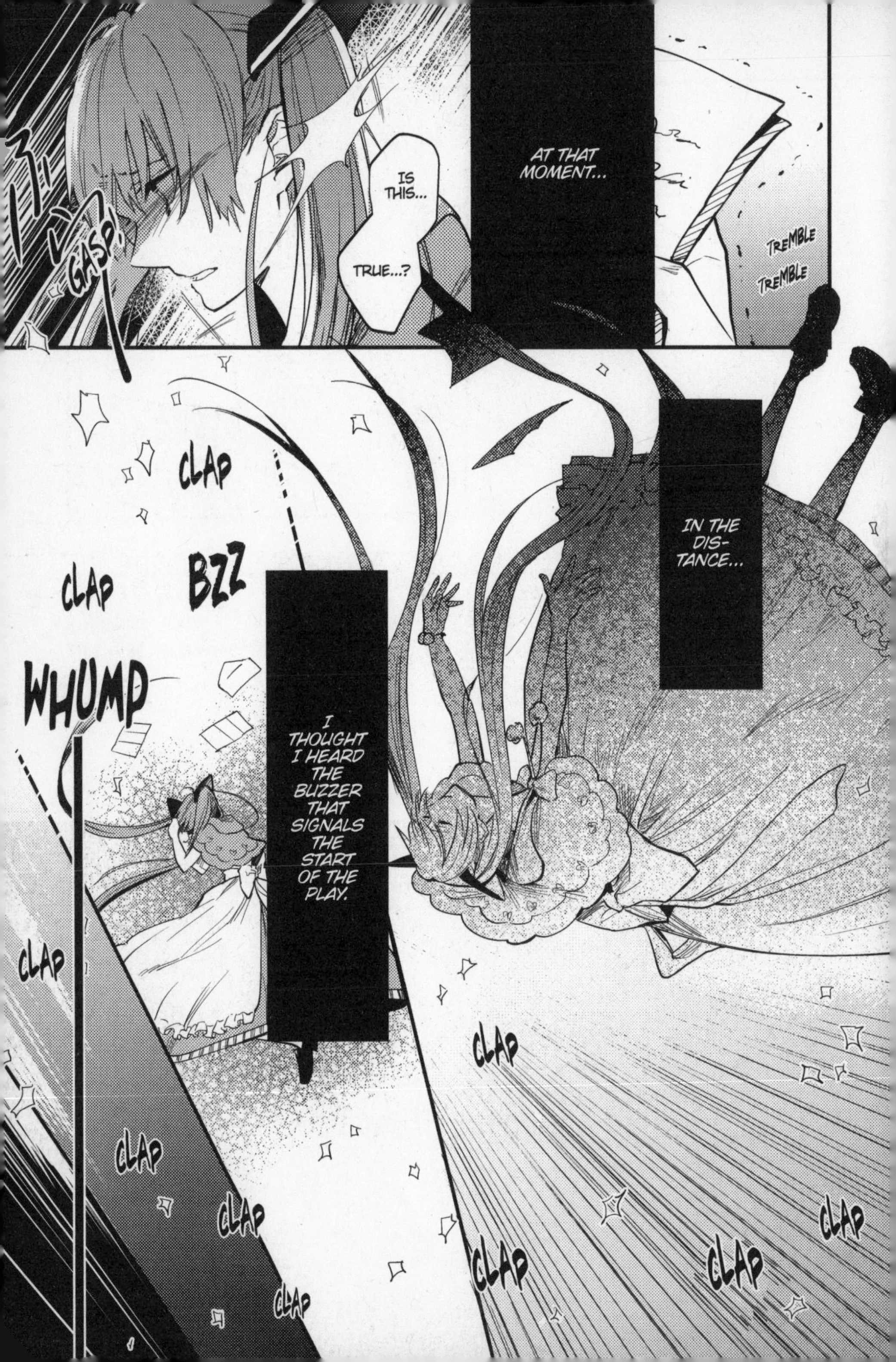
TREMBLE
TREMBLE
AT THAT MOMENT...
IS THIS...
TRUE...?
GASP!
IN THE DISTANCE...
I THOUGHT I HEARD THE BUZZER THAT SIGNALS THE START OF THE PLAY.
BZZ
CLAP
CLAP
WHUMP
CLAP
CLAP
CLAP
CLAP
CLAP
CLAP
CLAP
CLAP

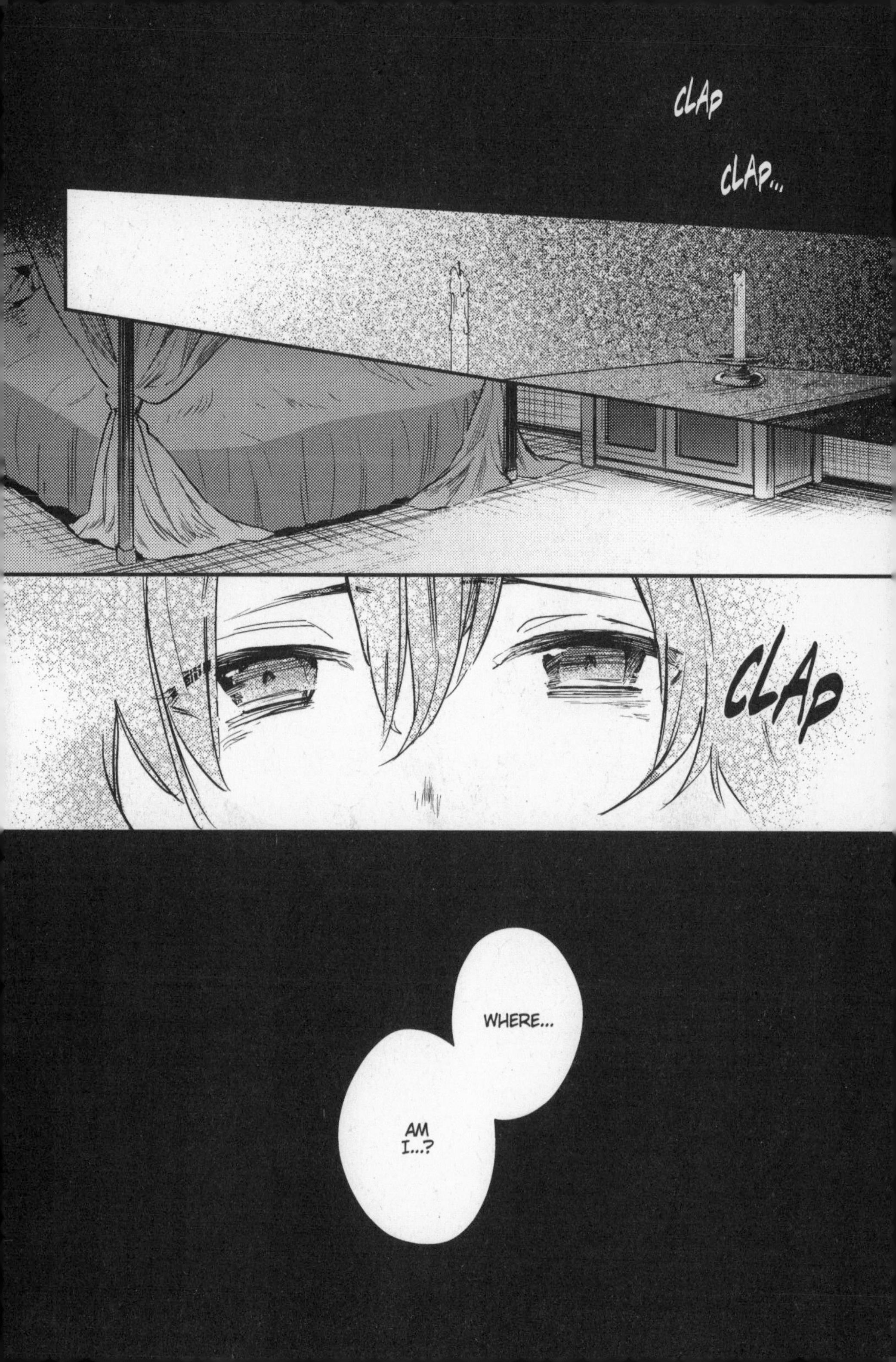
CLAP
CLAP...
CLAP
WHERE...
AM I...?

Act 2: Resolution

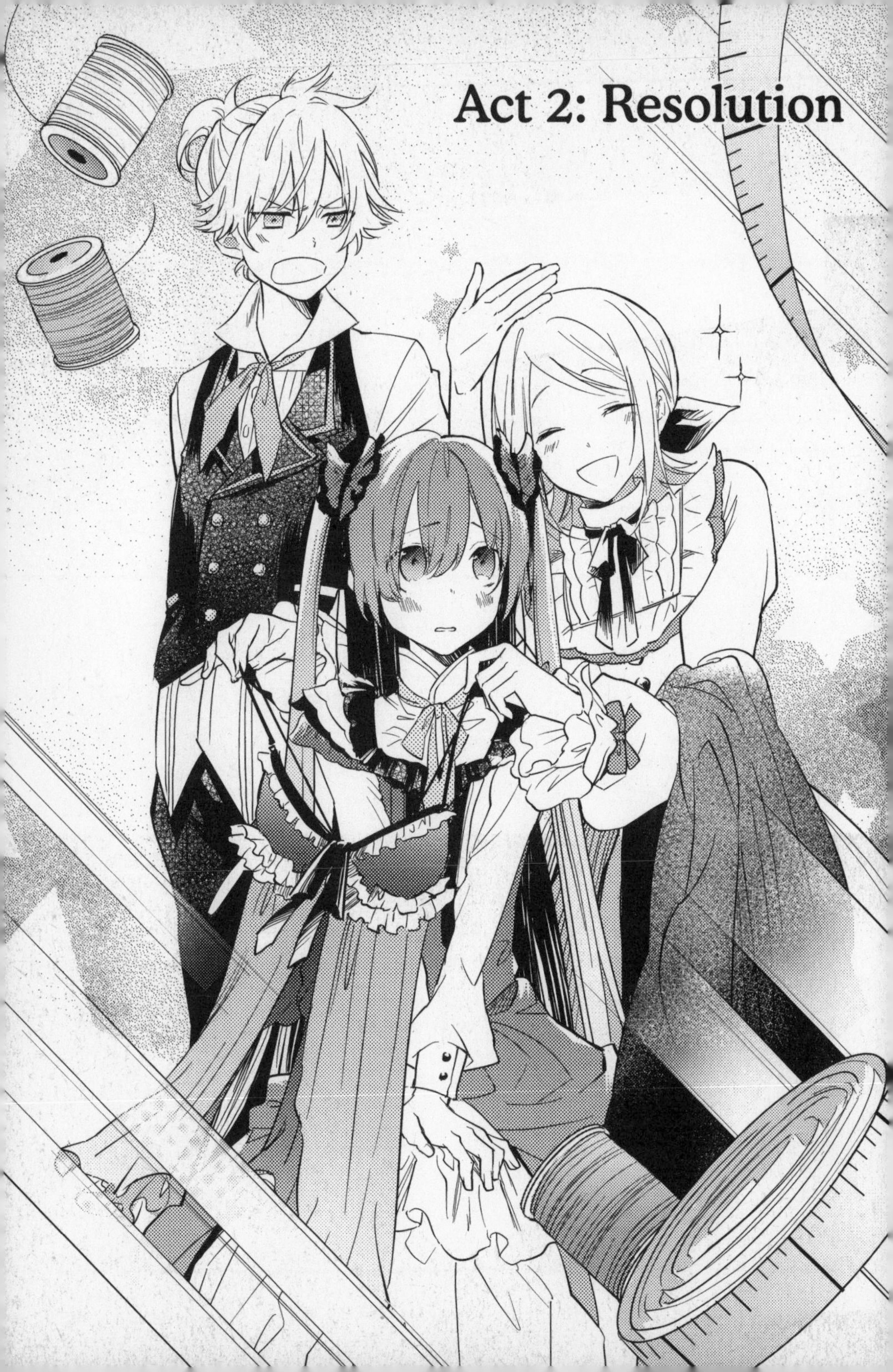

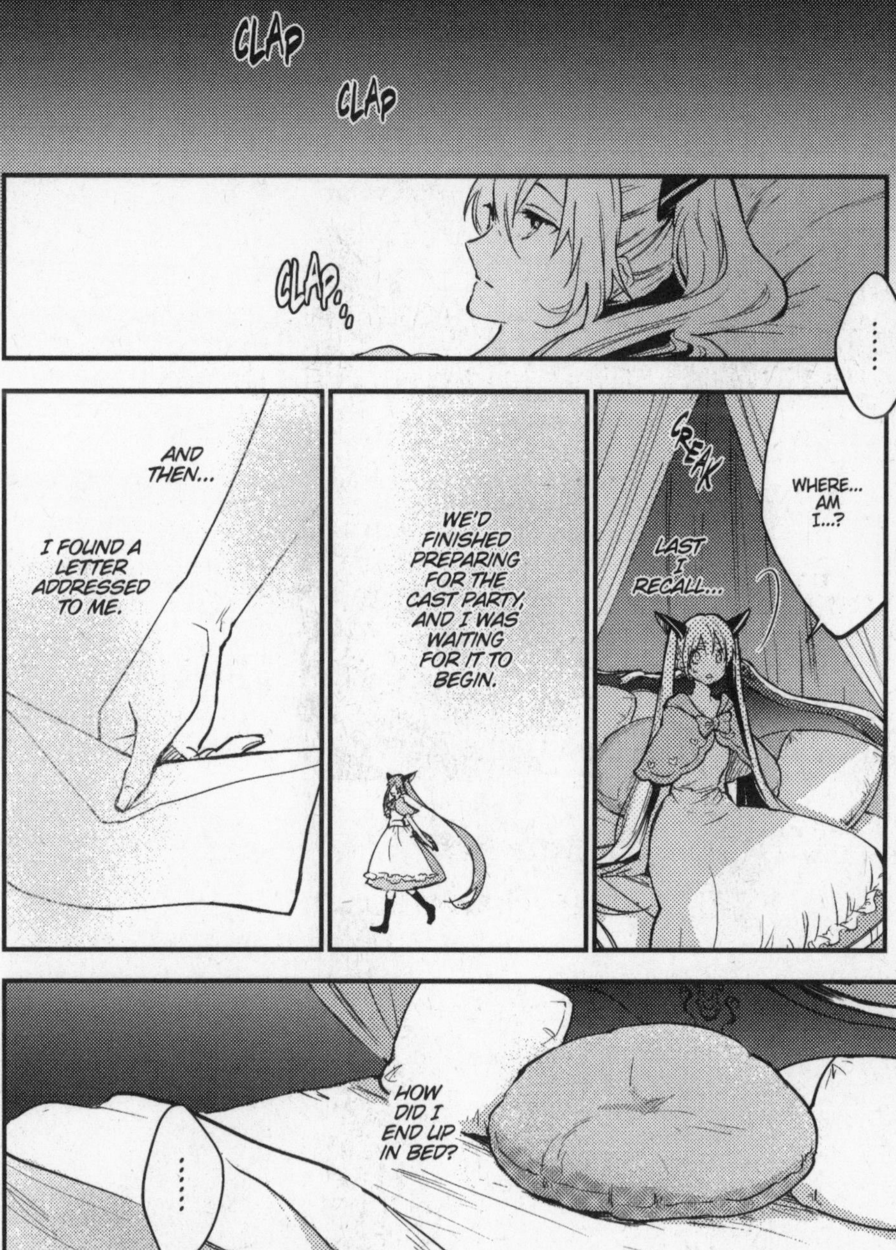
CLAP
CLAP
......
CLAP...
CREAK
WHERE... AM I...?
LAST I RECALL...
WE'D FINISHED PREPARING FOR THE CAST PARTY, AND I WAS WAITING FOR IT TO BEGIN.
AND THEN...
I FOUND A LETTER ADDRESSED TO ME.
HOW DID I END UP IN BED?
......

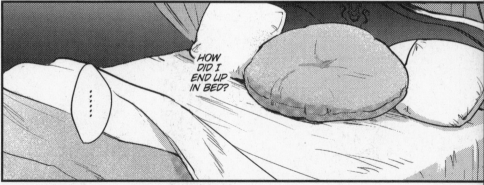

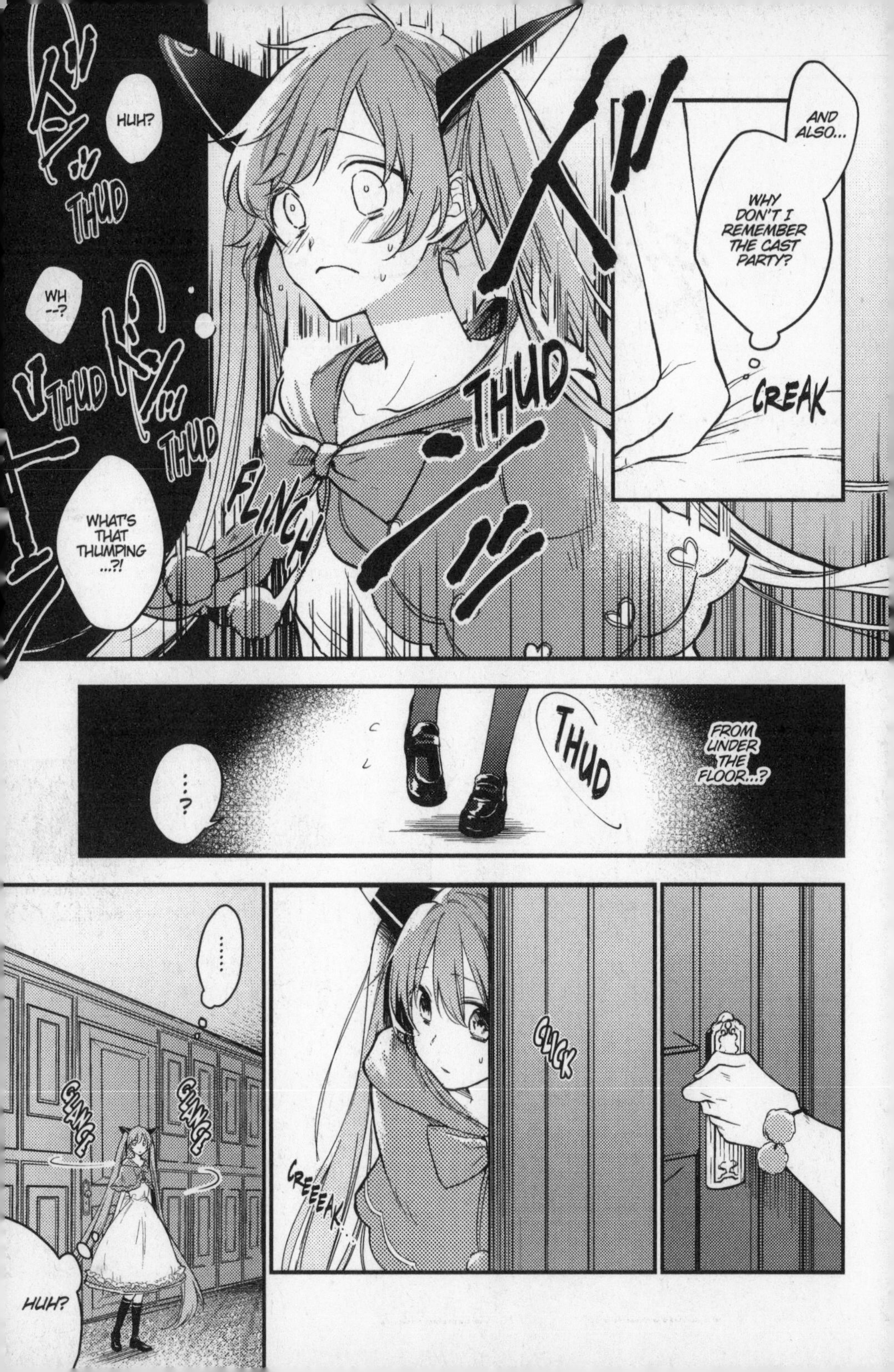
AND ALSO...
WHY DON'T I REMEMBER THE CAST PARTY?
CREAK
THUD
FLINCH
HUH?
THUD
WH--?
THUD
THUD
WHAT'S THAT THUMPING...?!
FROM UNDER THE FLOOR...?
THUD
...?
CLICK
CREEEAK!
......
GLANCE
GLANCE
HUH?

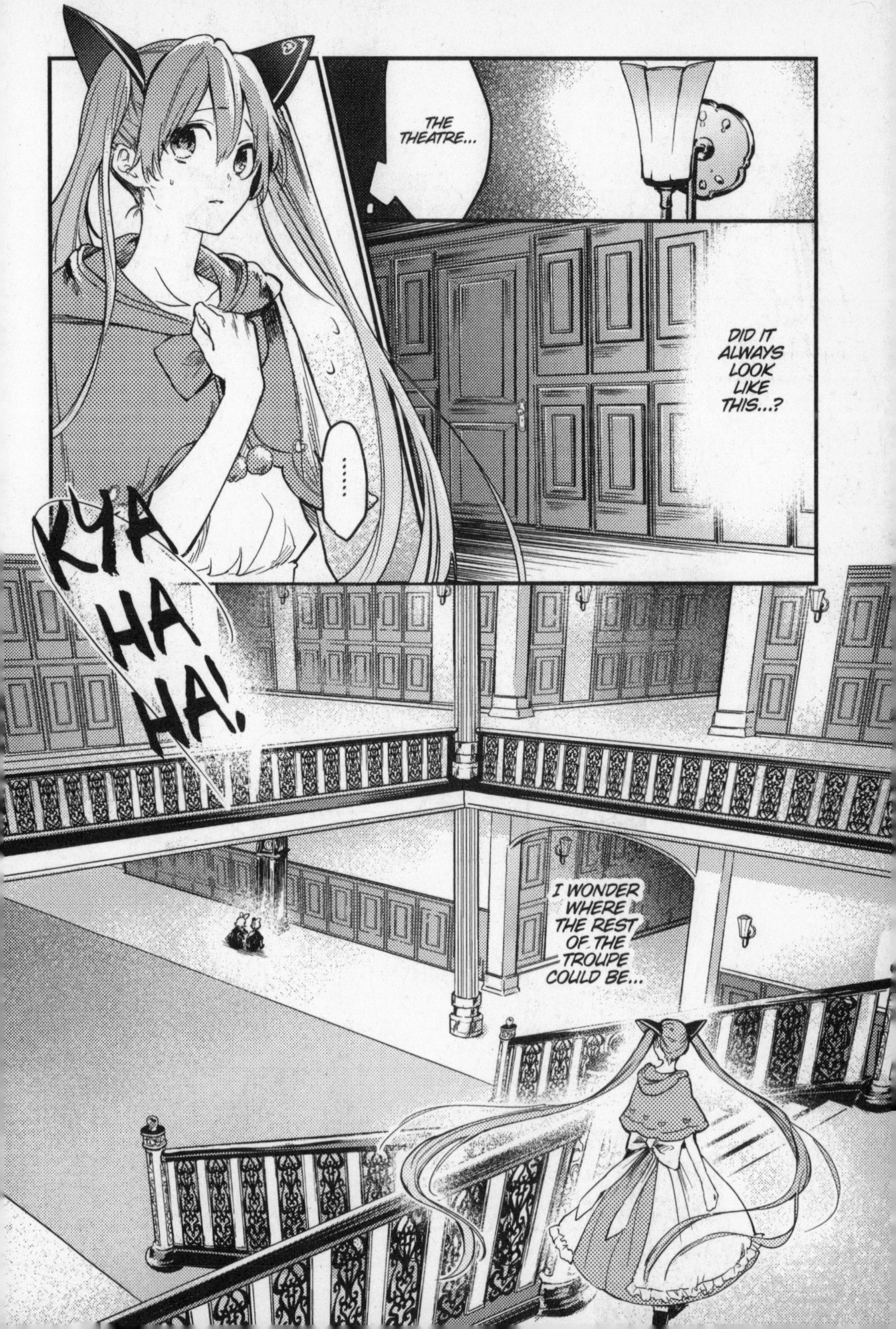
THE THEATRE...
DID IT ALWAYS LOOK LIKE THIS...?
......
KYA HA HA HA!
I WONDER WHERE THE REST OF THE TROUPE COULD BE...

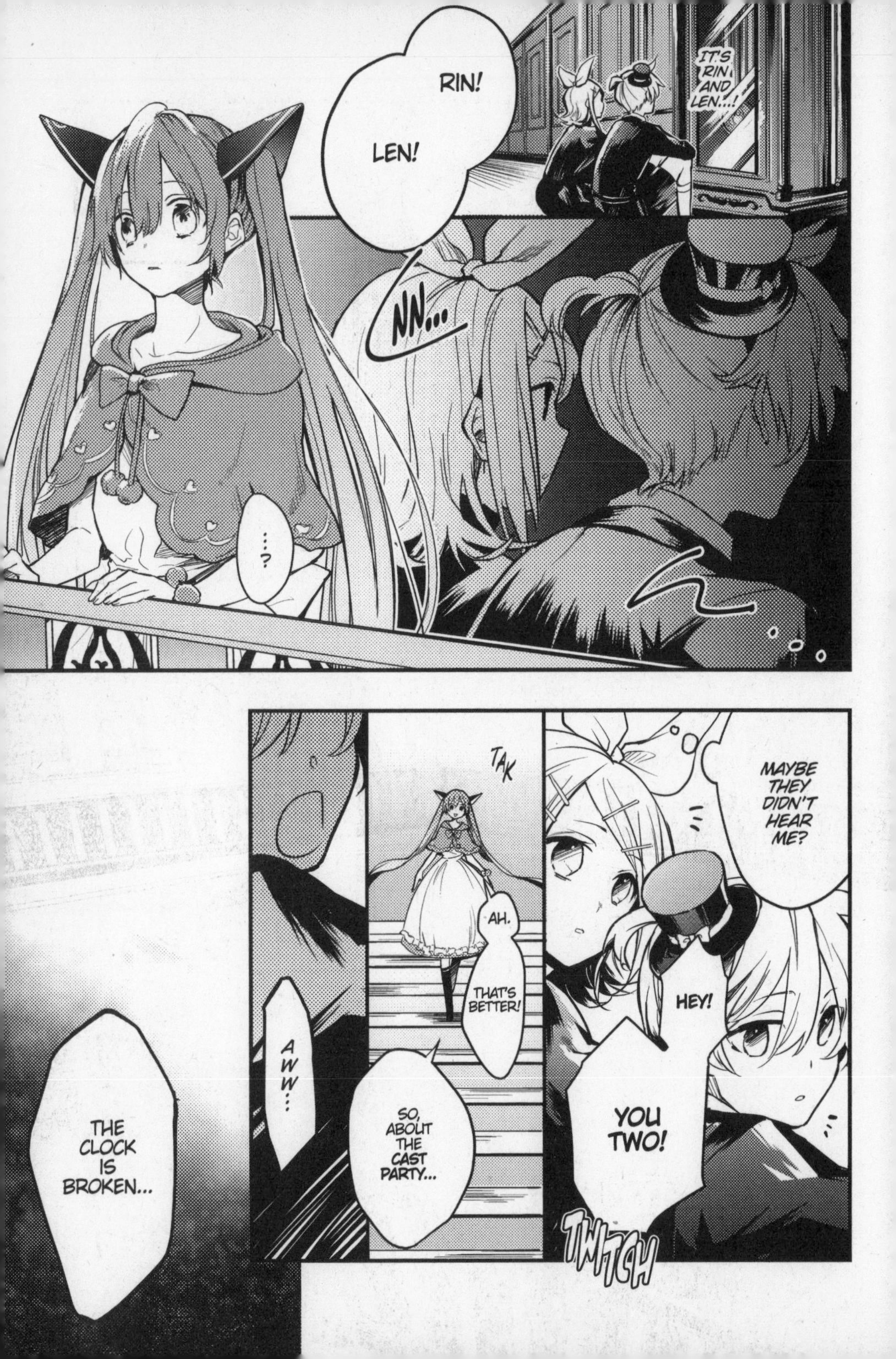
IT'S RIN AND LEN...!
RIN!
LEN!
NN...
...?
MAYBE THEY DIDN'T HEAR ME?
HEY!
YOU TWO!
TWITCH
TAK
AH.
THAT'S BETTER!
SO, ABOUT THE CAST PARTY...
AWW...
THE CLOCK IS BROKEN...

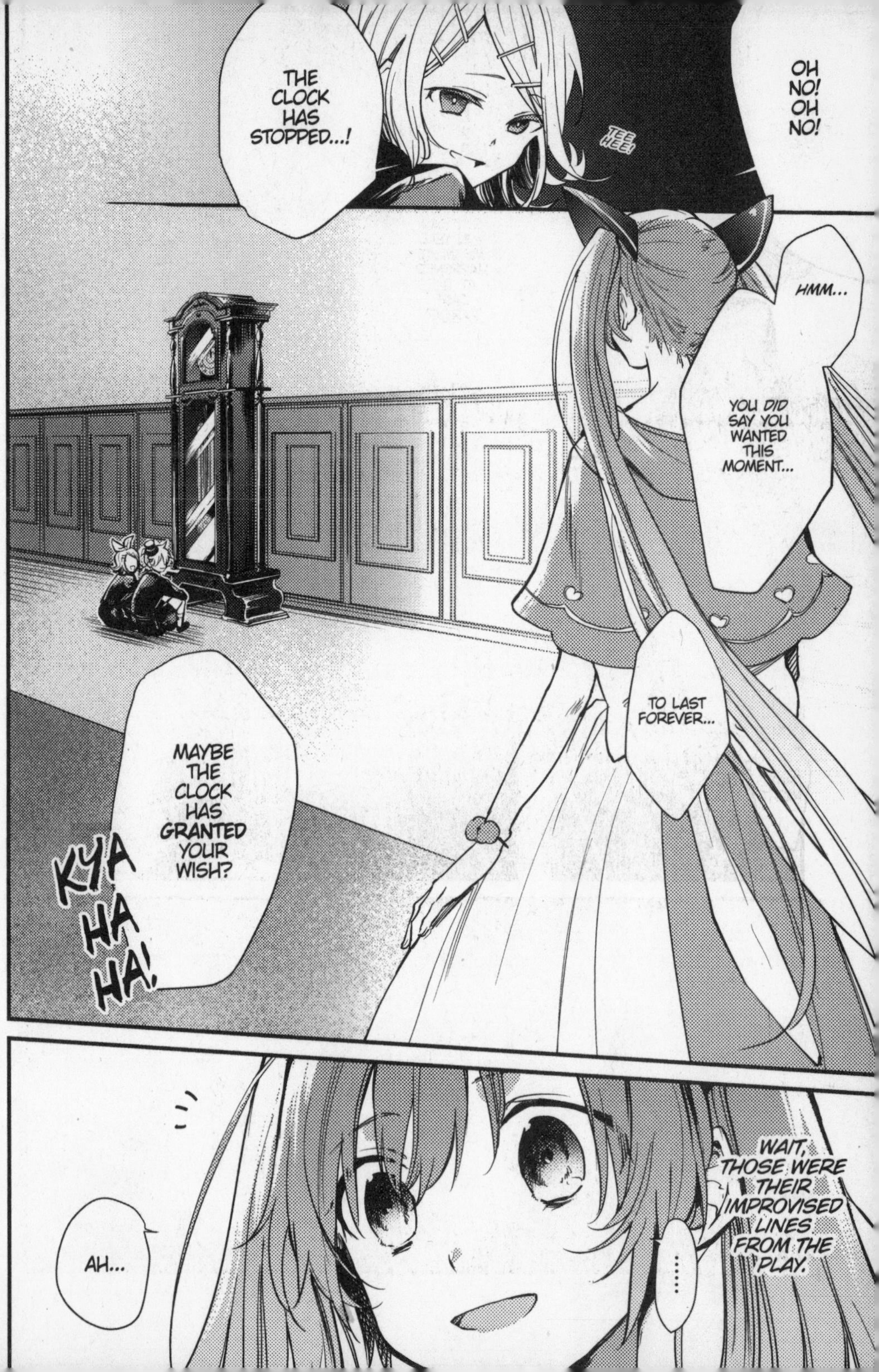
OH NO! OH NO!
TEE HEE!
THE CLOCK HAS STOPPED...!
HMM...
YOU DID SAY YOU WANTED THIS MOMENT...
TO LAST FOREVER...
MAYBE THE CLOCK HAS GRANTED YOUR WISH?
KYA HA HA HA!
WAIT, THOSE WERE THEIR IMPROVISED LINES FROM THE PLAY.
......
AH...

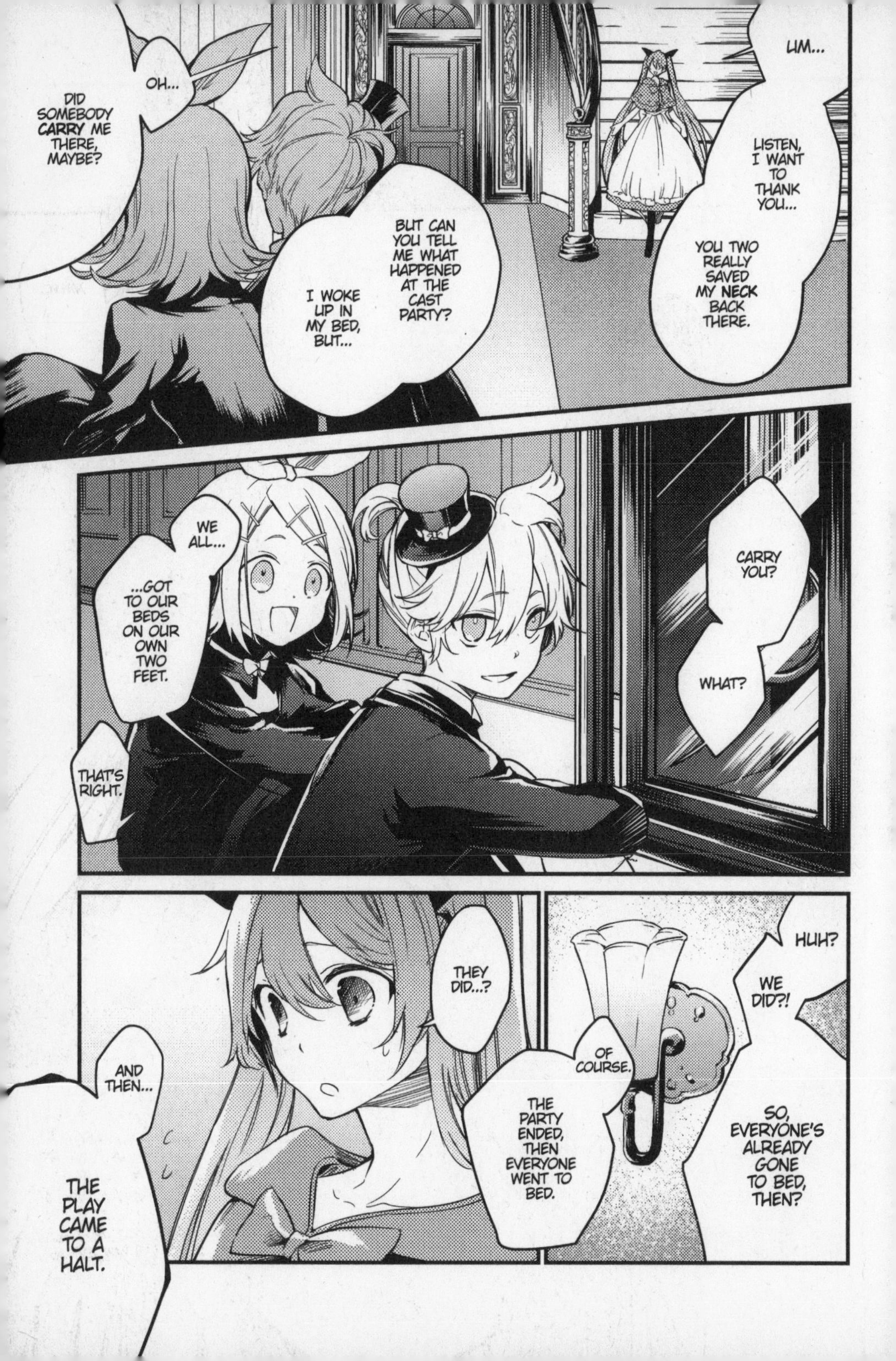
UM...
LISTEN, I WANT TO THANK YOU...
YOU TWO REALLY SAVED MY NECK BACK THERE.
BUT CAN YOU TELL ME WHAT HAPPENED AT THE CAST PARTY?
I WOKE UP IN MY BED, BUT...
OH...
DID SOMEBODY CARRY ME THERE, MAYBE?
CARRY YOU?
WHAT?
WE ALL...
...GOT TO OUR BEDS ON OUR OWN TWO FEET.
THAT'S RIGHT.
HUH?
WE DID?!
OF COURSE.
THE PARTY ENDED, THEN EVERYONE WENT TO BED.
SO, EVERYONE'S ALREADY GONE TO BED, THEN?
THEY DID...?
AND THEN...
THE PLAY CAME TO A HALT.

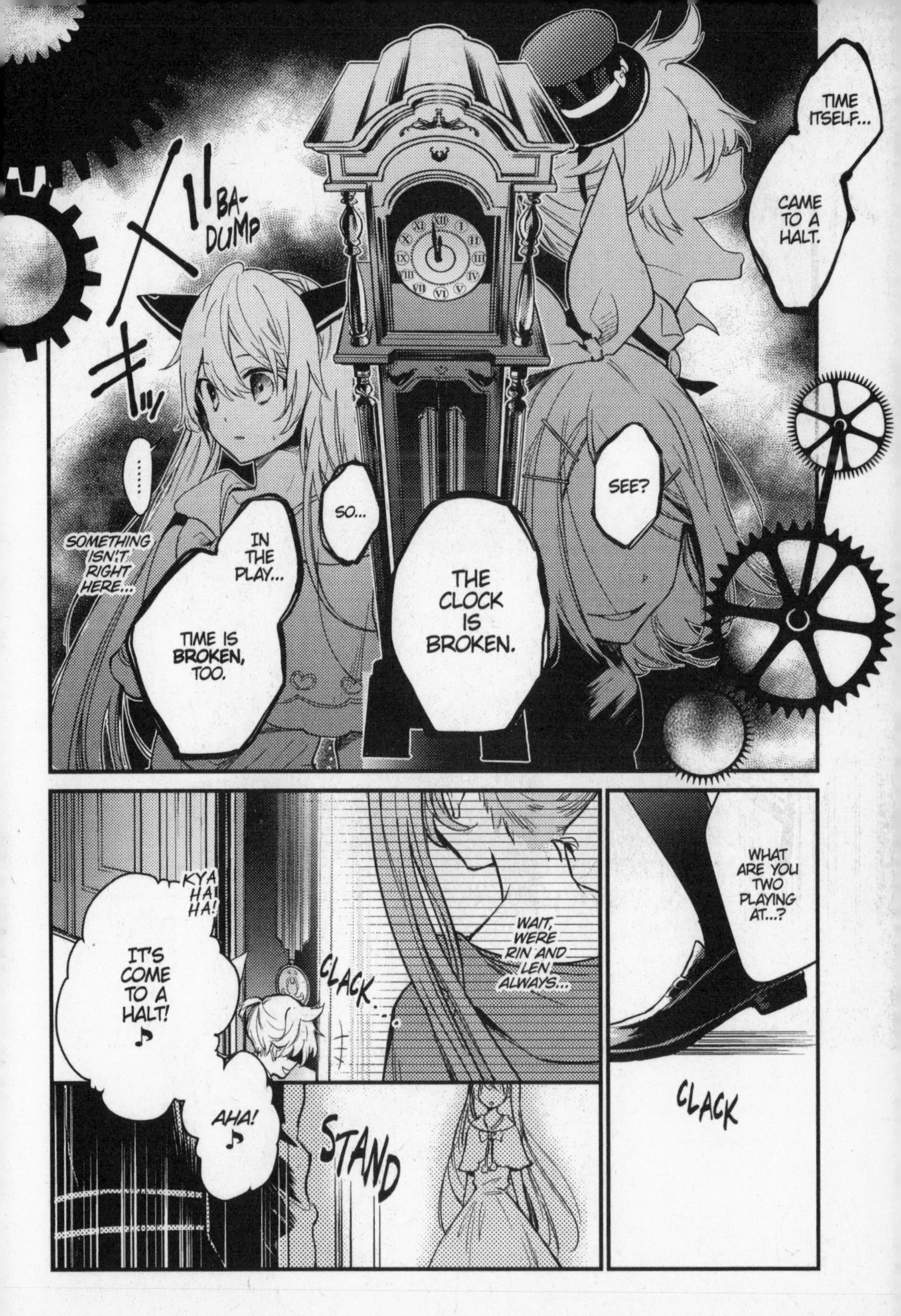
TIME ITSELF...
CAME TO A HALT.
BA-DUMP
SEE?
THE CLOCK IS BROKEN.
SO...
IN THE PLAY...
TIME IS BROKEN, TOO.
......
SOMETHING ISN'T RIGHT HERE...
WHAT ARE YOU TWO PLAYING AT...?
CLACK
WAIT, WERE RIN AND LEN ALWAYS...
CLACK
KYA HA HA!
IT'S COME TO A HALT! ♪
AHA! ♪
STAND

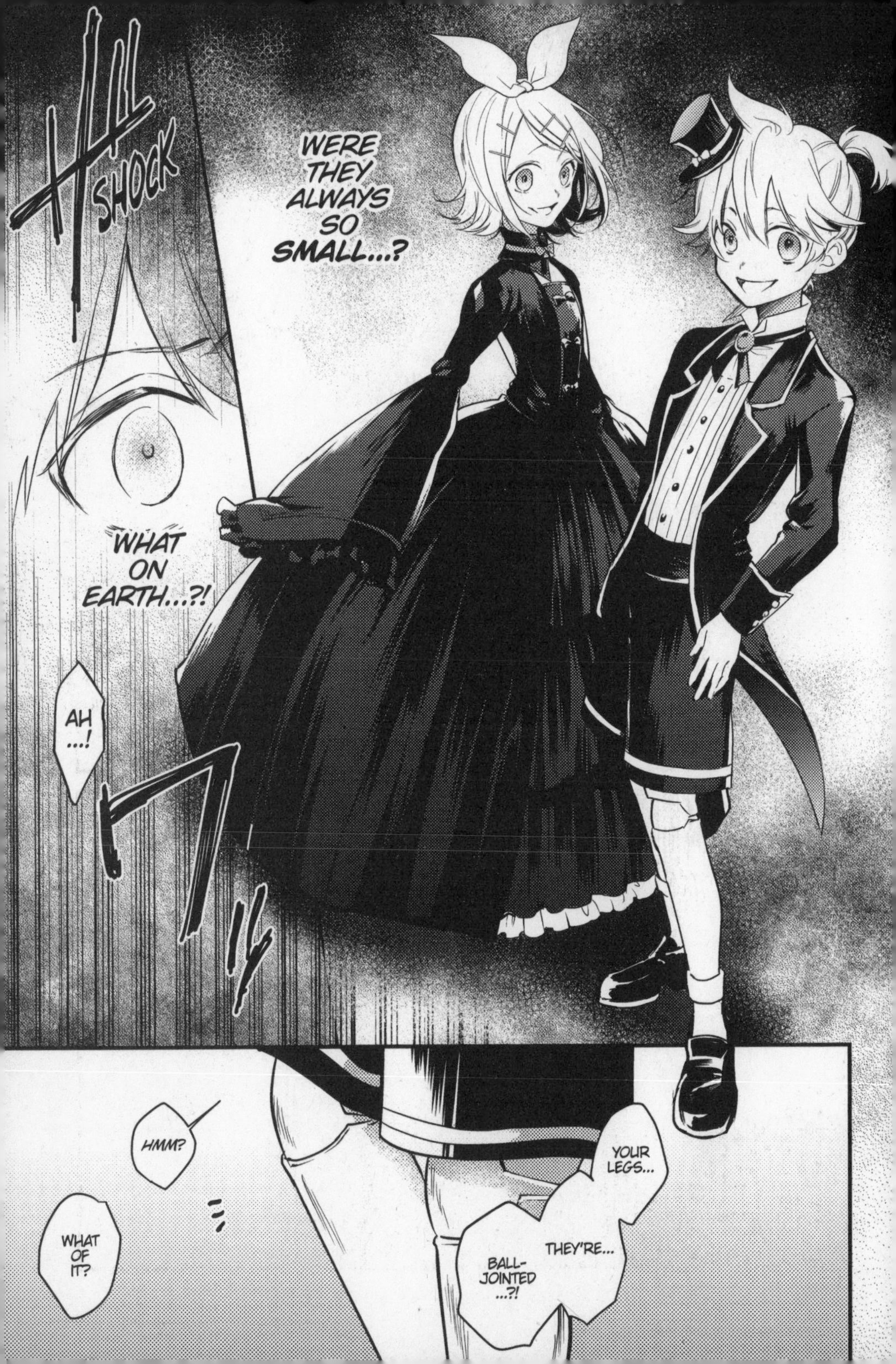

WERE THEY ALWAYS SO SMALL...?
SHOCK
WHAT ON EARTH...?!
AH...!
YOUR LEGS...
HMM?
THEY'RE...
BALL-JOINTED...?!
WHAT OF IT?

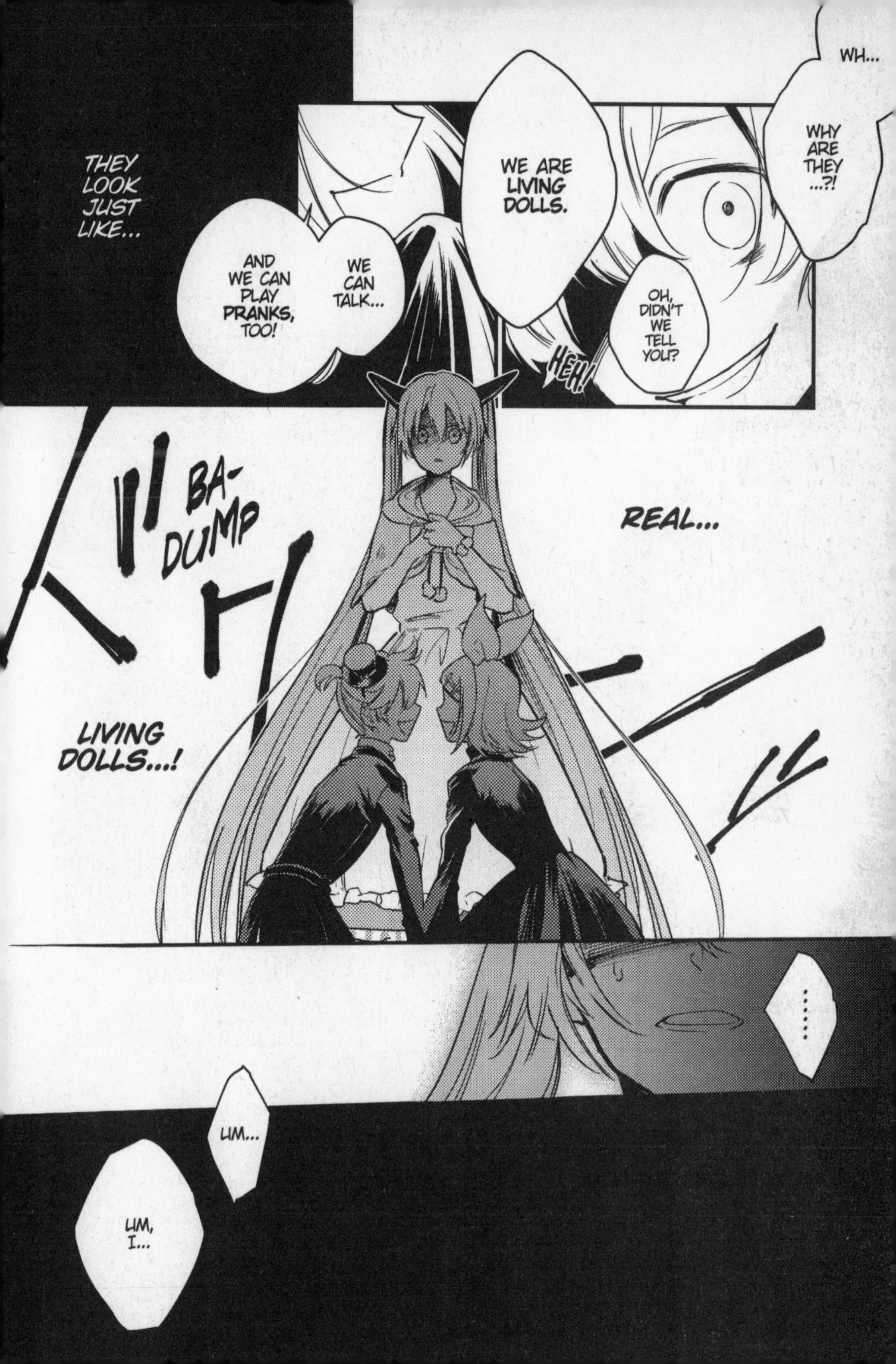
WH...
WHY ARE THEY ...?!
OH, DIDN'T WE TELL YOU?
HEH!
WE ARE LIVING DOLLS.
WE CAN TALK...
AND WE CAN PLAY PRANKS, TOO!
THEY LOOK JUST LIKE...
REAL...
BA-DUMP
LIVING DOLLS...!
......
UM...
UM, I...

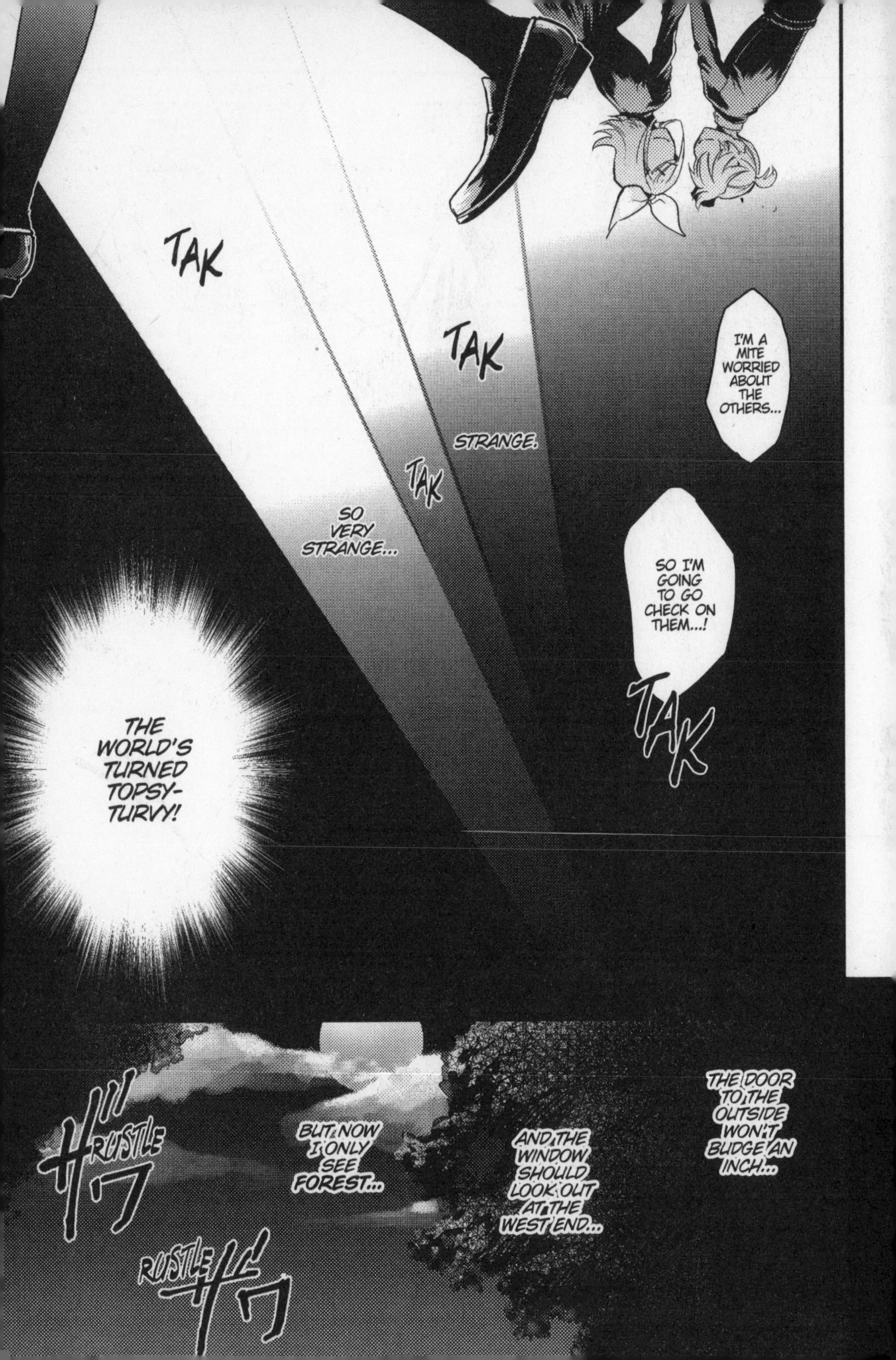

I'M A MITE WORRIED ABOUT THE OTHERS...
SO I'M GOING TO GO CHECK ON THEM...!
TAK
TAK
TAK
STRANGE.
TAK
SO VERY STRANGE...
THE WORLD'S TURNED TOPSY-TURVY!
THE DOOR TO THE OUTSIDE WON'T BUDGE AN INCH...
AND THE WINDOW SHOULD LOOK OUT AT THE WEST END...
BUT NOW I ONLY SEE FOREST...
ザワ RUSTLE
ザワ RUSTLE

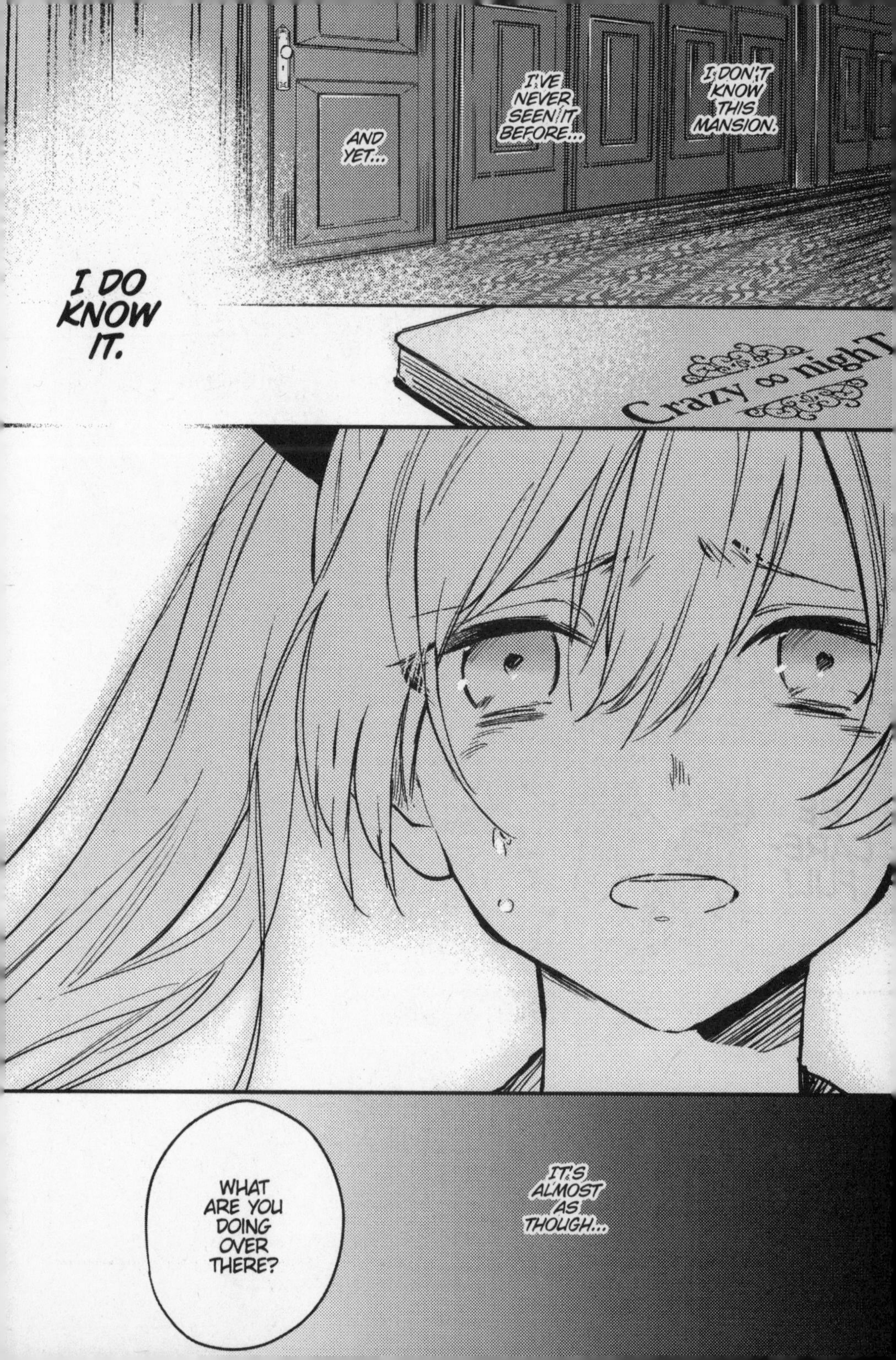

I DON'T KNOW THIS MANSION.
I'VE NEVER SEEN IT BEFORE...
AND YET...
I DO KNOW IT.
Crazy ∞ nighT
IT'S ALMOST AS THOUGH...
WHAT ARE YOU DOING OVER THERE?

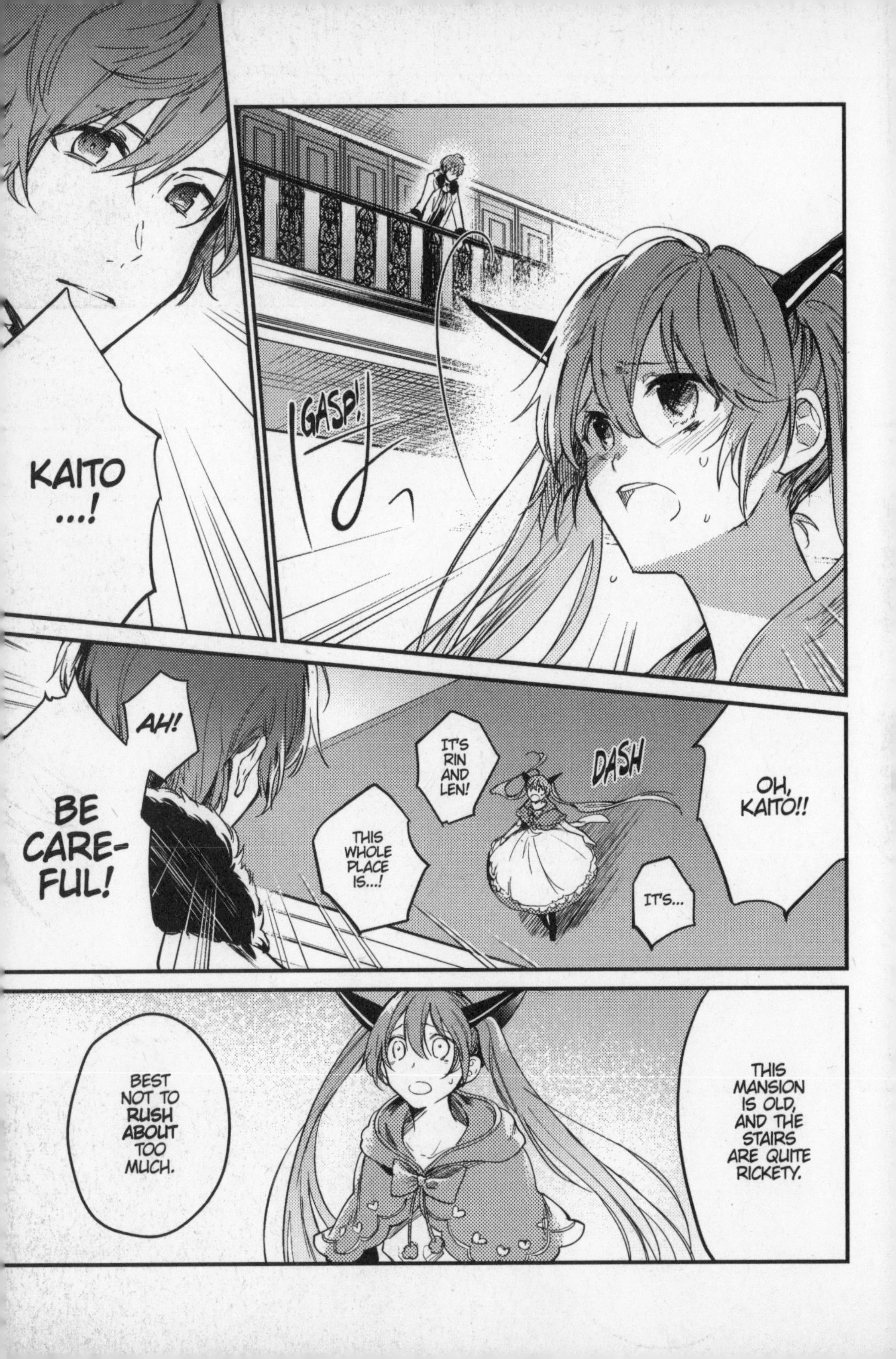
GASP!
KAITO ...!
OH, KAITO!!
DASH
IT'S...
IT'S RIN AND LEN!
THIS WHOLE PLACE IS...!
AH!
BE CARE-FUL!
THIS MANSION IS OLD, AND THE STAIRS ARE QUITE RICKETY.
BEST NOT TO RUSH ABOUT TOO MUCH.

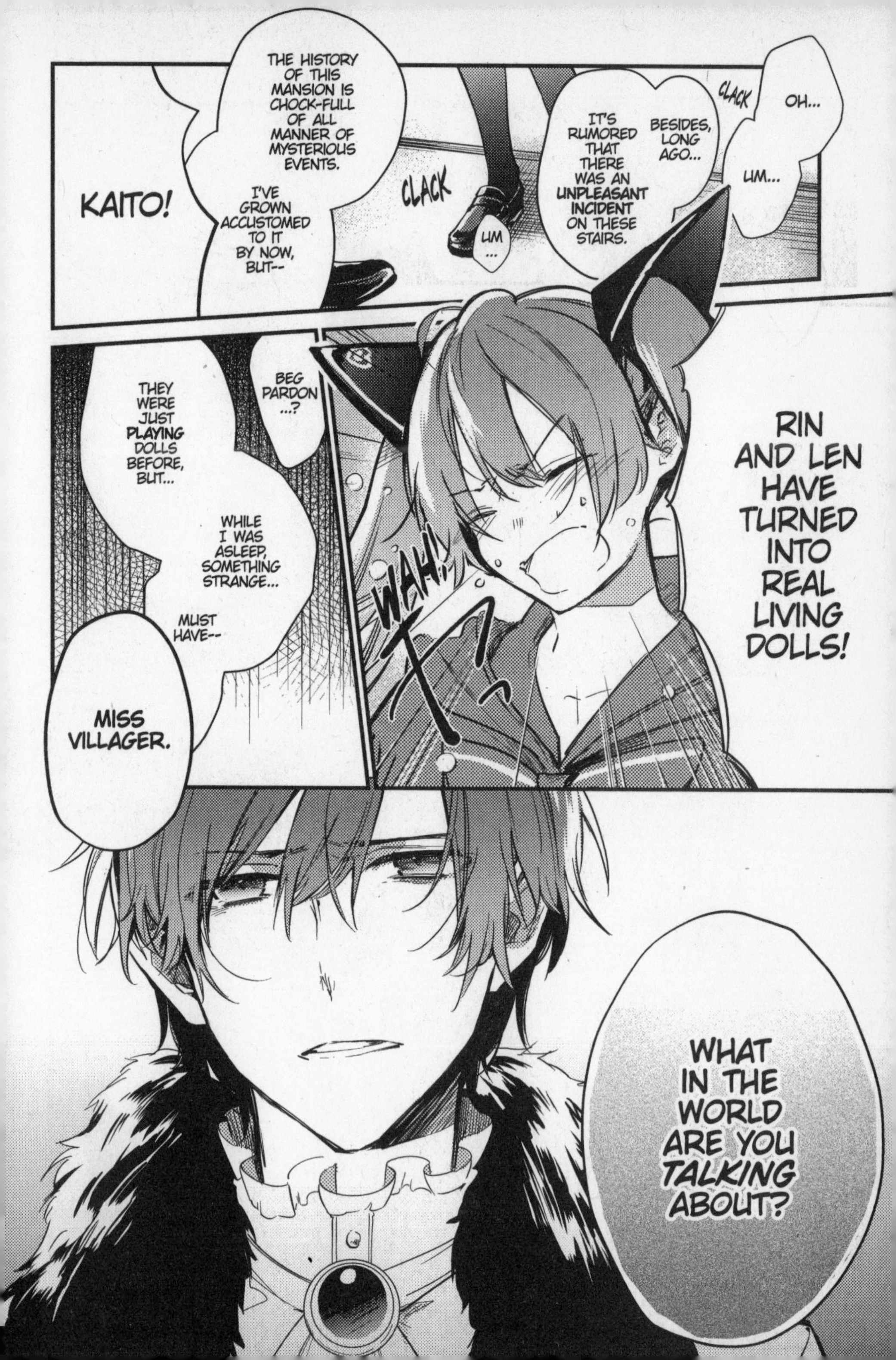
OH...
UM...
CLACK
BESIDES, LONG AGO...
IT'S RUMORED THAT THERE WAS AN UNPLEASANT INCIDENT ON THESE STAIRS.
UM ...
CLACK
THE HISTORY OF THIS MANSION IS CHOCK-FULL OF ALL MANNER OF MYSTERIOUS EVENTS.
I'VE GROWN ACCUSTOMED TO IT BY NOW, BUT--
KAITO!
RIN AND LEN HAVE TURNED INTO REAL LIVING DOLLS!
WAH!
BEG PARDON ...?
THEY WERE JUST PLAYING DOLLS BEFORE, BUT...
WHILE I WAS ASLEEP, SOMETHING STRANGE...
MUST HAVE--
MISS VILLAGER.
WHAT IN THE WORLD ARE YOU TALKING ABOUT?

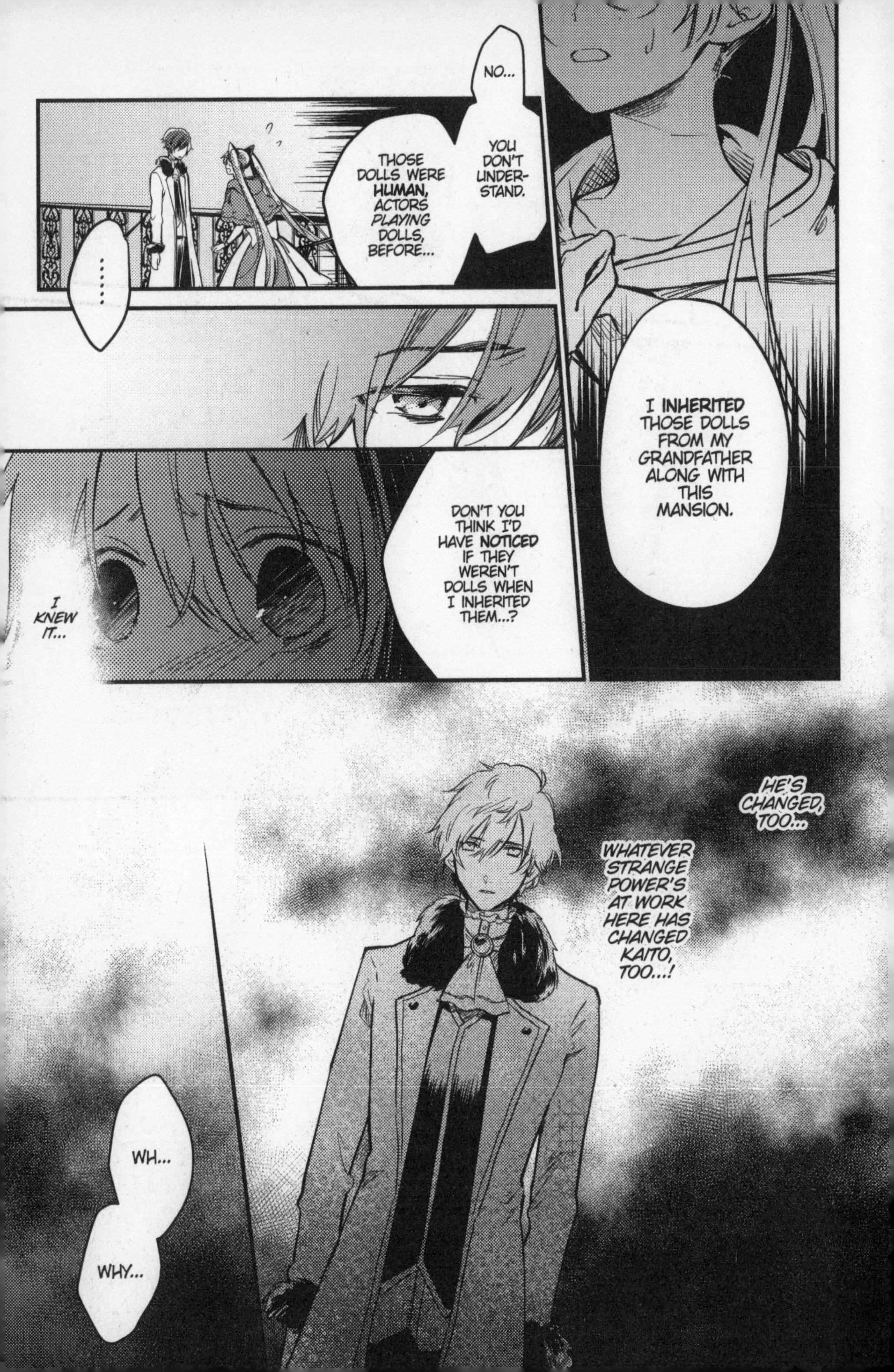
NO...
YOU DON'T UNDER-STAND.
THOSE DOLLS WERE HUMAN, ACTORS PLAYING DOLLS, BEFORE...
......
I INHERITED THOSE DOLLS FROM MY GRANDFATHER ALONG WITH THIS MANSION.
DON'T YOU THINK I'D HAVE NOTICED IF THEY WEREN'T DOLLS WHEN I INHERITED THEM...?
I KNEW IT...
HE'S CHANGED, TOO...
WHATEVER STRANGE POWER'S AT WORK HERE HAS CHANGED KAITO, TOO...!
WH...
WHY...

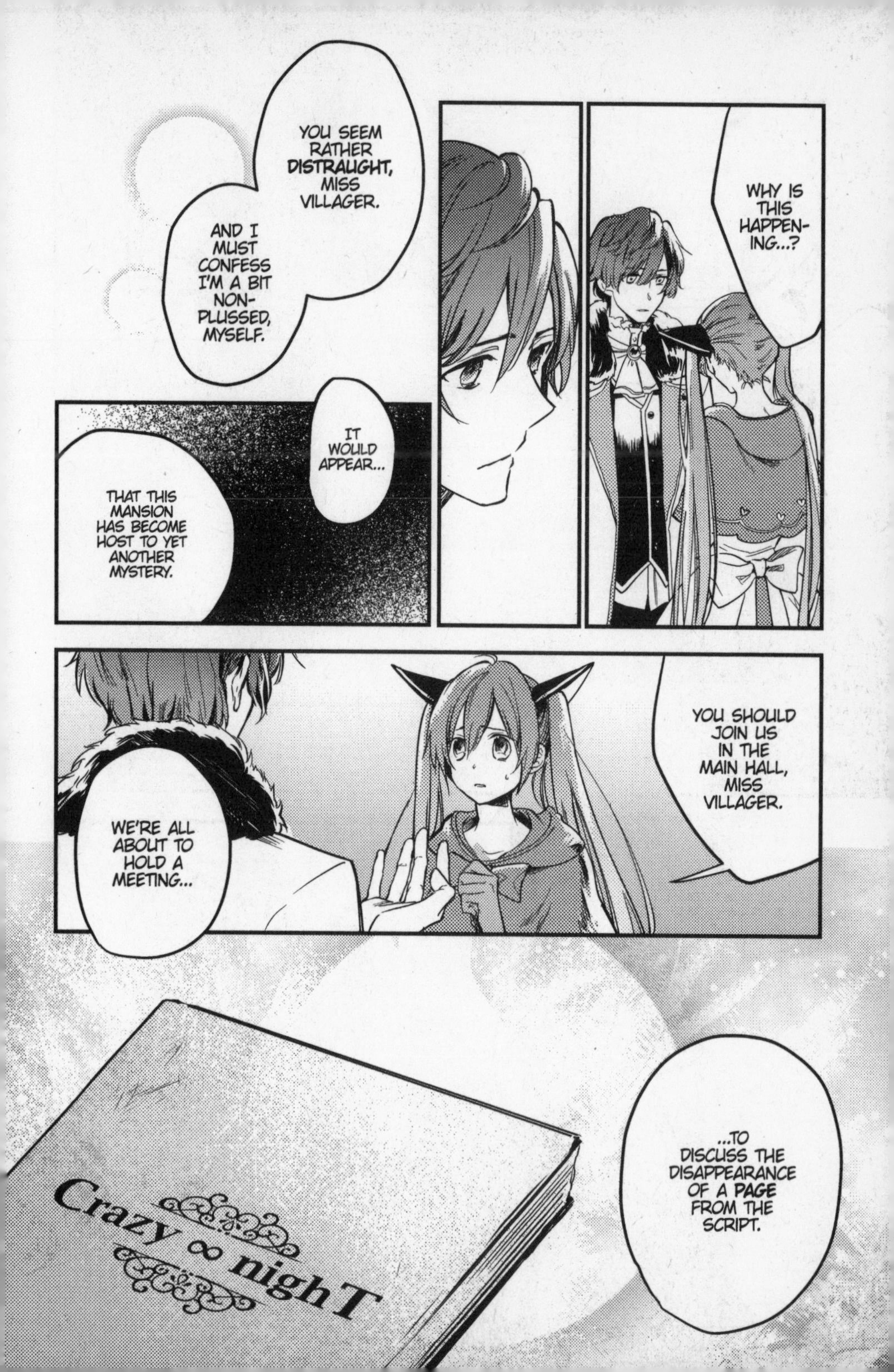
WHY IS THIS HAPPENING...?
YOU SEEM RATHER DISTRAUGHT, MISS VILLAGER.
AND I MUST CONFESS I'M A BIT NONPLUSSED, MYSELF.
IT WOULD APPEAR...
THAT THIS MANSION HAS BECOME HOST TO YET ANOTHER MYSTERY.
YOU SHOULD JOIN US IN THE MAIN HALL, MISS VILLAGER.
WE'RE ALL ABOUT TO HOLD A MEETING...
...TO DISCUSS THE DISAPPEARANCE OF A PAGE FROM THE SCRIPT.
Crazy ∞ nighT

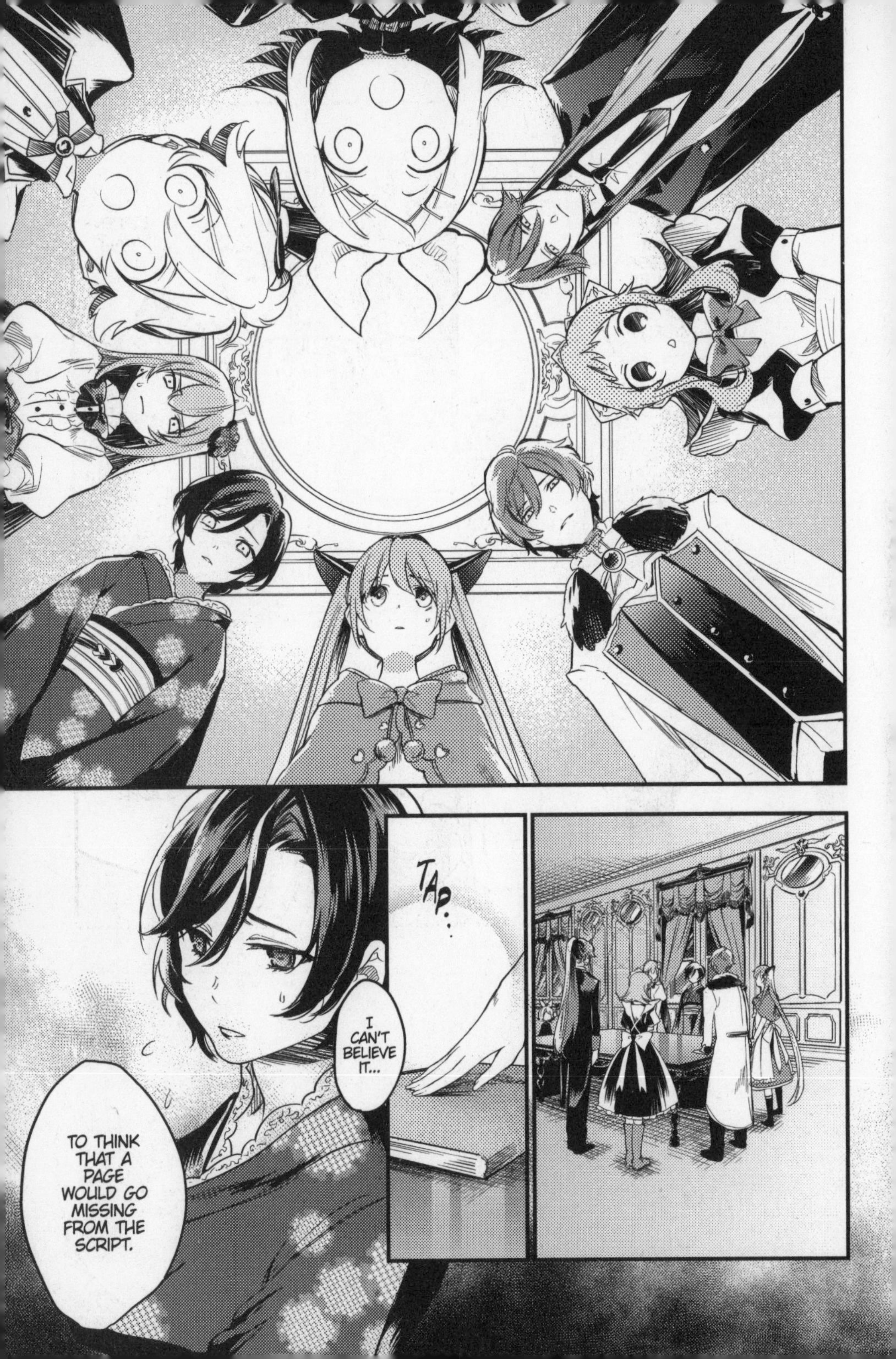
TAP...
I CAN'T BELIEVE IT...
TO THINK THAT A PAGE WOULD GO MISSING FROM THE SCRIPT.

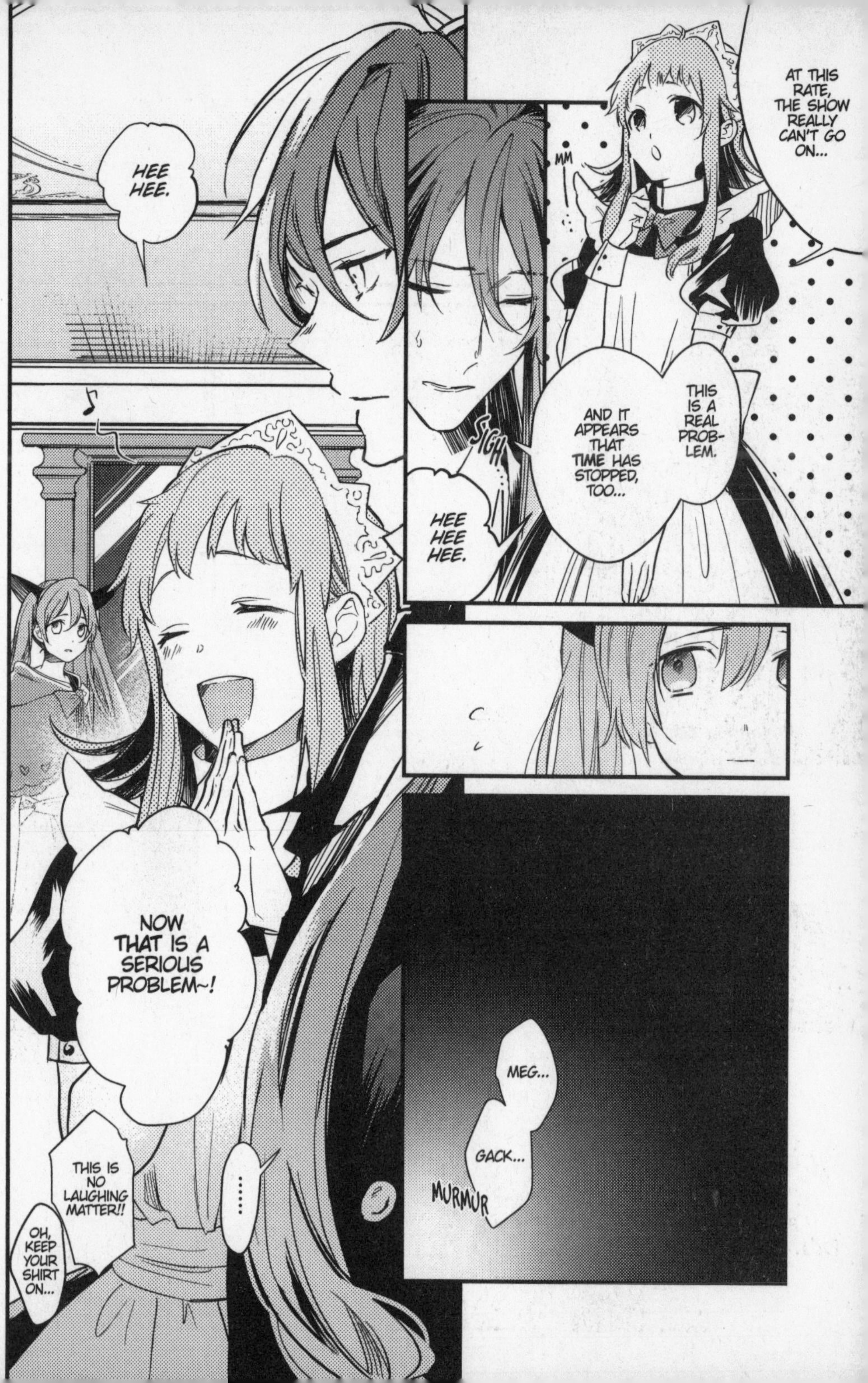

AT THIS RATE, THE SHOW REALLY CAN'T GO ON...
MM...
THIS IS A REAL PROBLEM.
AND IT APPEARS THAT TIME HAS STOPPED, TOO...
SIGH...
HEE HEE HEE.
MEG...
GACK...
MURMUR
HEE HEE.
♪
NOW THAT IS A SERIOUS PROBLEM~!
......
THIS IS NO LAUGHING MATTER!!
OH, KEEP YOUR SHIRT ON...

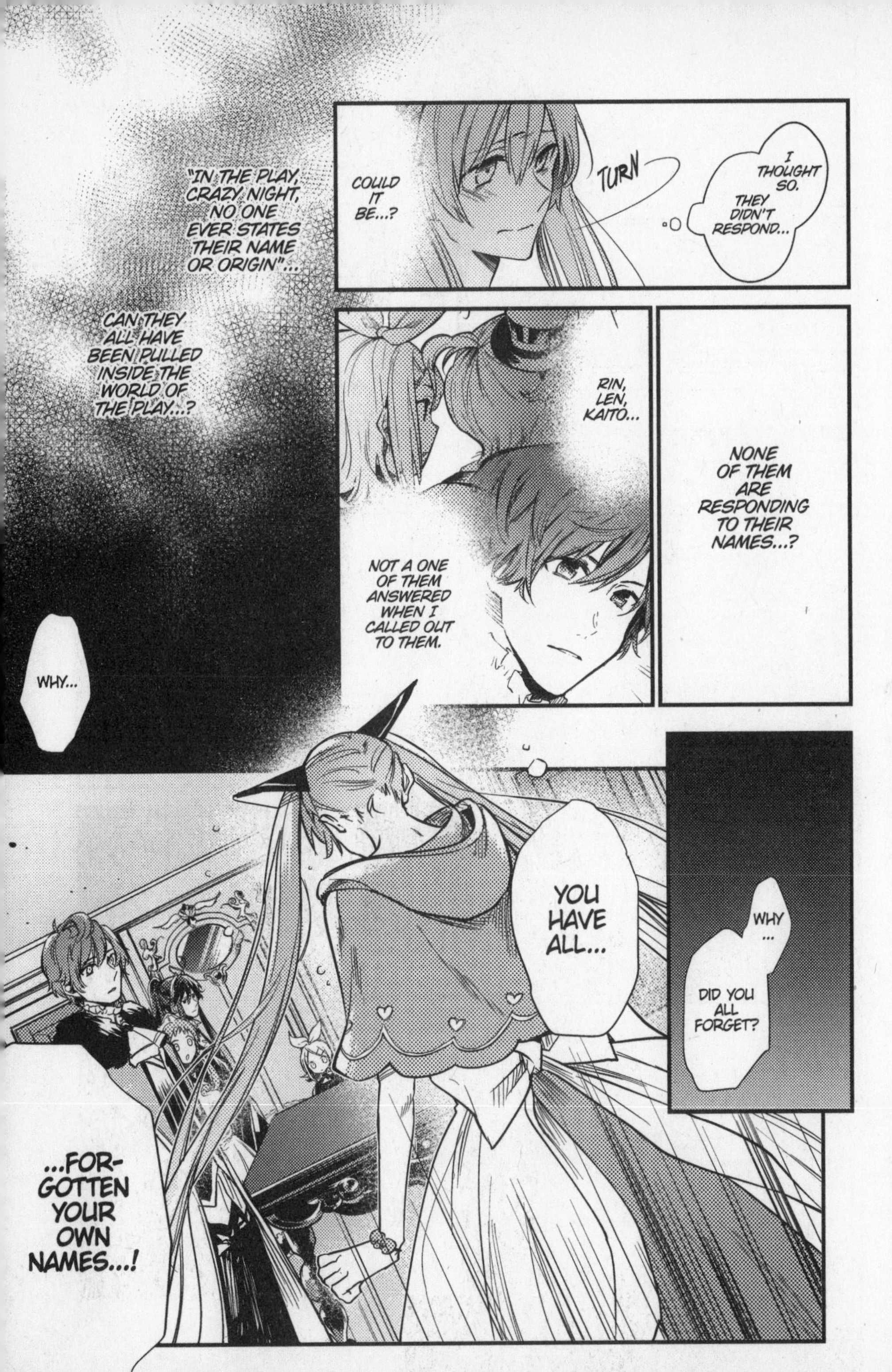

I THOUGHT SO.
THEY DIDN'T RESPOND...
TURN
COULD IT BE...?
"IN THE PLAY, CRAZY NIGHT, NO ONE EVER STATES THEIR NAME OR ORIGIN"...
CAN THEY ALL HAVE BEEN PULLED INSIDE THE WORLD OF THE PLAY...?
NONE OF THEM ARE RESPONDING TO THEIR NAMES...?
RIN, LEN, KAITO...
NOT A ONE OF THEM ANSWERED WHEN I CALLED OUT TO THEM.
WHY...
WHY...
DID YOU ALL FORGET?
YOU HAVE ALL...
...FOR-GOTTEN YOUR OWN NAMES...!

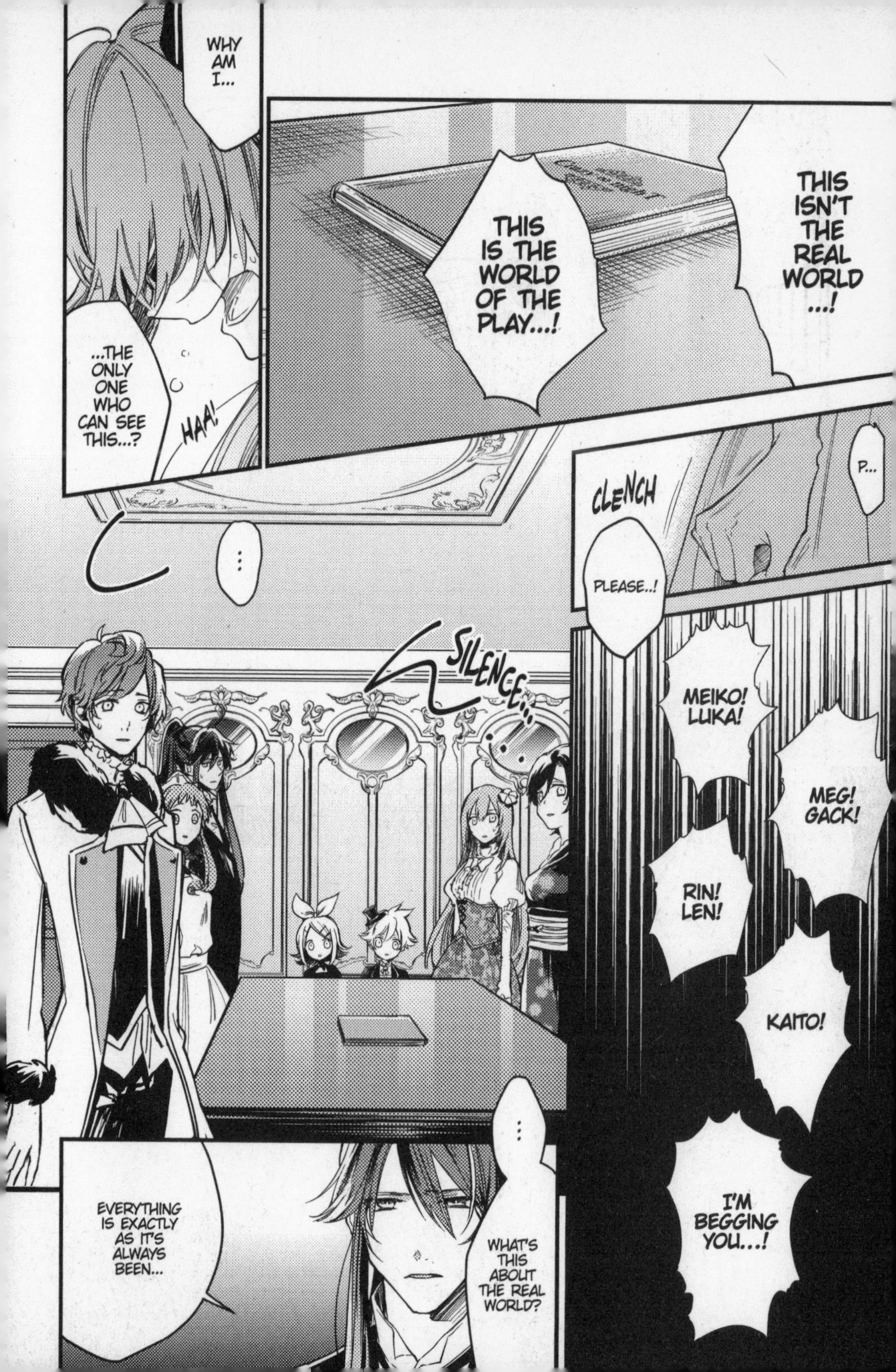
THIS ISN'T THE REAL WORLD ...!
THIS IS THE WORLD OF THE PLAY...!
WHY AM I...
...THE ONLY ONE WHO CAN SEE THIS...?
HAA!
P...
CLENCH
PLEASE..!
...
MEIKO! LUKA!
MEG! GACK!
RIN! LEN!
KAITO!
I'M BEGGING YOU...!
SILENCE...
...
WHAT'S THIS ABOUT THE REAL WORLD?
EVERYTHING IS EXACTLY AS IT'S ALWAYS BEEN...

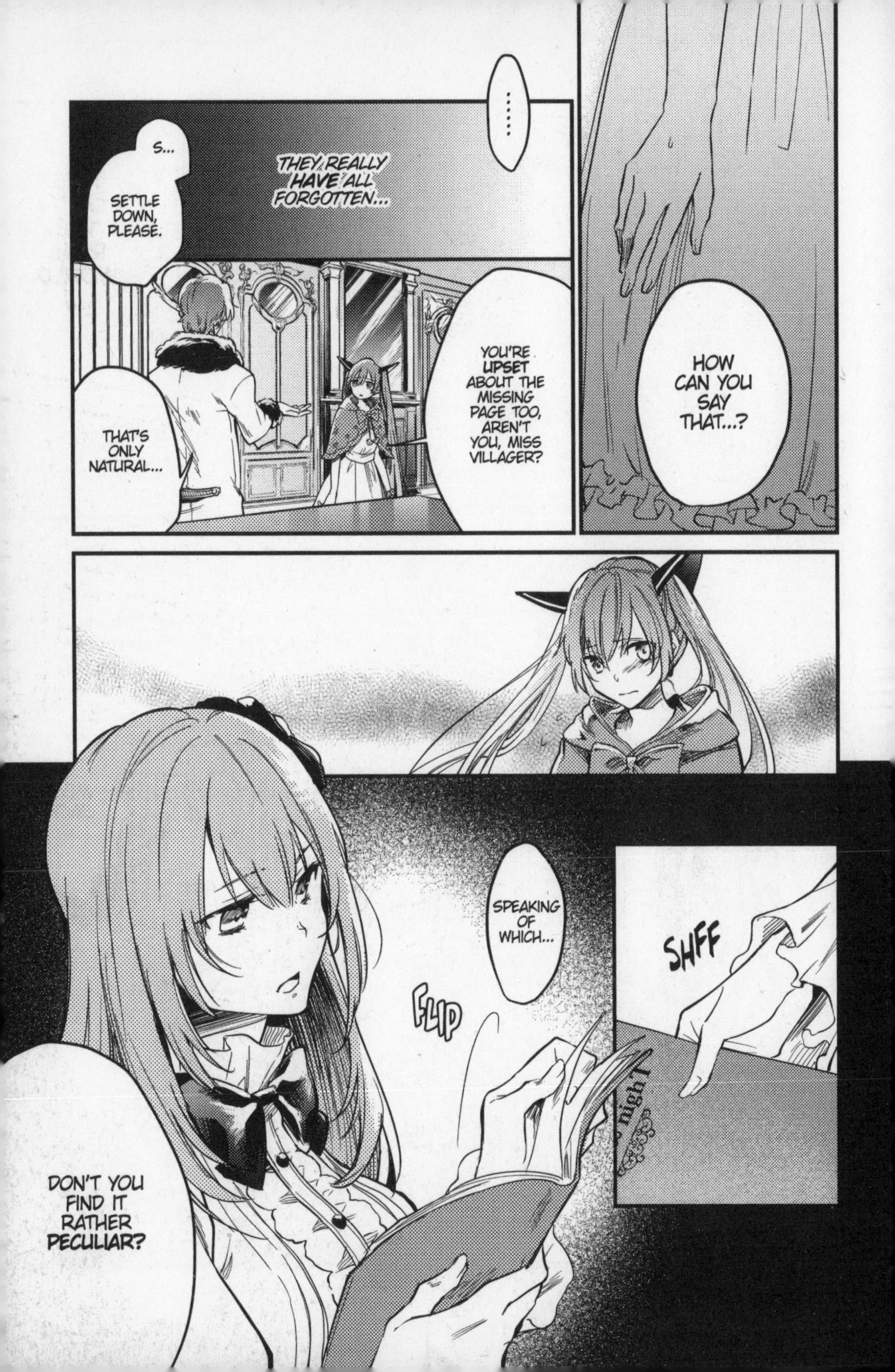
HOW CAN YOU SAY THAT...?
......
THEY REALLY HAVE ALL FORGOTTEN...
S...
SETTLE DOWN, PLEASE.
YOU'RE UPSET ABOUT THE MISSING PAGE TOO, AREN'T YOU, MISS VILLAGER?
THAT'S ONLY NATURAL...
SHFF
SPEAKING OF WHICH...
FLIP
DON'T YOU FIND IT RATHER PECULIAR?

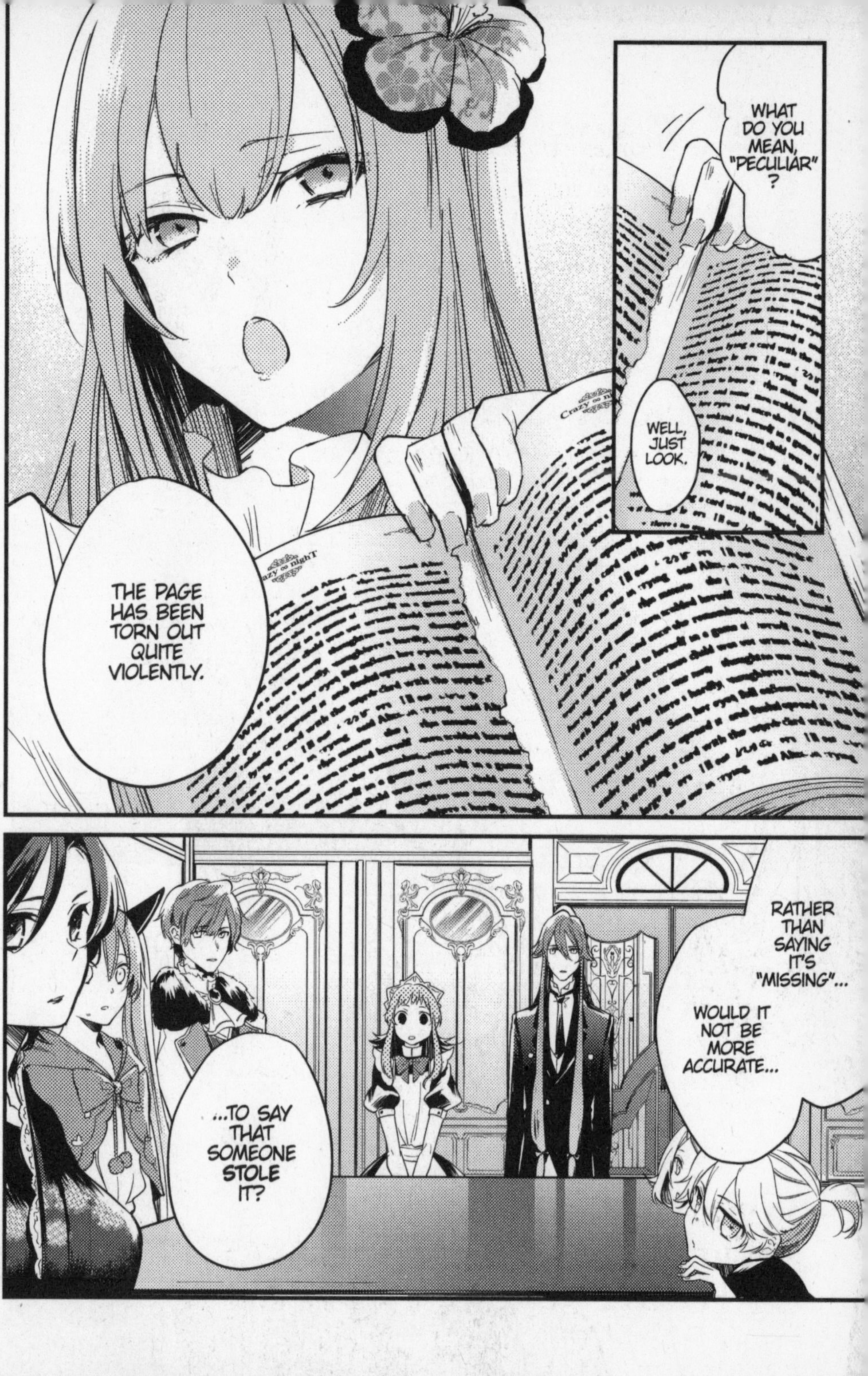
WHAT DO YOU MEAN, "PECULIAR"?
WELL, JUST LOOK.
THE PAGE HAS BEEN TORN OUT QUITE VIOLENTLY.
RATHER THAN SAYING IT'S "MISSING"...
WOULD IT NOT BE MORE ACCURATE...
...TO SAY THAT SOMEONE STOLE IT?

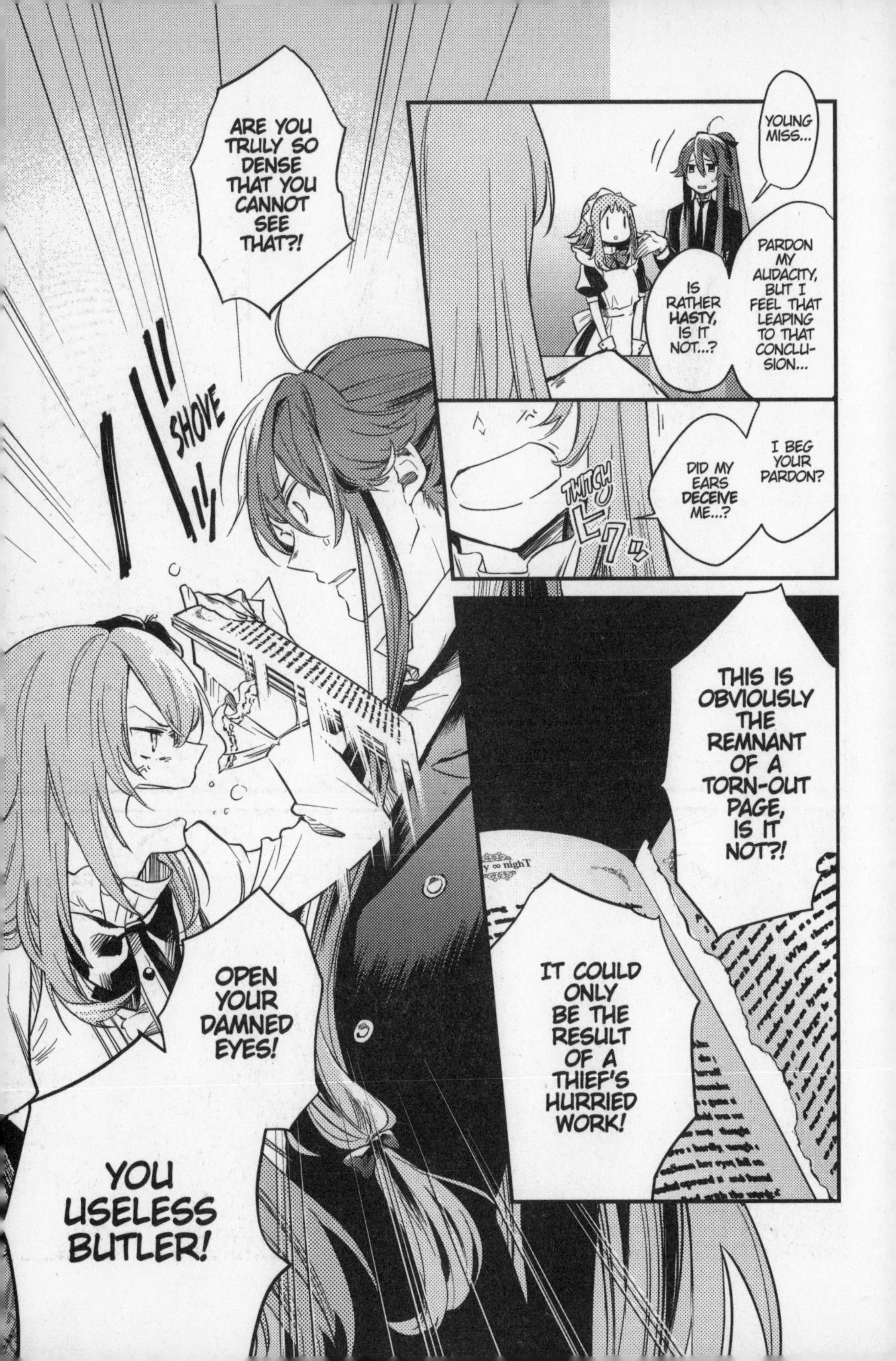
YOUNG MISS...
PARDON MY AUDACITY, BUT I FEEL THAT LEAPING TO THAT CONCLUSION...
IS RATHER HASTY, IS IT NOT...?
I BEG YOUR PARDON?
DID MY EARS DECEIVE ME...?
TWITCH
THIS IS OBVIOUSLY THE REMNANT OF A TORN-OUT PAGE, IS IT NOT?!
IT COULD ONLY BE THE RESULT OF A THIEF'S HURRIED WORK!
ARE YOU TRULY SO DENSE THAT YOU CANNOT SEE THAT?!
SHOVE
OPEN YOUR DAMNED EYES!
YOU USELESS BUTLER!

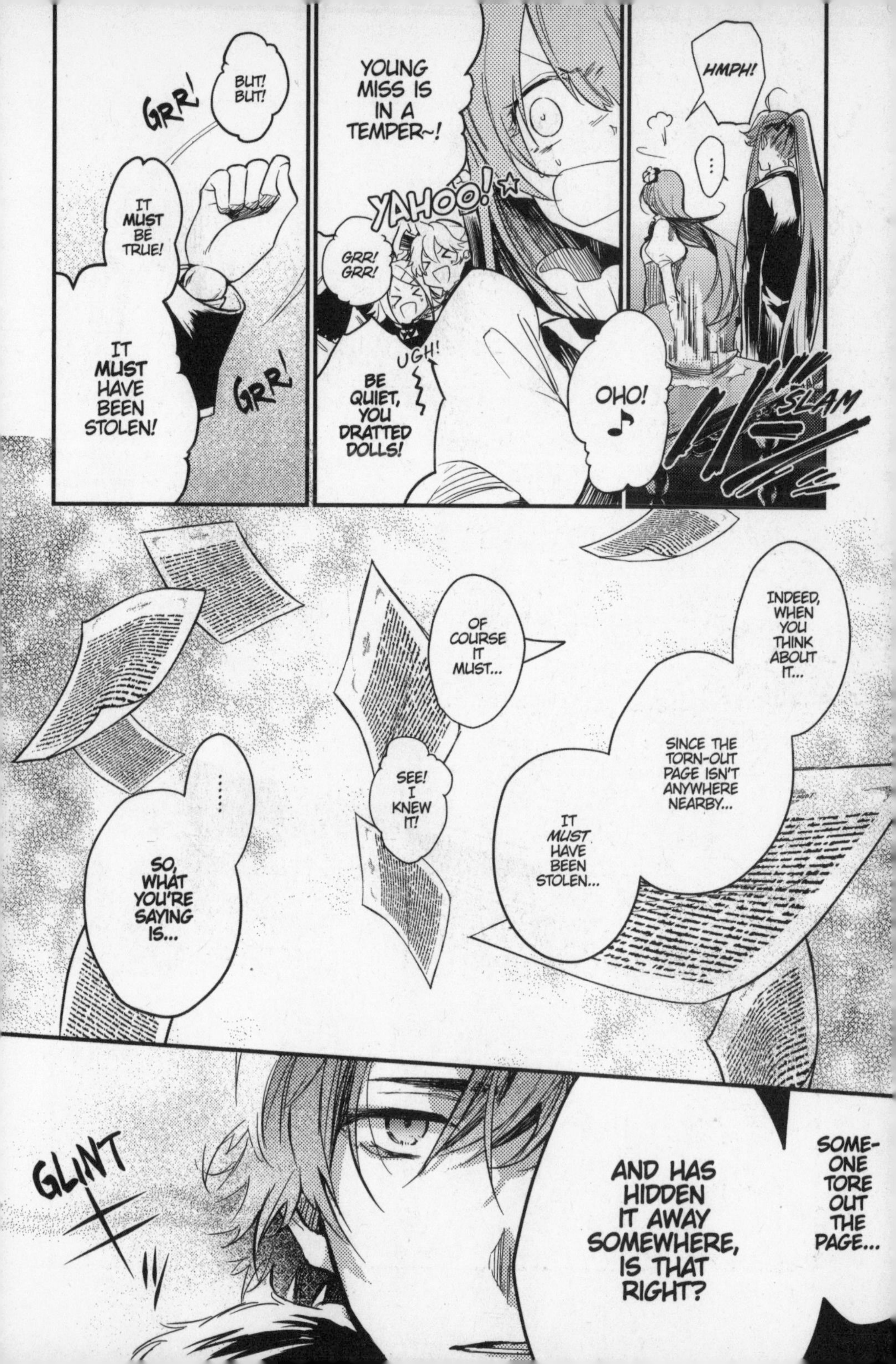
HMPH!
...
SLAM
OHO! ♪
YOUNG MISS IS IN A TEMPER~!
YAHOO!☆
GRR! GRR!
UGH!
BE QUIET, YOU DRATTED DOLLS!
BUT! BUT!
GRR!
IT MUST BE TRUE!
IT MUST HAVE BEEN STOLEN!
GRR!
INDEED, WHEN YOU THINK ABOUT IT...
SINCE THE TORN-OUT PAGE ISN'T ANYWHERE NEARBY...
IT *MUST* HAVE BEEN STOLEN...
OF COURSE IT MUST...
SEE! I KNEW IT!
......
SO, WHAT YOU'RE SAYING IS...
SOME-ONE TORE OUT THE PAGE...
AND HAS HIDDEN IT AWAY SOMEWHERE, IS THAT RIGHT?
GLINT

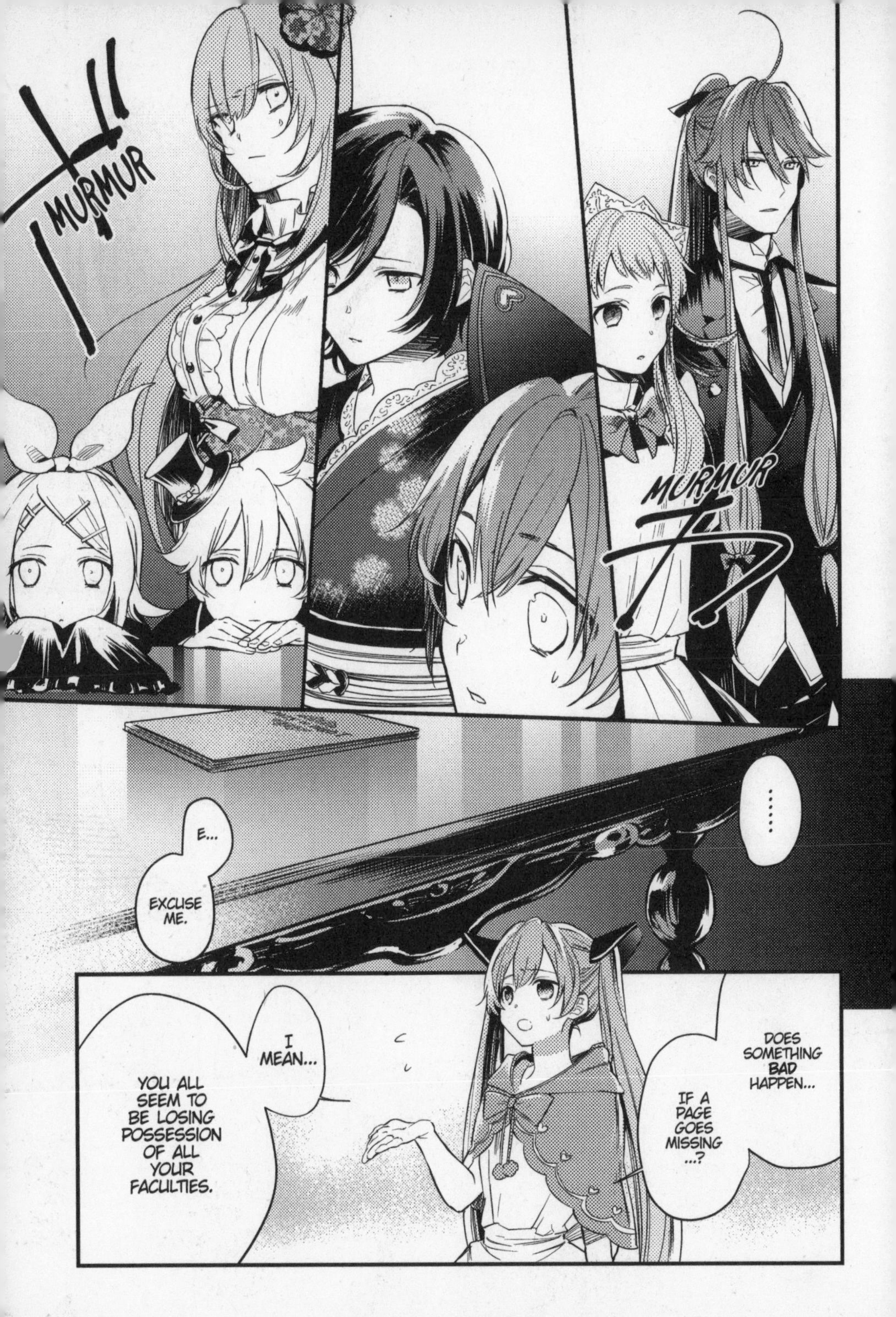
MURMUR
MURMUR
......
E...
EXCUSE ME.
DOES SOMETHING BAD HAPPEN...
IF A PAGE GOES MISSING ...?
I MEAN...
YOU ALL SEEM TO BE LOSING POSSESSION OF ALL YOUR FACULTIES.

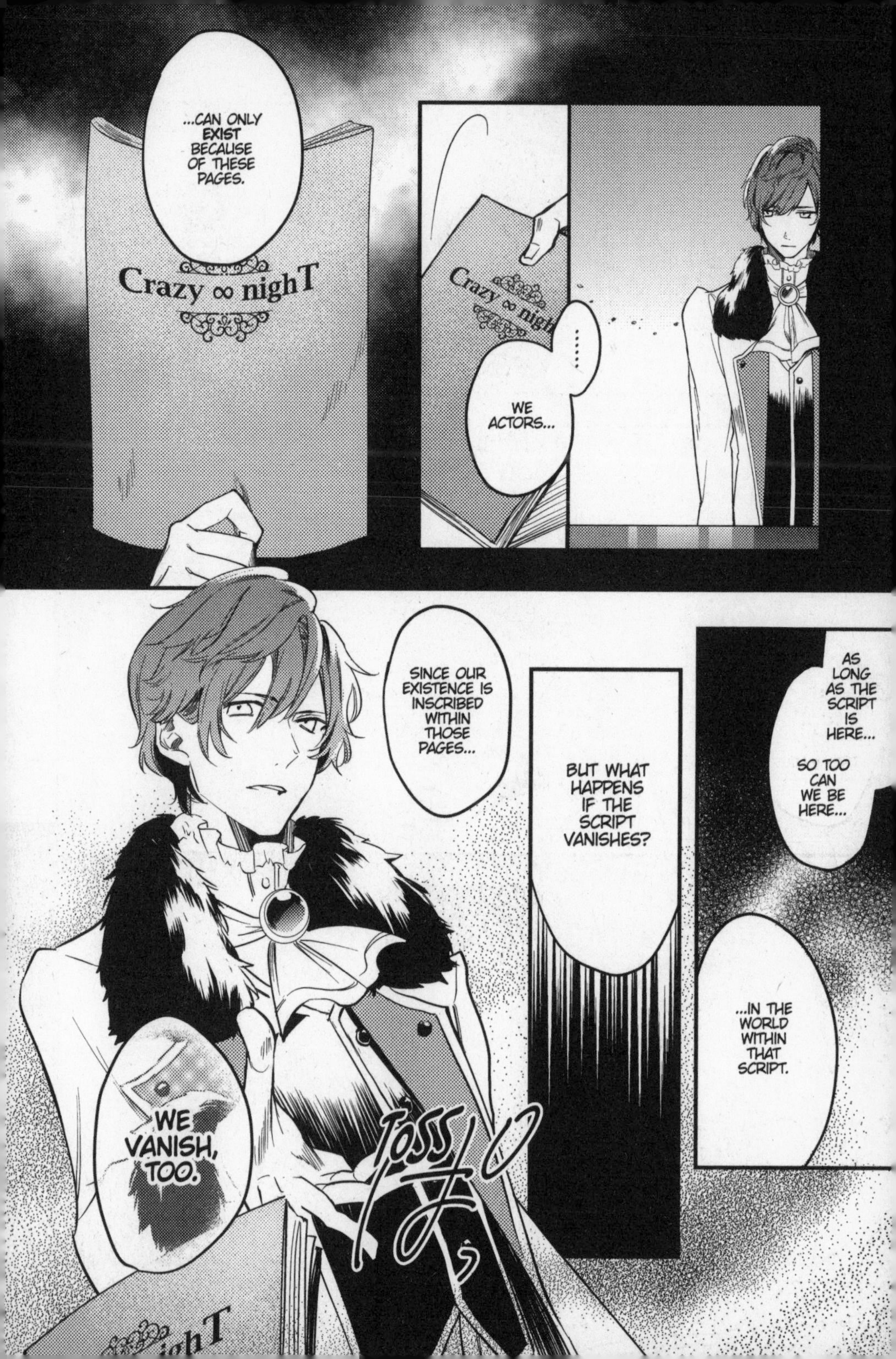
.....
WE ACTORS...
Crazy ∞ nighT
Crazy ∞ nighT
...CAN ONLY EXIST BECAUSE OF THESE PAGES.
AS LONG AS THE SCRIPT IS HERE...
SO TOO CAN WE BE HERE...
...IN THE WORLD WITHIN THAT SCRIPT.
BUT WHAT HAPPENS IF THE SCRIPT VANISHES?
SINCE OUR EXISTENCE IS INSCRIBED WITHIN THOSE PAGES...
WE VANISH, TOO.
TOSS

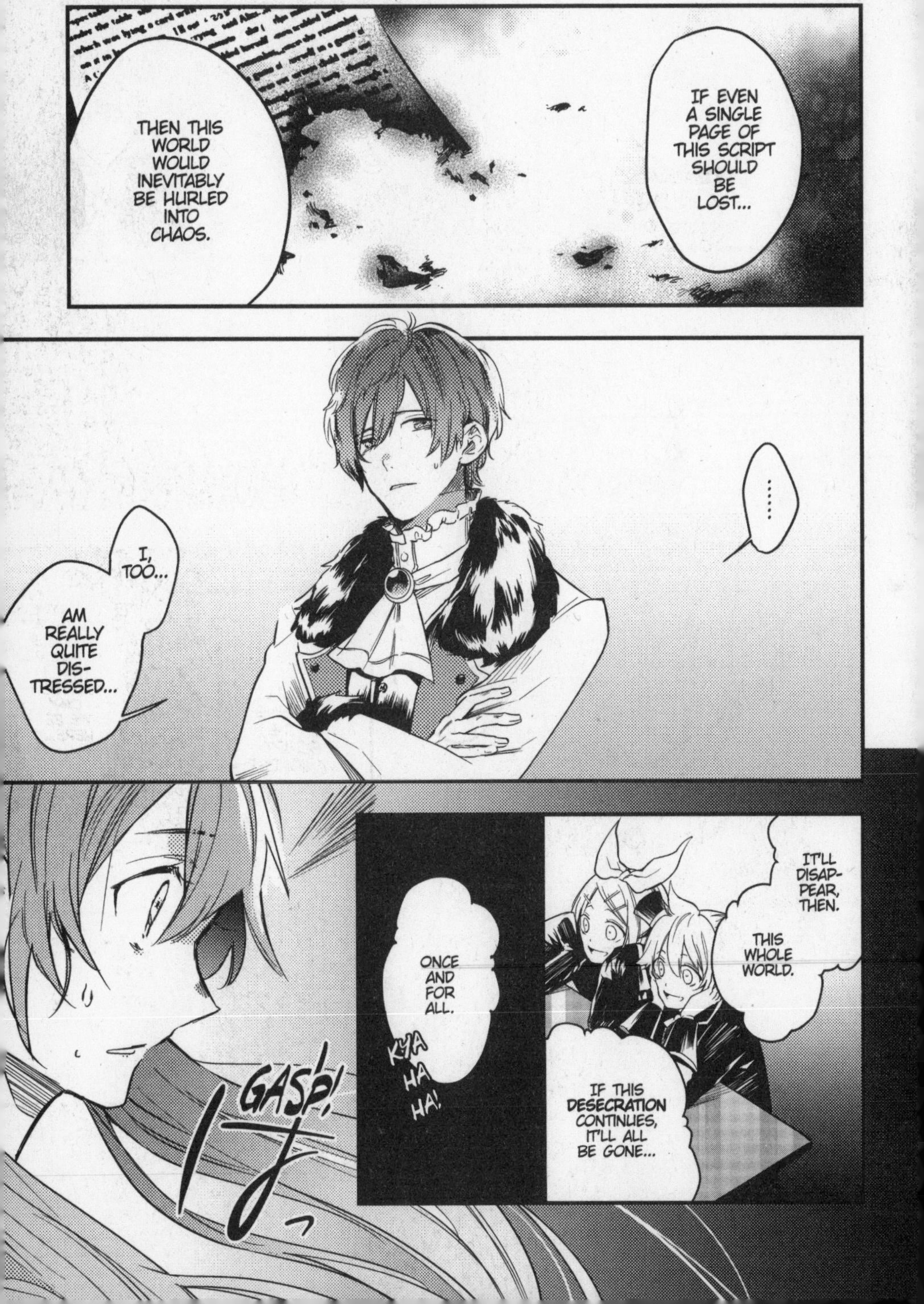
IF EVEN A SINGLE PAGE OF THIS SCRIPT SHOULD BE LOST...
THEN THIS WORLD WOULD INEVITABLY BE HURLED INTO CHAOS.
......
I, TOO...
AM REALLY QUITE DIS-TRESSED...
IT'LL DISAP-PEAR, THEN.
THIS WHOLE WORLD.
IF THIS DESECRATION CONTINUES, IT'LL ALL BE GONE...
ONCE AND FOR ALL.
KYA HA HA!
GASP!

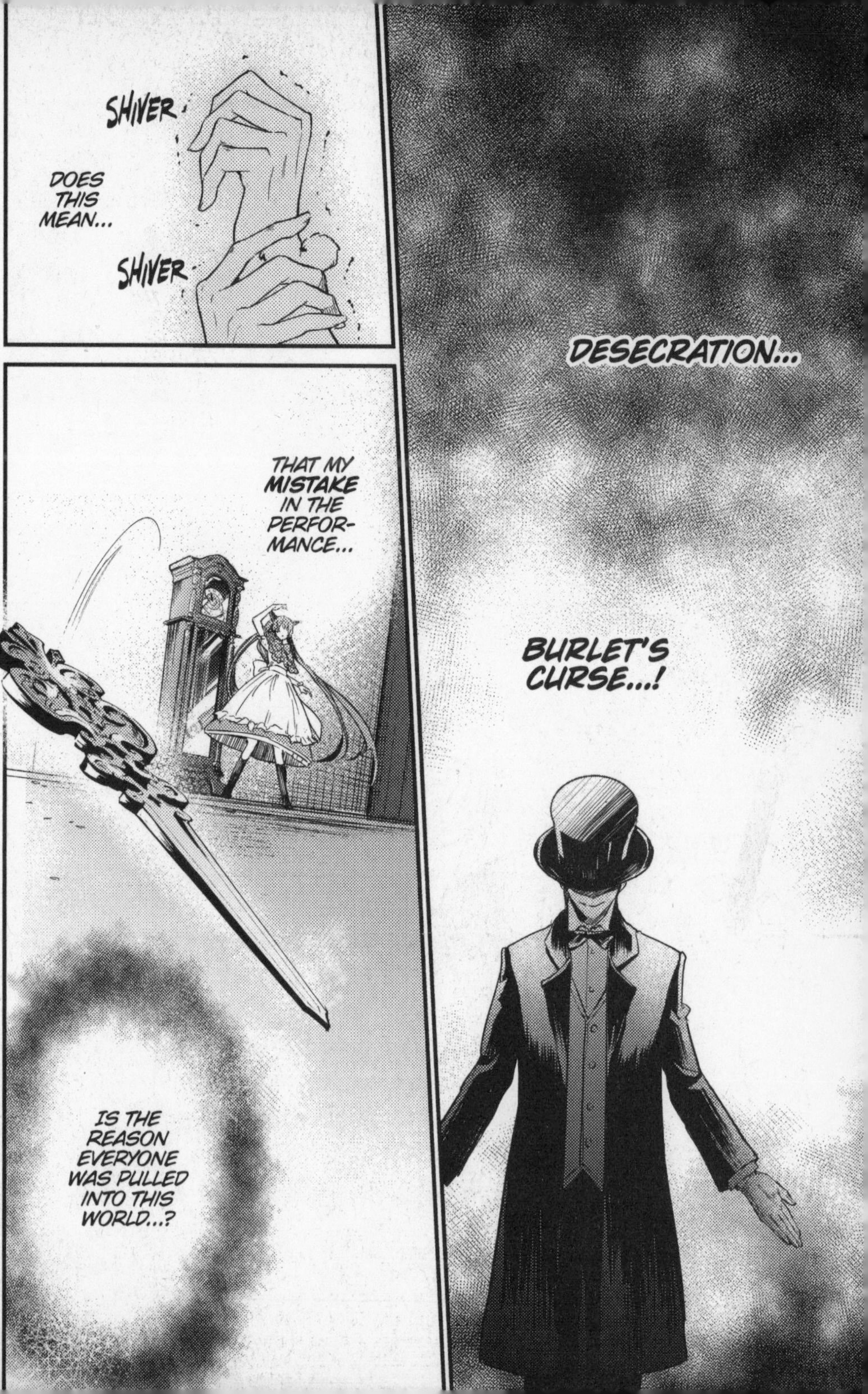
DESECRATION...
BURLET'S CURSE...!
SHIVER
DOES THIS MEAN...
SHIVER
THAT MY MISTAKE IN THE PERFORMANCE...
IS THE REASON EVERYONE WAS PULLED INTO THIS WORLD...?

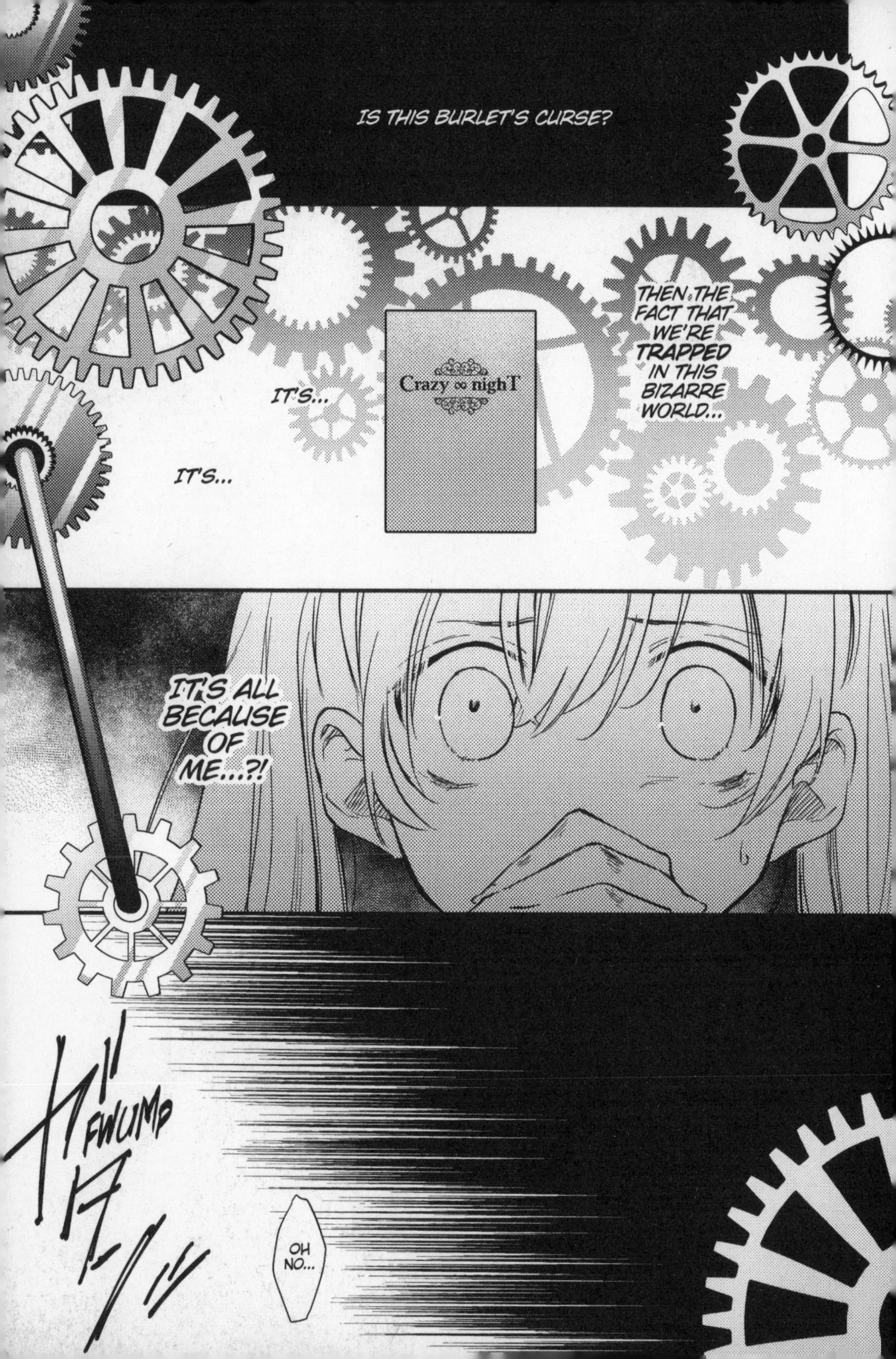
IS THIS BURLET'S CURSE?
THEN THE FACT THAT WE'RE TRAPPED IN THIS BIZARRE WORLD...
Crazy ∞ nighT
IT'S...
IT'S...
IT'S ALL BECAUSE OF ME...?!
FWUMP
OH NO...

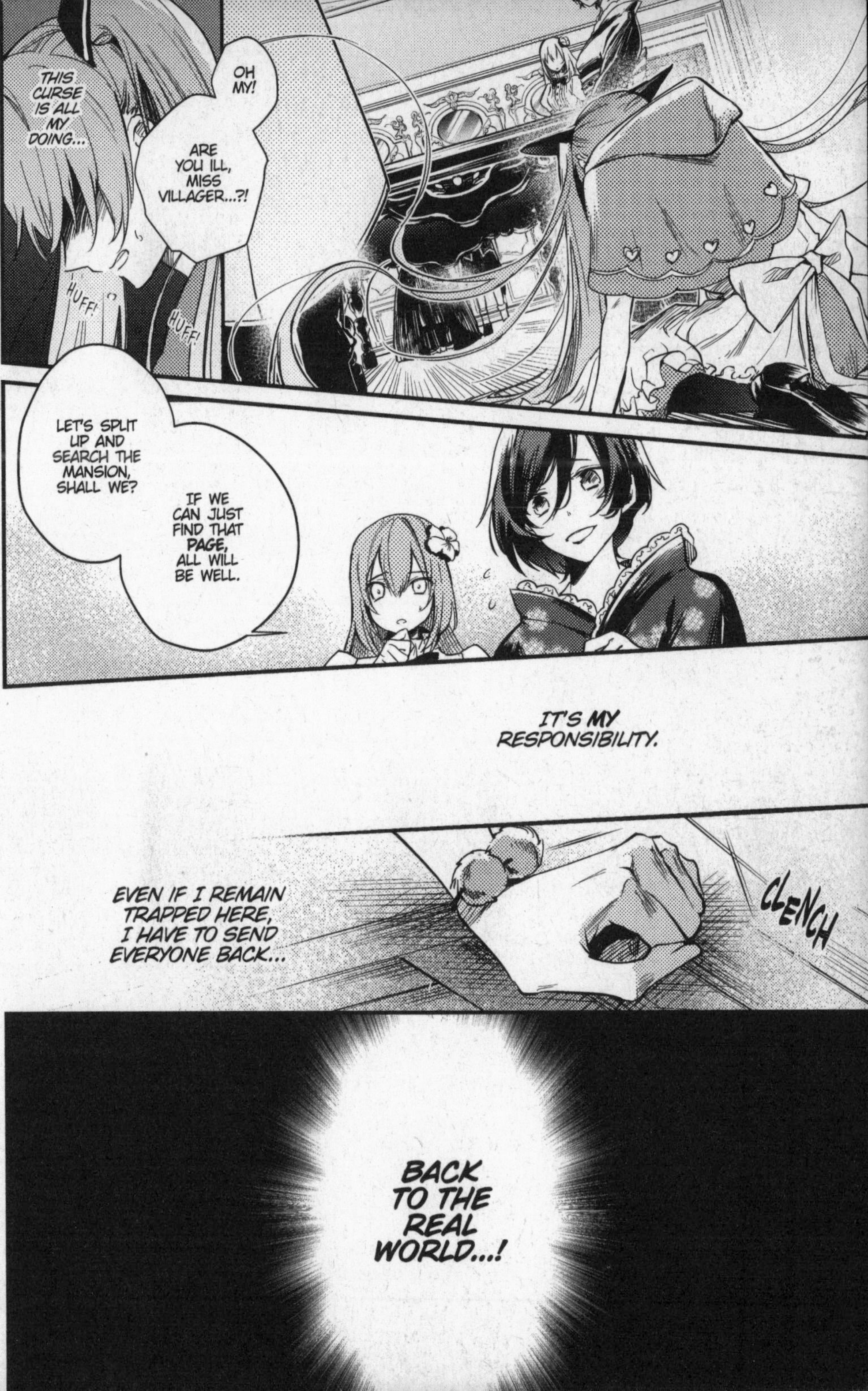
OH MY!
ARE YOU ILL, MISS VILLAGER...?!
THIS CURSE IS ALL MY DOING...
HUFF!
HUFF!
LET'S SPLIT UP AND SEARCH THE MANSION, SHALL WE?
IF WE CAN JUST FIND THAT PAGE, ALL WILL BE WELL.
IT'S MY RESPONSIBILITY.
CLENCH
EVEN IF I REMAIN TRAPPED HERE, I HAVE TO SEND EVERYONE BACK...
BACK TO THE REAL WORLD...!

~ Hatsune Miku ~

Bad∞End∞Night

Act 3: Blade

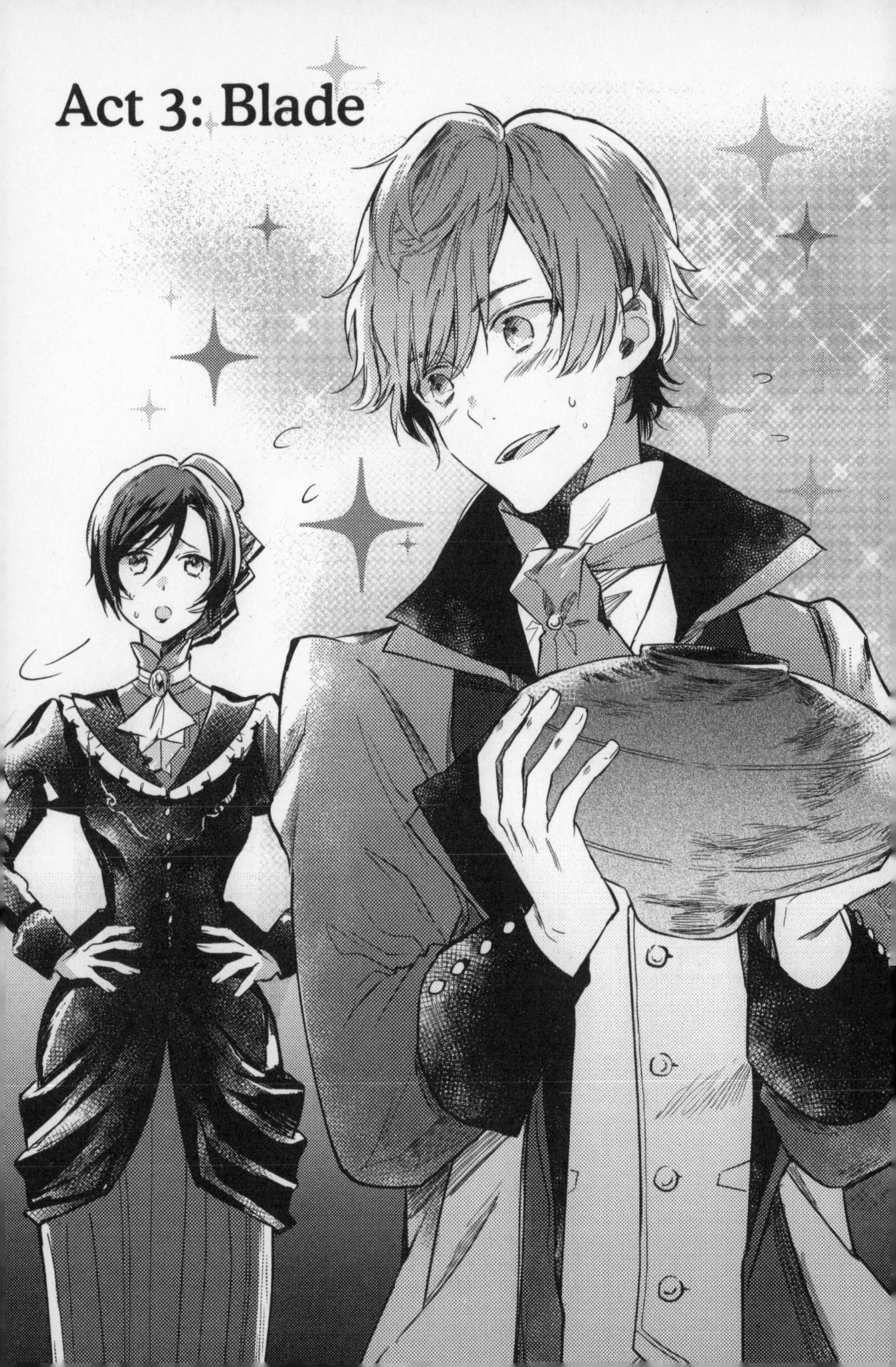

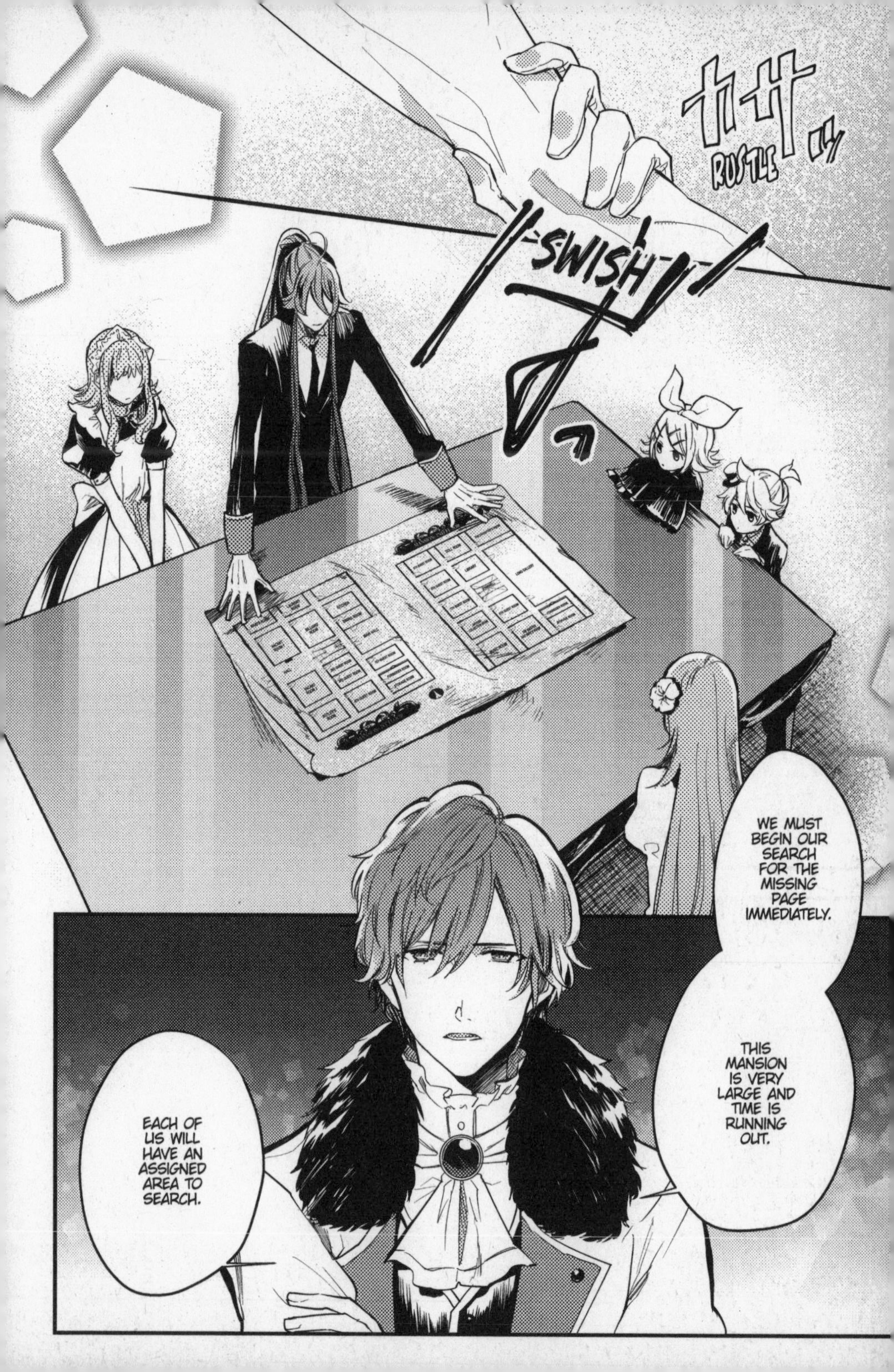
RUSTLE
SWISH
WE MUST BEGIN OUR SEARCH FOR THE MISSING PAGE IMMEDIATELY.
THIS MANSION IS VERY LARGE AND TIME IS RUNNING OUT.
EACH OF US WILL HAVE AN ASSIGNED AREA TO SEARCH.

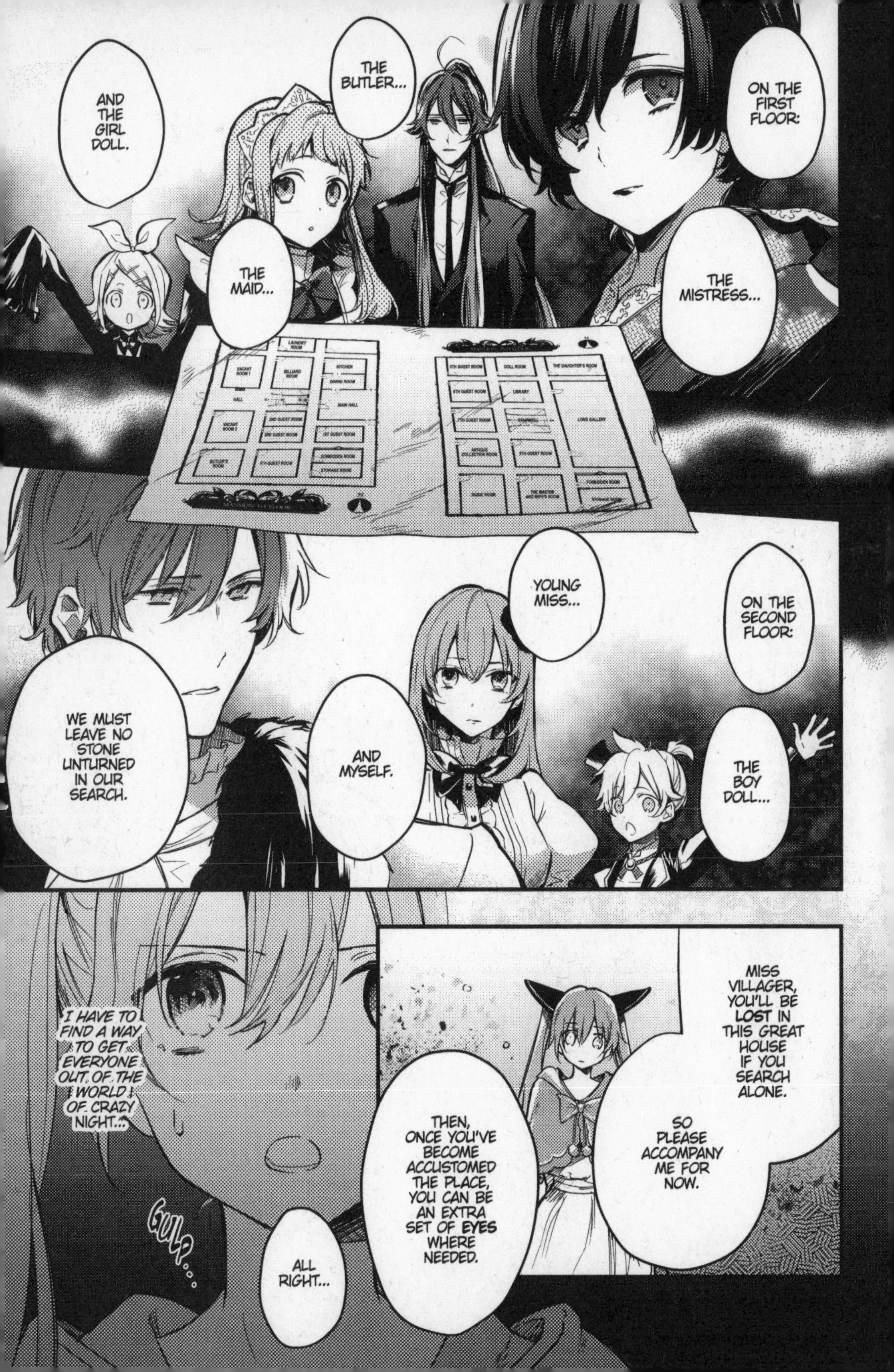
ON THE FIRST FLOOR:
THE MISTRESS...
THE BUTLER...
THE MAID...
AND THE GIRL DOLL.
ON THE SECOND FLOOR:
YOUNG MISS...
THE BOY DOLL...
AND MYSELF.
WE MUST LEAVE NO STONE UNTURNED IN OUR SEARCH.
MISS VILLAGER, YOU'LL BE LOST IN THIS GREAT HOUSE IF YOU SEARCH ALONE.
SO PLEASE ACCOMPANY ME FOR NOW.
THEN, ONCE YOU'VE BECOME ACCUSTOMED THE PLACE, YOU CAN BE AN EXTRA SET OF EYES WHERE NEEDED.
ALL RIGHT...
I HAVE TO FIND A WAY TO GET EVERYONE OUT OF THE WORLD OF CRAZY NIGHT...
GULP...

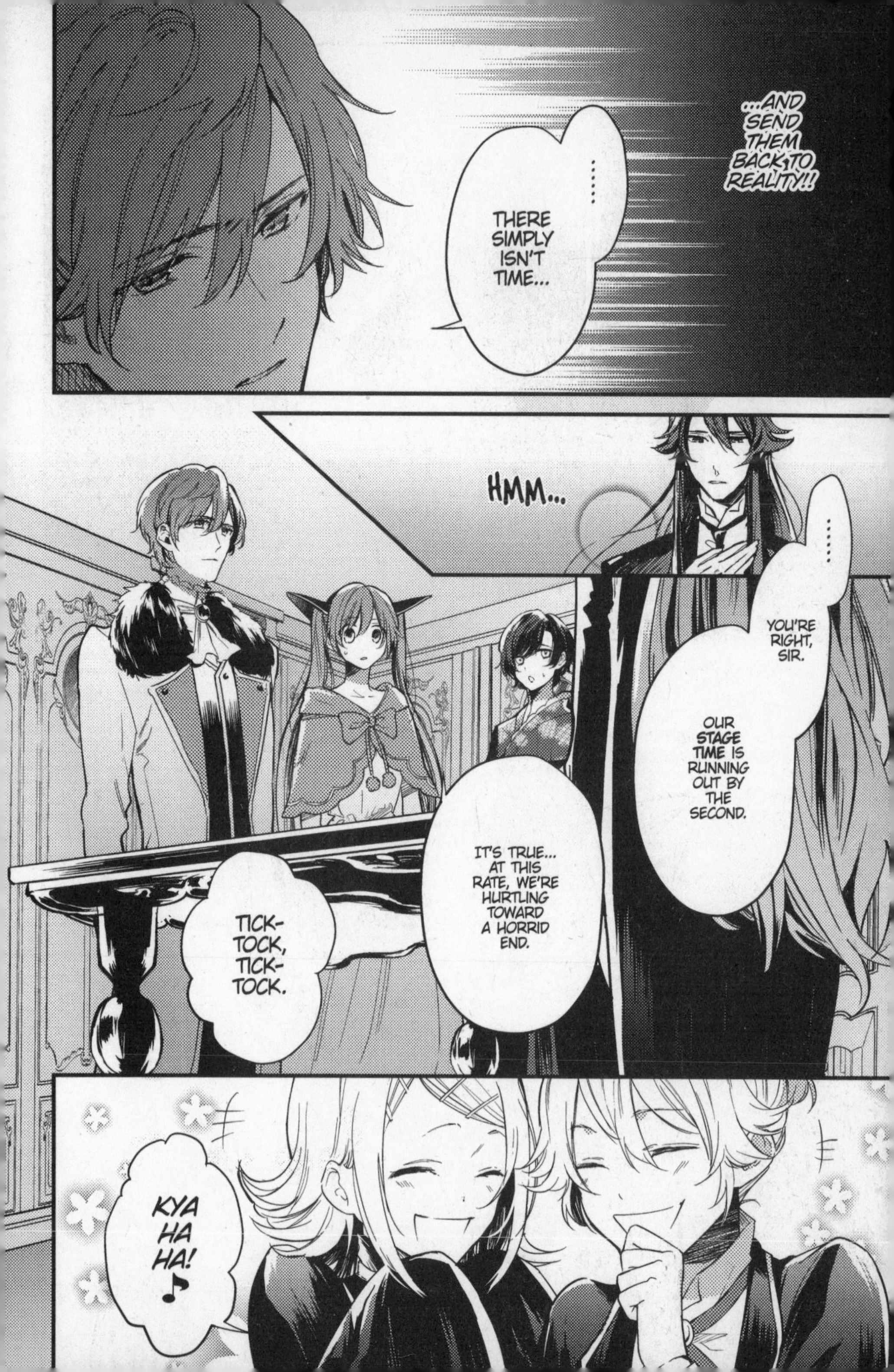
...AND SEND THEM BACK TO REALITY!!
...... THERE SIMPLY ISN'T TIME...
......
HMM...
YOU'RE RIGHT, SIR.
OUR STAGE TIME IS RUNNING OUT BY THE SECOND.
IT'S TRUE... AT THIS RATE, WE'RE HURTLING TOWARD A HORRID END.
TICK-TOCK, TICK-TOCK.
KYA HA HA! ♪

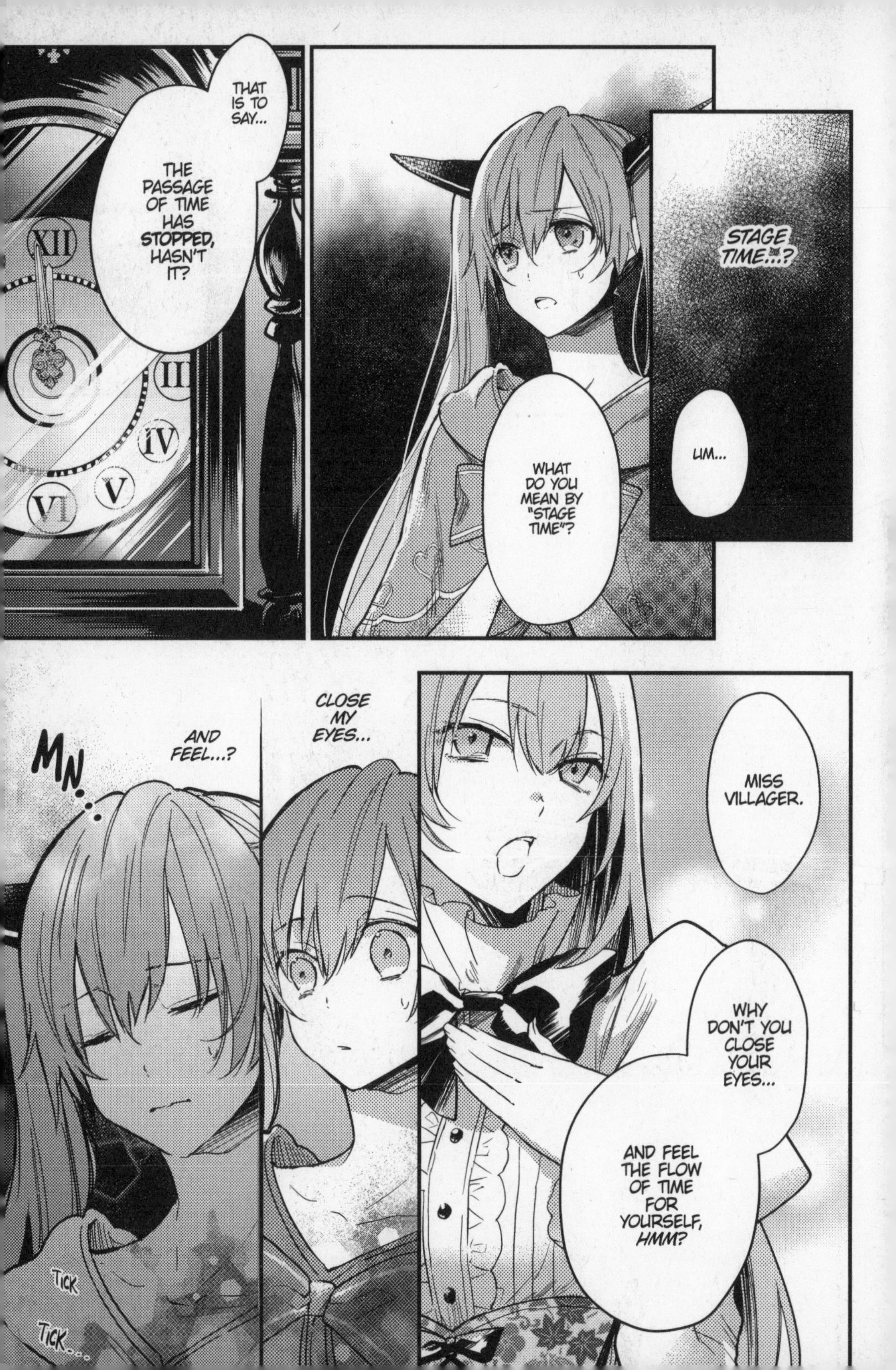
STAGE TIME...?
UM...
WHAT DO YOU MEAN BY "STAGE TIME"?
THAT IS TO SAY...
THE PASSAGE OF TIME HAS STOPPED, HASN'T IT?
MISS VILLAGER.
WHY DON'T YOU CLOSE YOUR EYES...
AND FEEL THE FLOW OF TIME FOR YOURSELF, *HMM*?
CLOSE MY EYES...
AND FEEL...?
MN...
TICK
TICK...

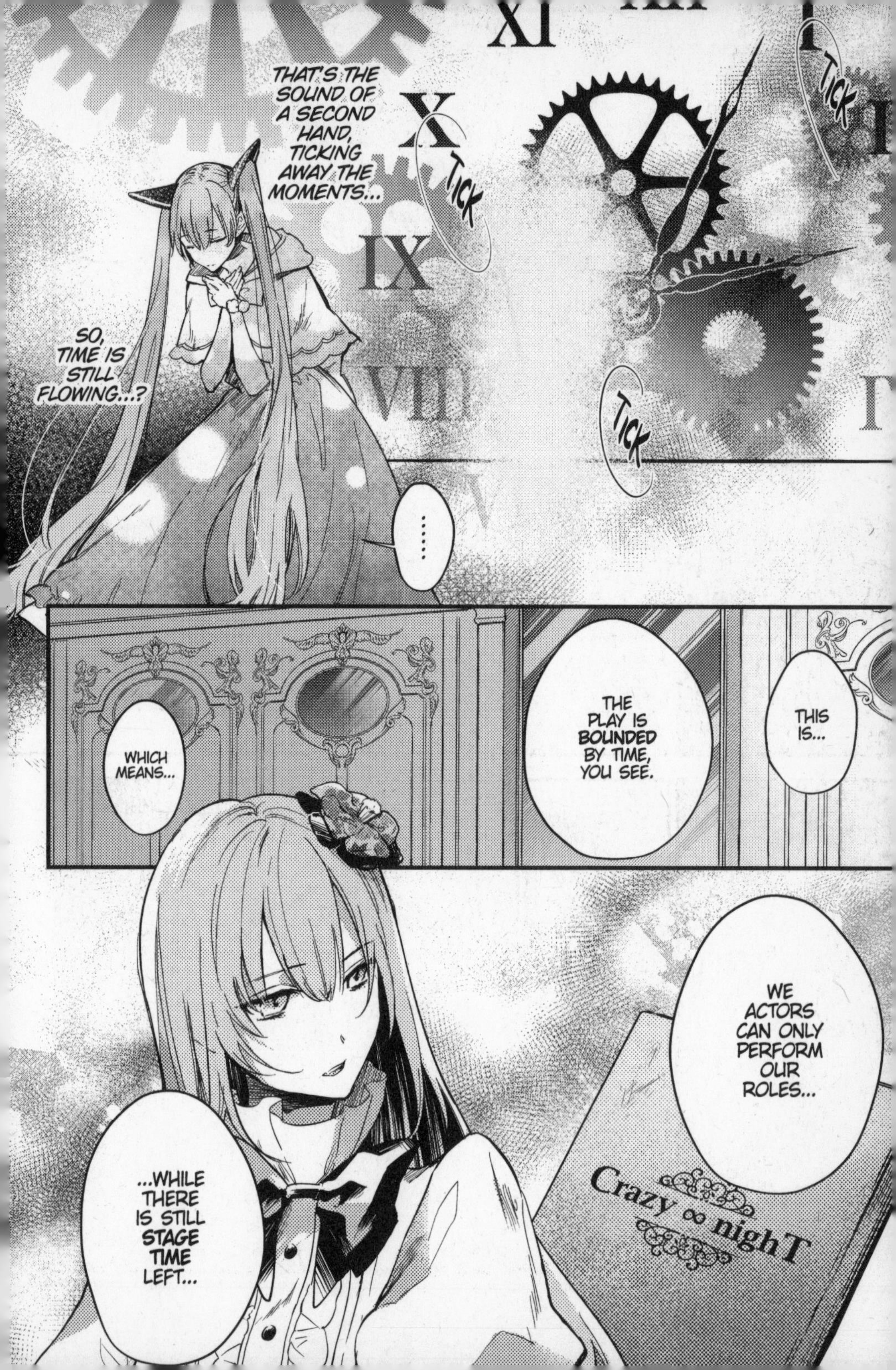
TICK
THAT'S THE SOUND OF A SECOND HAND, TICKING AWAY THE MOMENTS...
TICK
TICK
SO, TIME IS STILL FLOWING...?
......
THIS IS...
THE PLAY IS BOUNDED BY TIME, YOU SEE.
WHICH MEANS...
WE ACTORS CAN ONLY PERFORM OUR ROLES...
Crazy ∞ nighT
...WHILE THERE IS STILL STAGE TIME LEFT...

WHAT IF WE CANNOT FIND THE MISSING PAGE...

BA-DUMP...

WILL WE...

DISAPPEAR...?

AND THUS CANNOT COMPLETE THE PLAY...?

SNFF

WE'RE RUNNING OUT OF TIME.

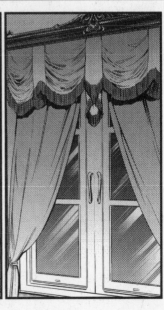

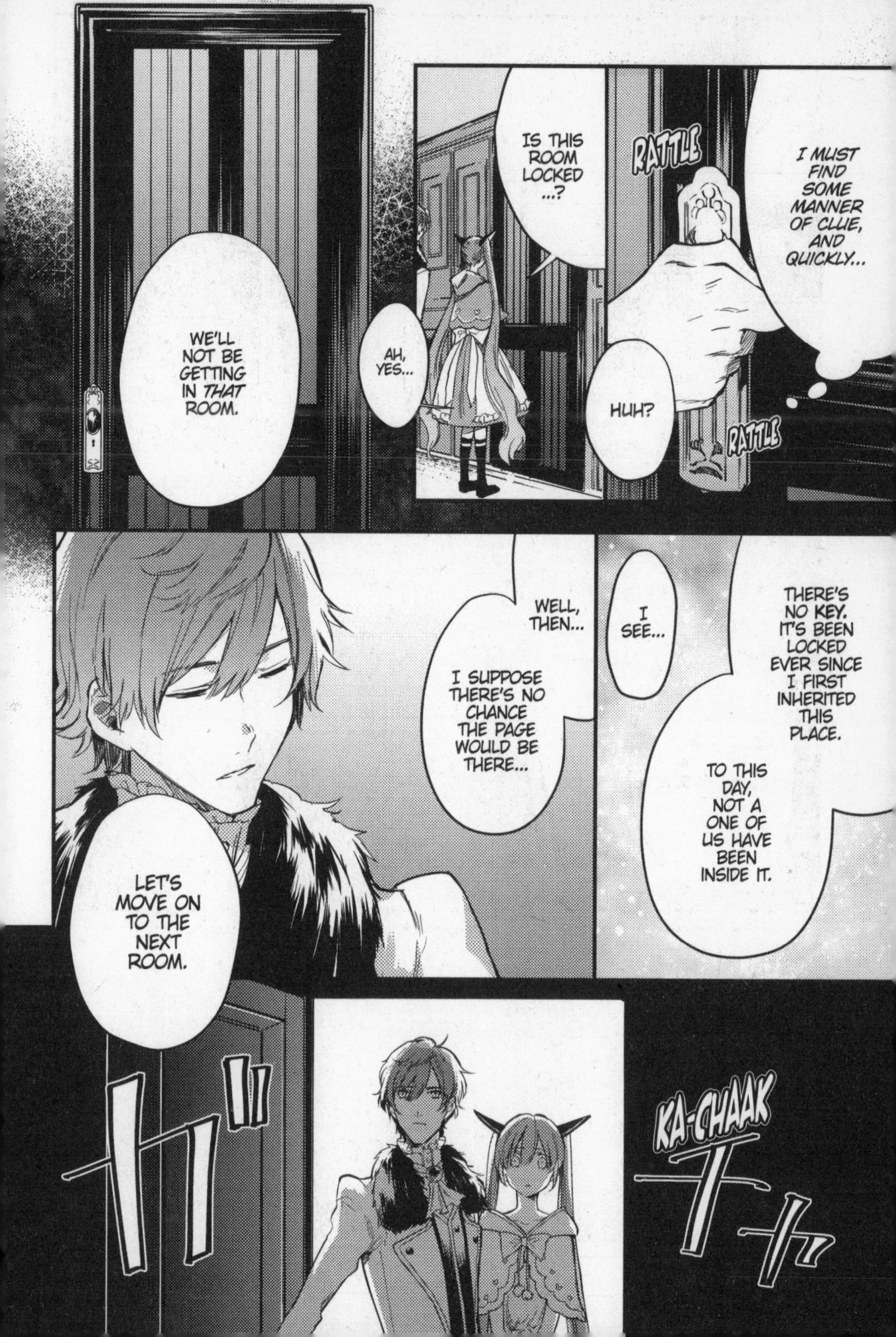
I MUST FIND SOME MANNER OF CLUE, AND QUICKLY...
RATTLE
RATTLE
HUH?
IS THIS ROOM LOCKED ...?
AH, YES...
WE'LL NOT BE GETTING IN *THAT* ROOM.
THERE'S NO KEY. IT'S BEEN LOCKED EVER SINCE I FIRST INHERITED THIS PLACE.
TO THIS DAY, NOT A ONE OF US HAVE BEEN INSIDE IT.
I SEE...
WELL, THEN...
I SUPPOSE THERE'S NO CHANCE THE PAGE WOULD BE THERE...
LET'S MOVE ON TO THE NEXT ROOM.
KA-CHAAK

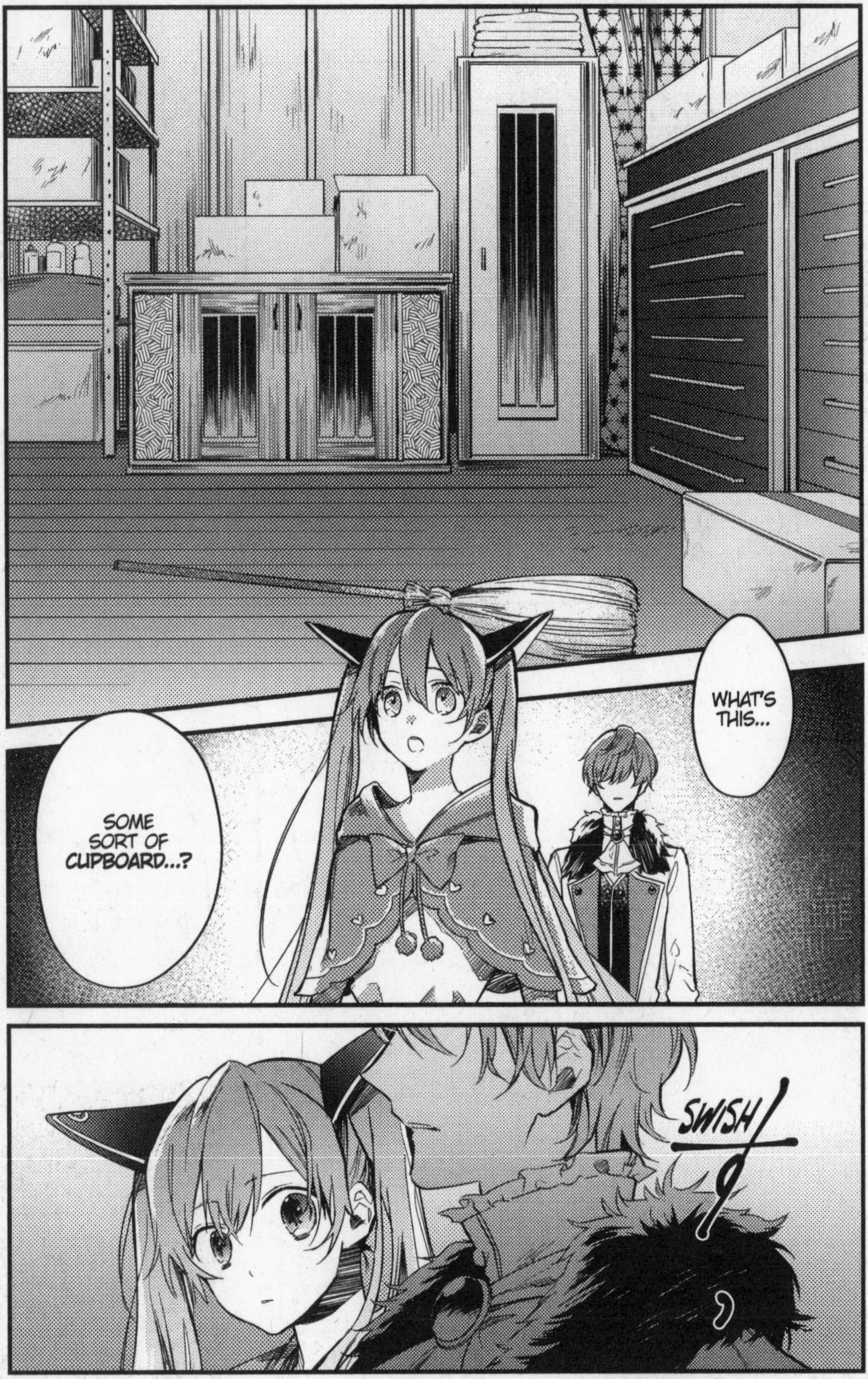
WHAT'S THIS...
SOME SORT OF CUPBOARD...?
SWISH

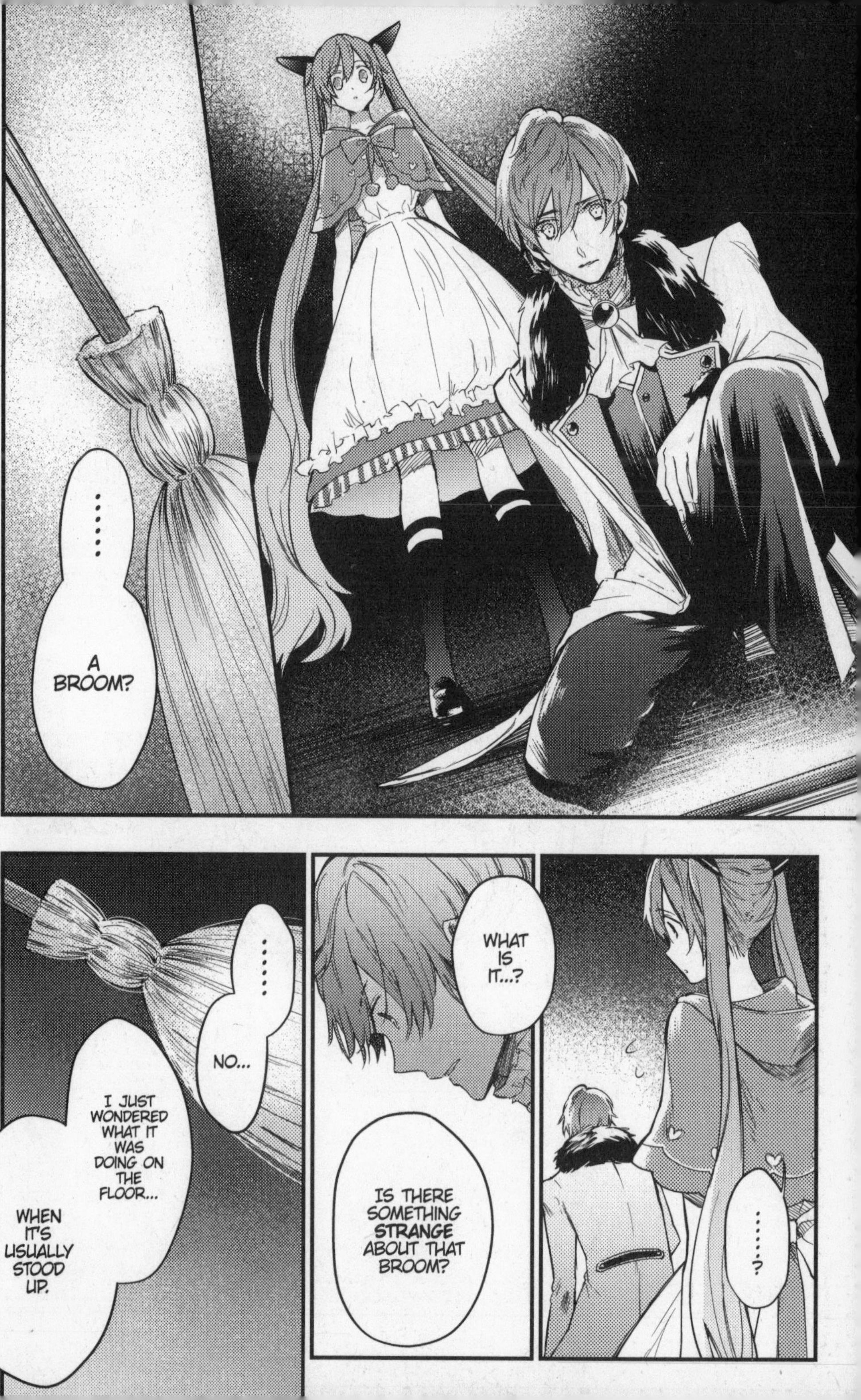
......
A BROOM?
......?
WHAT IS IT...?
IS THERE SOMETHING STRANGE ABOUT THAT BROOM?
......
NO...
I JUST WONDERED WHAT IT WAS DOING ON THE FLOOR...
WHEN IT'S USUALLY STOOD UP.

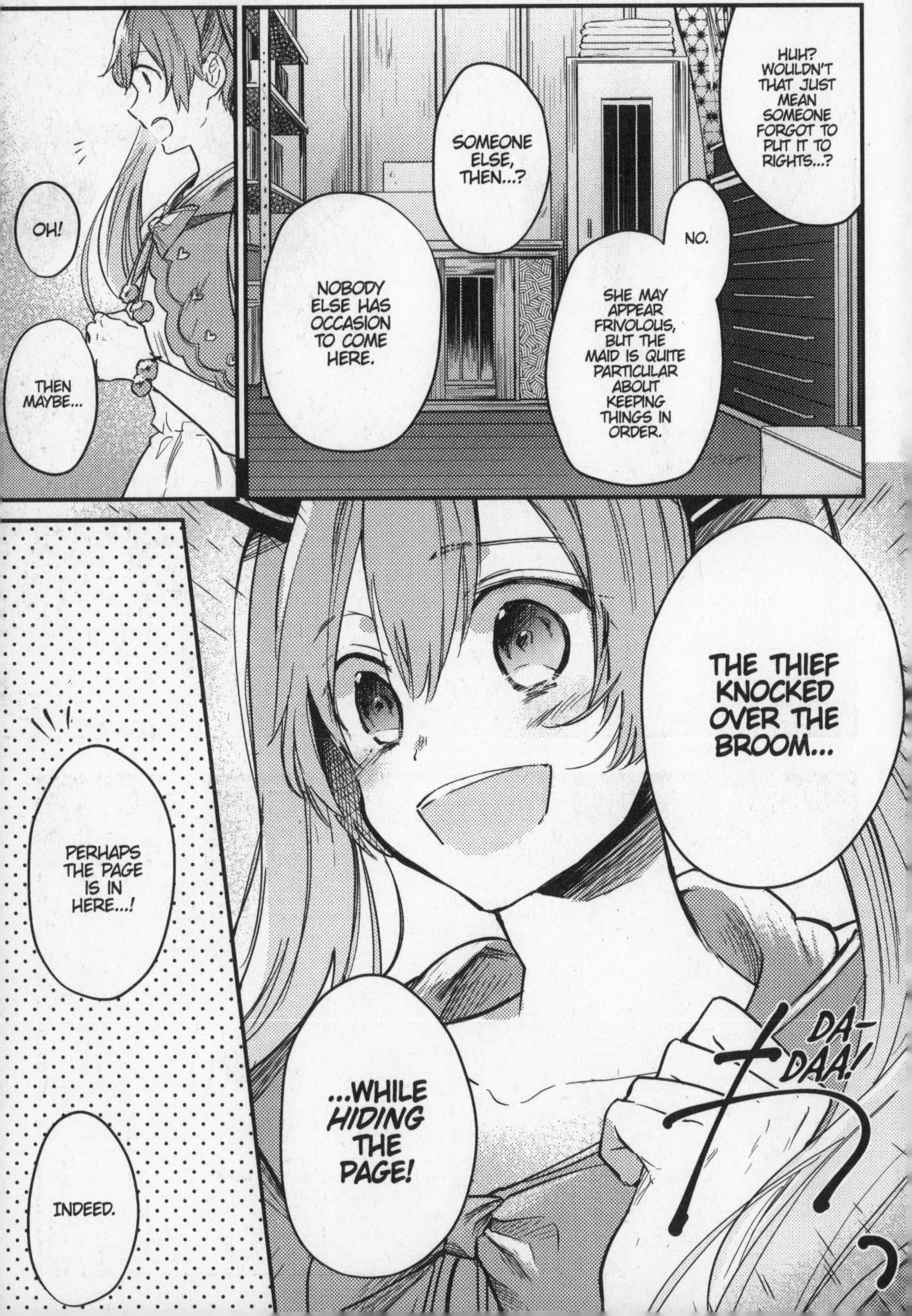
HUH? WOULDN'T THAT JUST MEAN SOMEONE FORGOT TO PUT IT TO RIGHTS...?
NO.
SHE MAY APPEAR FRIVOLOUS, BUT THE MAID IS QUITE PARTICULAR ABOUT KEEPING THINGS IN ORDER.
SOMEONE ELSE, THEN...?
NOBODY ELSE HAS OCCASION TO COME HERE.
OH!
THEN MAYBE...
THE THIEF KNOCKED OVER THE BROOM...
...WHILE *HIDING* THE PAGE!
DA-DAA!
PERHAPS THE PAGE IS IN HERE...!
INDEED.

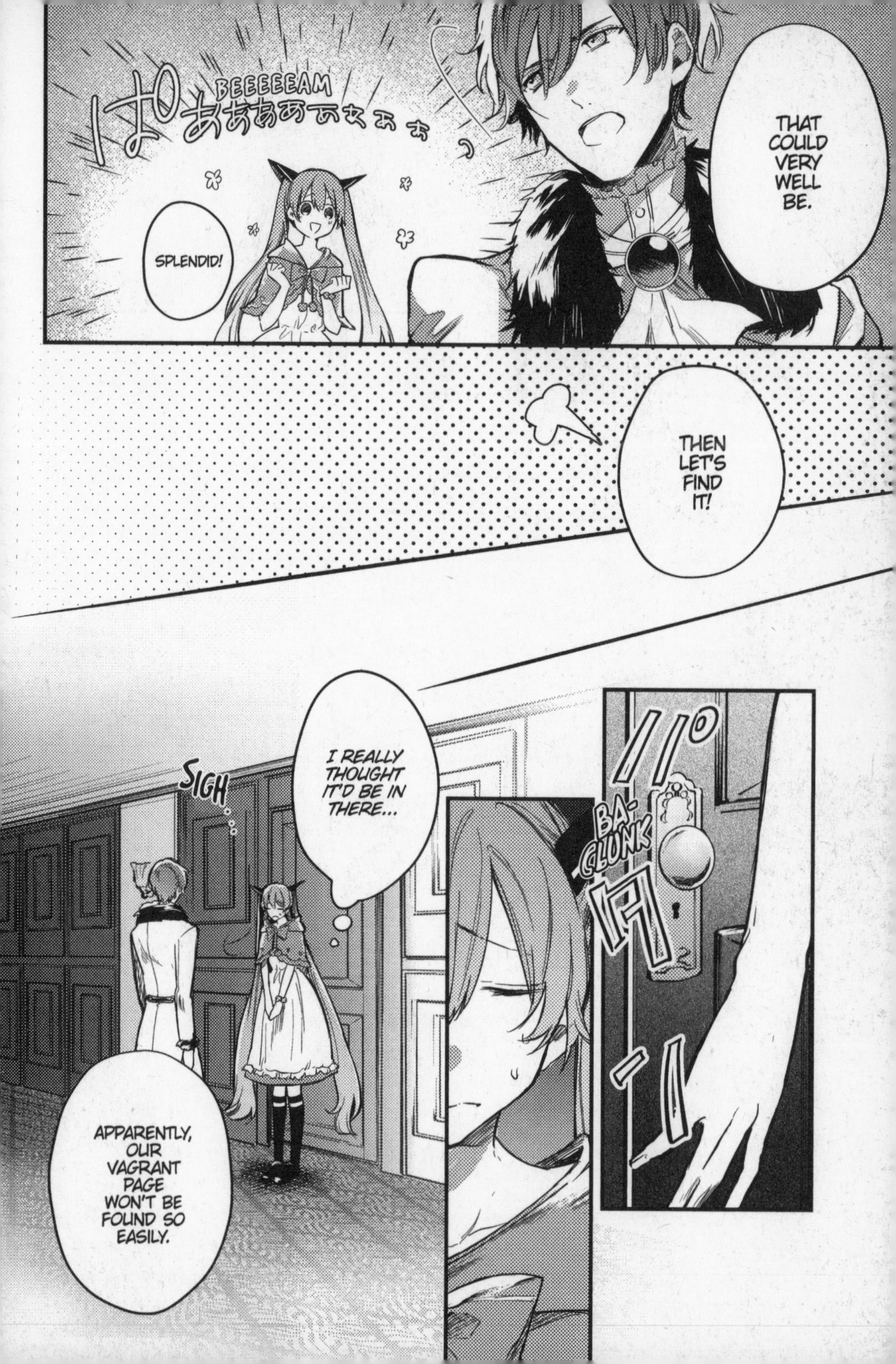
THAT COULD VERY WELL BE.
BEEEEEAM
SPLENDID!
THEN LET'S FIND IT!
BA-CLUNK
I REALLY THOUGHT IT'D BE IN THERE...
SIGH
APPARENTLY, OUR VAGRANT PAGE WON'T BE FOUND SO EASILY.

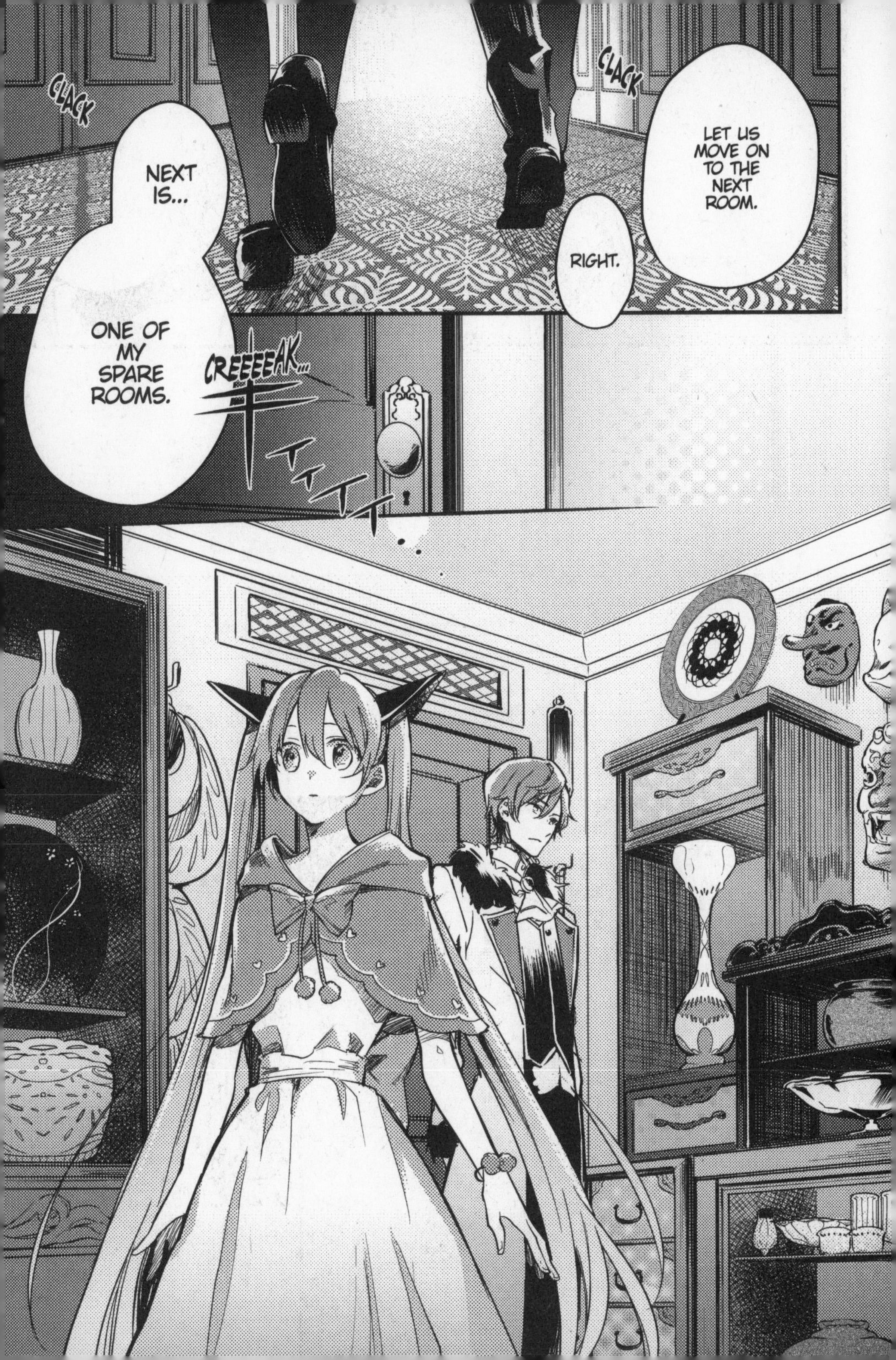
CLACK
LET US MOVE ON TO THE NEXT ROOM.
RIGHT.
CLACK
NEXT IS...
ONE OF MY SPARE ROOMS.
CREEEEAK...

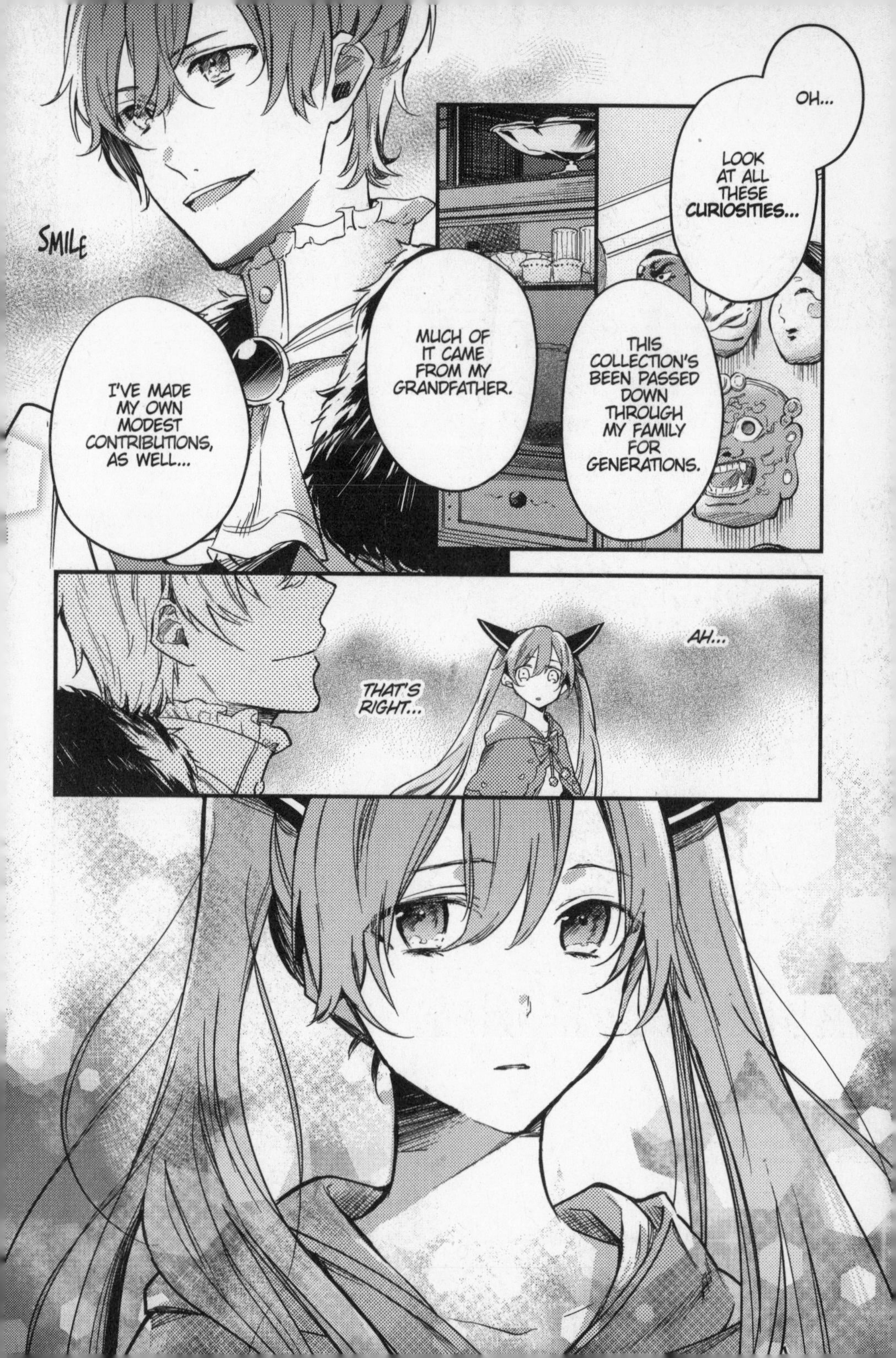
OH...
LOOK AT ALL THESE CURIOSITIES...
THIS COLLECTION'S BEEN PASSED DOWN THROUGH MY FAMILY FOR GENERATIONS.
MUCH OF IT CAME FROM MY GRANDFATHER.
I'VE MADE MY OWN MODEST CONTRIBUTIONS, AS WELL...
SMILE
AH...
THAT'S RIGHT...

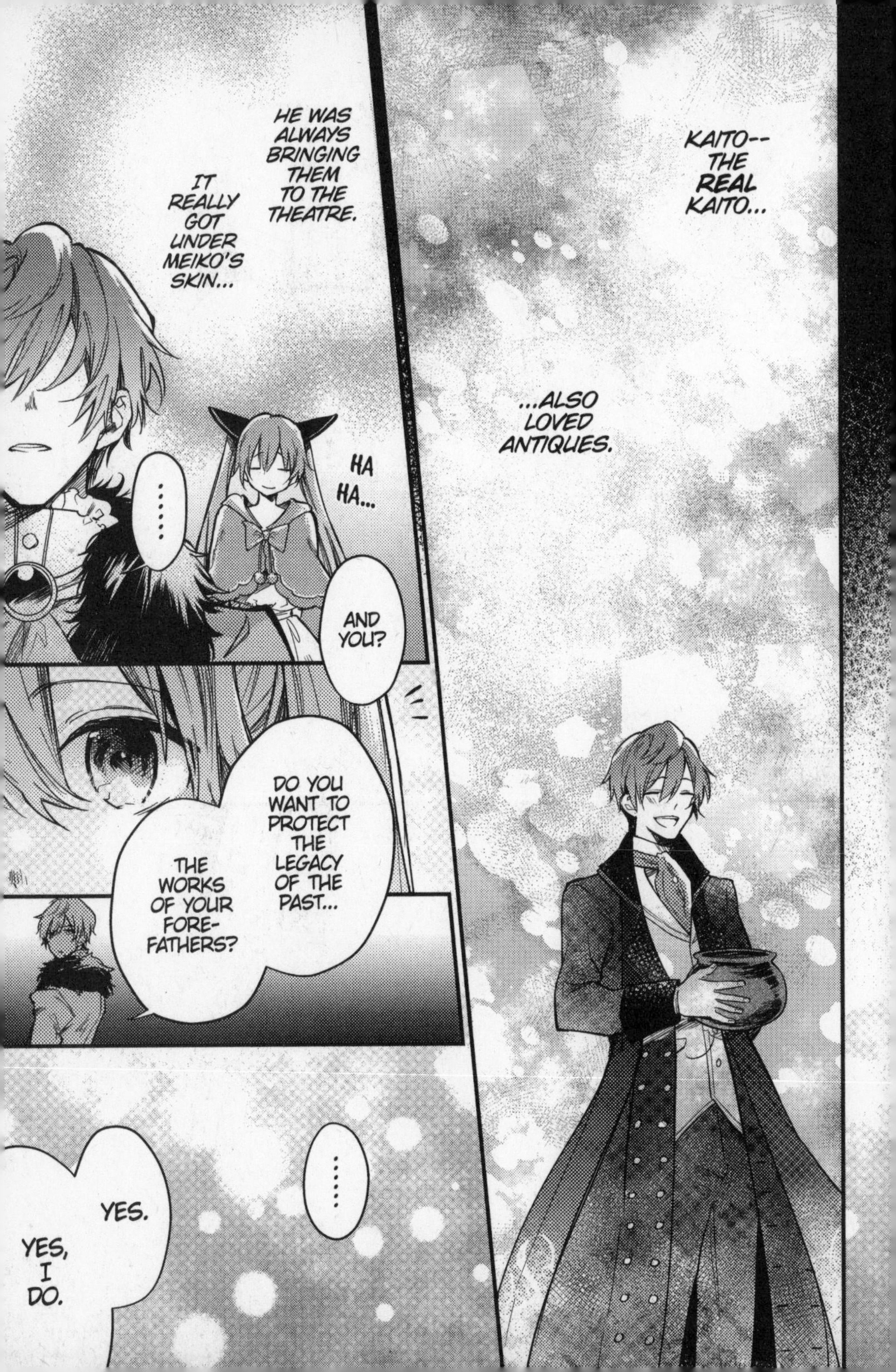
KAITO-- THE REAL KAITO...
...ALSO LOVED ANTIQUES.
HE WAS ALWAYS BRINGING THEM TO THE THEATRE.
IT REALLY GOT UNDER MEIKO'S SKIN...
......
HA HA...
AND YOU?
DO YOU WANT TO PROTECT THE LEGACY OF THE PAST...
THE WORKS OF YOUR FORE-FATHERS?
......
YES.
YES, I DO.

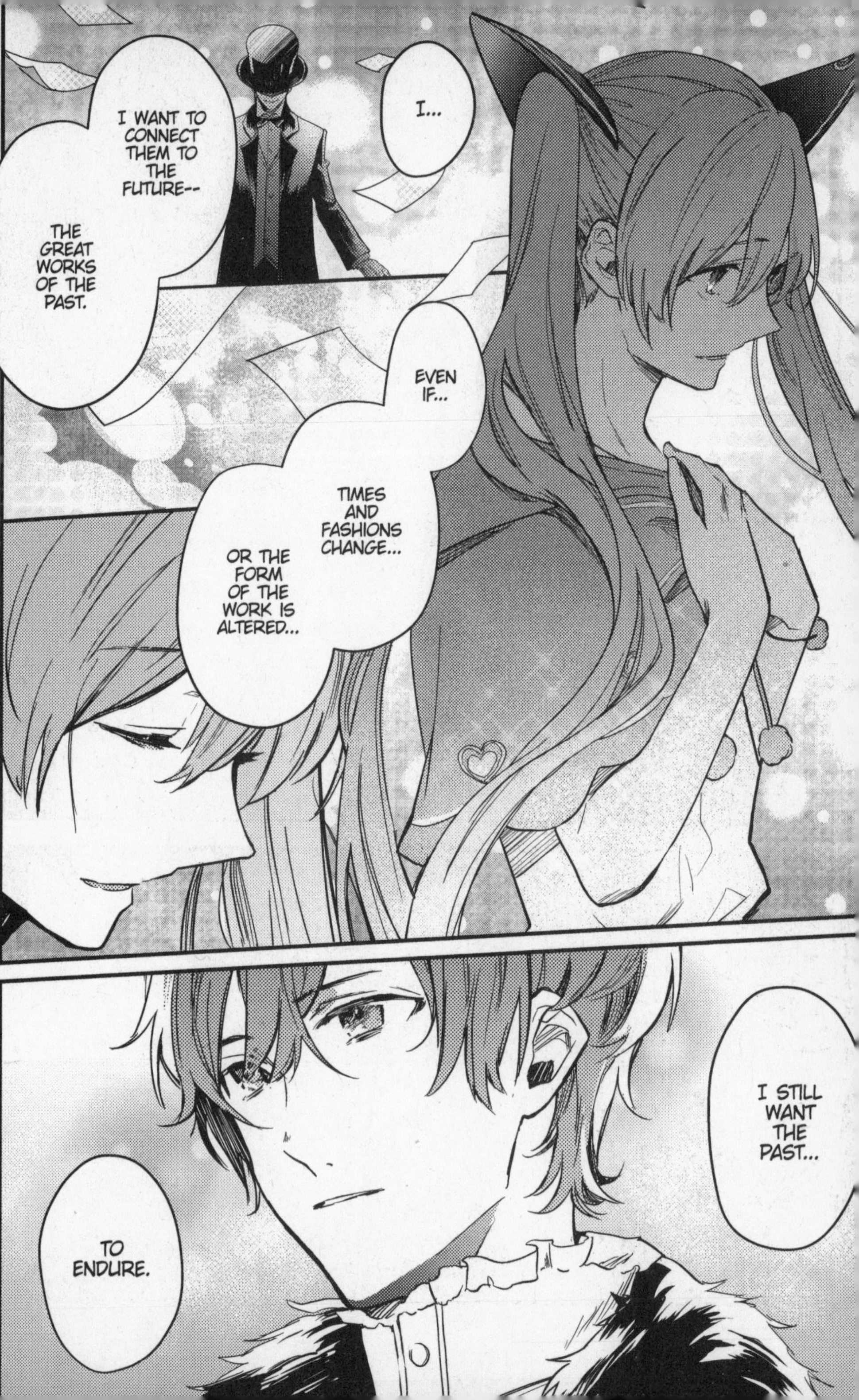
I...
EVEN IF...
TIMES AND FASHIONS CHANGE...
OR THE FORM OF THE WORK IS ALTERED...
I WANT TO CONNECT THEM TO THE FUTURE--
THE GREAT WORKS OF THE PAST.
I STILL WANT THE PAST...
TO ENDURE.

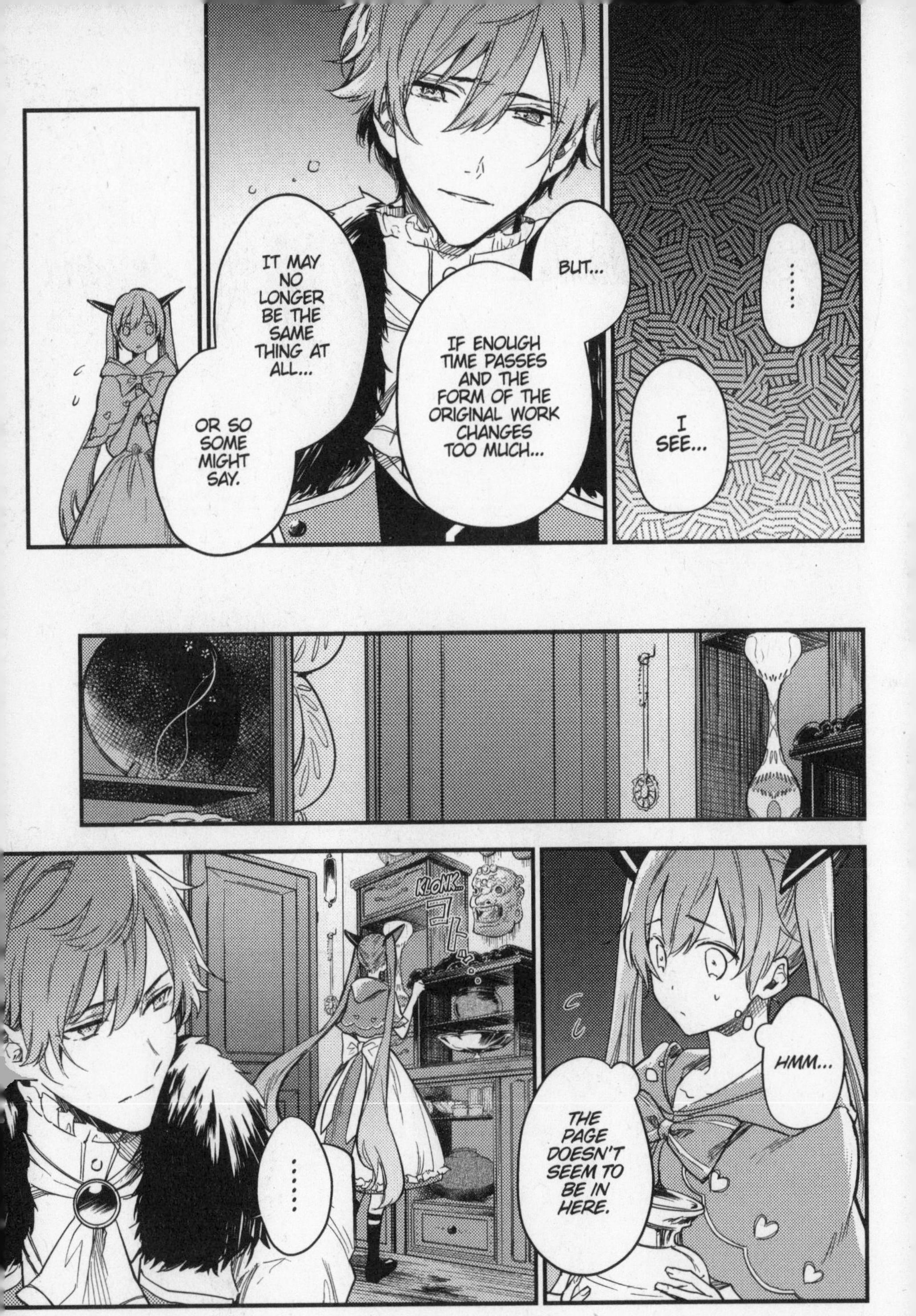
......
I SEE...
BUT...
IF ENOUGH TIME PASSES AND THE FORM OF THE ORIGINAL WORK CHANGES TOO MUCH...
IT MAY NO LONGER BE THE SAME THING AT ALL...
OR SO SOME MIGHT SAY.
HMM...
THE PAGE DOESN'T SEEM TO BE IN HERE.
KLONK...
......

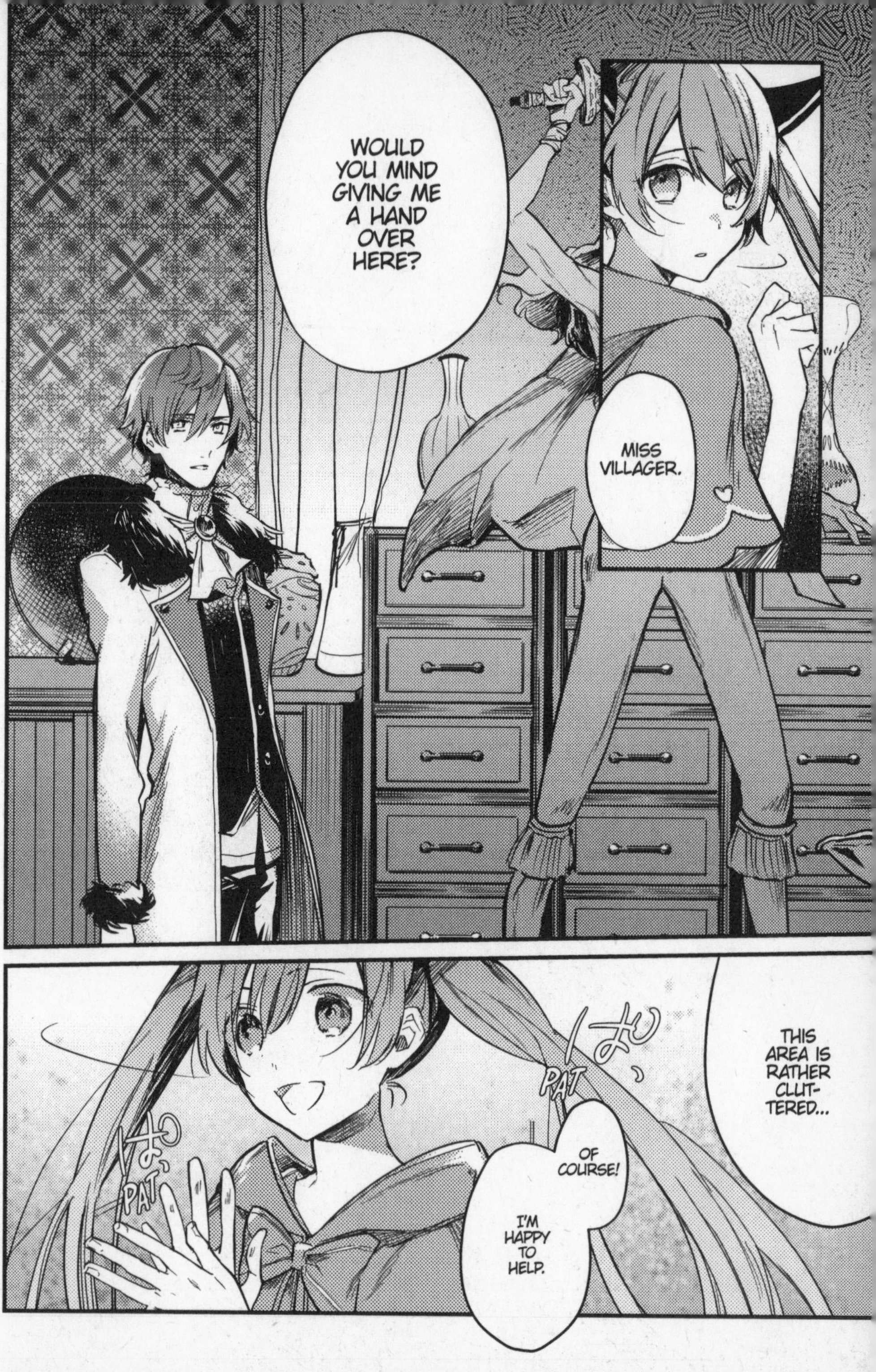
MISS VILLAGER.
WOULD YOU MIND GIVING ME A HAND OVER HERE?
THIS AREA IS RATHER CLUT-TERED...
PAT
OF COURSE!
I'M HAPPY TO HELP.
PAT

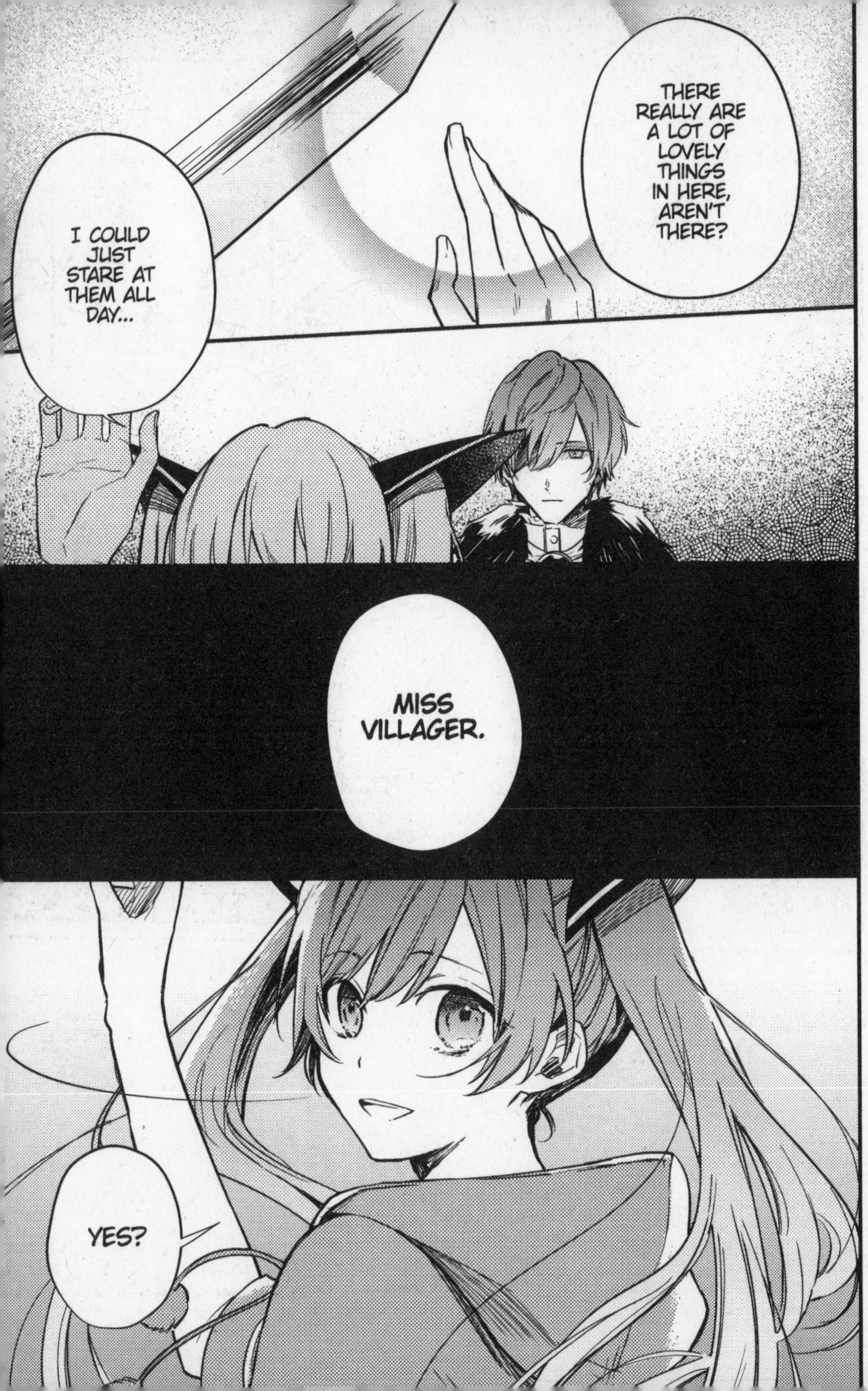
THERE REALLY ARE A LOT OF LOVELY THINGS IN HERE, AREN'T THERE?
I COULD JUST STARE AT THEM ALL DAY...
MISS VILLAGER.
YES?

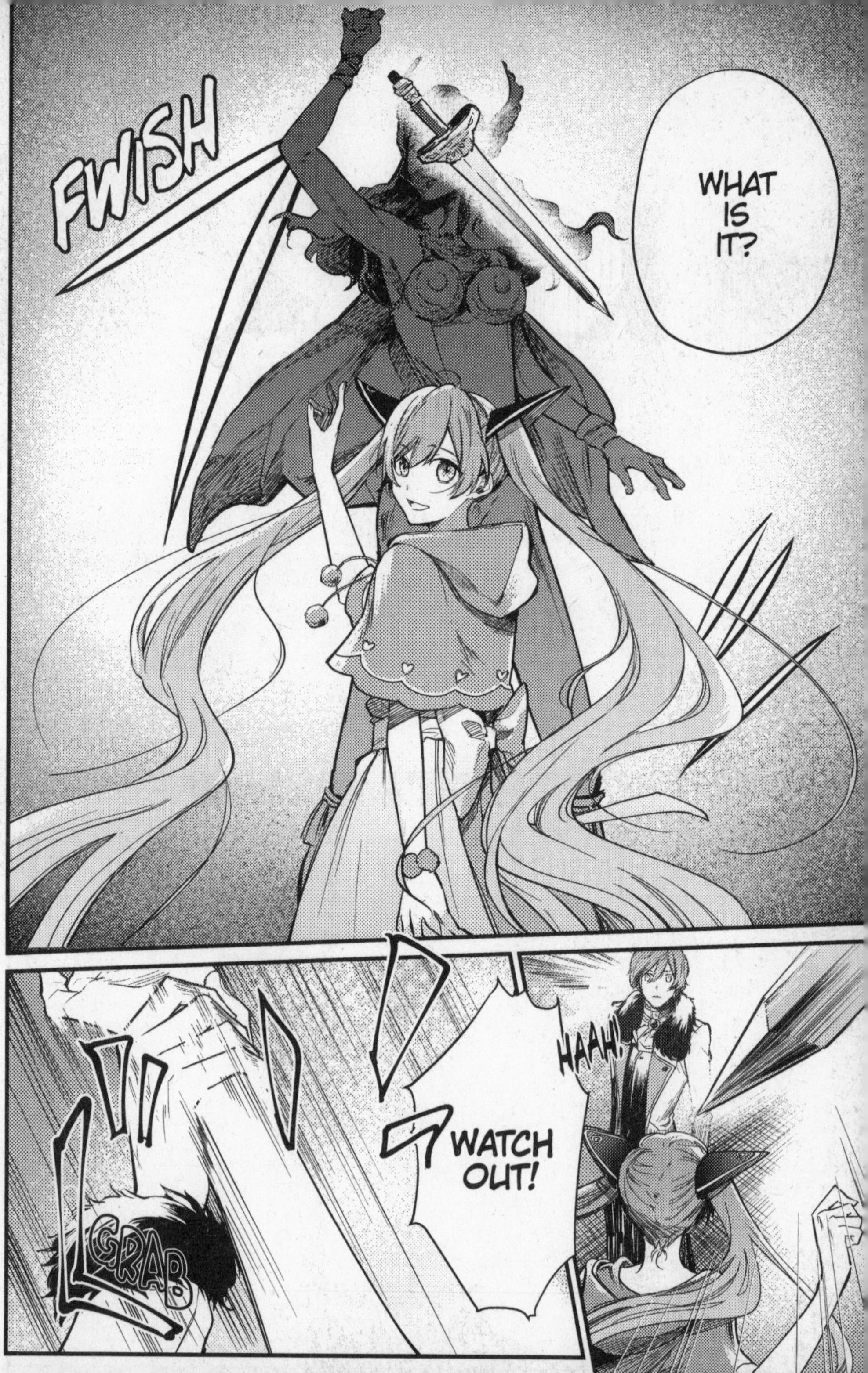
WHAT IS IT?
FWISH
HAAH!
WATCH OUT!
GRAB

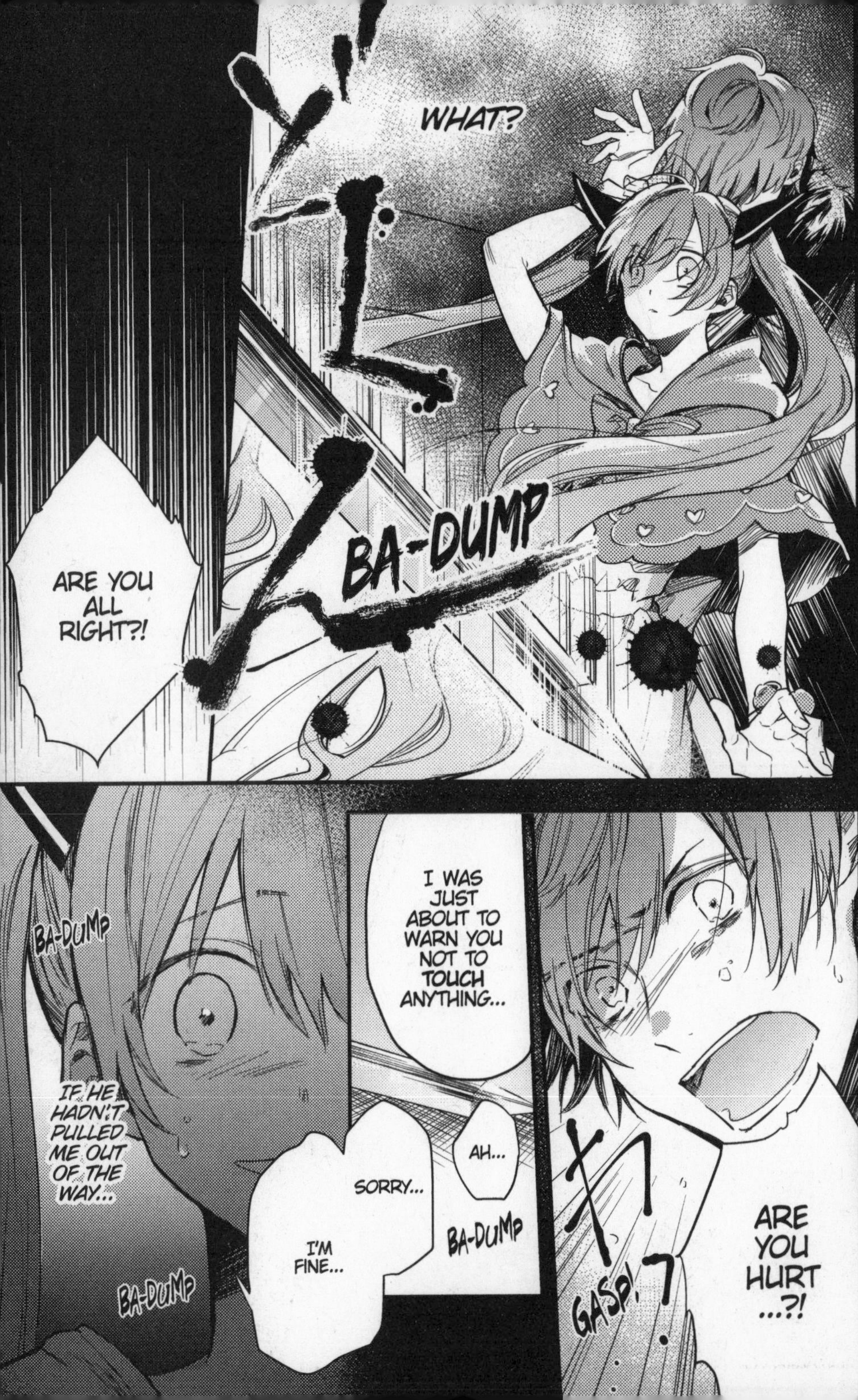
WHAT?
BA-DUMP
ARE YOU ALL RIGHT?!
ARE YOU HURT ...?!
GASP!
I WAS JUST ABOUT TO WARN YOU NOT TO TOUCH ANYTHING...
AH...
BA-DUMP
SORRY... I'M FINE...
BA-DUMP
IF HE HADN'T PULLED ME OUT OF THE WAY...
BA-DUMP

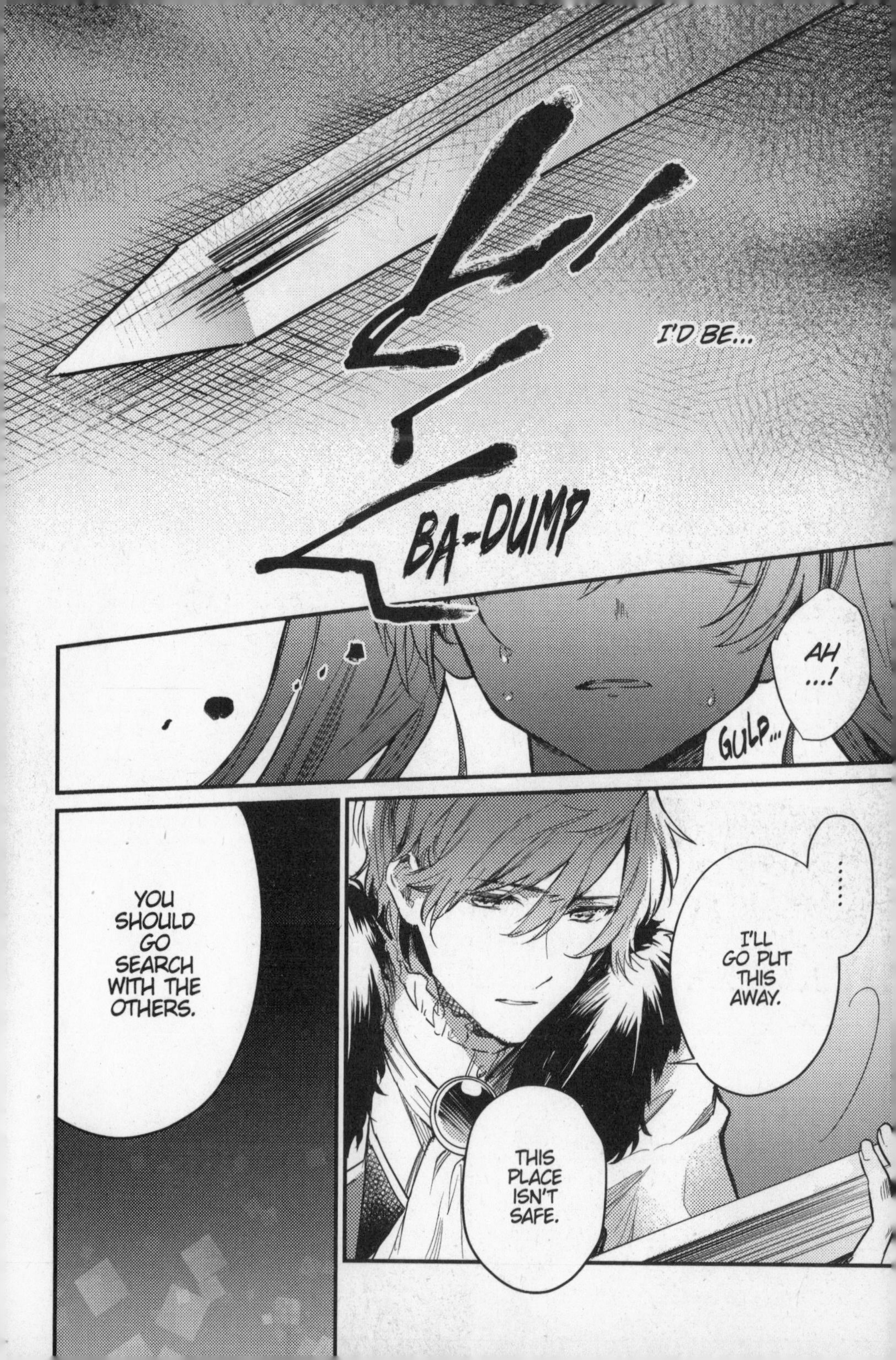

I'D BE...
BA-DUMP
AH ...!
GULP...
......
I'LL GO PUT THIS AWAY.
THIS PLACE ISN'T SAFE.
YOU SHOULD GO SEARCH WITH THE OTHERS.

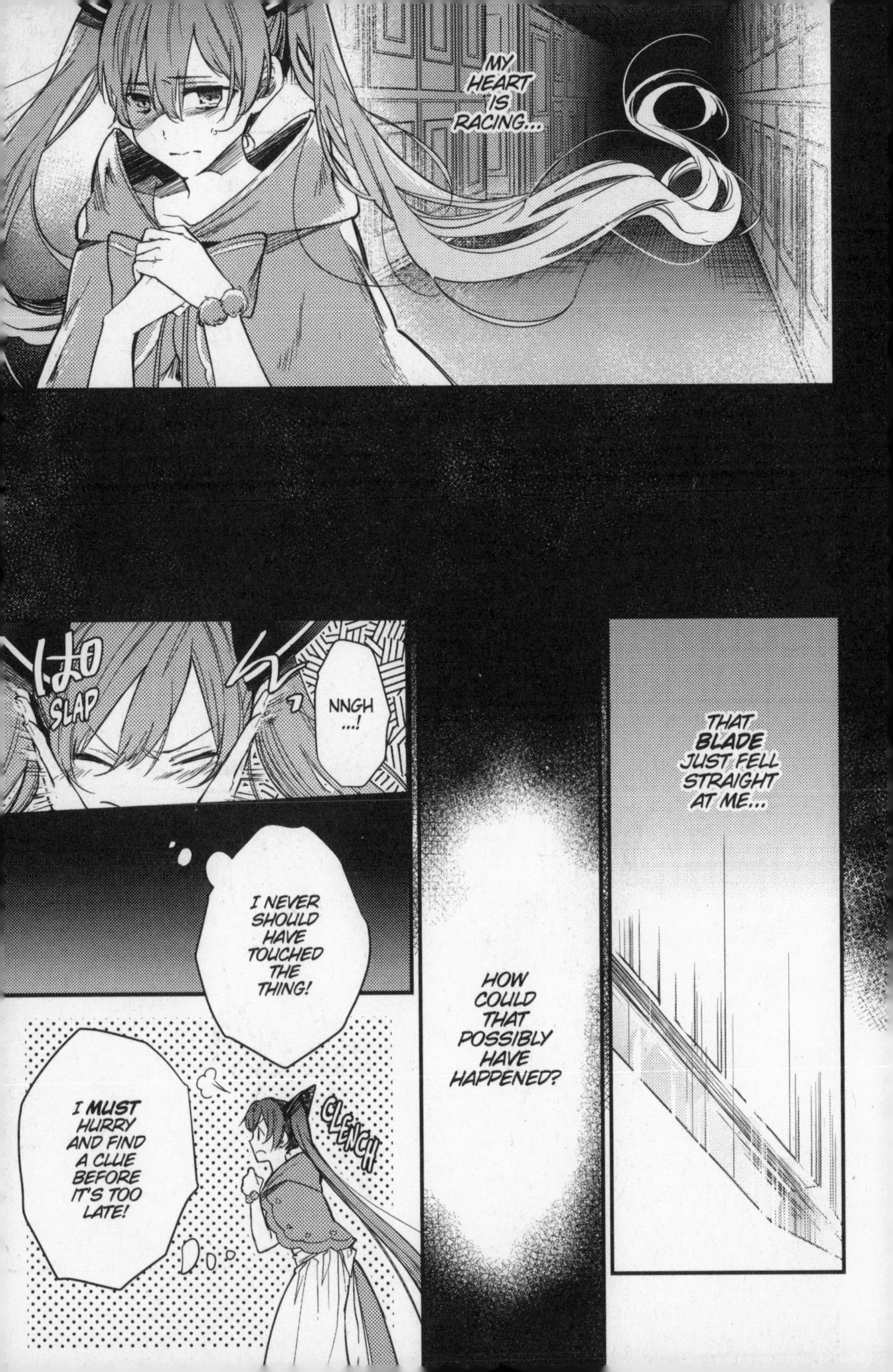
MY HEART IS RACING...
THAT BLADE JUST FELL STRAIGHT AT ME...
HOW COULD THAT POSSIBLY HAVE HAPPENED?
NNGH ...!
SLAP
I NEVER SHOULD HAVE TOUCHED THE THING!
I MUST HURRY AND FIND A CLUE BEFORE IT'S TOO LATE!
CLENCH

NOW, WHY ON EARTH WOULD SOMEONE HAVE DONE THIS...?

DID SOMEONE WANT THE PLAY TO FAIL?

OR...

DID THEY WANT TO STOP TIME AND DESTROY THIS WORLD?

CLACK

CLACK

BUT WHY WOULD ANYONE...?

IF THEY TORE A PAGE FROM THE BOOK...

...DOES THAT MEAN THEY DIDN'T WANT US FOLLOWING THE SCRIPT?

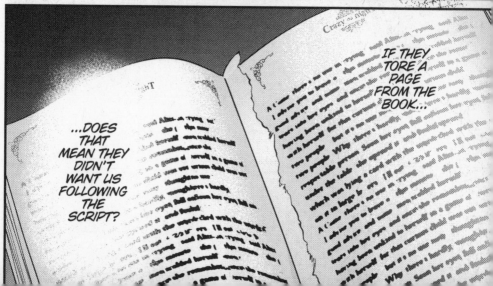

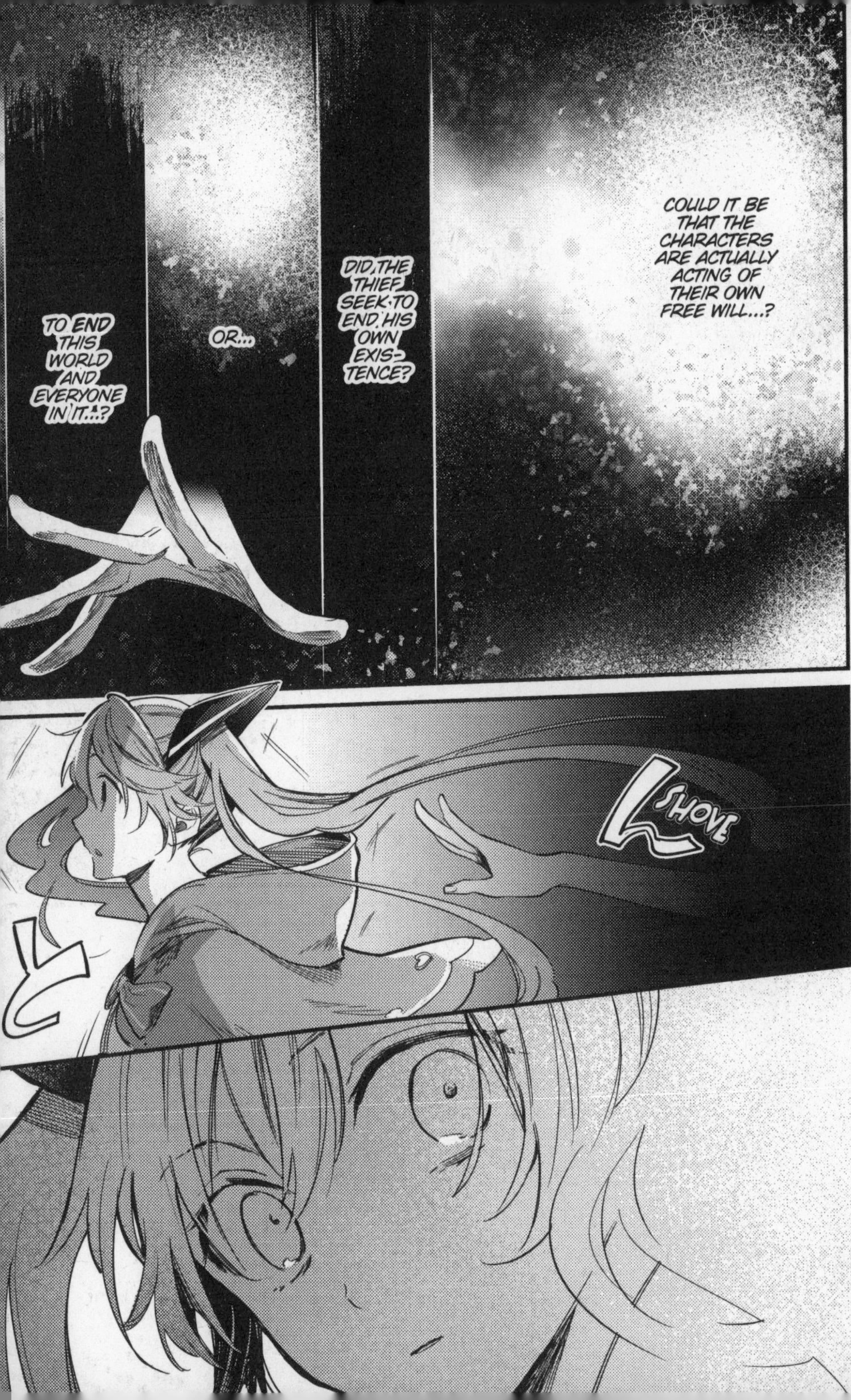
COULD IT BE THAT THE CHARACTERS ARE ACTUALLY ACTING OF THEIR OWN FREE WILL...?
DID THE THIEF SEEK TO END HIS OWN EXISTENCE?
OR...
TO END THIS WORLD AND EVERYONE IN IT...?
SHOVE

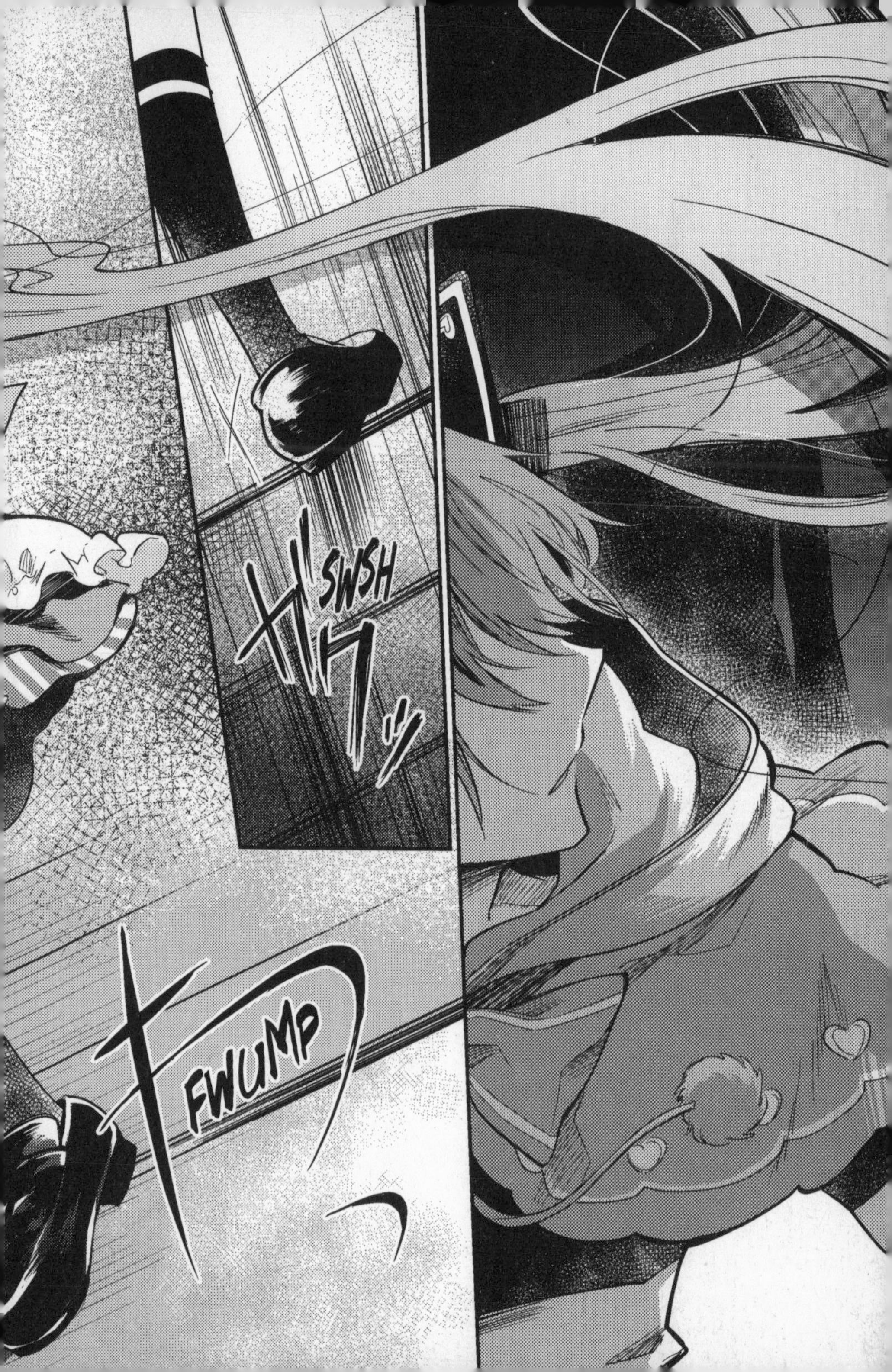
SWSH
FWUMP

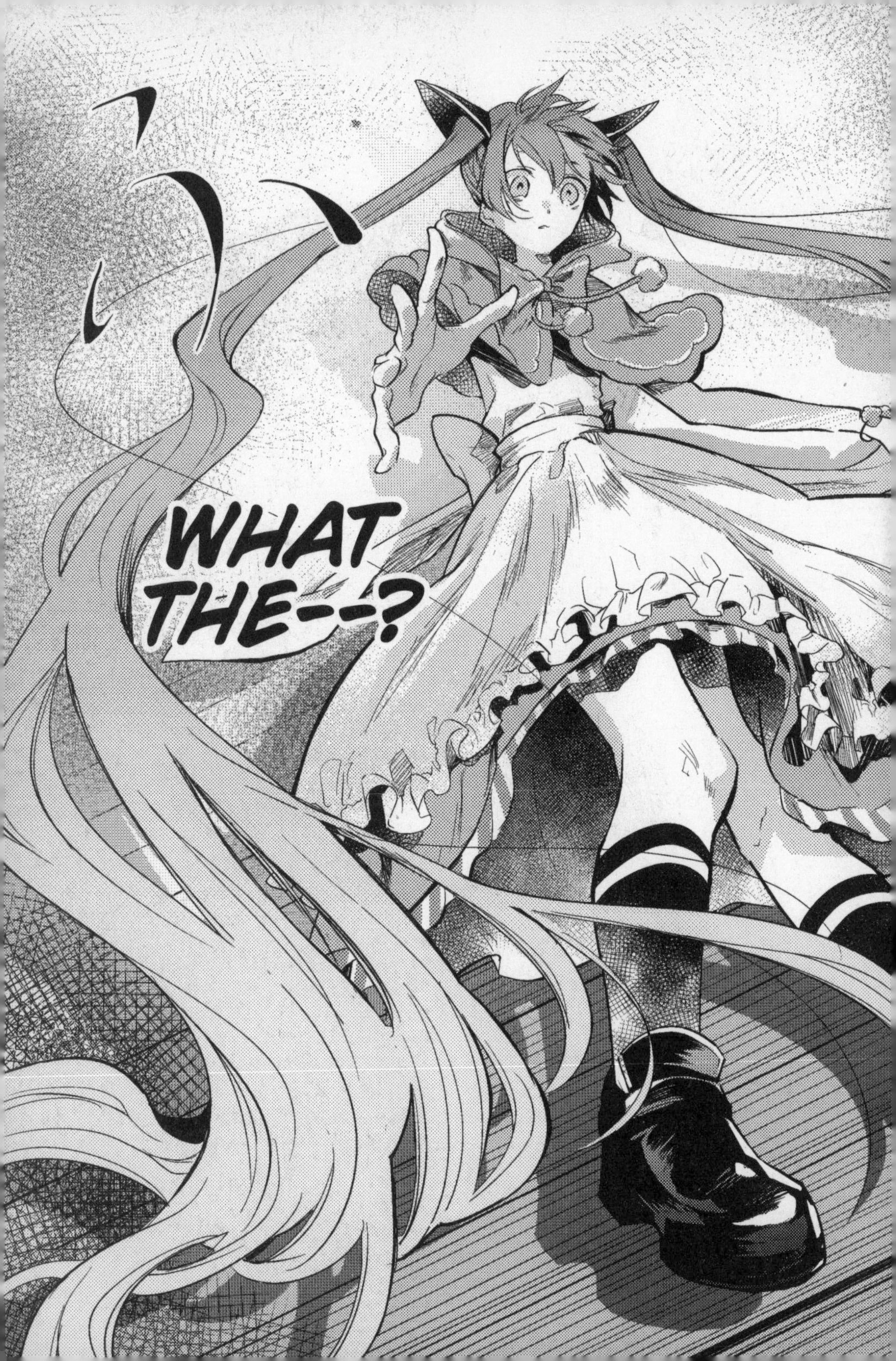
WHAT THE--?

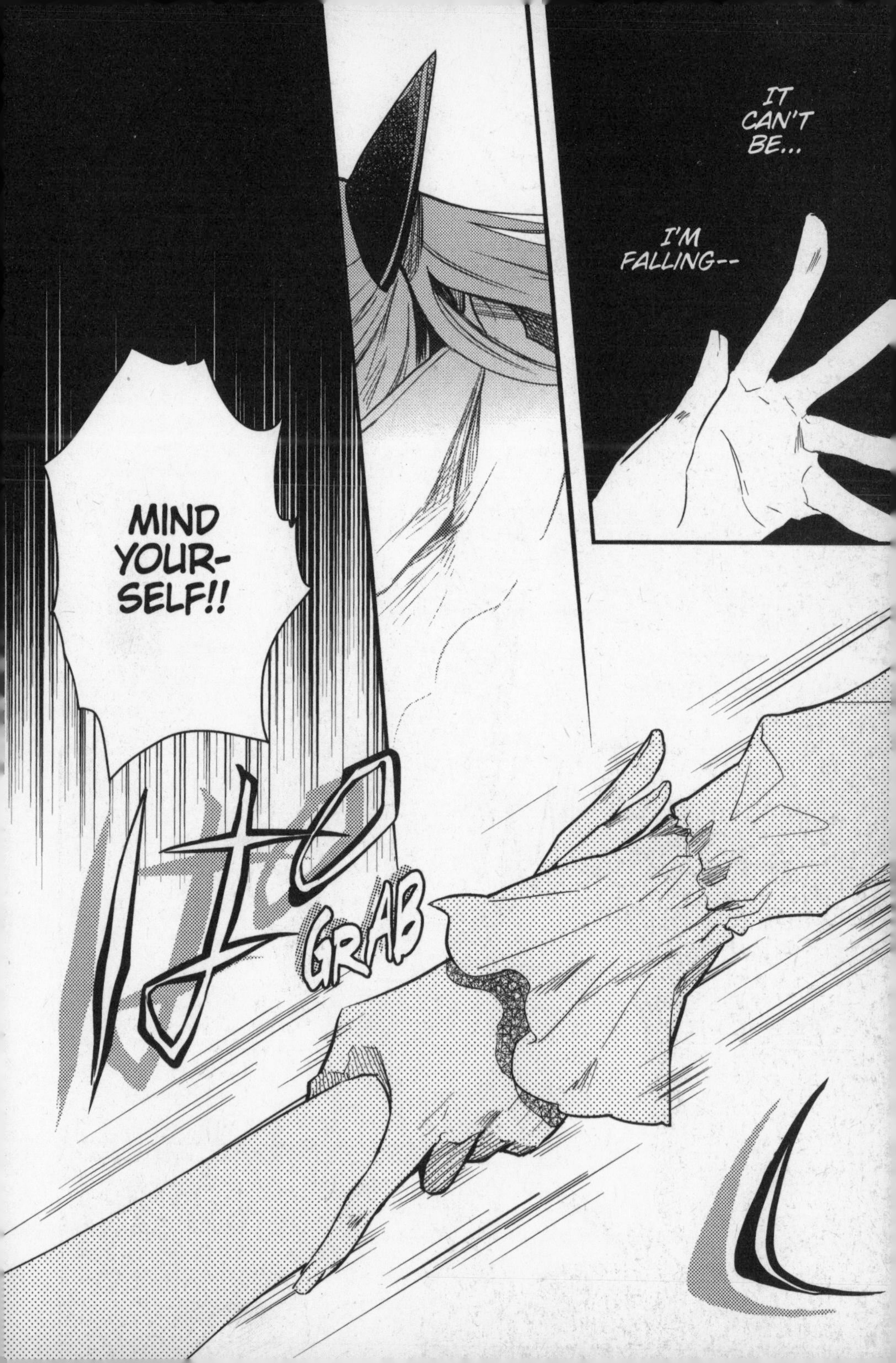
IT CAN'T BE...
I'M FALLING--
MIND YOUR-SELF!!
GRAB

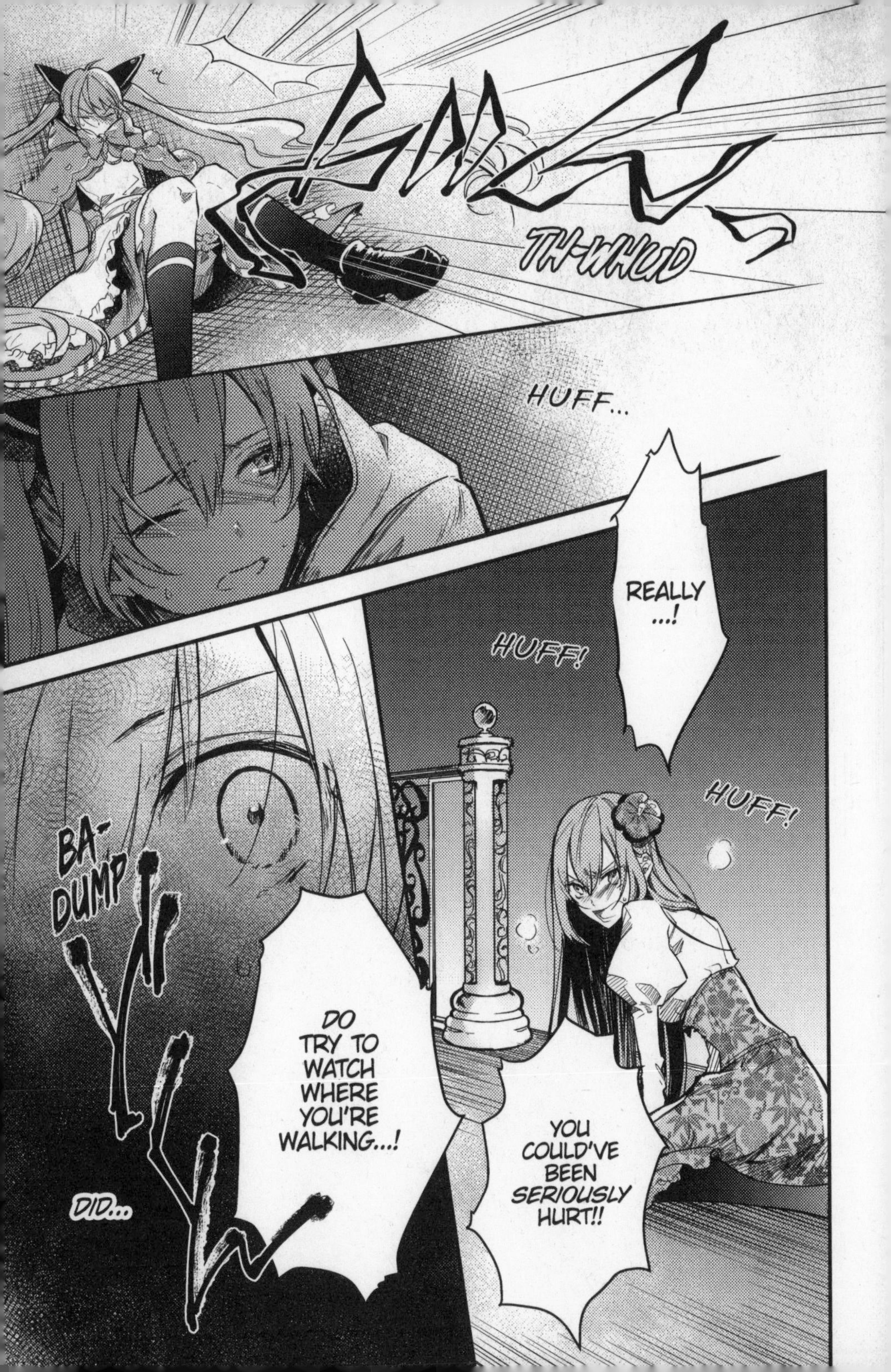
TH-WHUD
HUFF...
REALLY ...!
HUFF!
HUFF!
YOU COULD'VE BEEN SERIOUSLY HURT!!
DO TRY TO WATCH WHERE YOU'RE WALKING...!
BA-DUMP
DID...

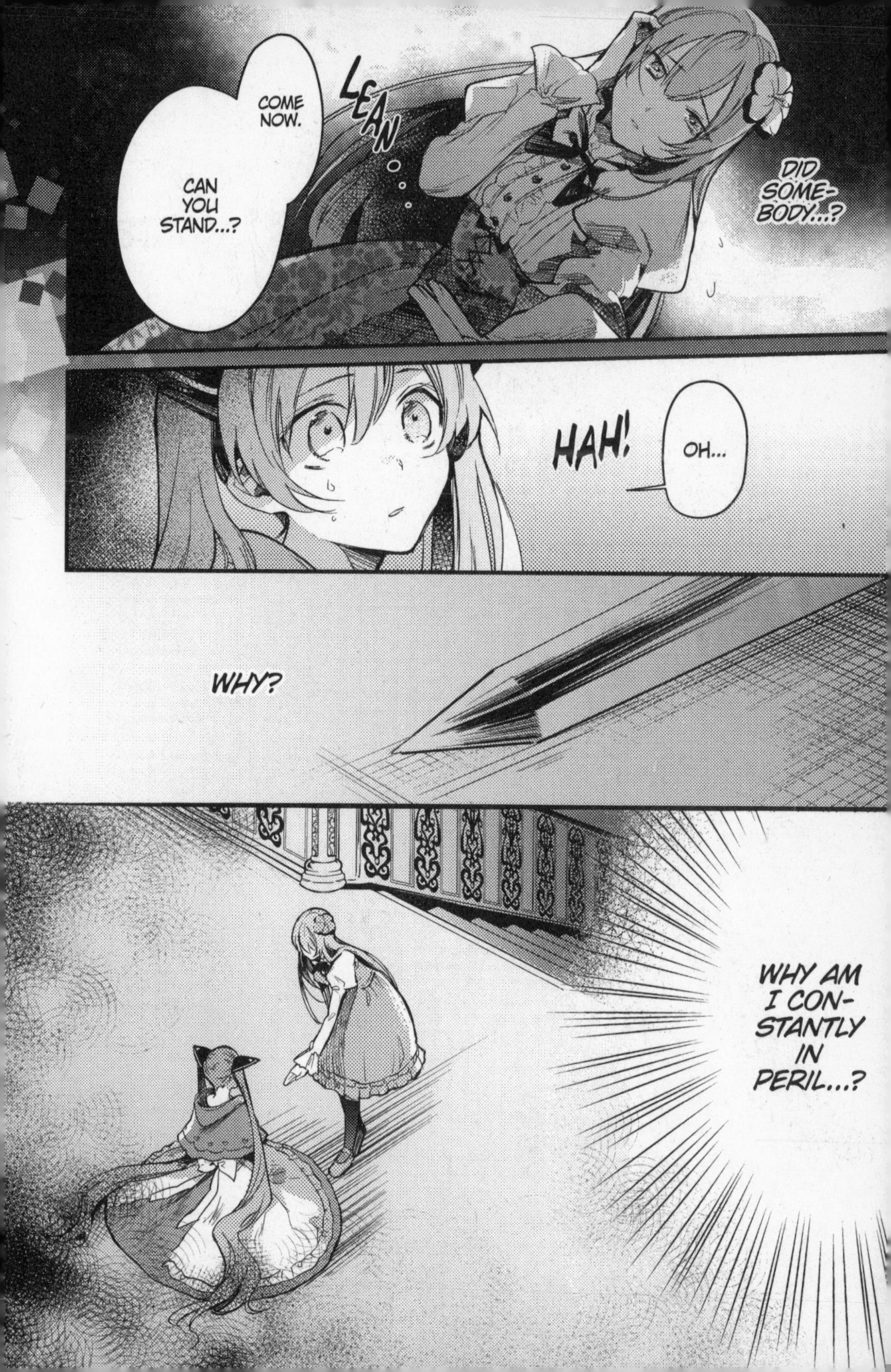
DID SOME-BODY...?
LEAN
COME NOW.
CAN YOU STAND...?
OH...
HAH!
WHY?
WHY AM I CON-STANTLY IN PERIL...?

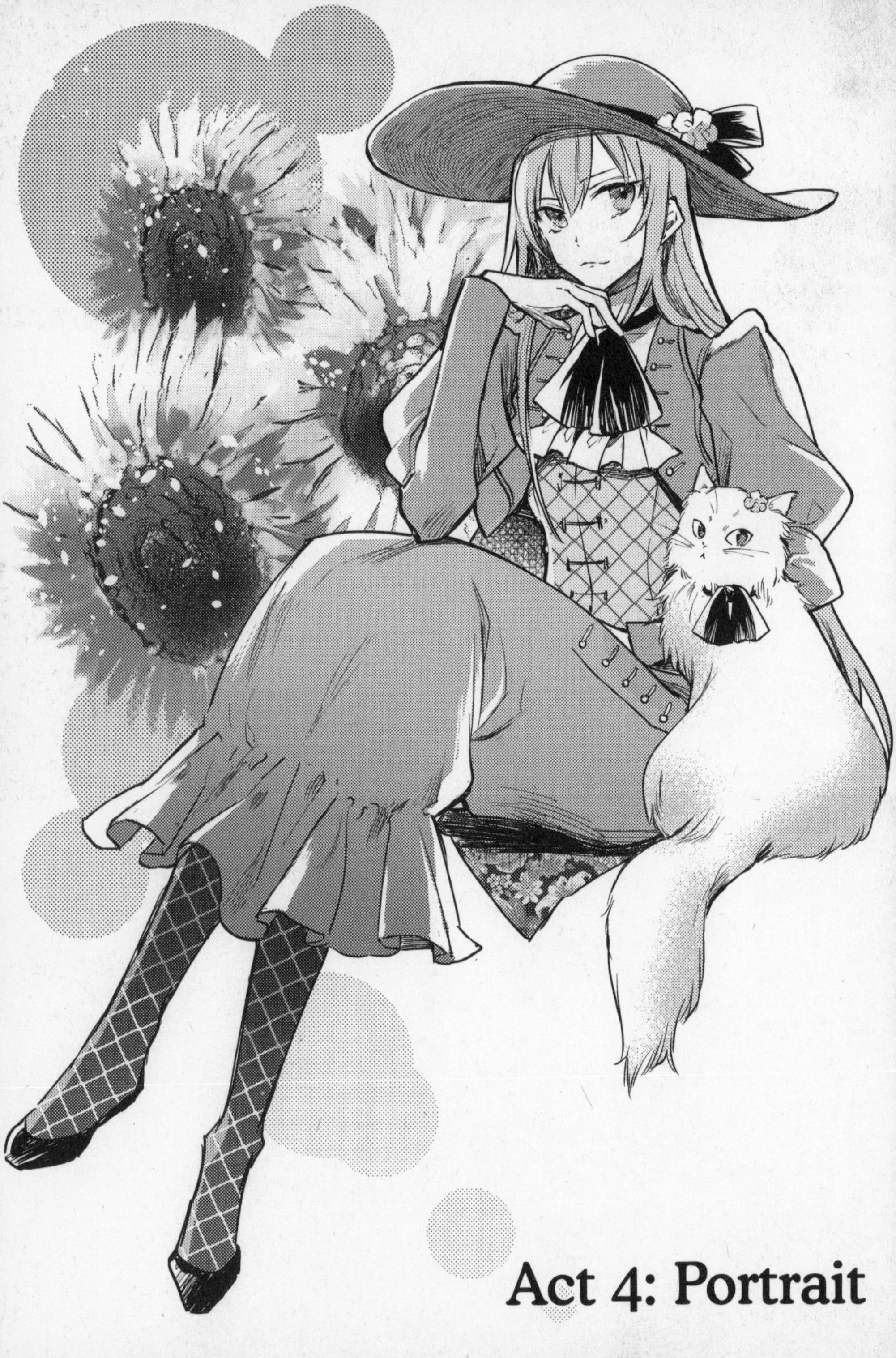

Act 4: Portrait

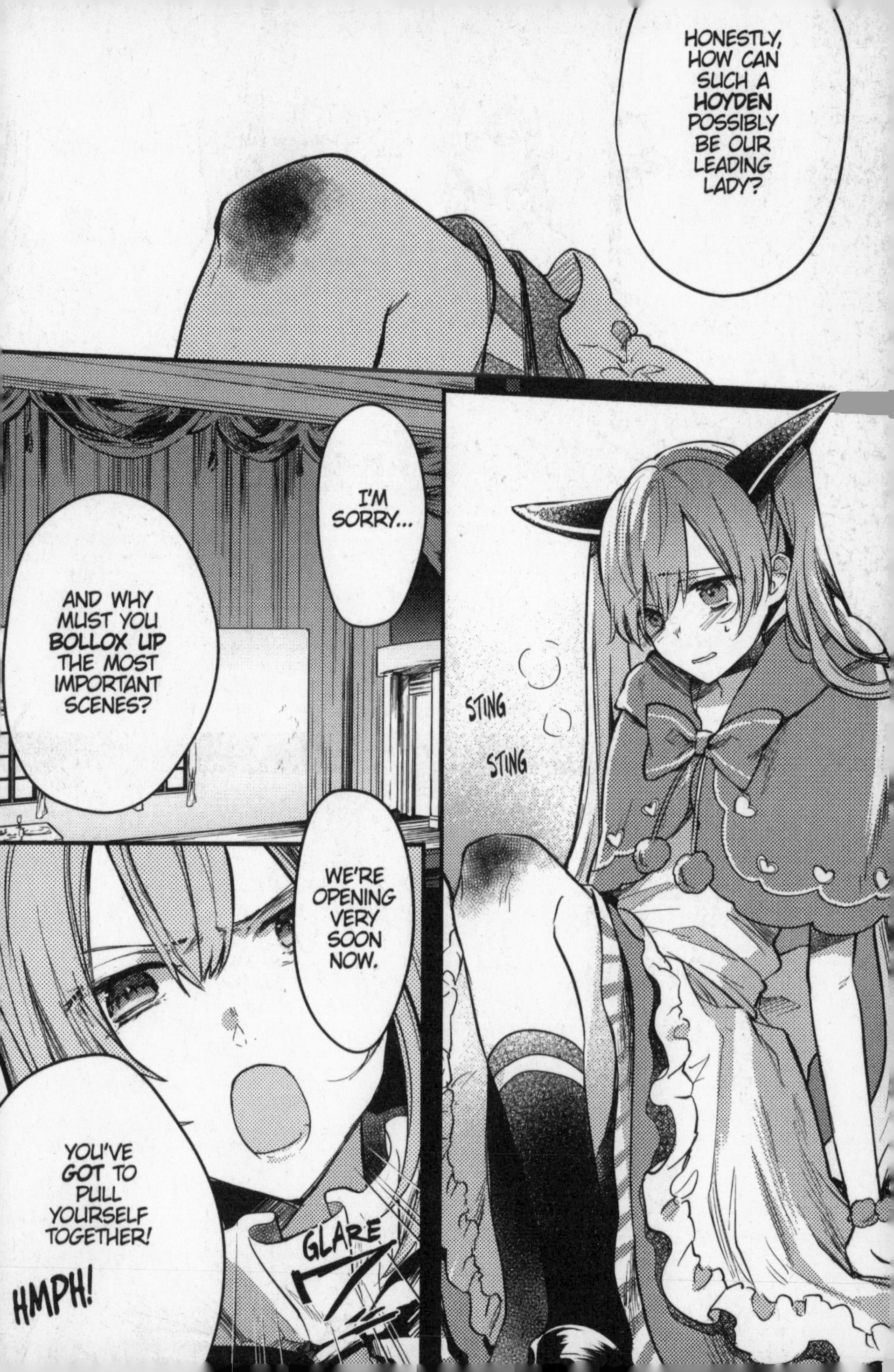
HONESTLY, HOW CAN SUCH A HOYDEN POSSIBLY BE OUR LEADING LADY?
STING
STING
I'M SORRY...
AND WHY MUST YOU BOLLOX UP THE MOST IMPORTANT SCENES?
WE'RE OPENING VERY SOON NOW.
YOU'VE GOT TO PULL YOURSELF TOGETHER!
GLARE
HMPH!

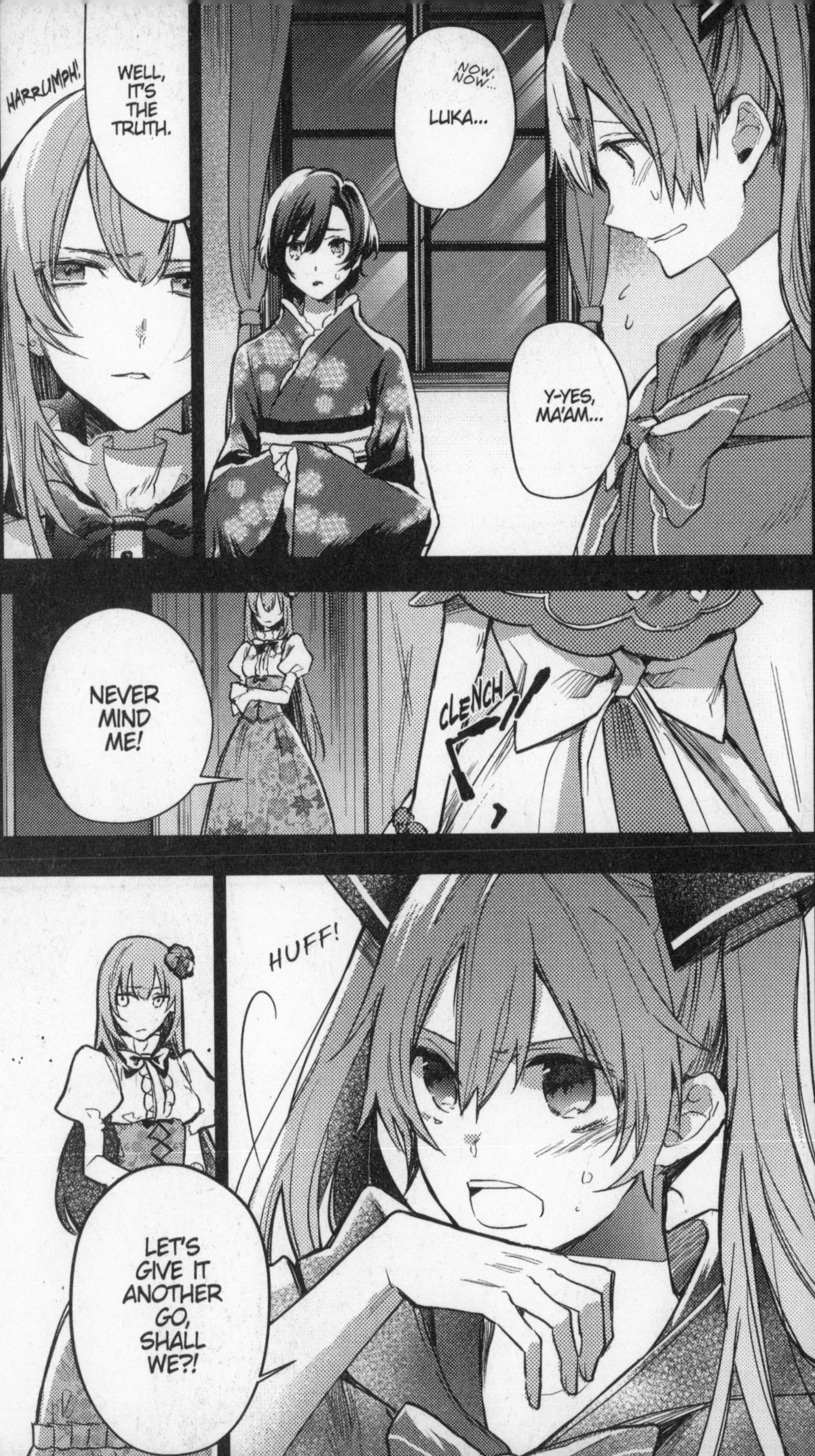
Y-YES, MA'AM...
NOW, NOW...
LUKA...
HARRUMPH!
WELL, IT'S THE TRUTH.
CLENCH
NEVER MIND ME!
HUFF!
LET'S GIVE IT ANOTHER GO, SHALL WE?!

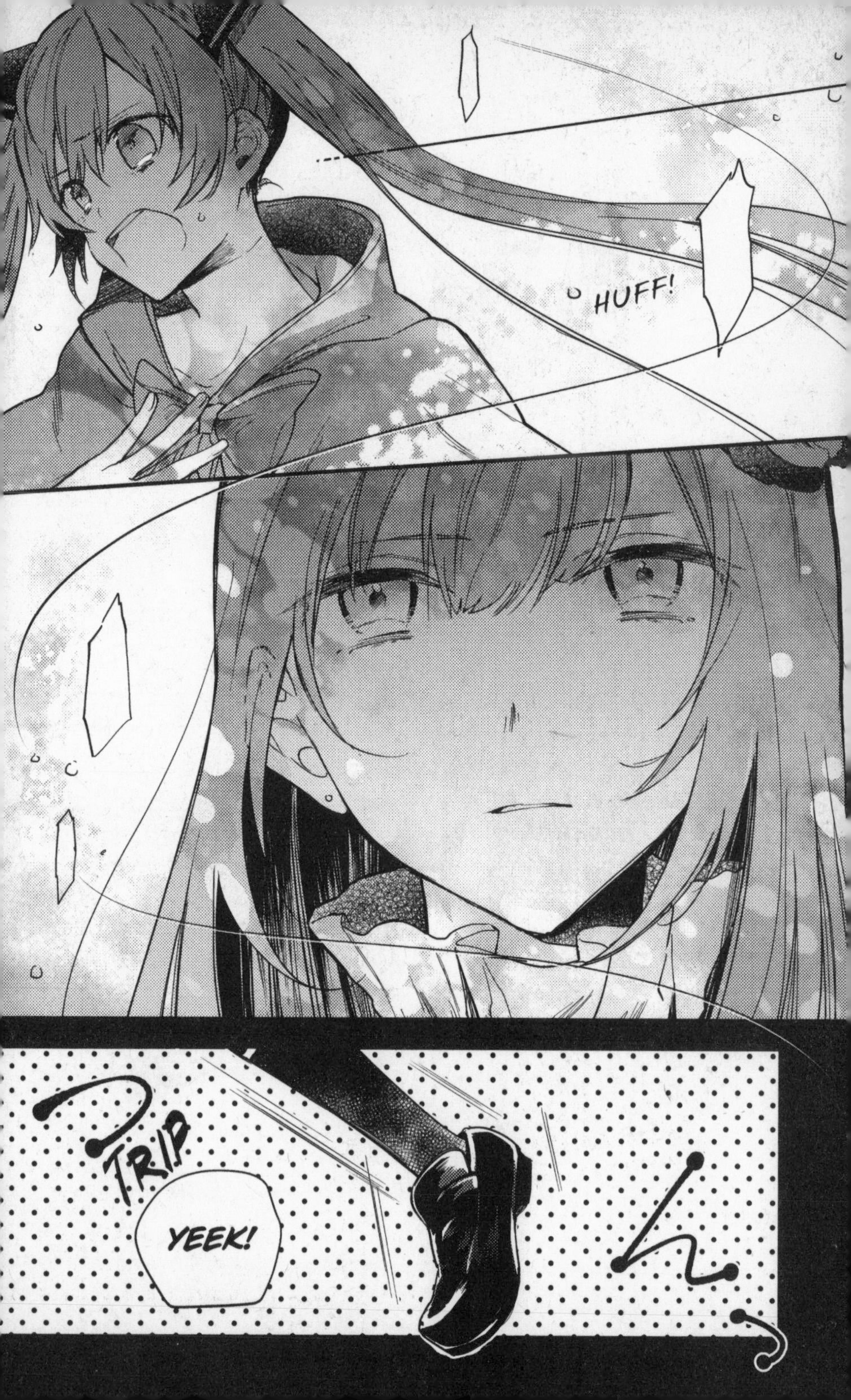
HUFF!
TRIP
YEEK!

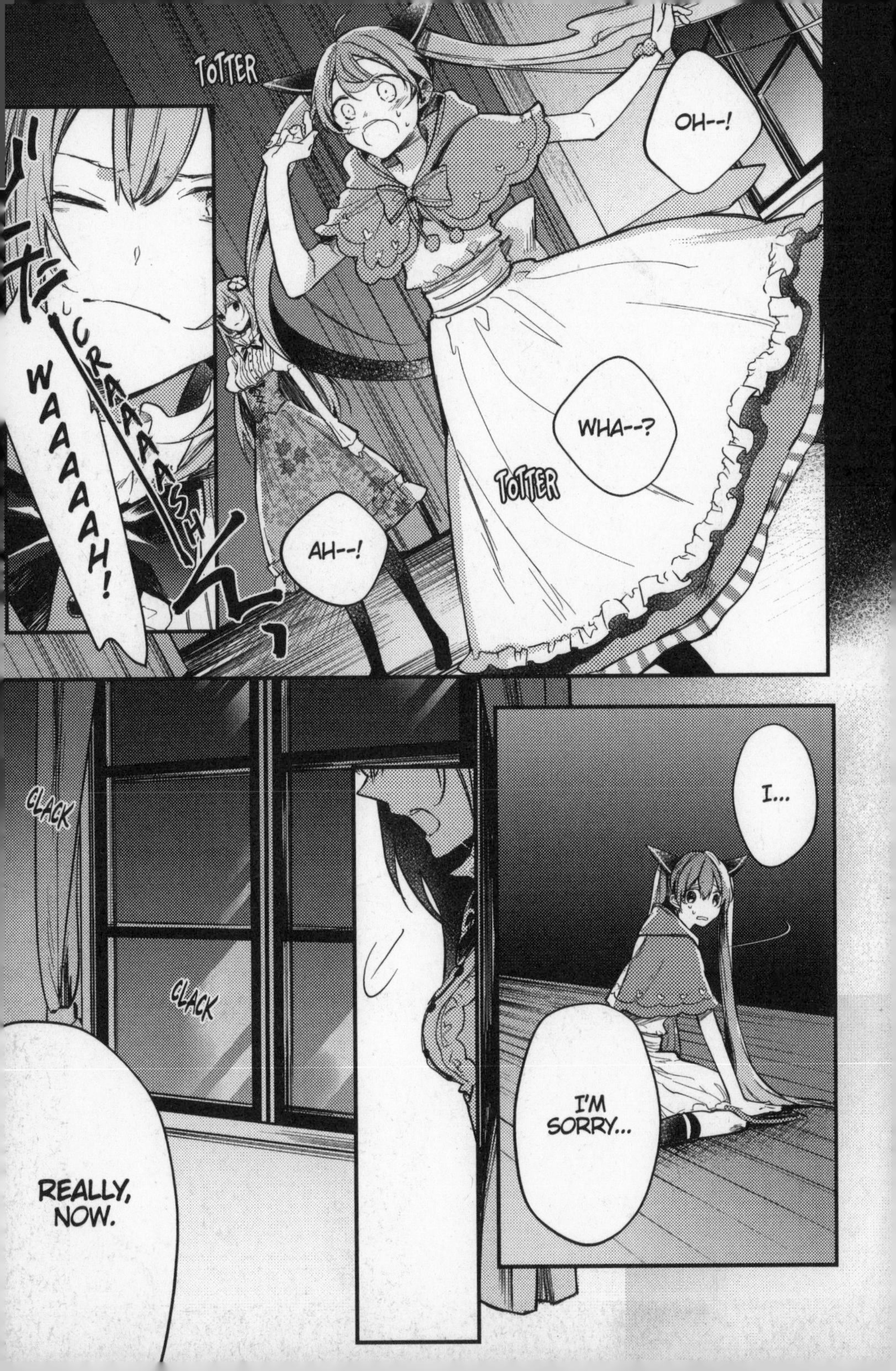

OH--!
TOTTER
WHA--?
TOTTER
AH--!
URAAAAASH
WAAAAAAH!
I...
I'M SORRY...
CLACK
CLACK
REALLY, NOW.

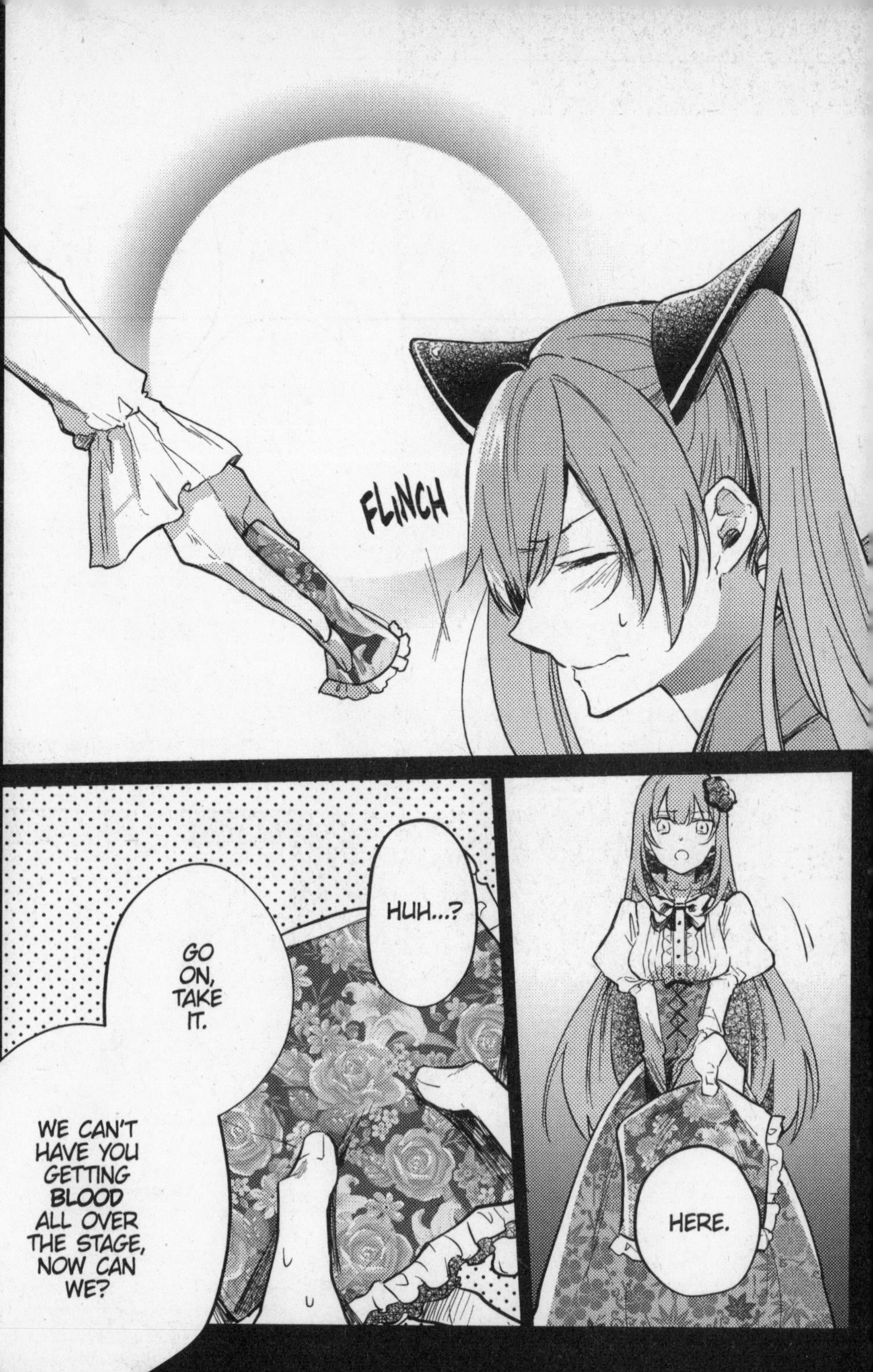
FLINCH
HERE.
HUH...?
GO ON, TAKE IT.
WE CAN'T HAVE YOU GETTING BLOOD ALL OVER THE STAGE, NOW CAN WE?

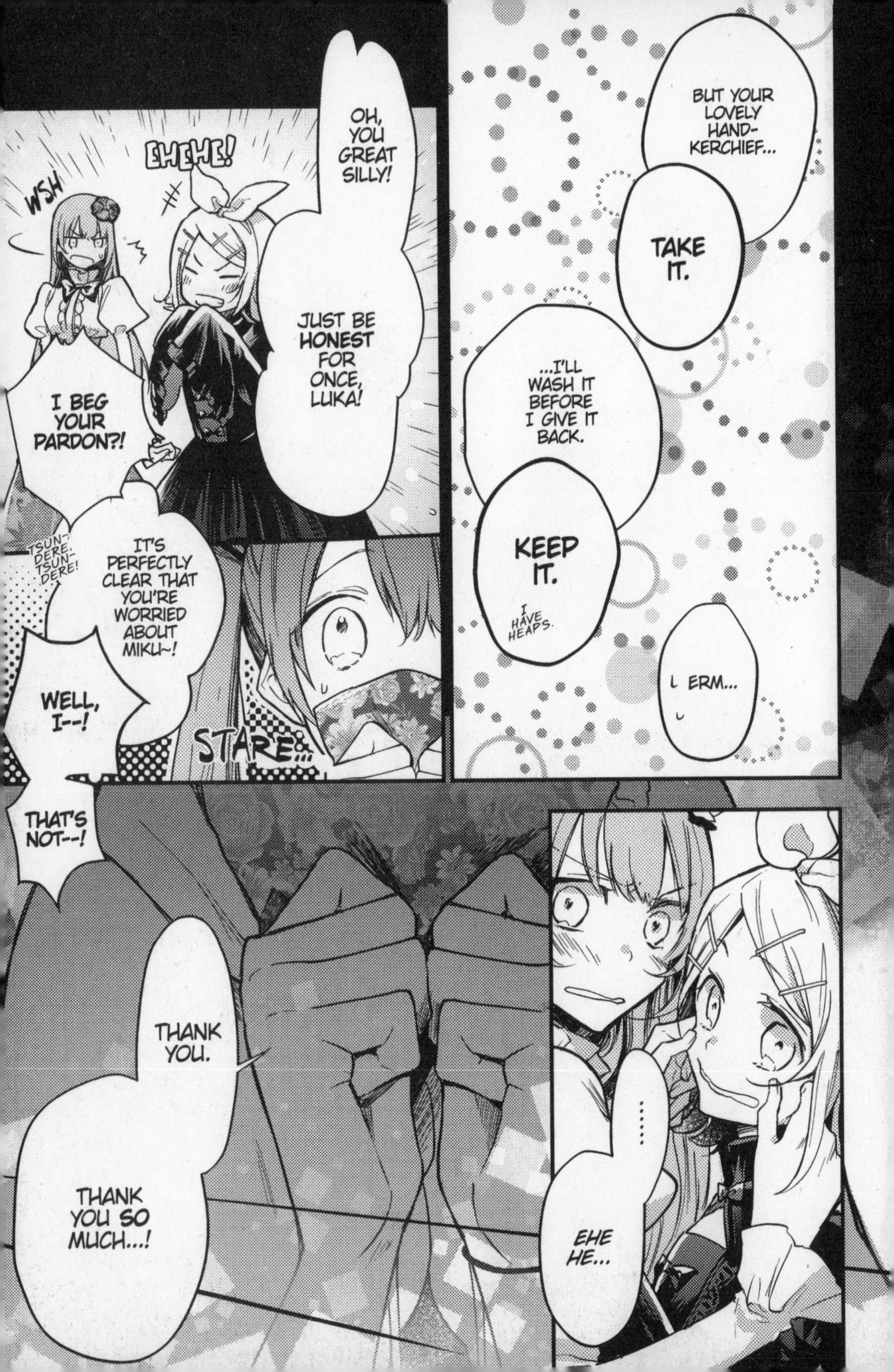

BUT YOUR LOVELY HAND-KERCHIEF...
TAKE IT.
...I'LL WASH IT BEFORE I GIVE IT BACK.
KEEP IT.
I HAVE HEAPS.
ERM...
EHEHE!
OH, YOU GREAT SILLY!
WSH
JUST BE HONEST FOR ONCE, LUKA!
I BEG YOUR PARDON?!
TSUN-DERE, TSUN-DERE!
IT'S PERFECTLY CLEAR THAT YOU'RE WORRIED ABOUT MIKU~!
WELL, I--!
STARE...
THAT'S NOT--!
......
EHE HE...
THANK YOU.
THANK YOU SO MUCH...!

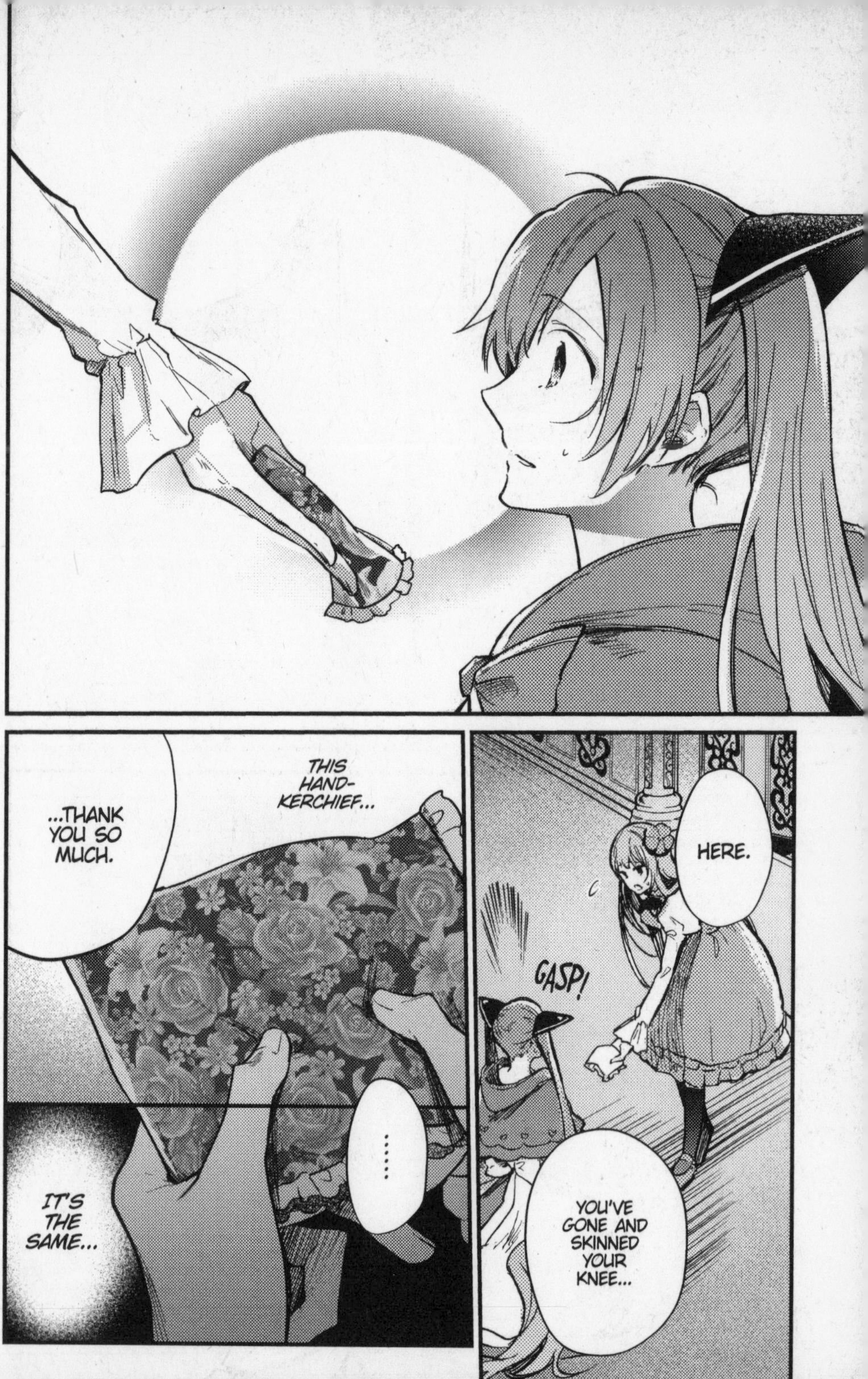
HERE.
GASP!
YOU'VE GONE AND SKINNED YOUR KNEE...
THIS HAND-KERCHIEF...
...THANK YOU SO MUCH.
......
IT'S THE SAME...

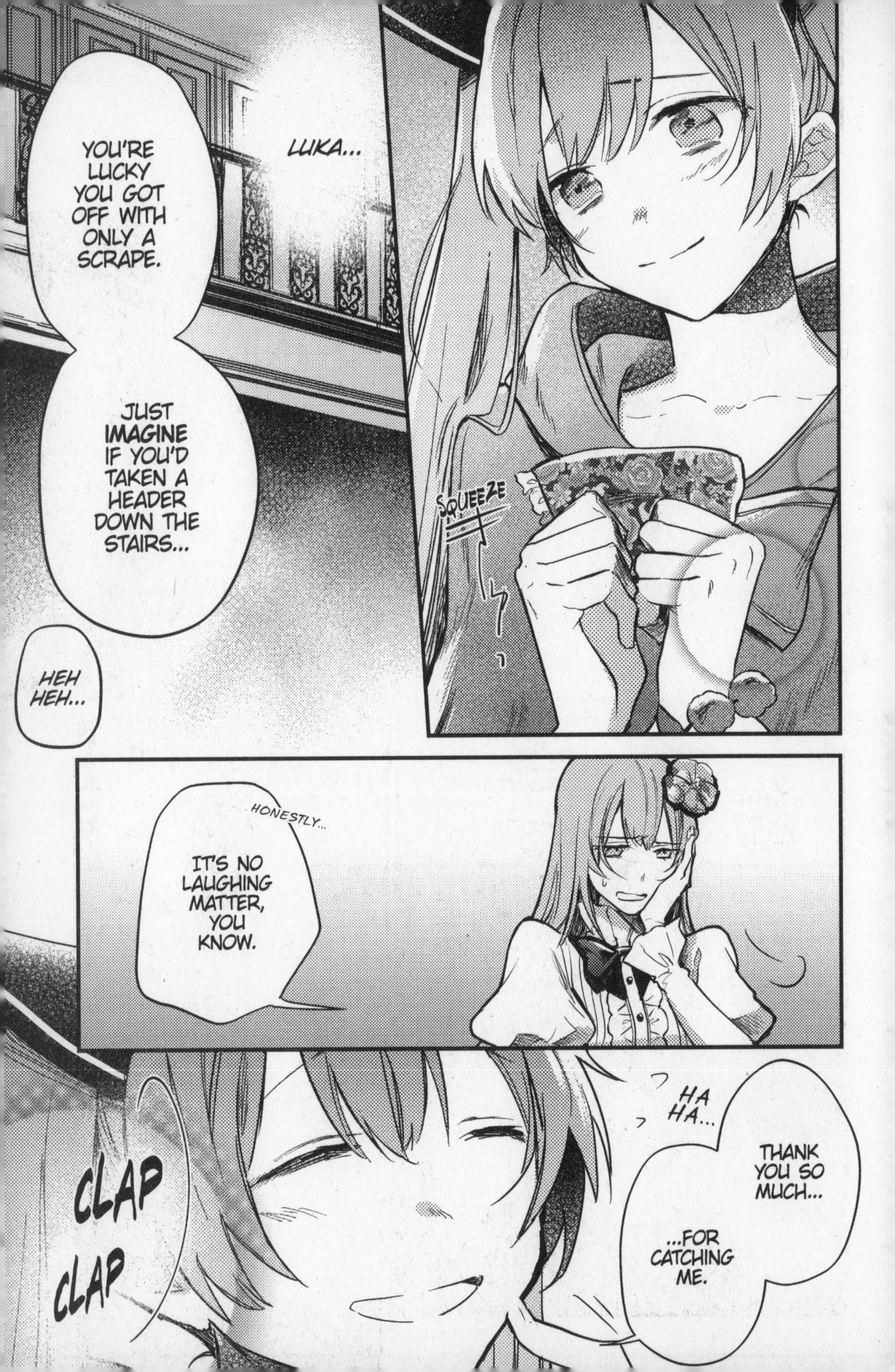
LUKA...
SQUEEZE
YOU'RE LUCKY YOU GOT OFF WITH ONLY A SCRAPE.
JUST IMAGINE IF YOU'D TAKEN A HEADER DOWN THE STAIRS...
HEH HEH...
HONESTLY...
IT'S NO LAUGHING MATTER, YOU KNOW.
HA HA...
THANK YOU SO MUCH...
...FOR CATCHING ME.
CLAP
CLAP

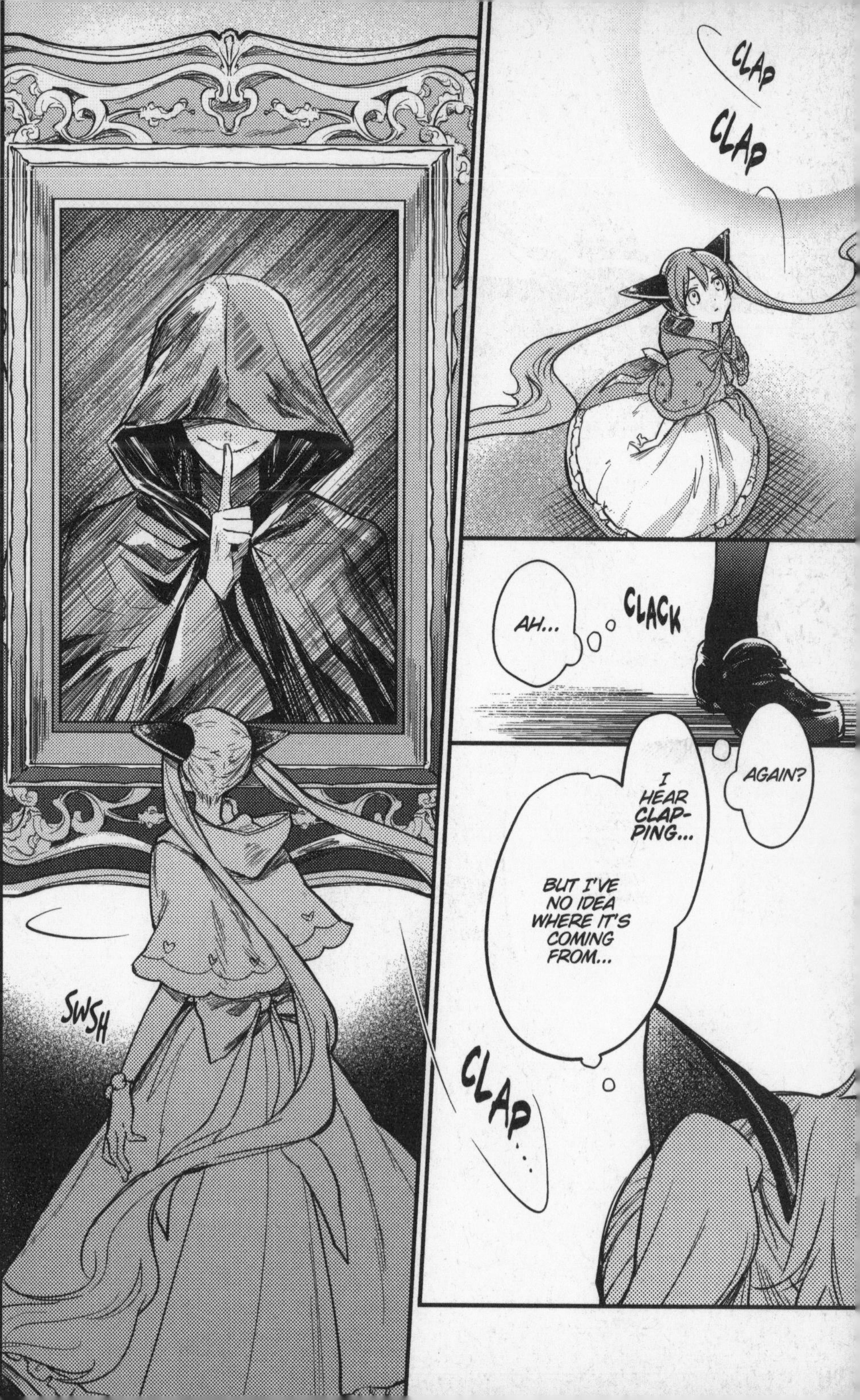
CLAP
CLAP
AH...
CLACK
AGAIN?
I HEAR CLAP-PING...
BUT I'VE NO IDEA WHERE IT'S COMING FROM...
CLAP...
SWSH

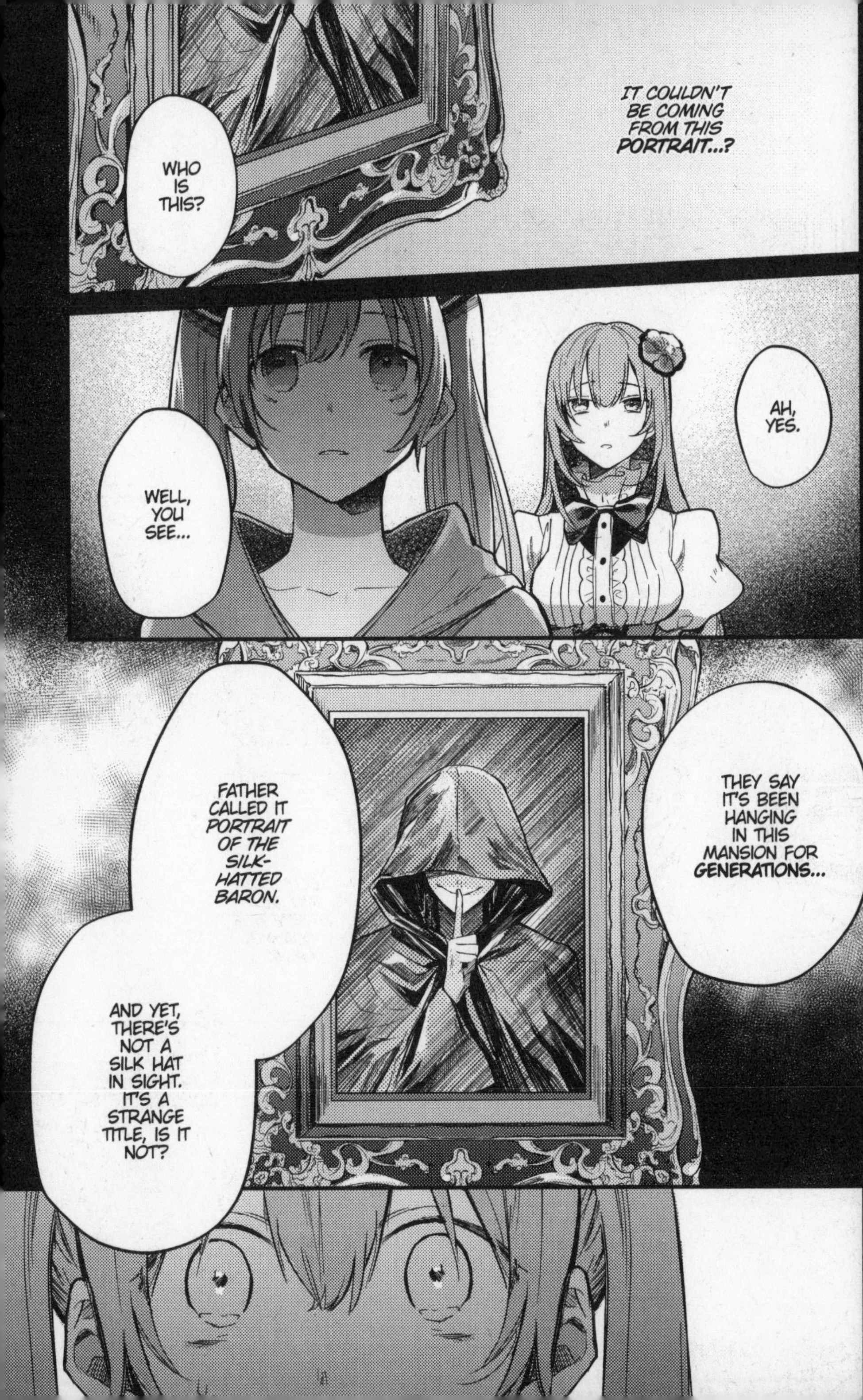
IT COULDN'T BE COMING FROM THIS PORTRAIT...?
WHO IS THIS?
AH, YES.
WELL, YOU SEE...
THEY SAY IT'S BEEN HANGING IN THIS MANSION FOR GENERATIONS...
FATHER CALLED IT PORTRAIT OF THE SILK-HATTED BARON.
AND YET, THERE'S NOT A SILK HAT IN SIGHT. IT'S A STRANGE TITLE, IS IT NOT?

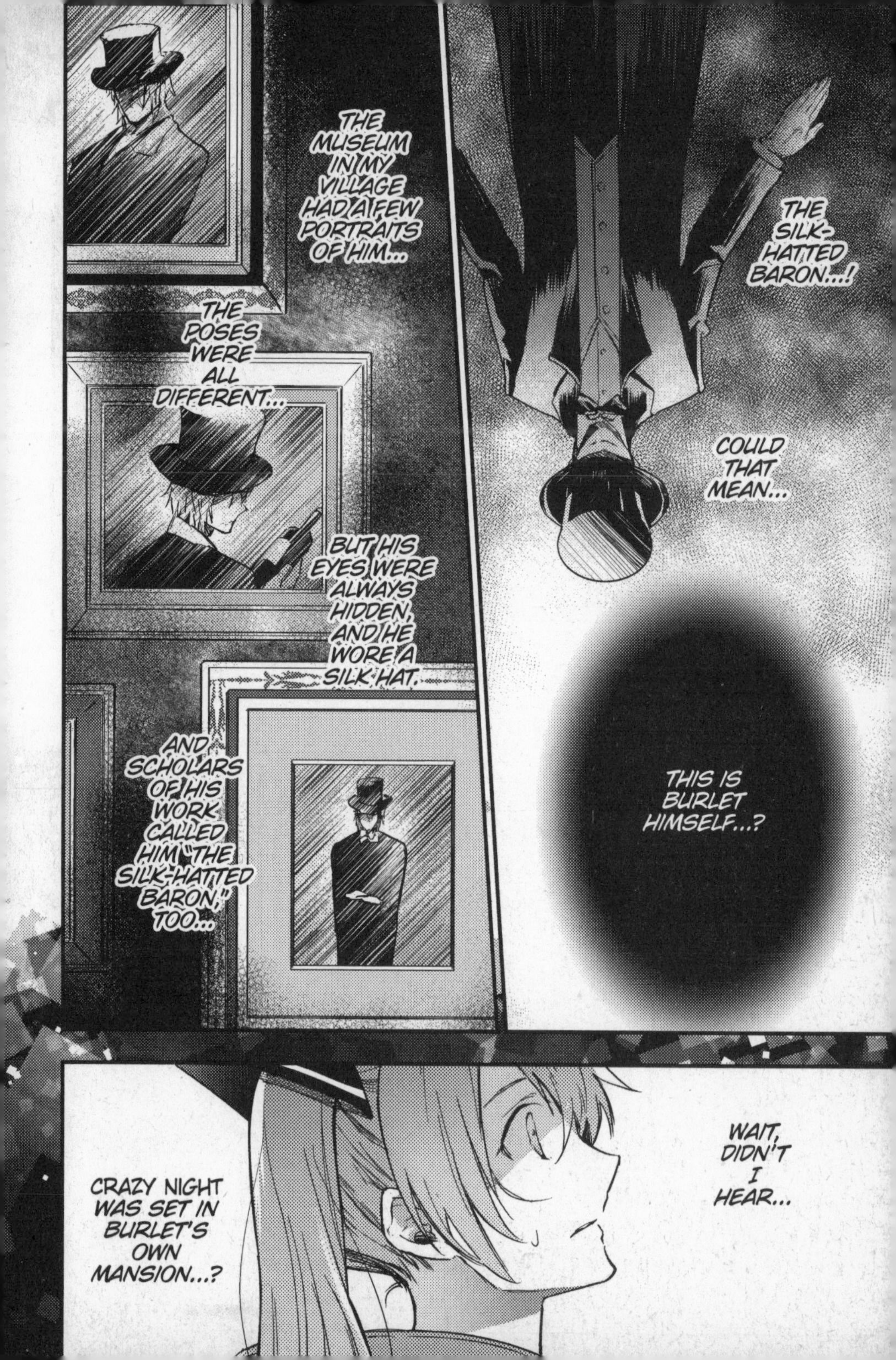
THE SILK-HATTED BARON...!
COULD THAT MEAN...
THIS IS BURLET HIMSELF...?
THE MUSEUM IN MY VILLAGE HAD A FEW PORTRAITS OF HIM...
THE POSES WERE ALL DIFFERENT...
BUT HIS EYES WERE ALWAYS HIDDEN, AND HE WORE A SILK HAT.
AND SCHOLARS OF HIS WORK CALLED HIM "THE SILK-HATTED BARON," TOO...
WAIT, DIDN'T I HEAR...
CRAZY NIGHT WAS SET IN BURLET'S OWN MANSION...?

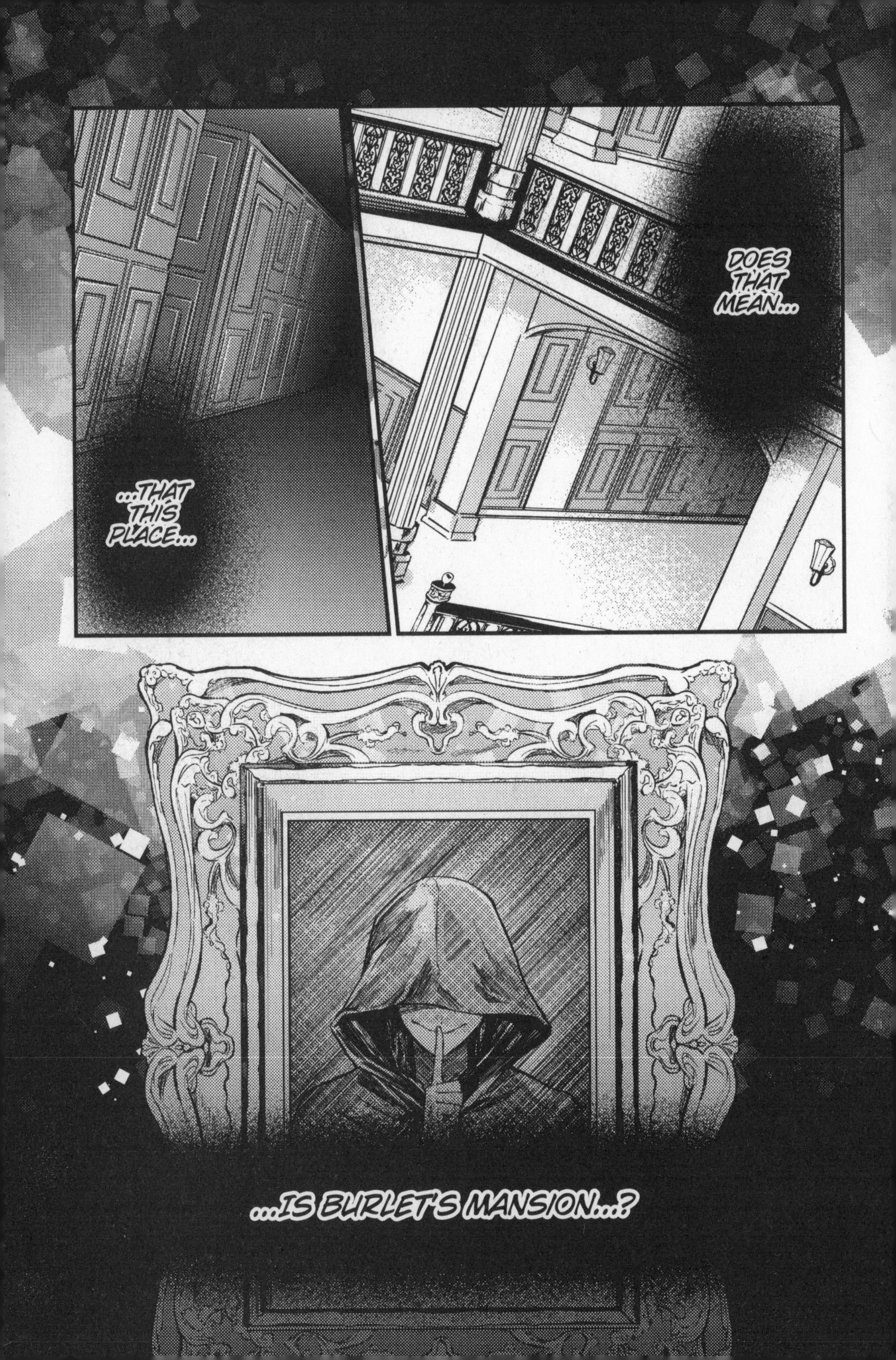
DOES THAT MEAN...
...THAT THIS PLACE...
...IS BURLET'S MANSION...?

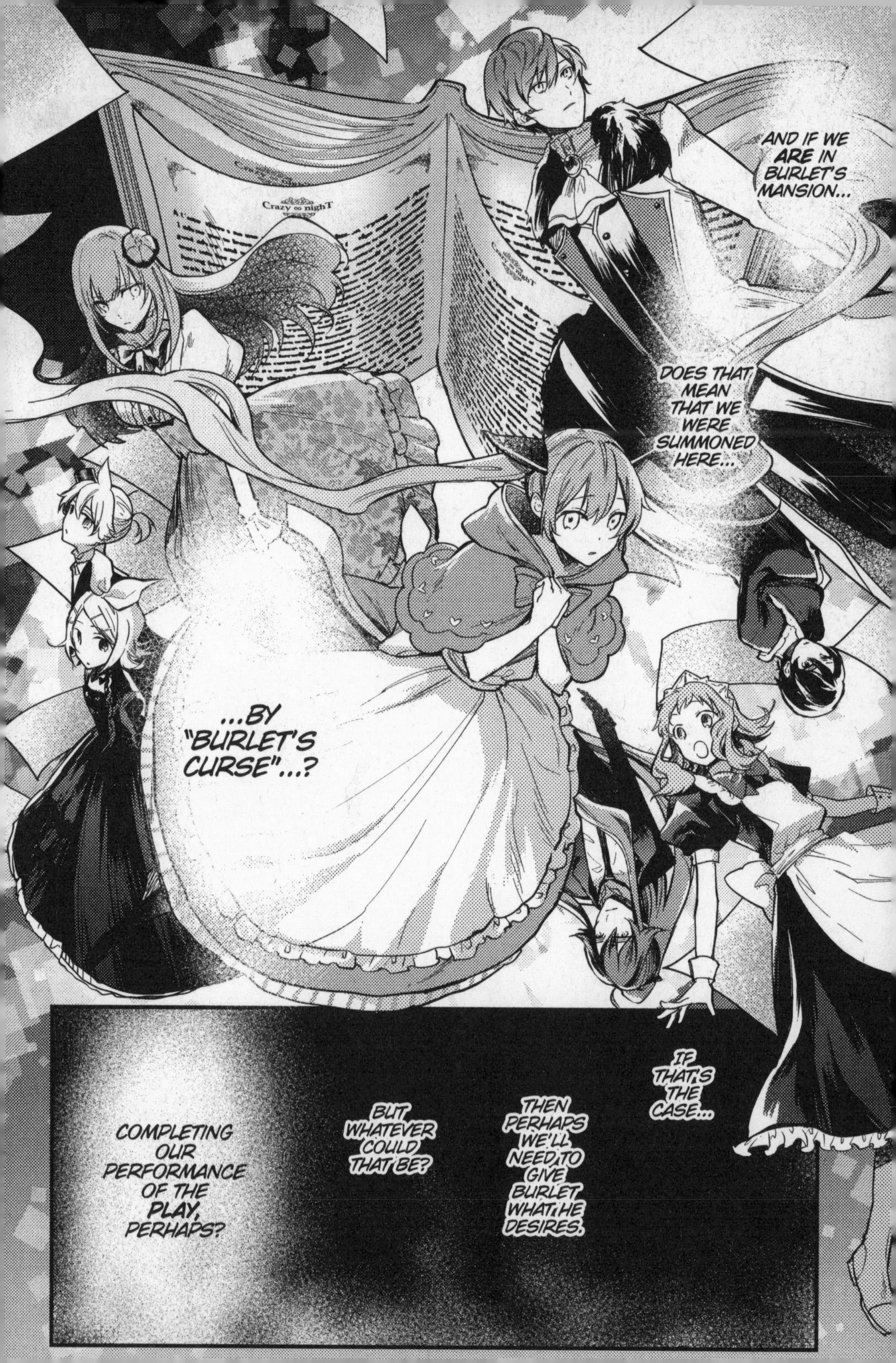
AND IF WE ARE IN BURLET'S MANSION...
DOES THAT MEAN THAT WE WERE SUMMONED HERE...
...BY "BURLET'S CURSE"...?
Crazy ∞ nighT
IF THAT'S THE CASE...
THEN PERHAPS WE'LL NEED TO GIVE BURLET WHAT HE DESIRES.
BUT WHATEVER COULD THAT BE?
COMPLETING OUR PERFORMANCE OF THE PLAY, PERHAPS?

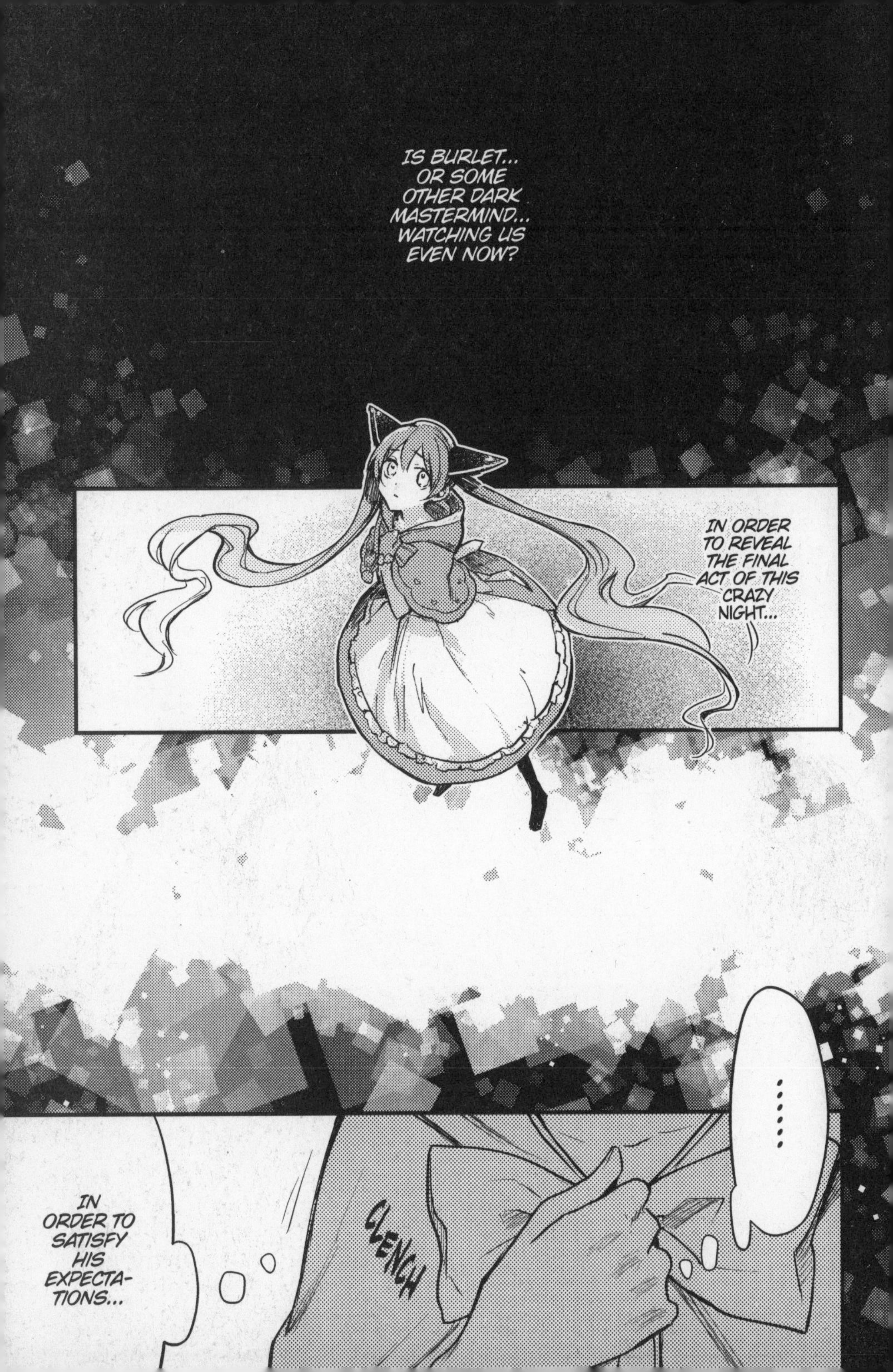
IS BURLET... OR SOME OTHER DARK MASTERMIND... WATCHING US EVEN NOW?
IN ORDER TO REVEAL THE FINAL ACT OF THIS CRAZY NIGHT...
......
CLENCH
IN ORDER TO SATISFY HIS EXPECTA-TIONS...

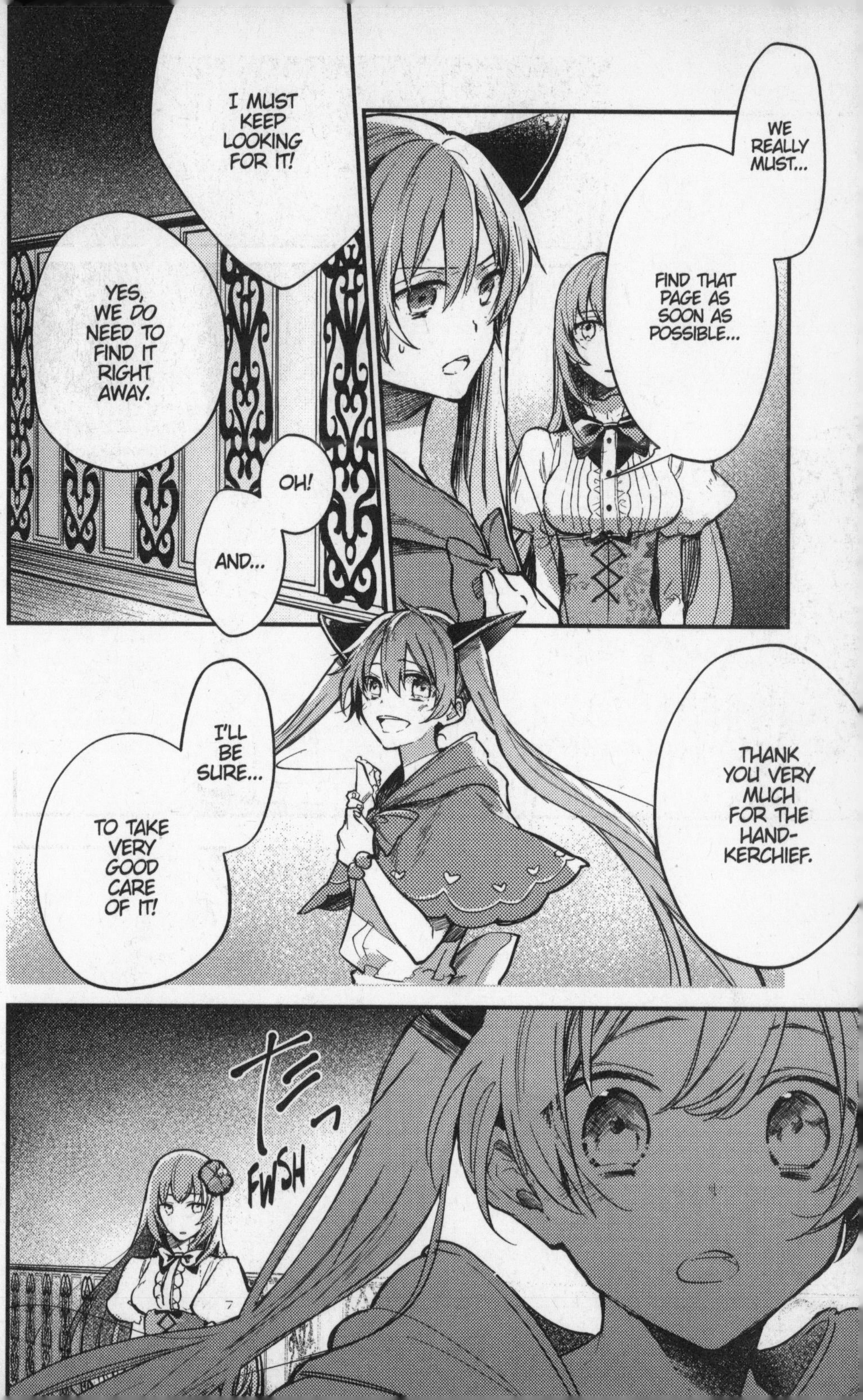
WE REALLY MUST...
FIND THAT PAGE AS SOON AS POSSIBLE...
I MUST KEEP LOOKING FOR IT!
YES, WE *DO* NEED TO FIND IT RIGHT AWAY.
OH!
AND...
THANK YOU VERY MUCH FOR THE HAND-KERCHIEF.
I'LL BE SURE...
TO TAKE VERY GOOD CARE OF IT!
FWSH

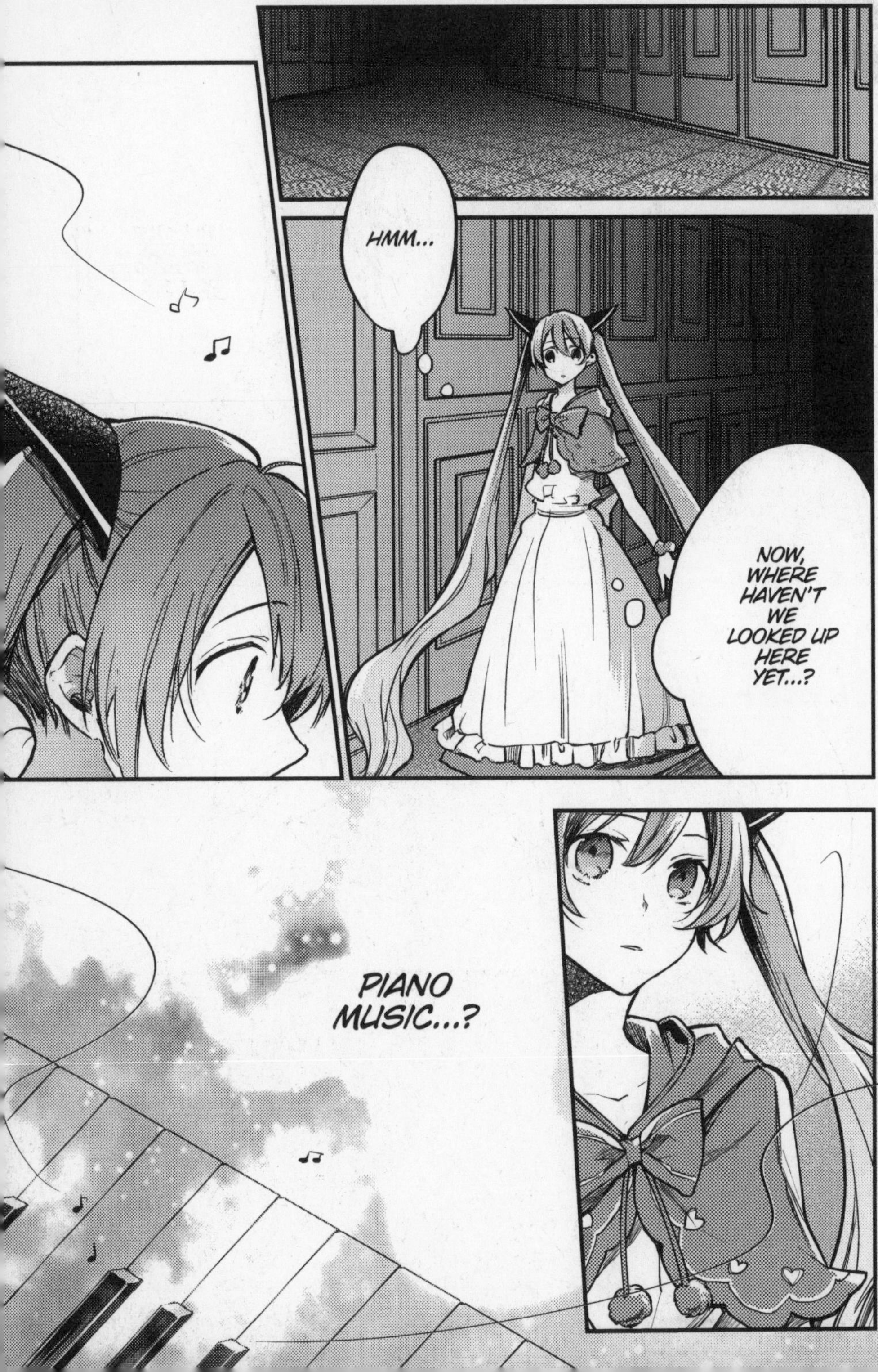
HMM...
NOW, WHERE HAVEN'T WE LOOKED UP HERE YET...?
PIANO MUSIC...?

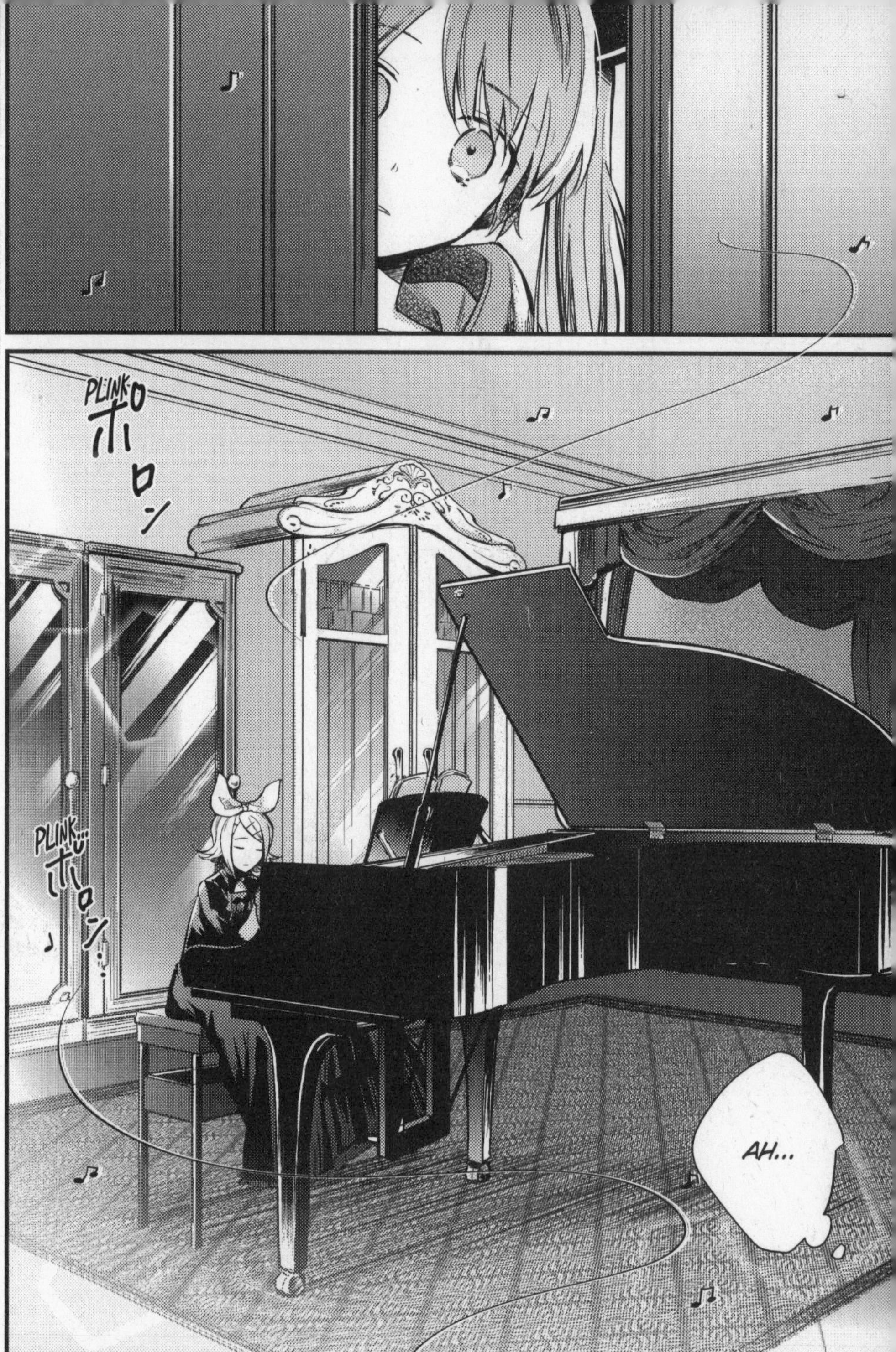
PLINK
ホロン
AH...
PLINK...
ホロン...

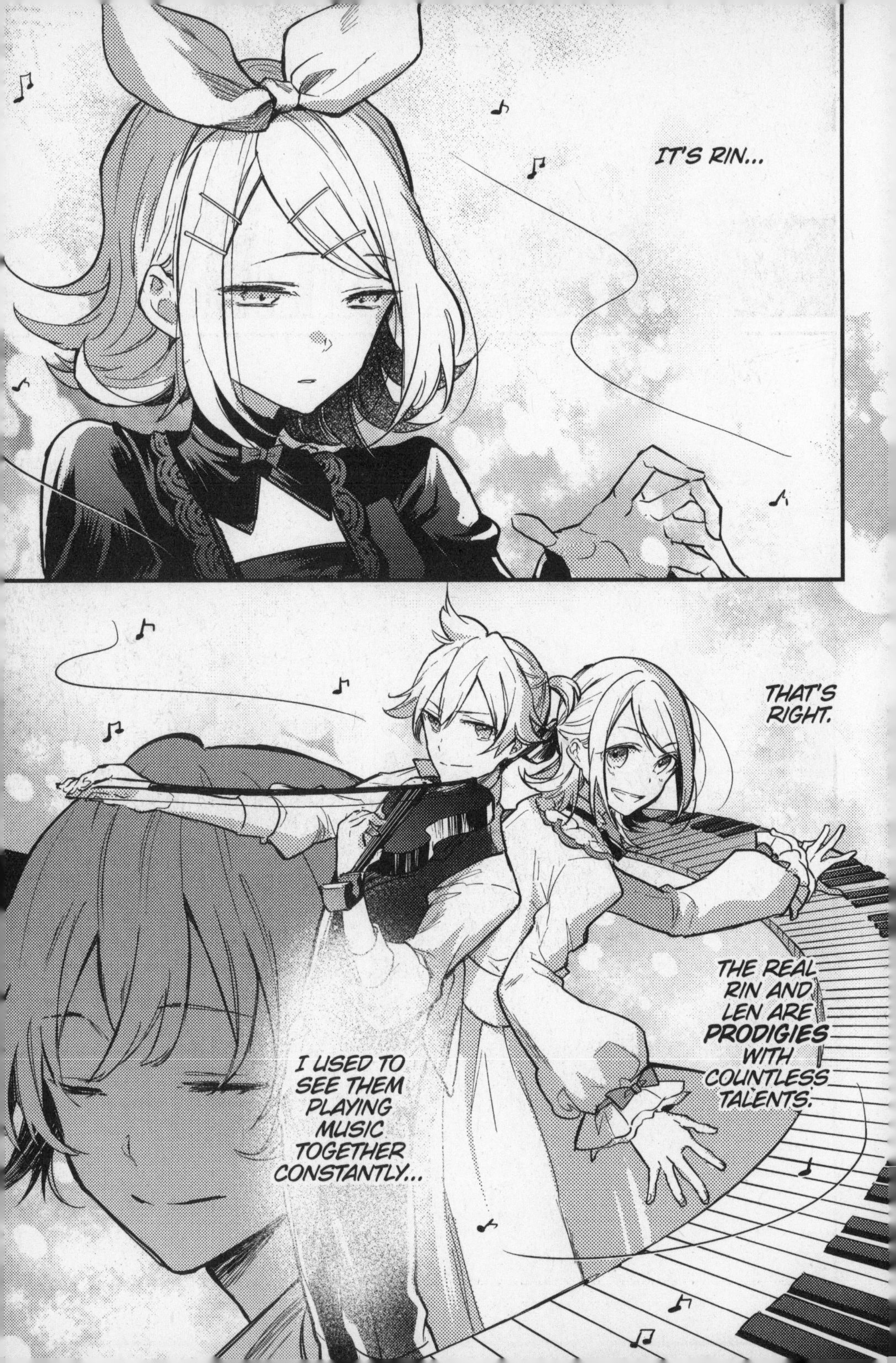
IT'S RIN...
THAT'S RIGHT.
THE REAL RIN AND LEN ARE PRODIGIES WITH COUNTLESS TALENTS.
I USED TO SEE THEM PLAYING MUSIC TOGETHER CONSTANTLY...

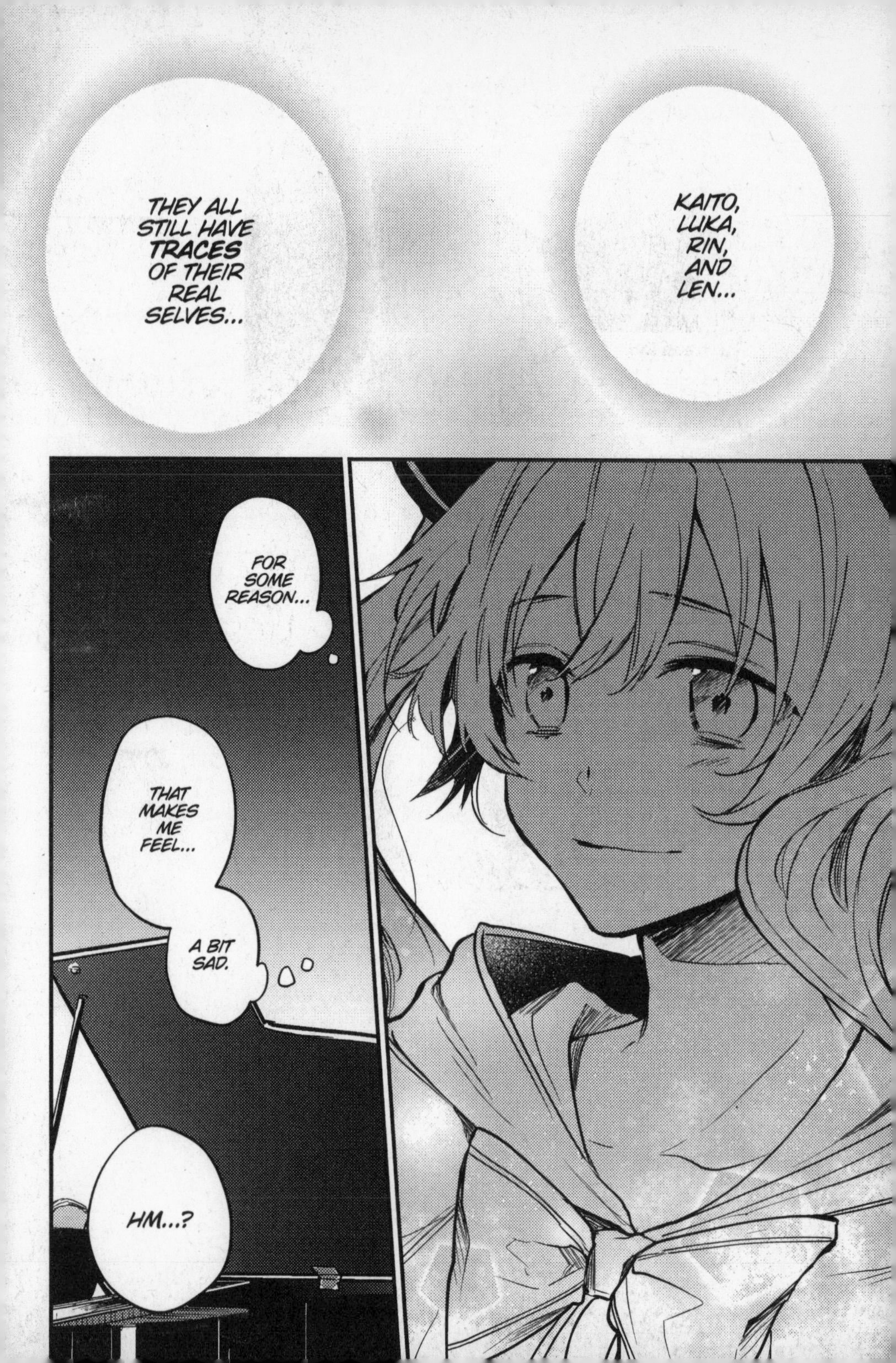
KAITO, LUKA, RIN, AND LEN...
THEY ALL STILL HAVE TRACES OF THEIR REAL SELVES...
FOR SOME REASON...
THAT MAKES ME FEEL...
A BIT SAD.
HM...?

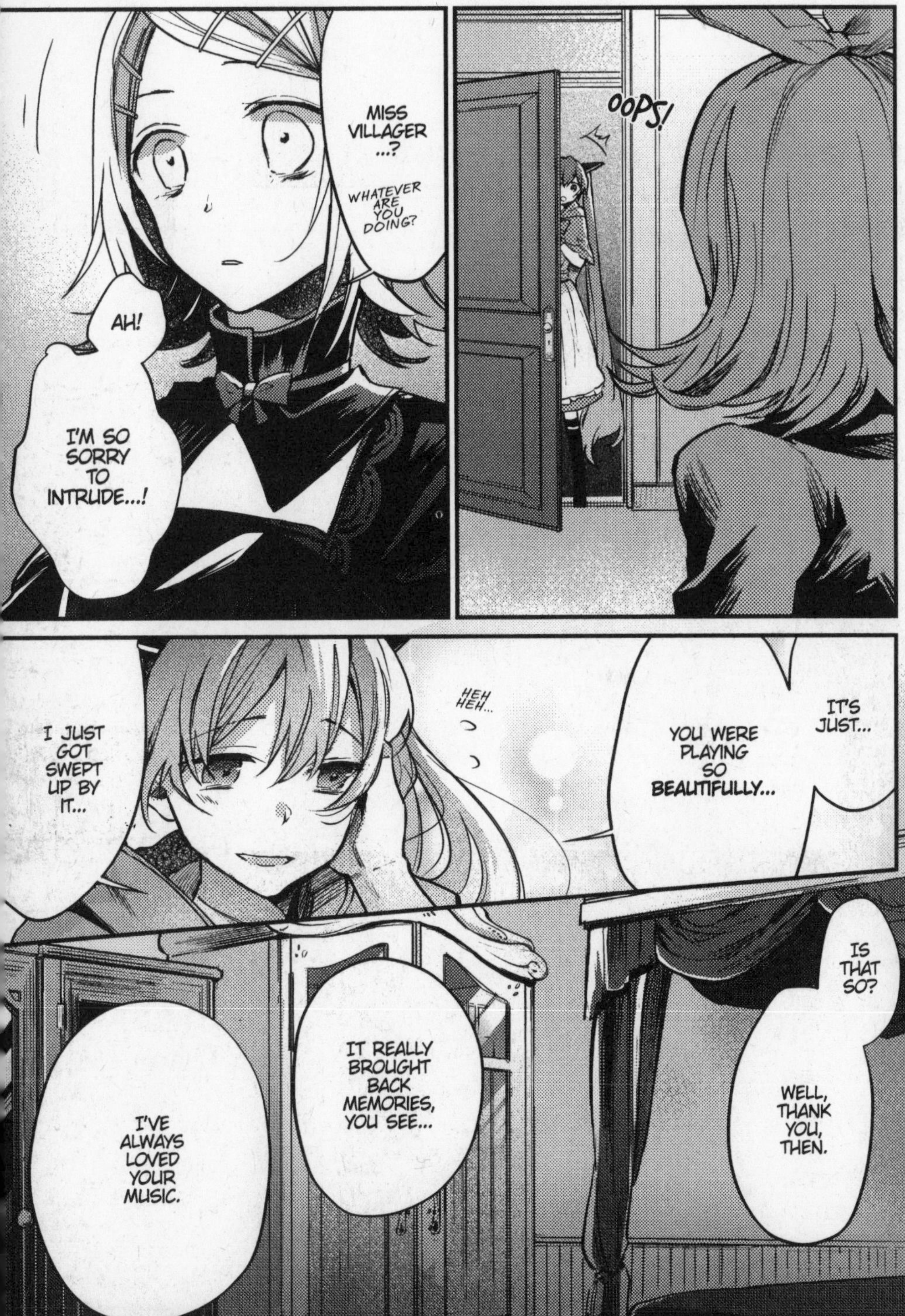
OOPS!
MISS VILLAGER ...?
WHATEVER ARE YOU DOING?
AH!
I'M SO SORRY TO INTRUDE...!
IT'S JUST...
YOU WERE PLAYING SO BEAUTIFULLY...
HEH HEH...
I JUST GOT SWEPT UP BY IT...
IS THAT SO?
WELL, THANK YOU, THEN.
IT REALLY BROUGHT BACK MEMORIES, YOU SEE...
I'VE ALWAYS LOVED YOUR MUSIC.

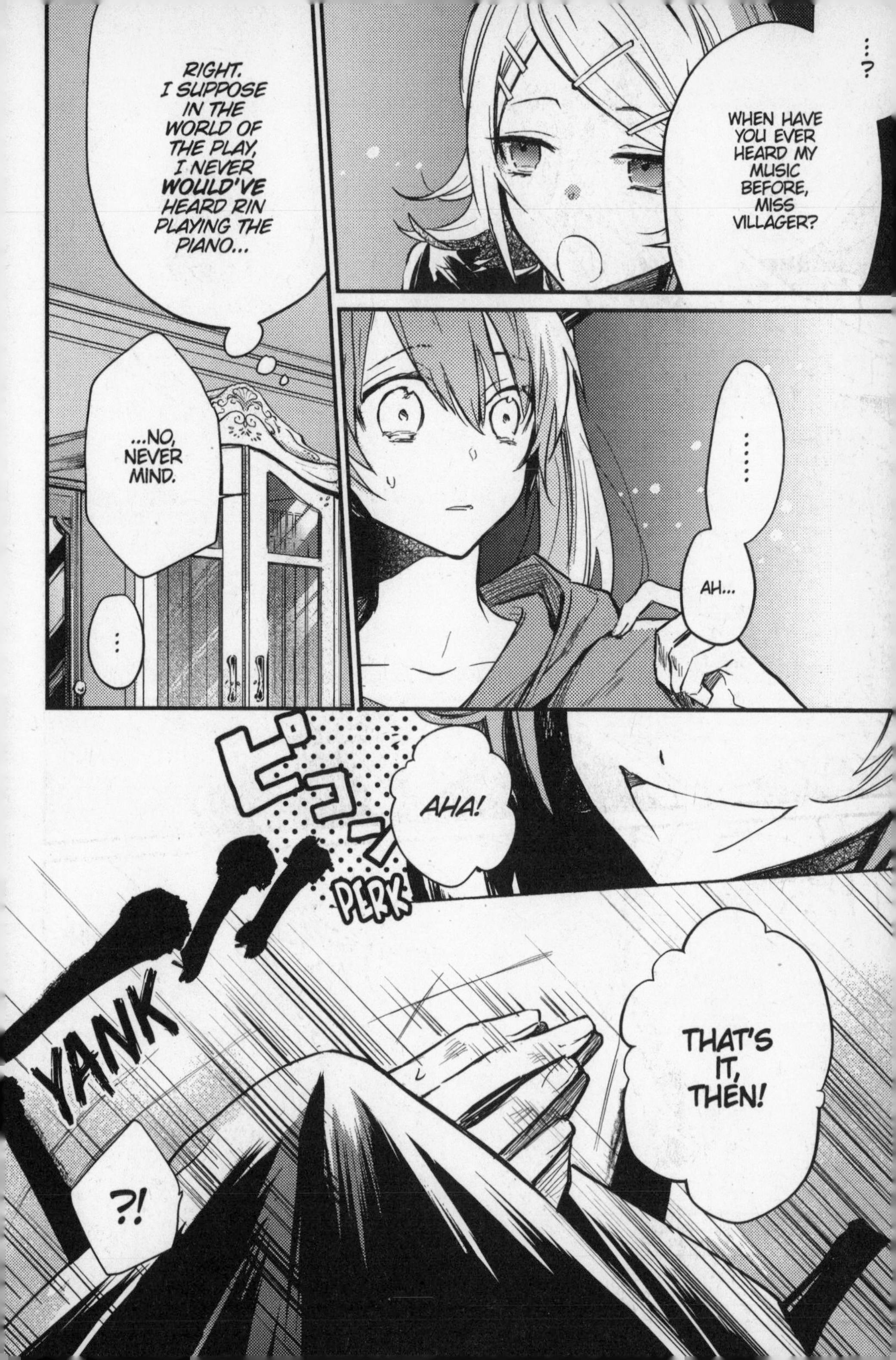

...?
WHEN HAVE YOU EVER HEARD MY MUSIC BEFORE, MISS VILLAGER?
......
AH...
RIGHT. I SUPPOSE IN THE WORLD OF THE PLAY, I NEVER WOULD'VE HEARD RIN PLAYING THE PIANO...
...NO, NEVER MIND.
...
AHA!
PERK
THAT'S IT, THEN!
YANK
?!

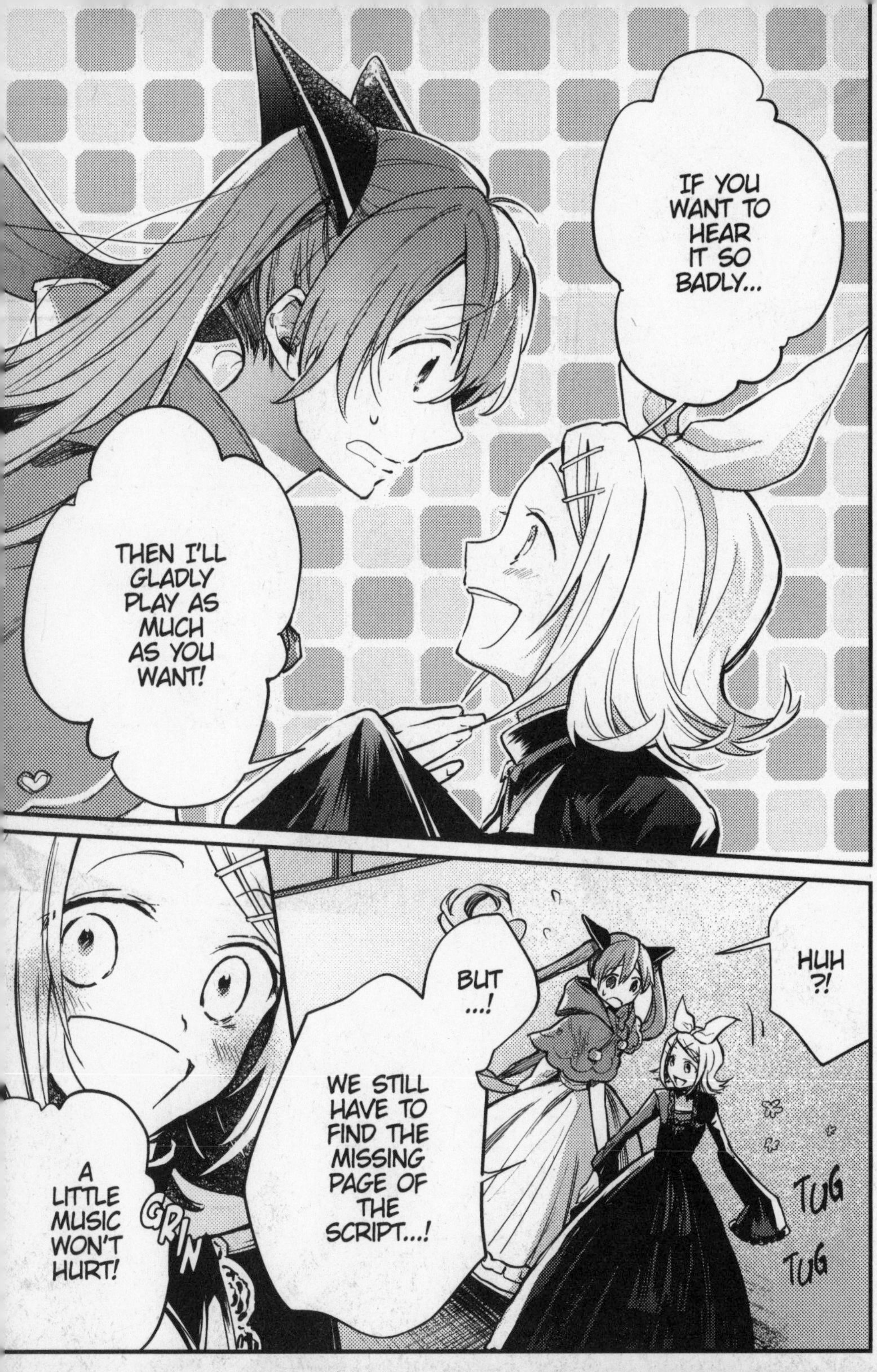
IF YOU WANT TO HEAR IT SO BADLY...
THEN I'LL GLADLY PLAY AS MUCH AS YOU WANT!
HUH ?!
TUG TUG
BUT ...!
WE STILL HAVE TO FIND THE MISSING PAGE OF THE SCRIPT...!
GRIN
A LITTLE MUSIC WON'T HURT!

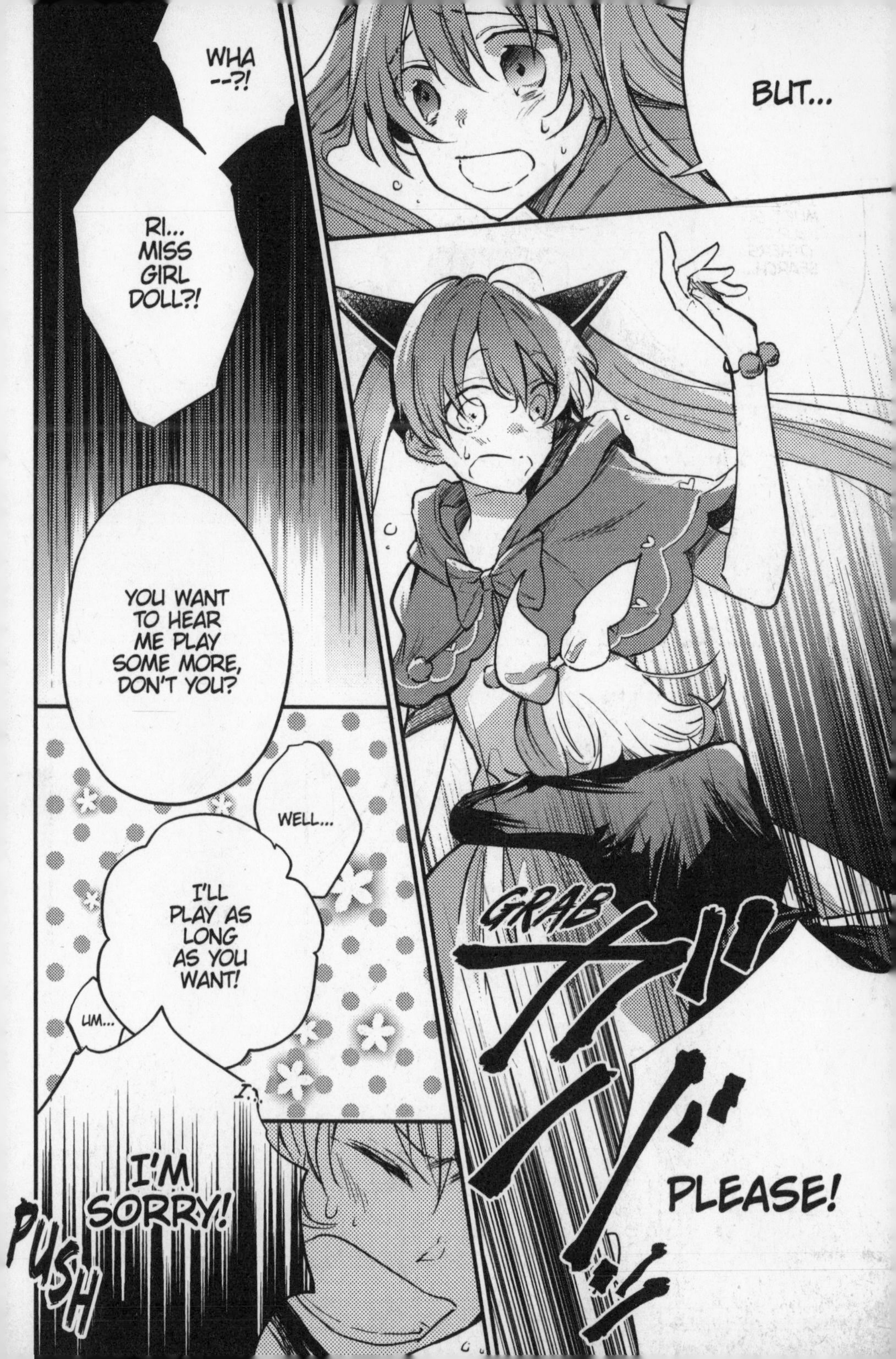
BUT...
GRAB
PLEASE!
WHA--?!
RI... MISS GIRL DOLL?!
YOU WANT TO HEAR ME PLAY SOME MORE, DON'T YOU?
WELL...
I'LL PLAY AS LONG AS YOU WANT!
UM...
I...
I'M SORRY!
PUSH

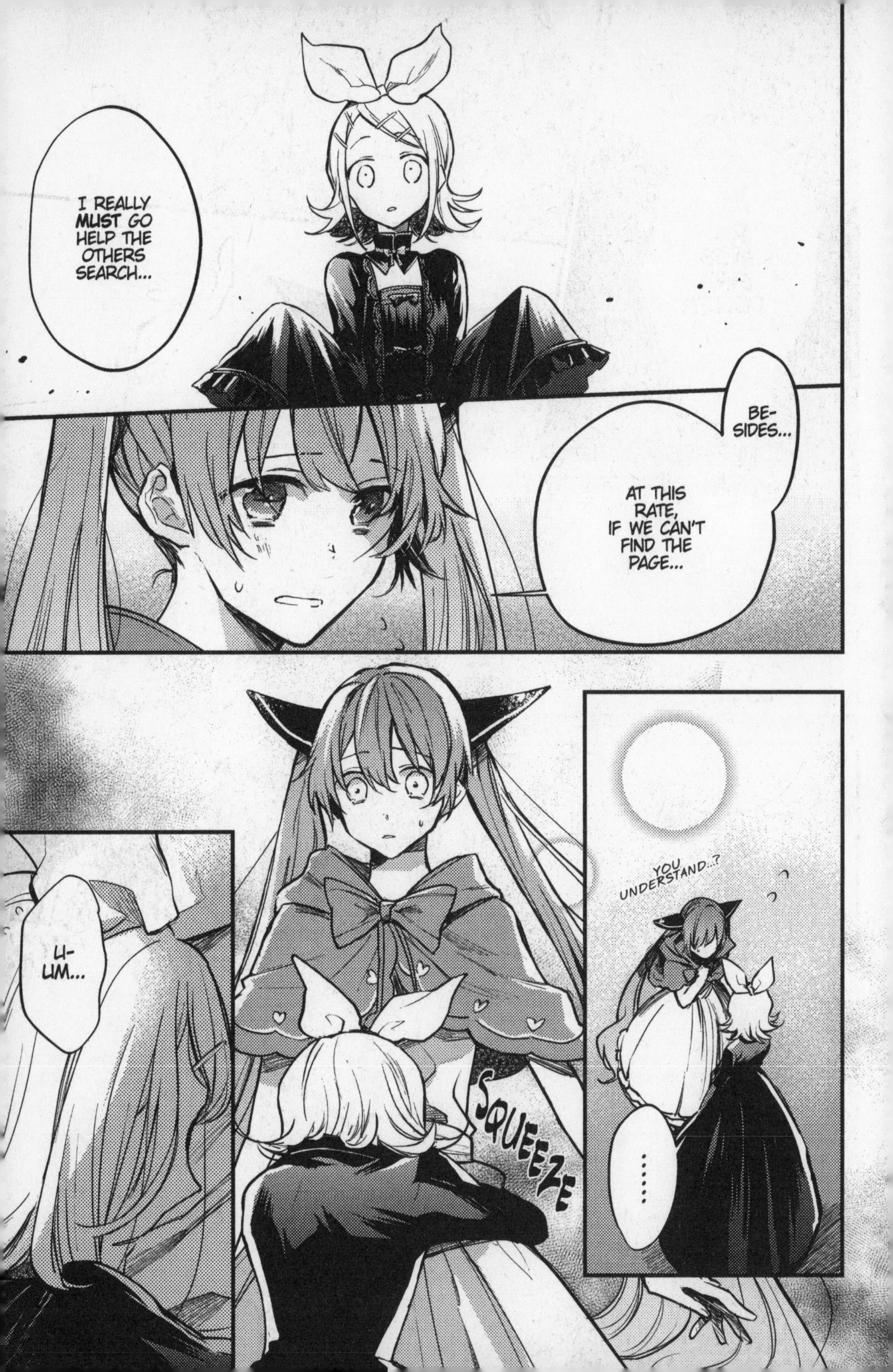
I REALLY MUST GO HELP THE OTHERS SEARCH...
BE-SIDES...
AT THIS RATE, IF WE CAN'T FIND THE PAGE...
YOU UNDERSTAND...?
......
SQUEEZE
U-UM...

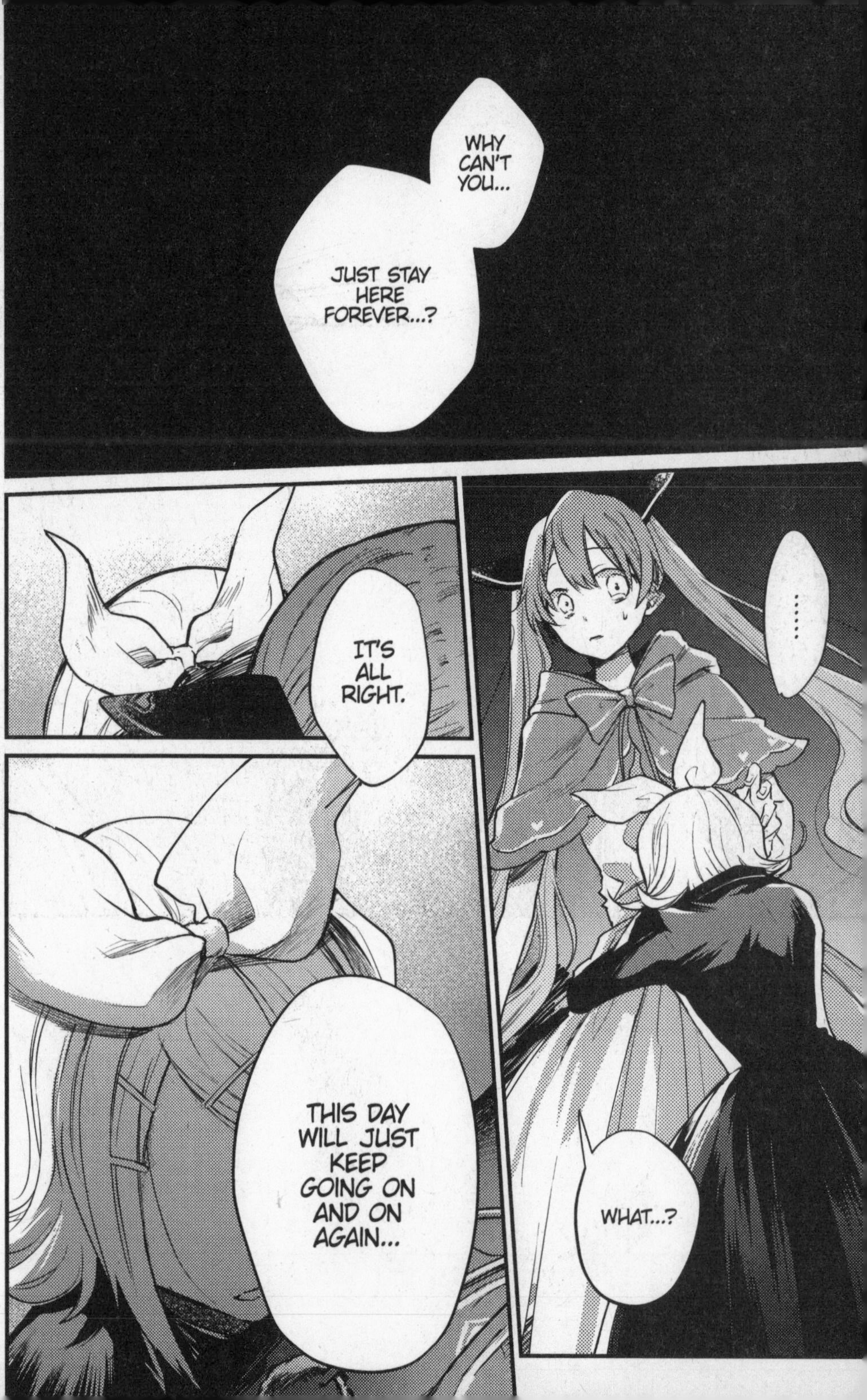
WHY CAN'T YOU...
JUST STAY HERE FOREVER...?
......
WHAT...?
IT'S ALL RIGHT.
THIS DAY WILL JUST KEEP GOING ON AND ON AGAIN...

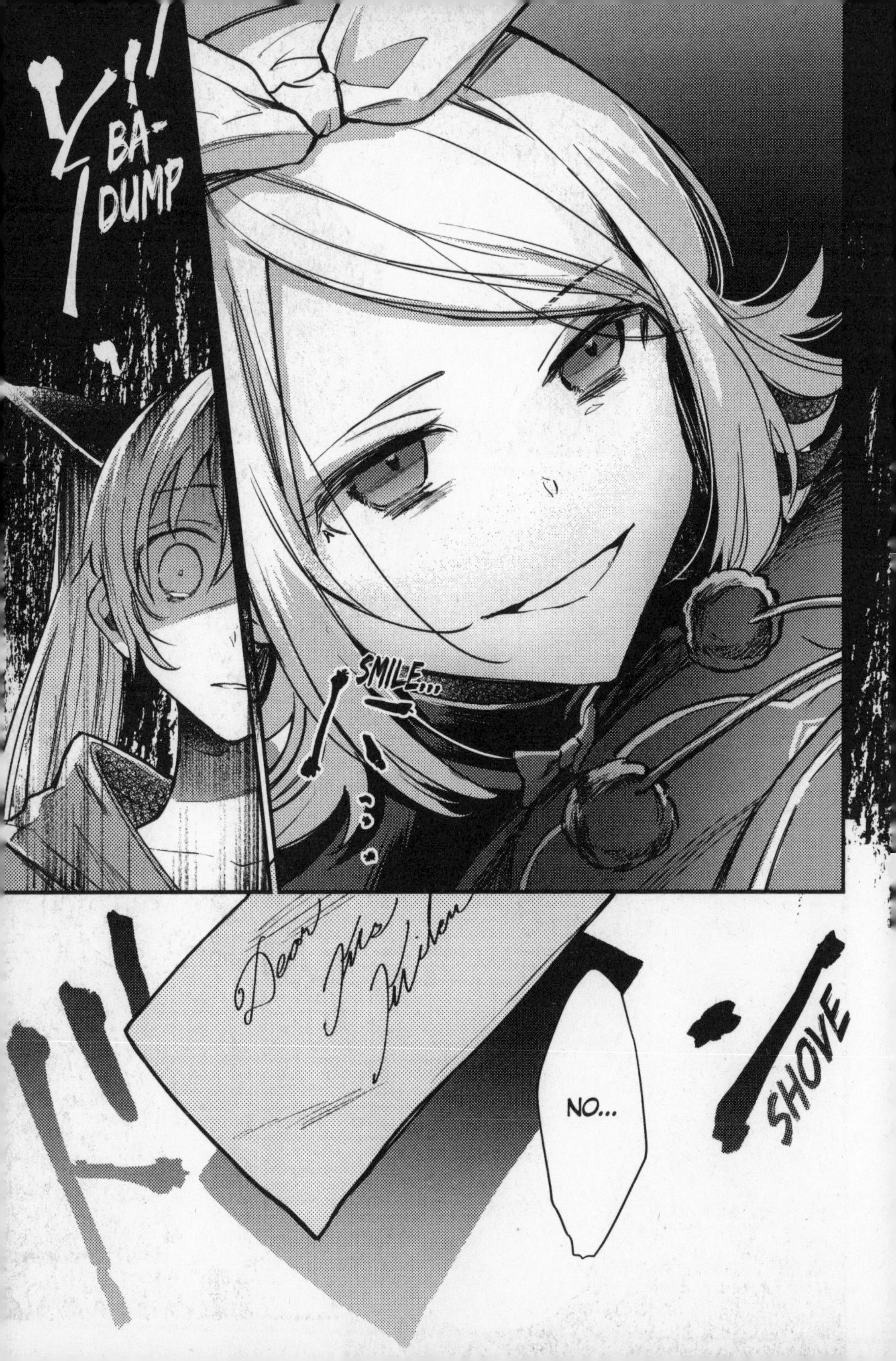

BA-DUMP
SMILE...
SHOVE
NO...

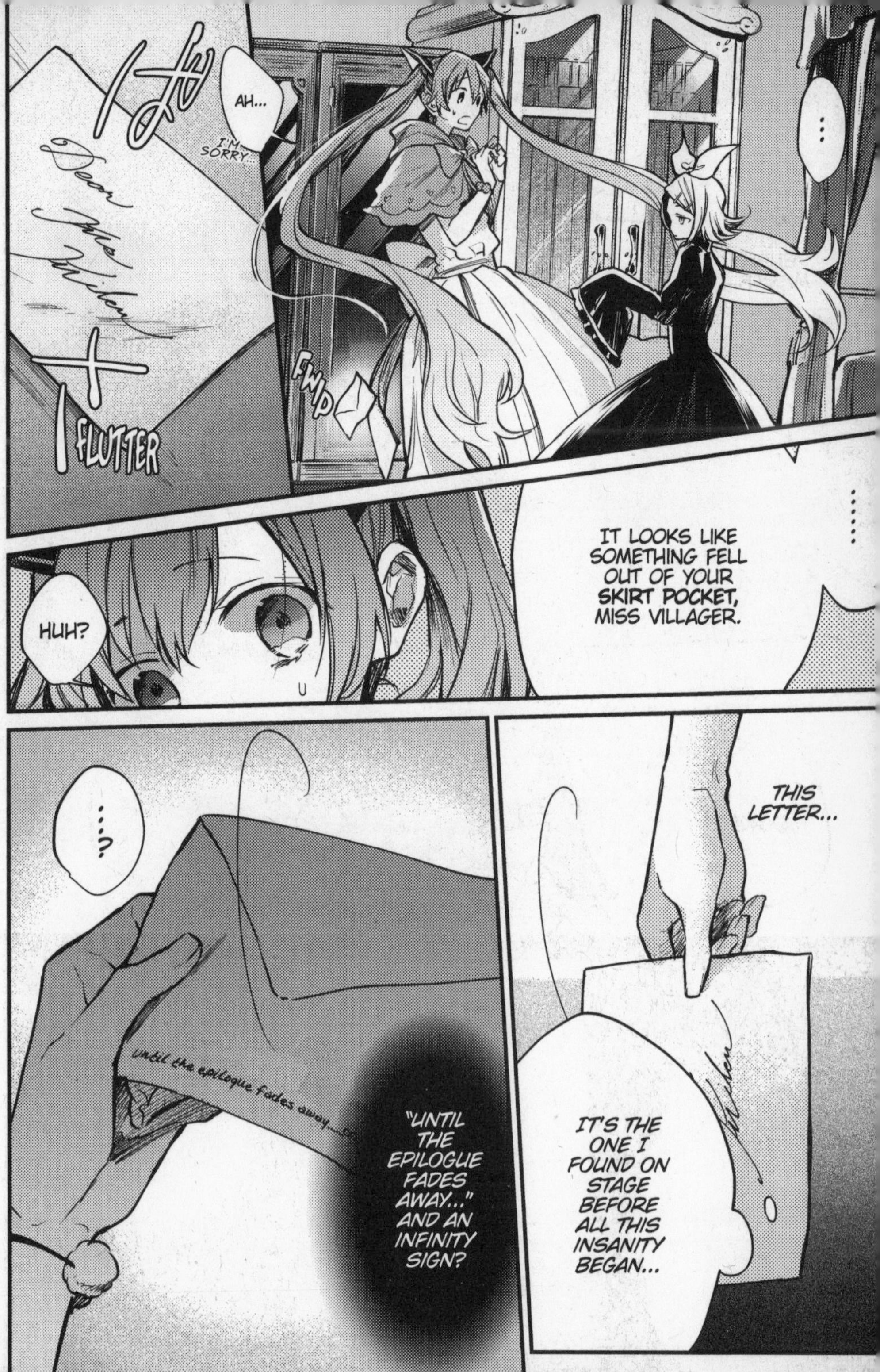
...
AH...
I'M SORRY...
FWIP
FLUTTER
......
IT LOOKS LIKE SOMETHING FELL OUT OF YOUR SKIRT POCKET, MISS VILLAGER.
HUH?
THIS LETTER...
IT'S THE ONE I FOUND ON STAGE BEFORE ALL THIS INSANITY BEGAN...
...?
until the epilogue fades away...
"UNTIL THE EPILOGUE FADES AWAY..." AND AN INFINITY SIGN?

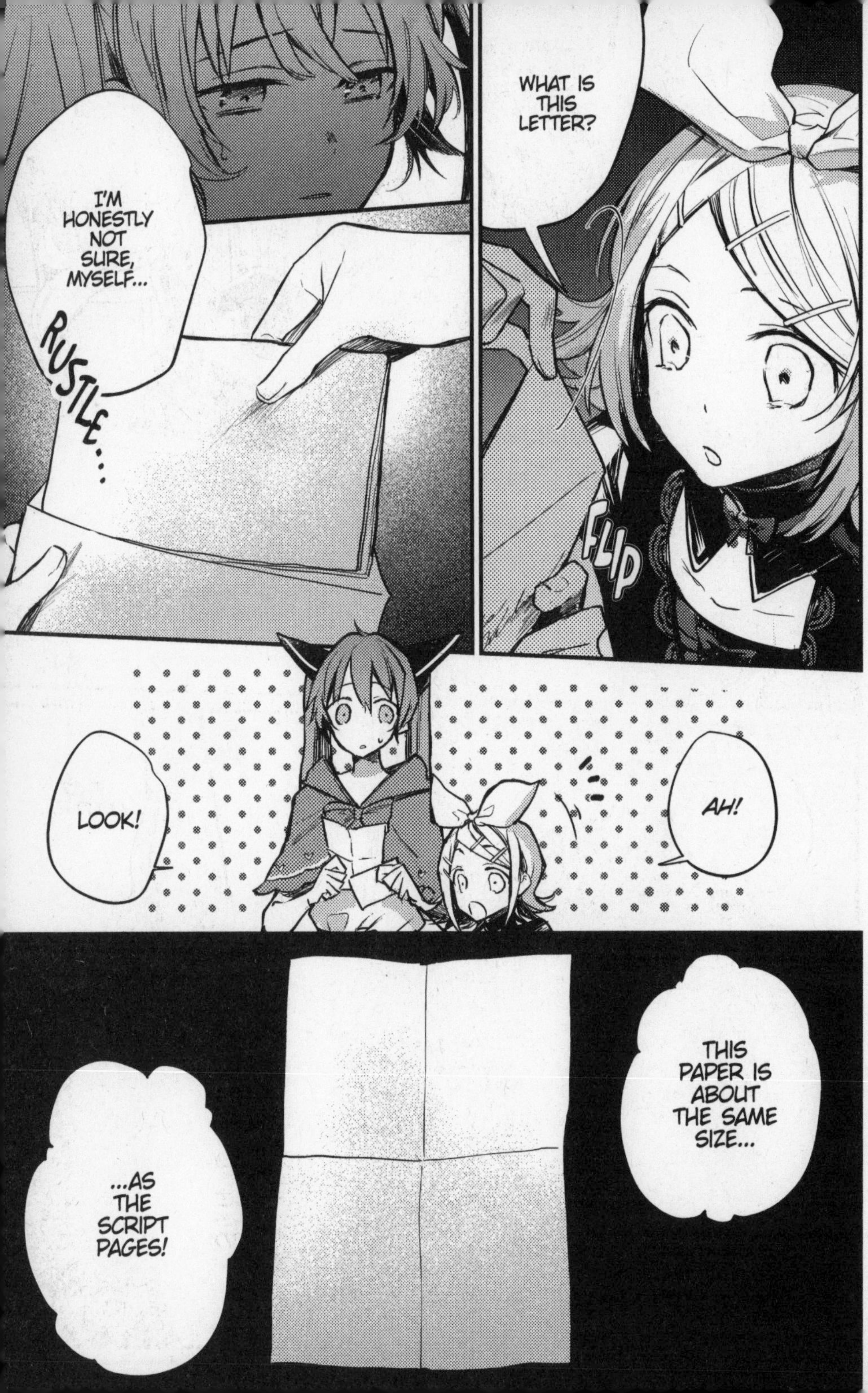
WHAT IS THIS LETTER?
FLIP
I'M HONESTLY NOT SURE, MYSELF...
RUSTLE...
AH!
LOOK!
THIS PAPER IS ABOUT THE SAME SIZE...
...AS THE SCRIPT PAGES!

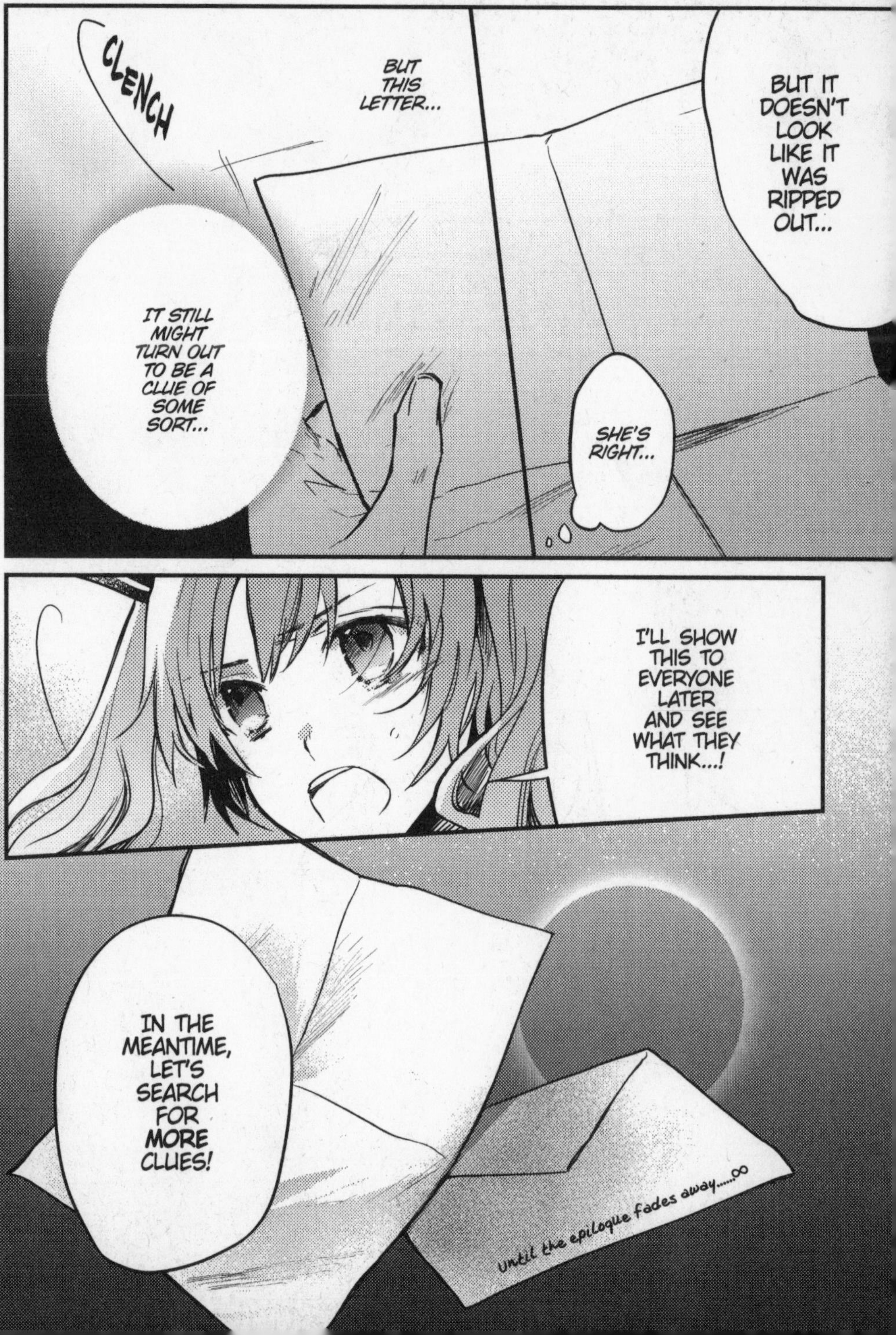
BUT IT DOESN'T LOOK LIKE IT WAS RIPPED OUT...
SHE'S RIGHT...
BUT THIS LETTER...
CLENCH
IT STILL MIGHT TURN OUT TO BE A CLUE OF SOME SORT...
I'LL SHOW THIS TO EVERYONE LATER AND SEE WHAT THEY THINK...!
IN THE MEANTIME, LET'S SEARCH FOR MORE CLUES!
Until the epilogue fades away.....∞

Act 5: Milk Tea

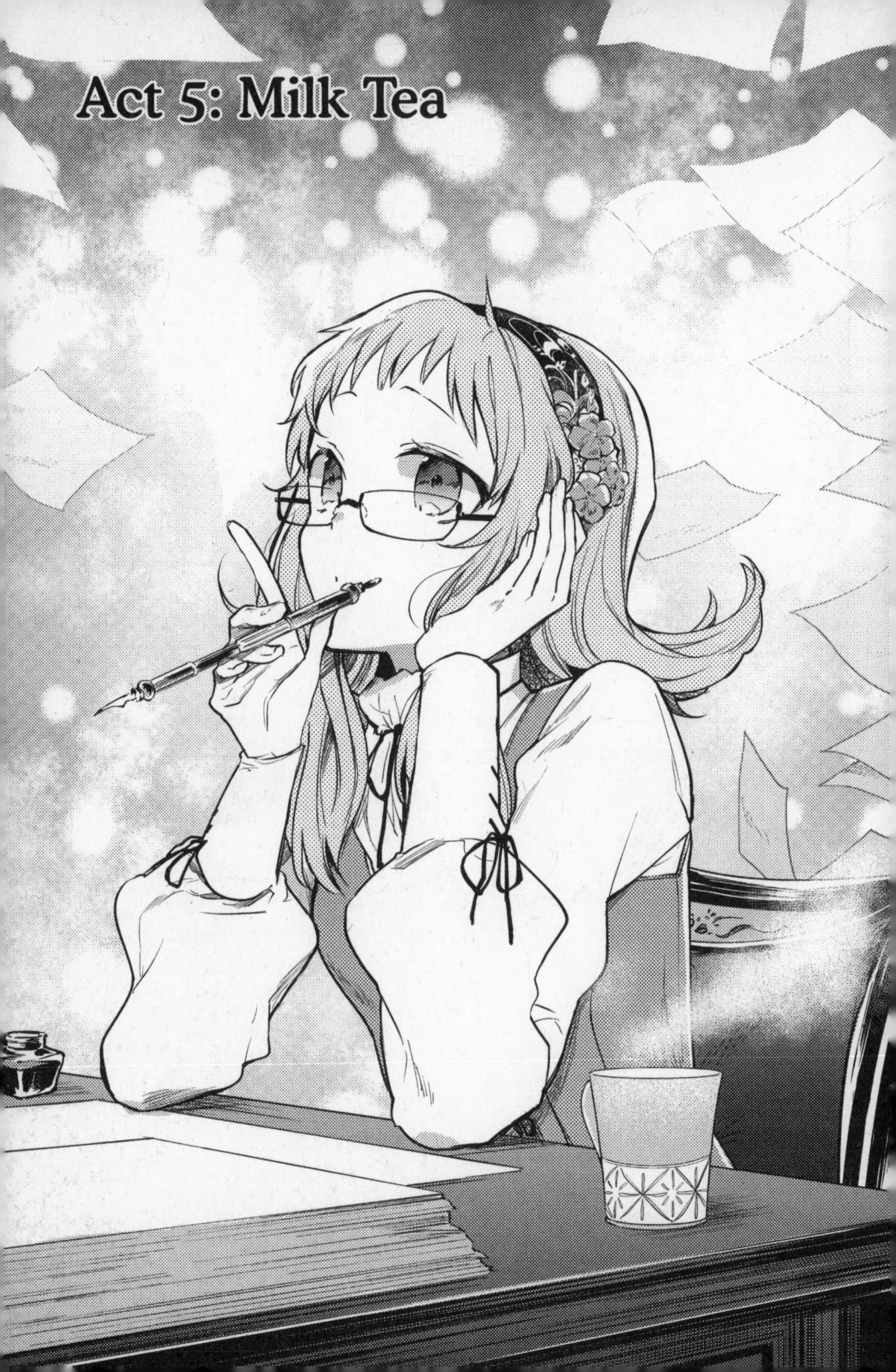

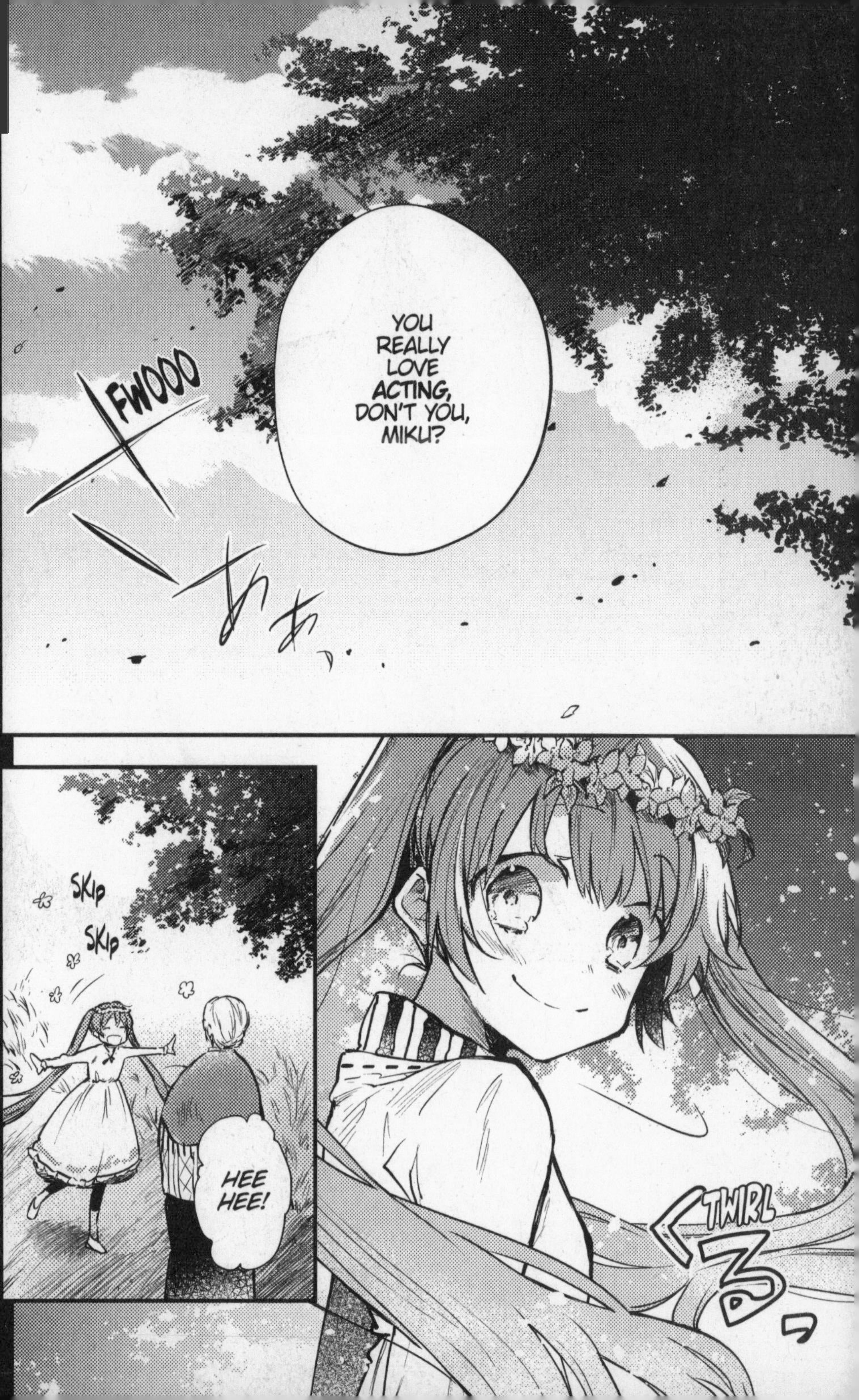
YOU REALLY LOVE ACTING, DON'T YOU, MIKU?
FWOOO
TWIRL
SKIP
SKIP
HEE HEE!

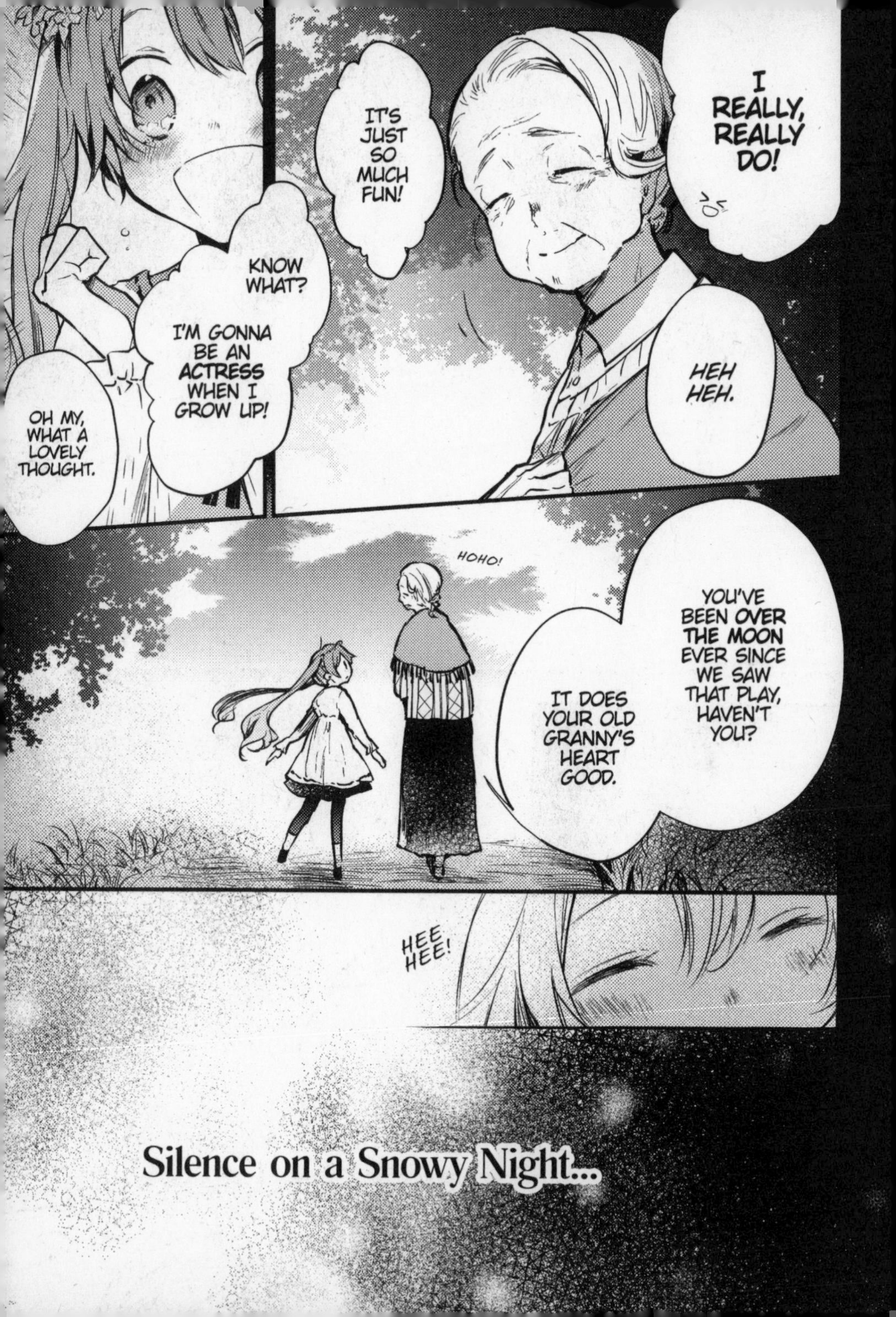
I REALLY, REALLY DO!
IT'S JUST SO MUCH FUN!
HEH HEH.
KNOW WHAT?
I'M GONNA BE AN ACTRESS WHEN I GROW UP!
OH MY, WHAT A LOVELY THOUGHT.
YOU'VE BEEN OVER THE MOON EVER SINCE WE SAW THAT PLAY, HAVEN'T YOU?
IT DOES YOUR OLD GRANNY'S HEART GOOD.
HOHO!
HEE HEE!
Silence on a Snowy Night...

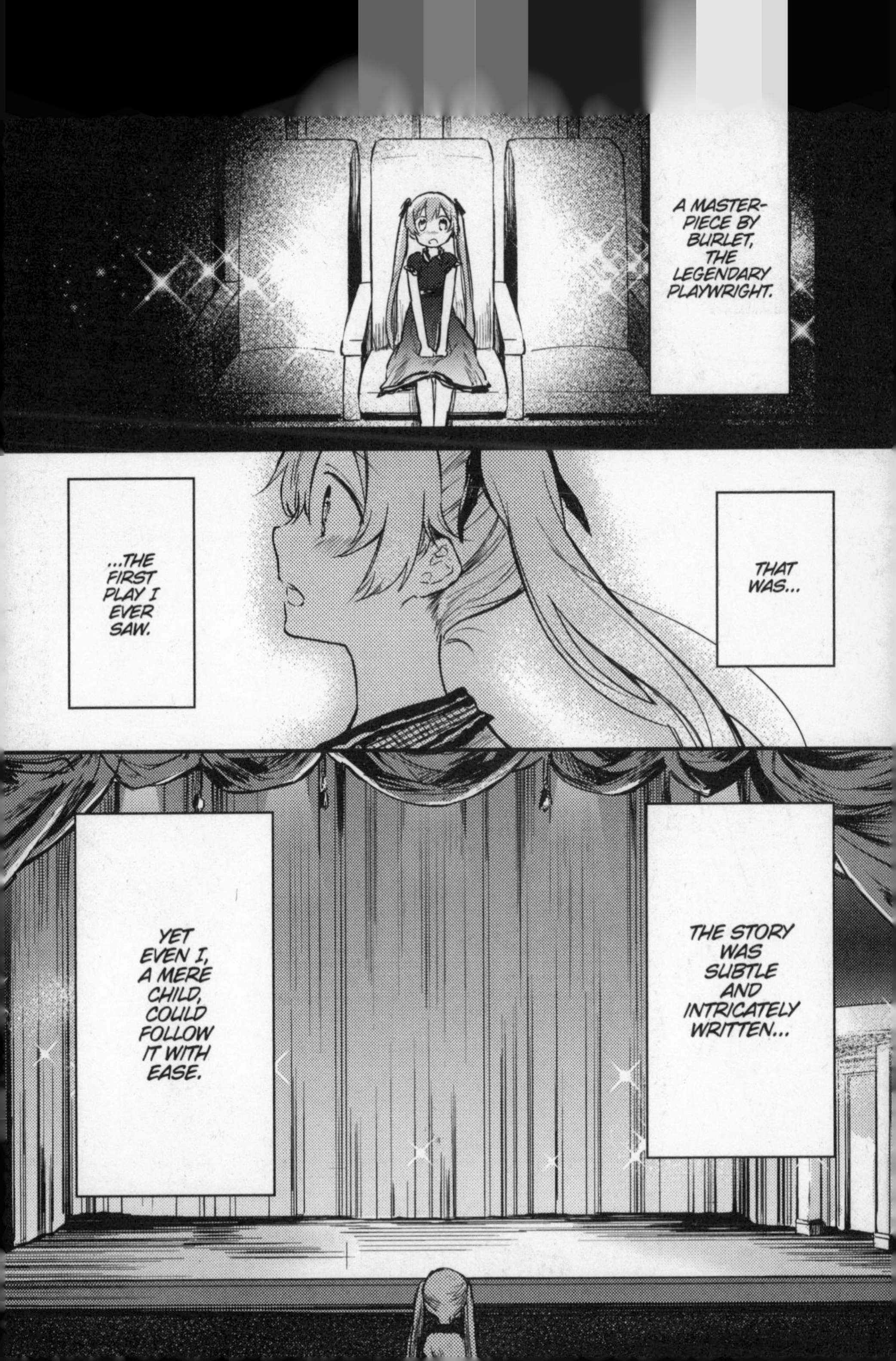
A MASTER-PIECE BY BURLET, THE LEGENDARY PLAYWRIGHT.
THAT WAS...
...THE FIRST PLAY I EVER SAW.
THE STORY WAS SUBTLE AND INTRICATELY WRITTEN...
YET EVEN I, A MERE CHILD, COULD FOLLOW IT WITH EASE.

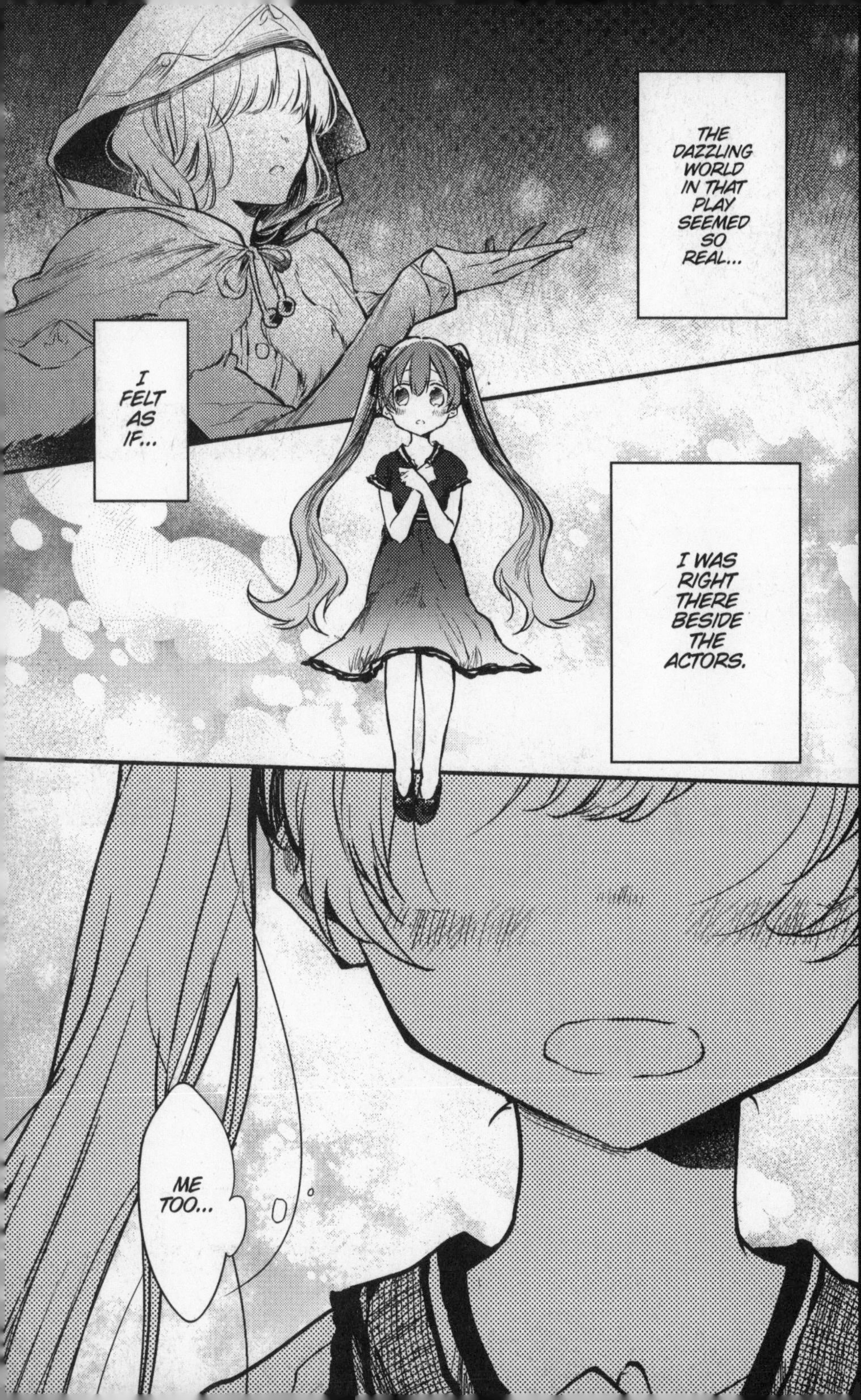
THE DAZZLING WORLD IN THAT PLAY SEEMED SO REAL...
I FELT AS IF...
I WAS RIGHT THERE BESIDE THE ACTORS.
ME TOO...

I WANT TO LIVE IN BURLET'S PLAYS, TOO!

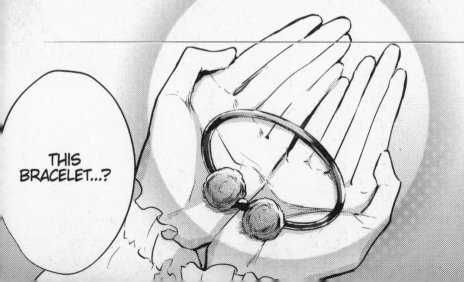

THIS BRACELET...?

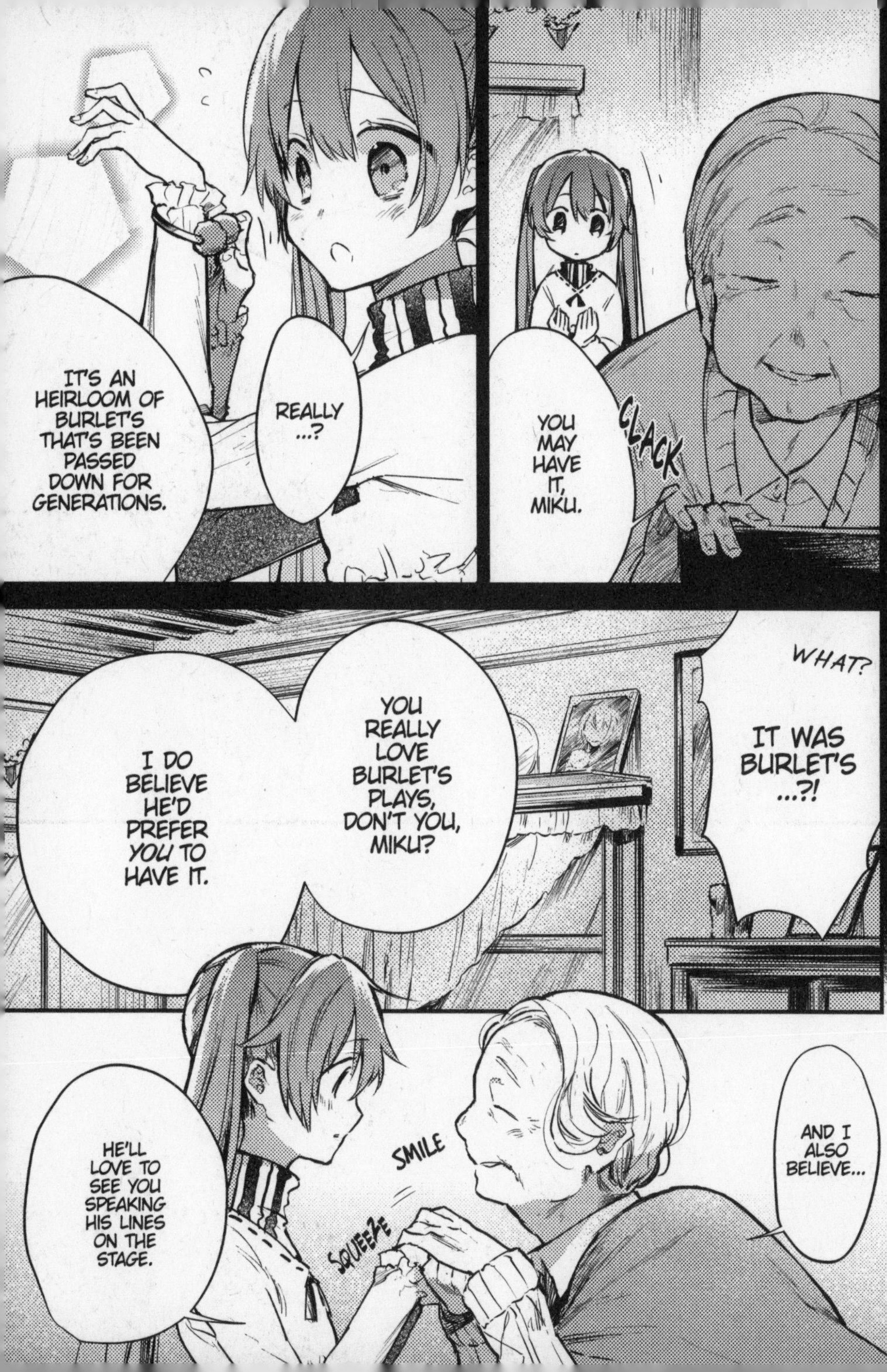
YOU MAY HAVE IT, MIKU.
CLACK
REALLY ...?
IT'S AN HEIRLOOM OF BURLET'S THAT'S BEEN PASSED DOWN FOR GENERATIONS.
WHAT?
IT WAS BURLET'S ...?!
YOU REALLY LOVE BURLET'S PLAYS, DON'T YOU, MIKU?
I DO BELIEVE HE'D PREFER *YOU* TO HAVE IT.
AND I ALSO BELIEVE...
SMILE
SQUEEZE
HE'LL LOVE TO SEE YOU SPEAKING HIS LINES ON THE STAGE.

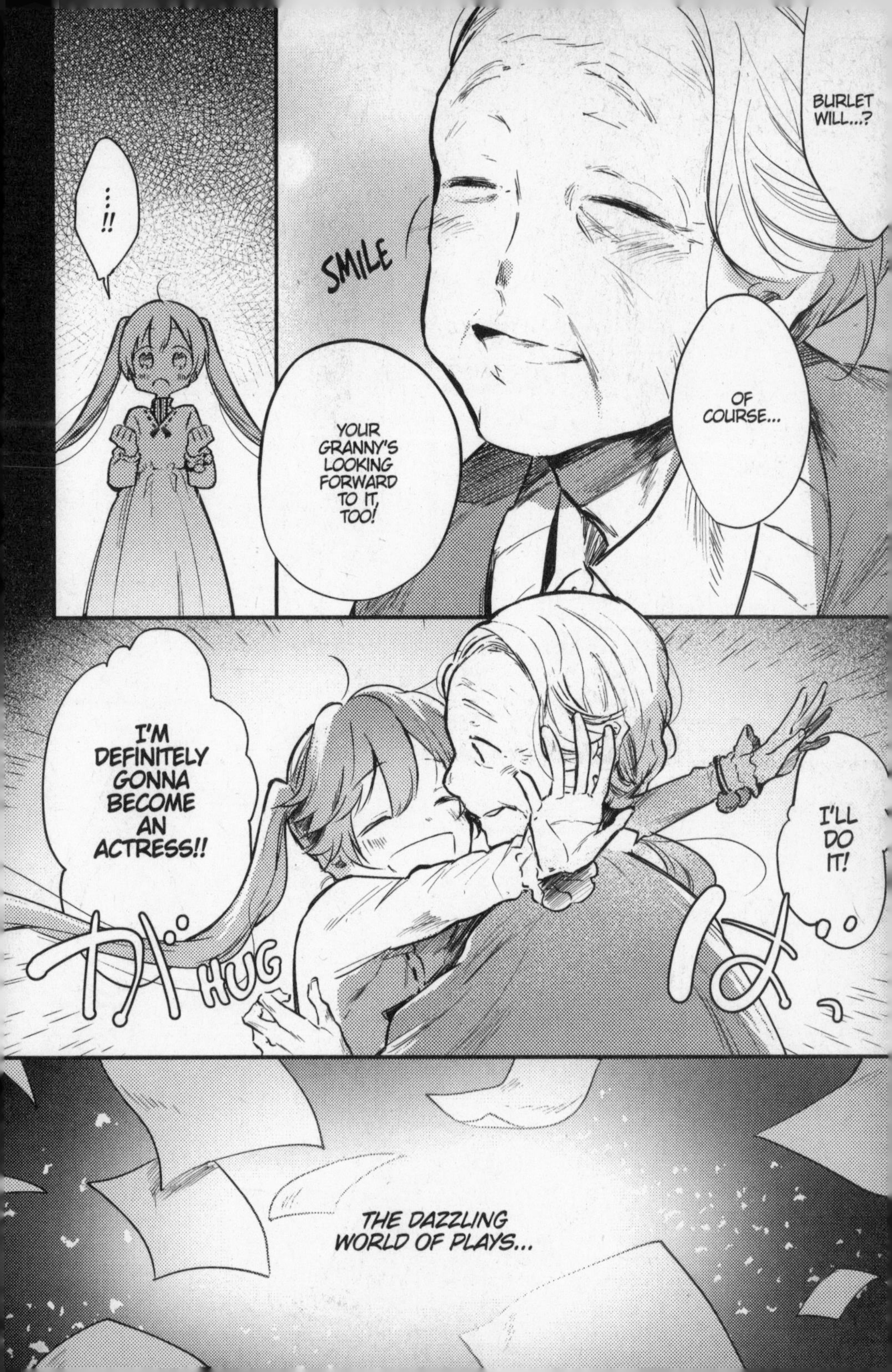
BURLET WILL...?
OF COURSE...
SMILE
YOUR GRANNY'S LOOKING FORWARD TO IT, TOO!
...!!
I'LL DO IT!
HUG
I'M DEFINITELY GONNA BECOME AN ACTRESS!!
THE DAZZLING WORLD OF PLAYS...

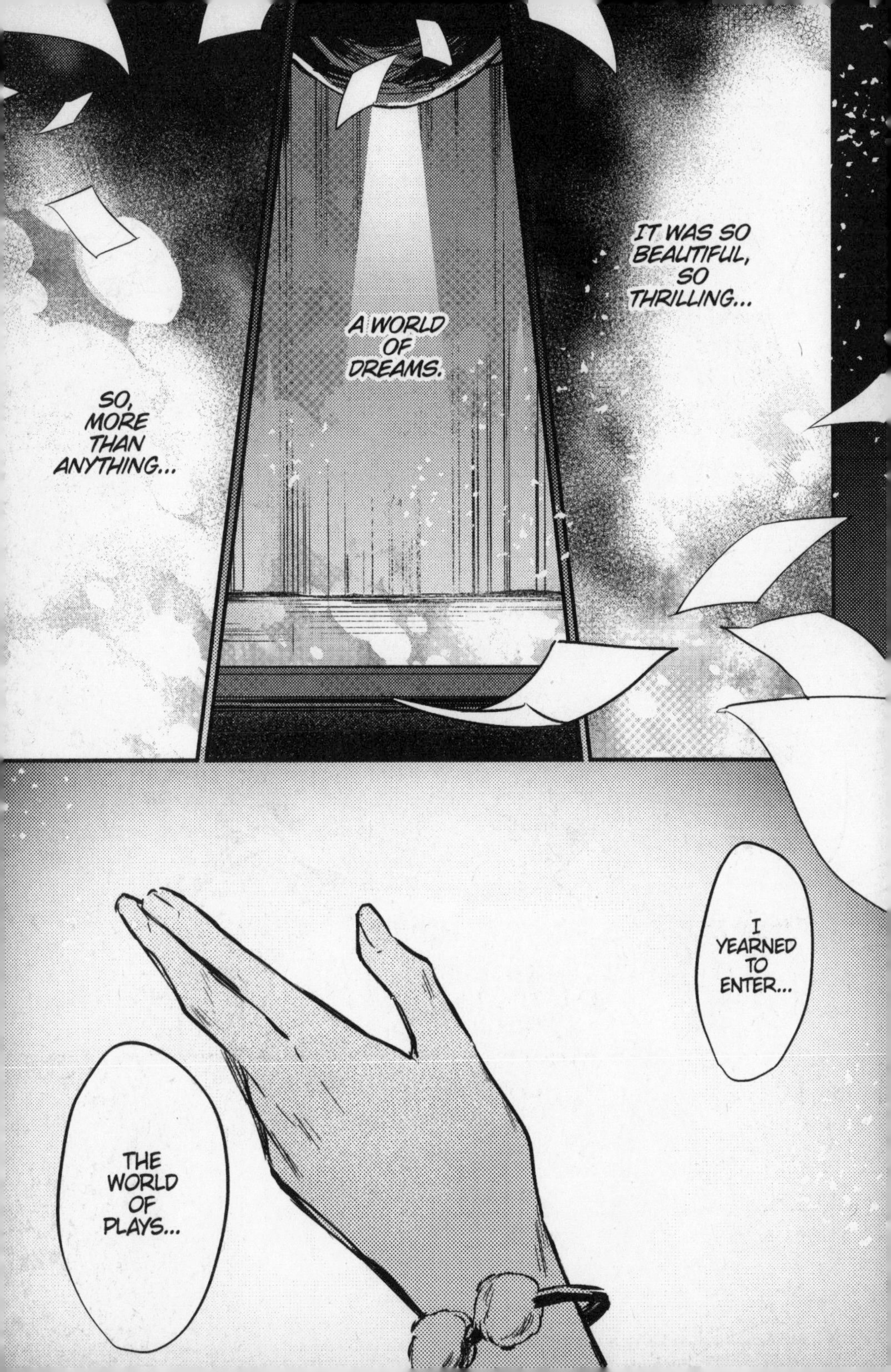
IT WAS SO BEAUTIFUL, SO THRILLING...
A WORLD OF DREAMS.
SO, MORE THAN ANYTHING...
I YEARNED TO ENTER...
THE WORLD OF PLAYS...

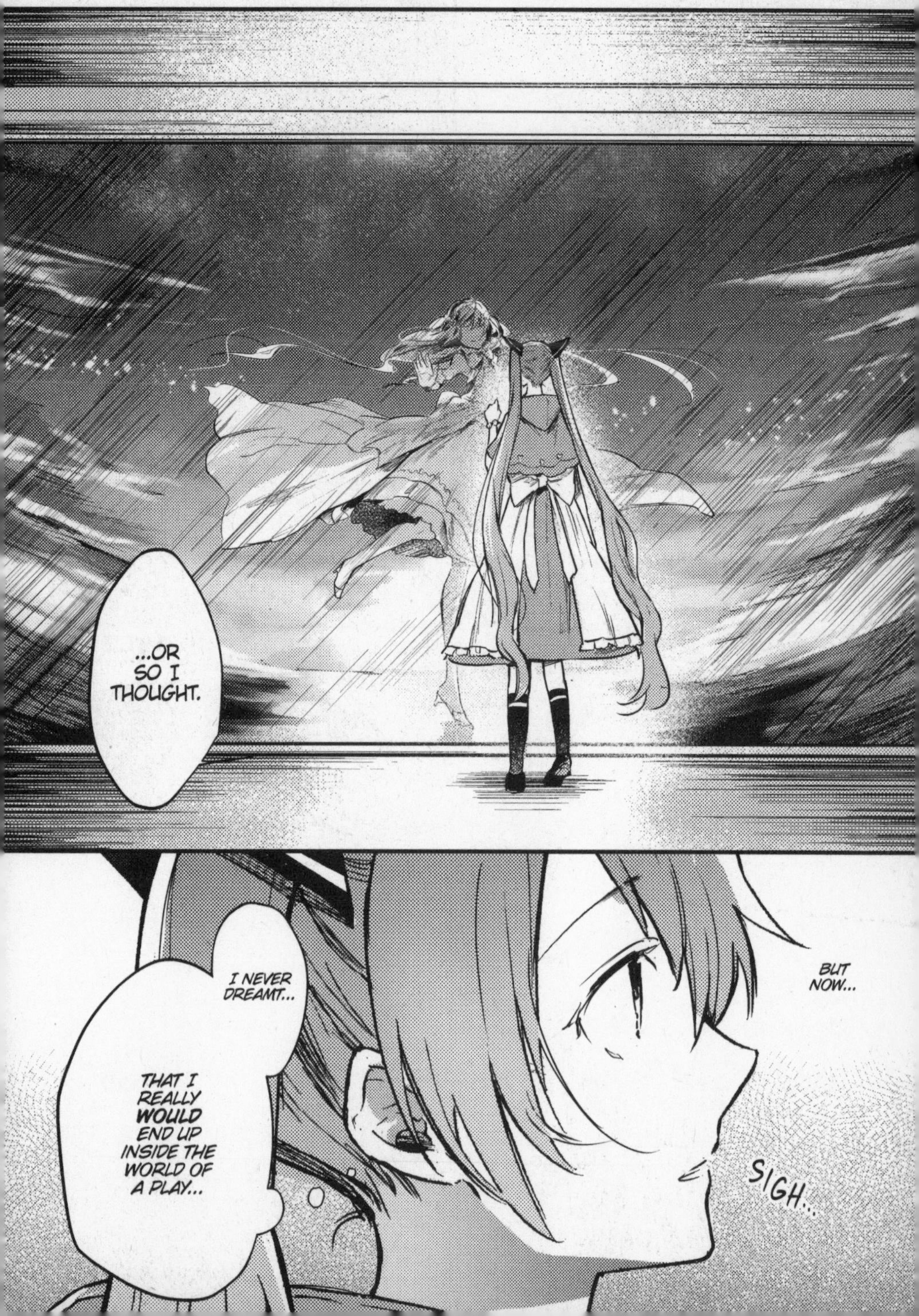
...OR SO I THOUGHT.
BUT NOW...
I NEVER DREAMT...
THAT I REALLY **WOULD** END UP INSIDE THE WORLD OF A PLAY...
SIGH...

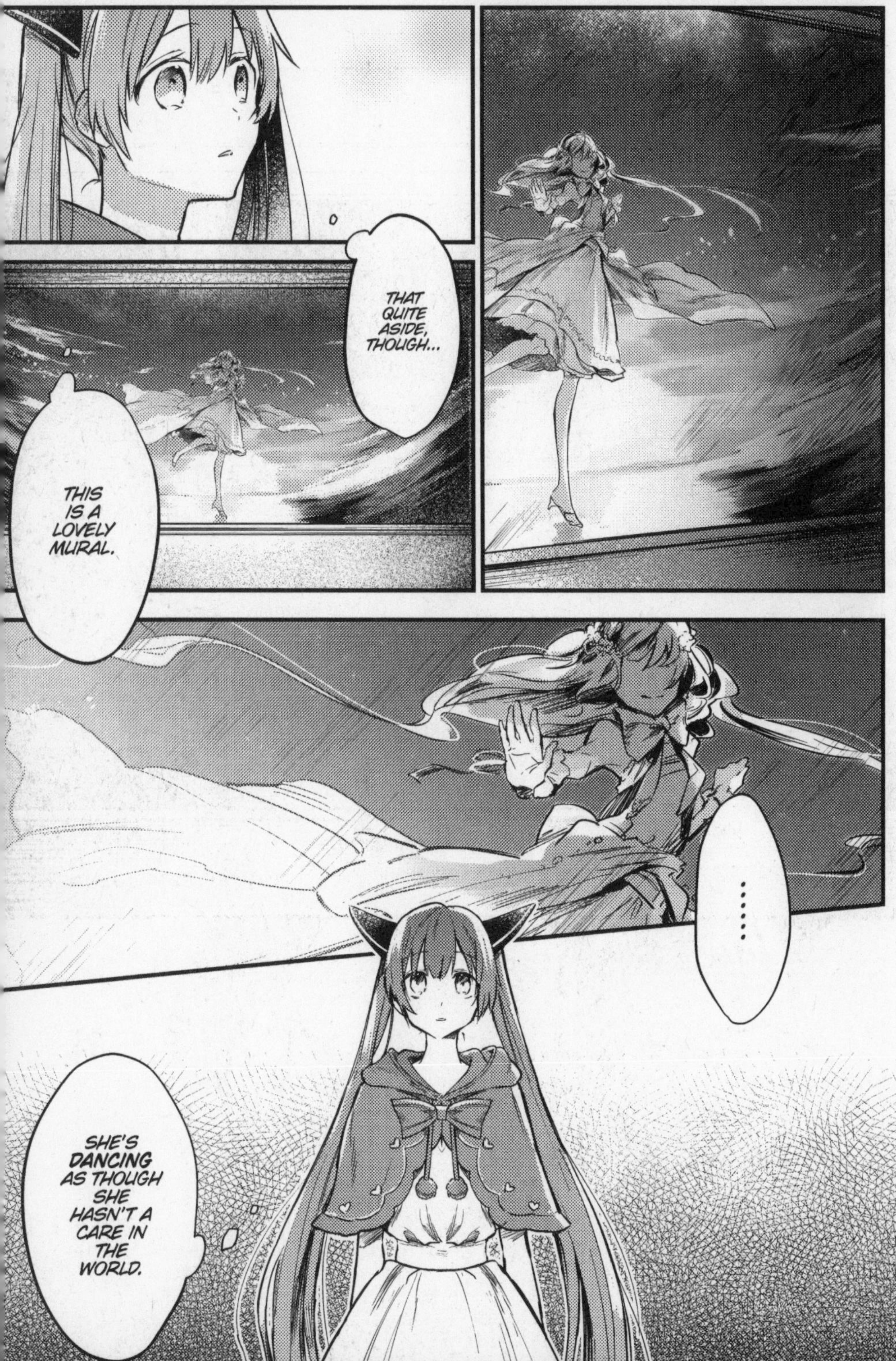
THAT QUITE ASIDE, THOUGH...
THIS IS A LOVELY MURAL.
......
SHE'S DANCING AS THOUGH SHE HASN'T A CARE IN THE WORLD.

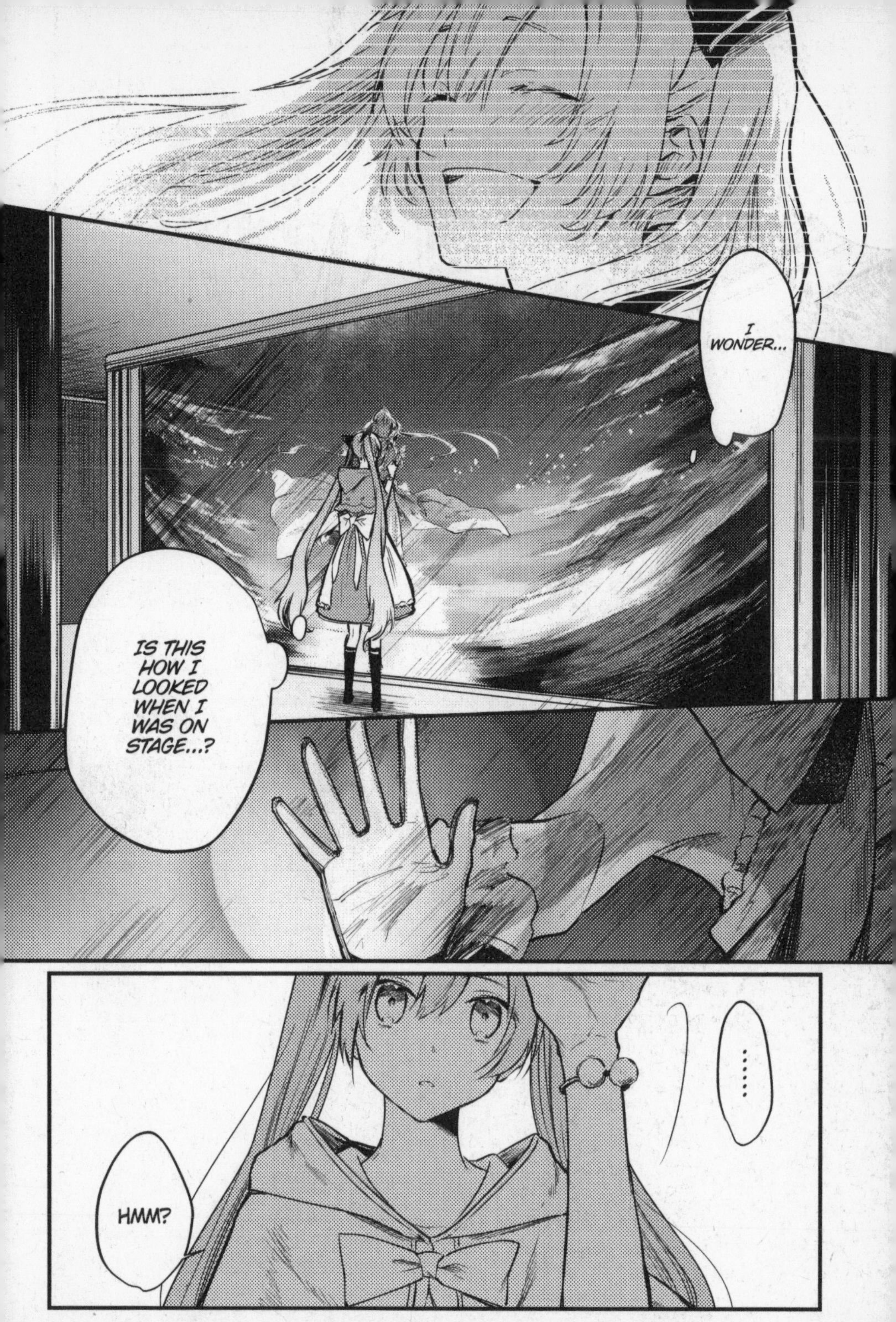
I WONDER...
IS THIS HOW I LOOKED WHEN I WAS ON STAGE...?
......
HMM?

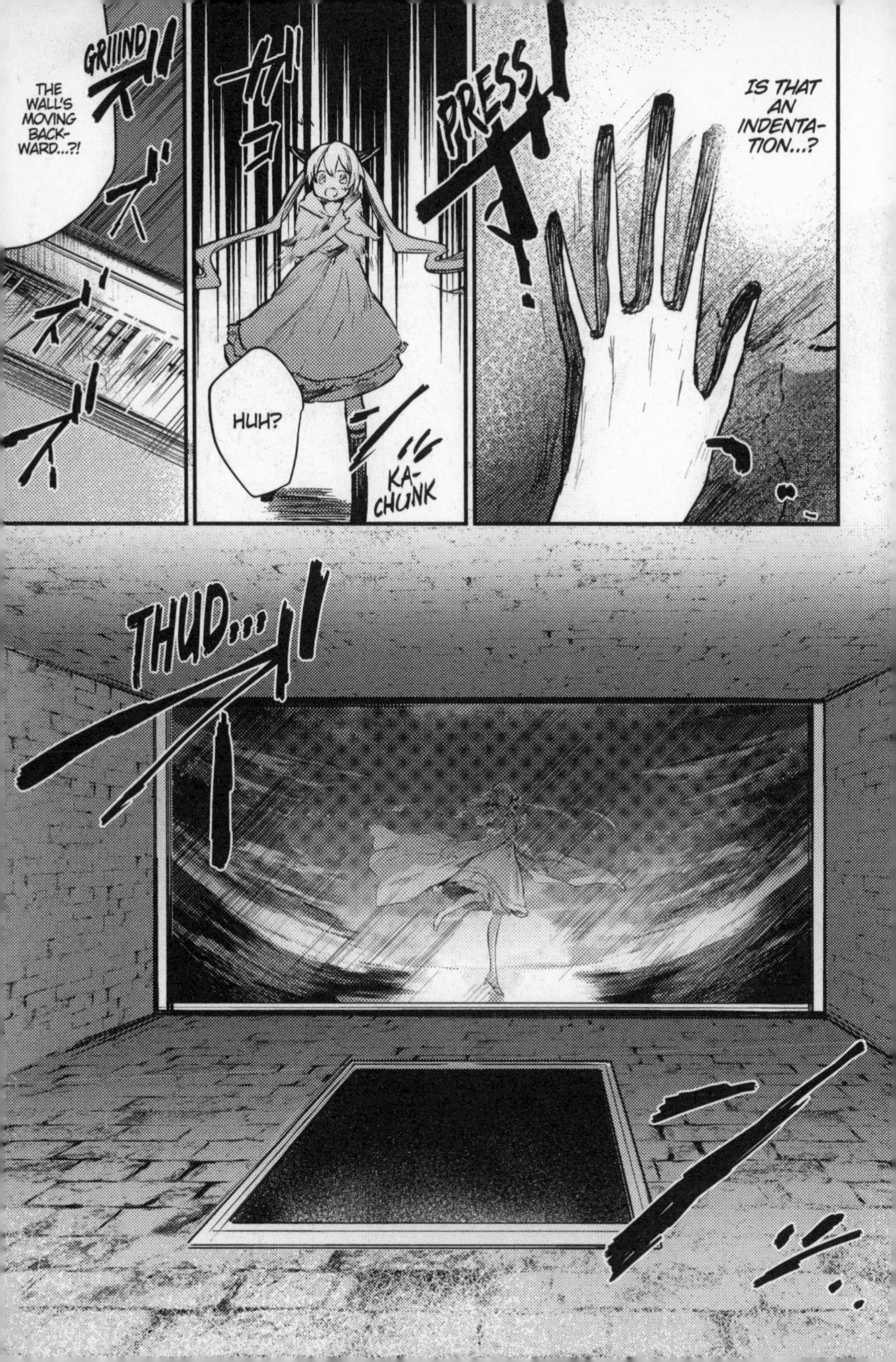
IS THAT AN INDENTATION...?
PRESS
HUH?
KA-CHUNK
GRIIIND
THE WALL'S MOVING BACKWARD...?!
THUD...

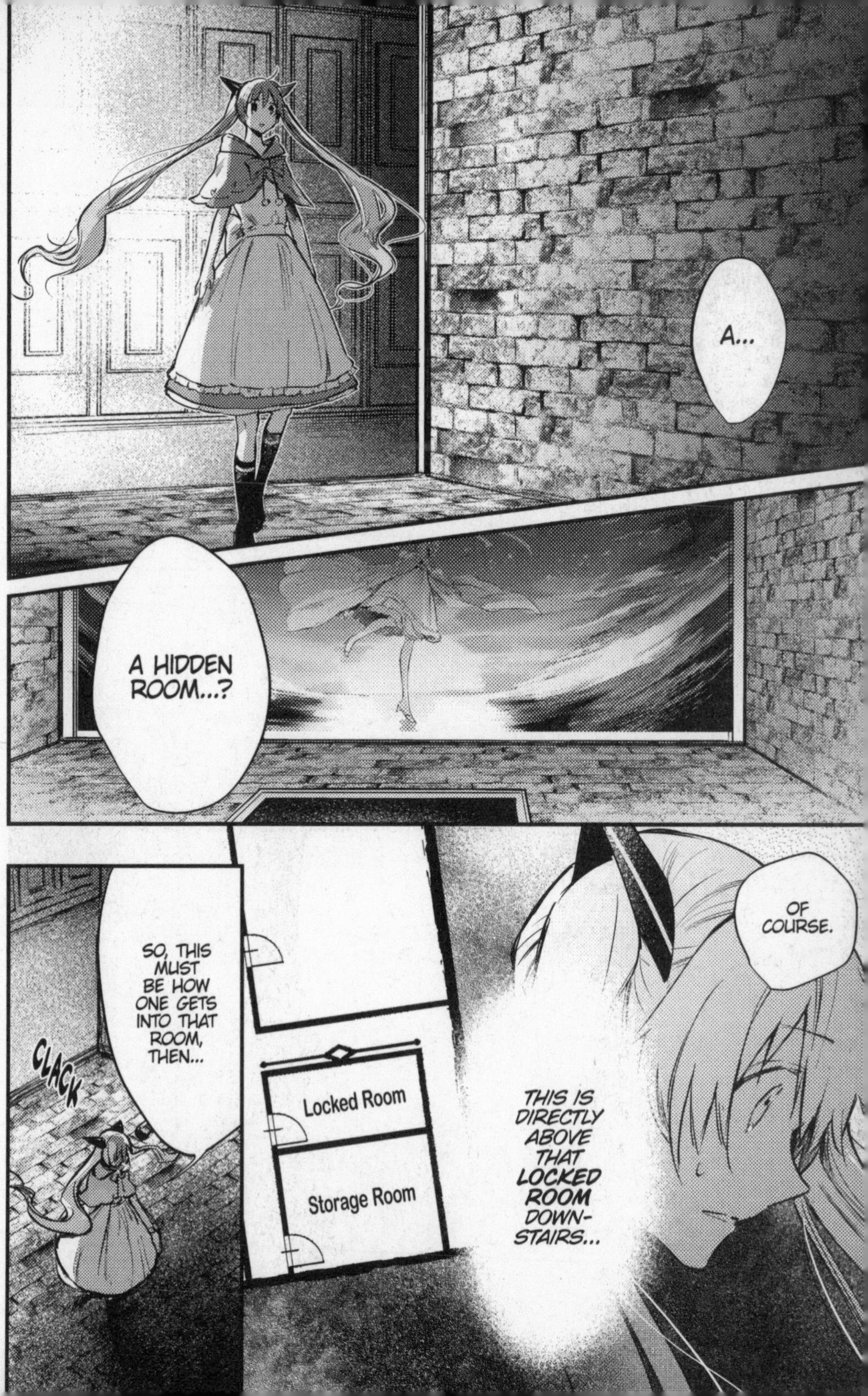
A...
A HIDDEN ROOM...?
OF COURSE.
THIS IS DIRECTLY ABOVE THAT LOCKED ROOM DOWNSTAIRS...
Locked Room
Storage Room
SO, THIS MUST BE HOW ONE GETS INTO THAT ROOM, THEN...
CLACK

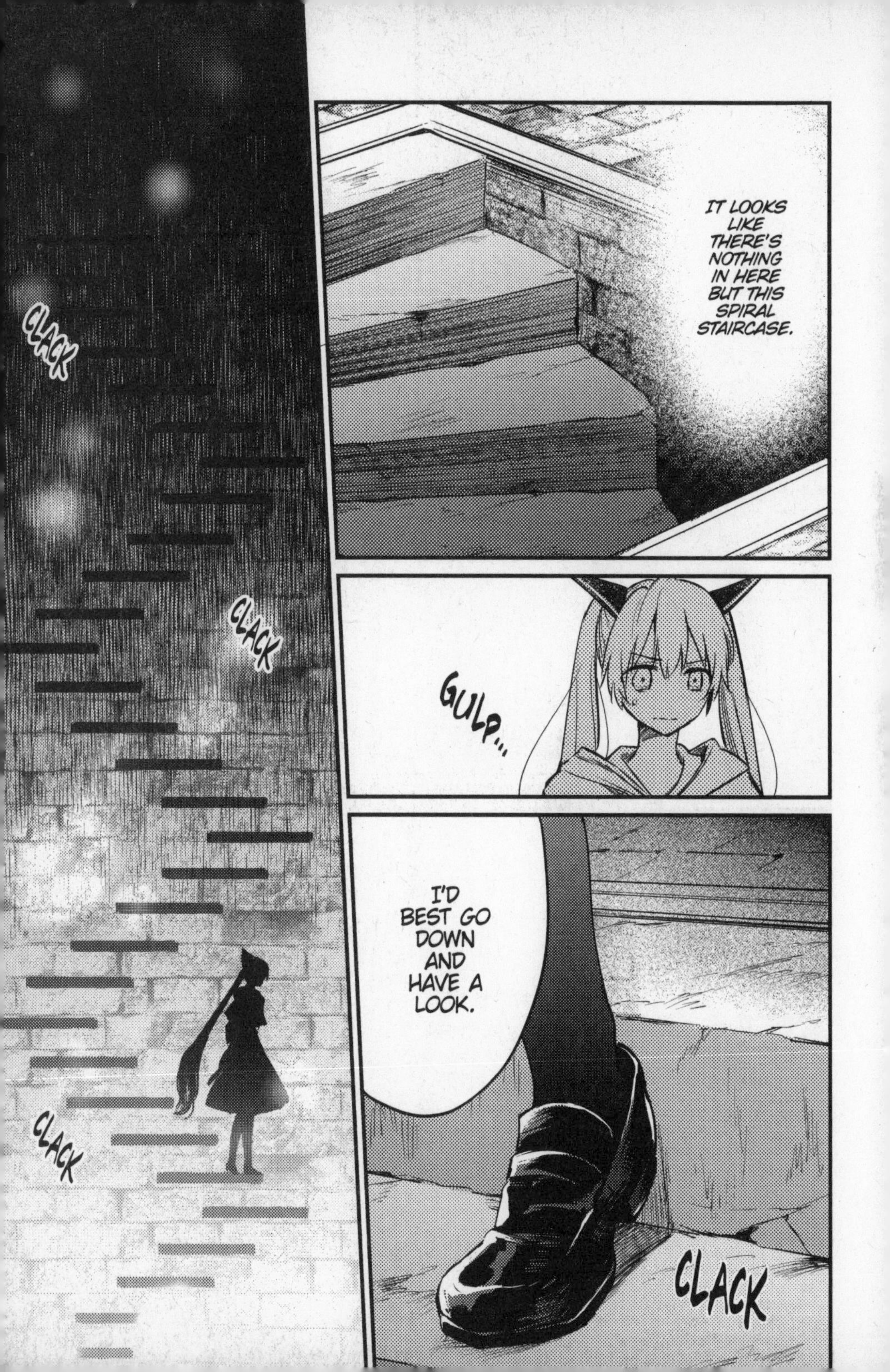
IT LOOKS LIKE THERE'S NOTHING IN HERE BUT THIS SPIRAL STAIRCASE.
GULP...
I'D BEST GO DOWN AND HAVE A LOOK.
CLACK
CLACK
CLACK
CLACK

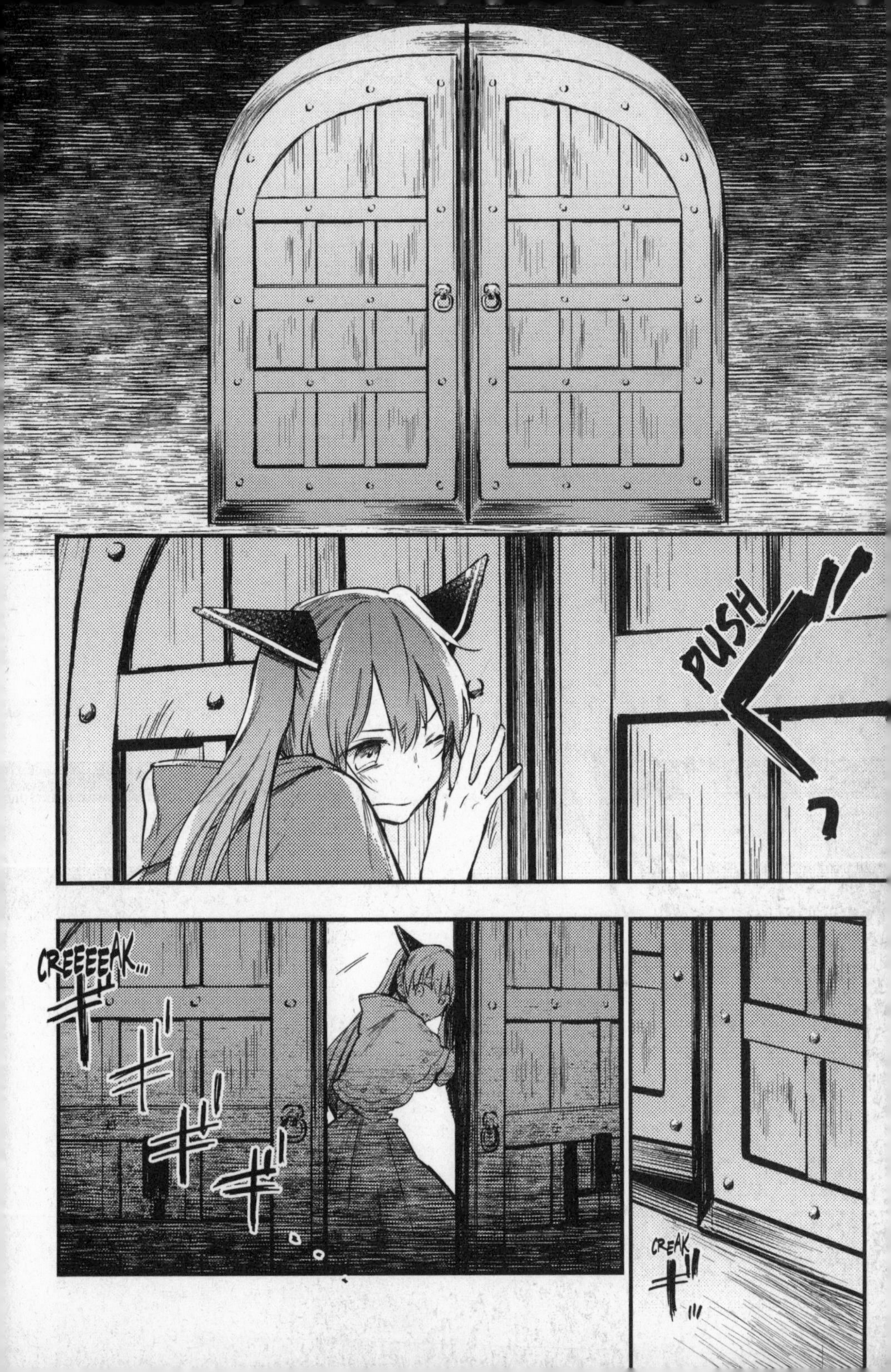
PUSH
CREAK
CREEEEAK...

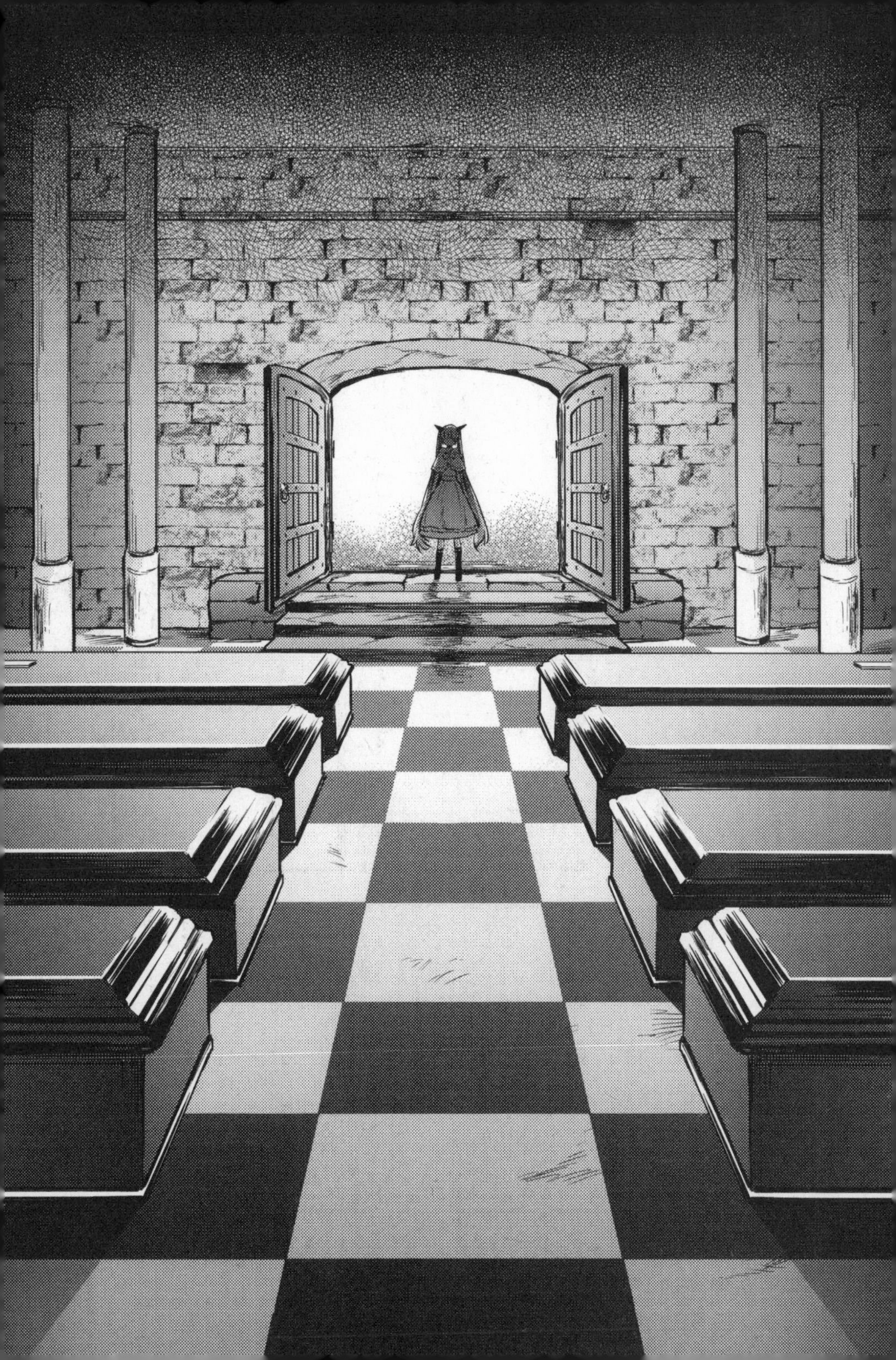

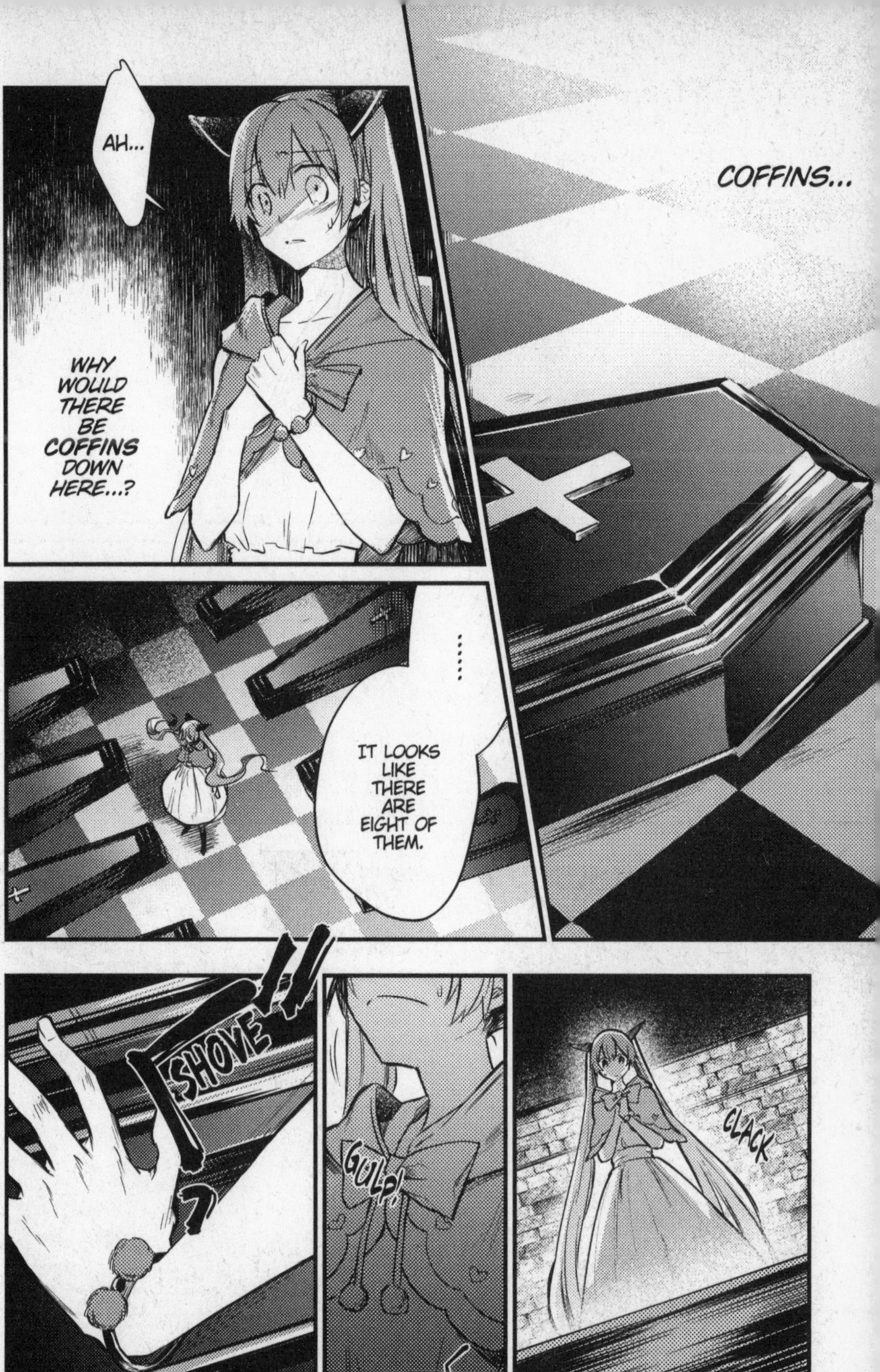
COFFINS...
AH...
WHY WOULD THERE BE COFFINS DOWN HERE...?
......
IT LOOKS LIKE THERE ARE EIGHT OF THEM.
CLACK
GULP!
SHOVE

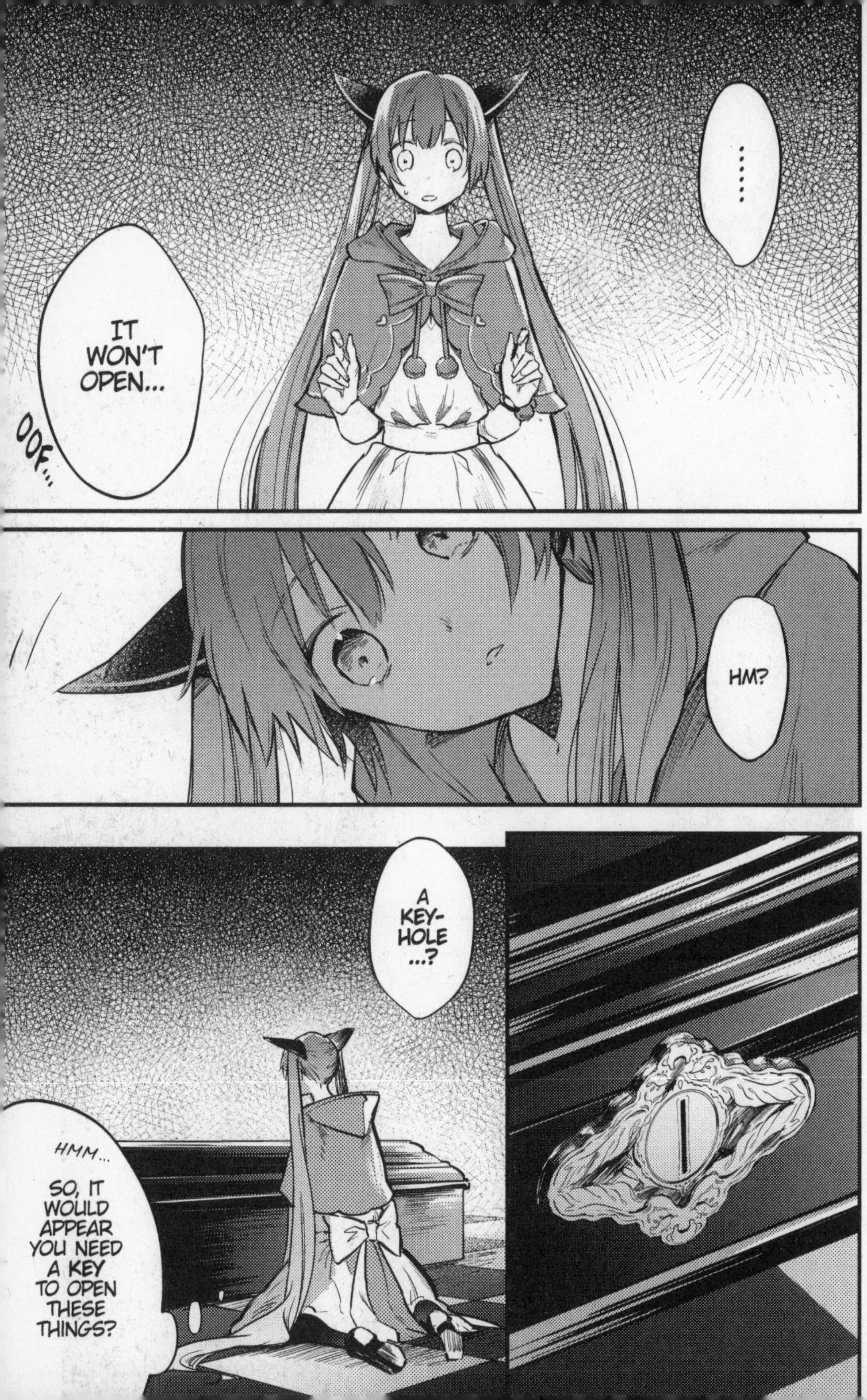
......
IT WON'T OPEN...
OOF...
HM?
A KEY-HOLE ...?
HMM...
SO, IT WOULD APPEAR YOU NEED A KEY TO OPEN THESE THINGS?

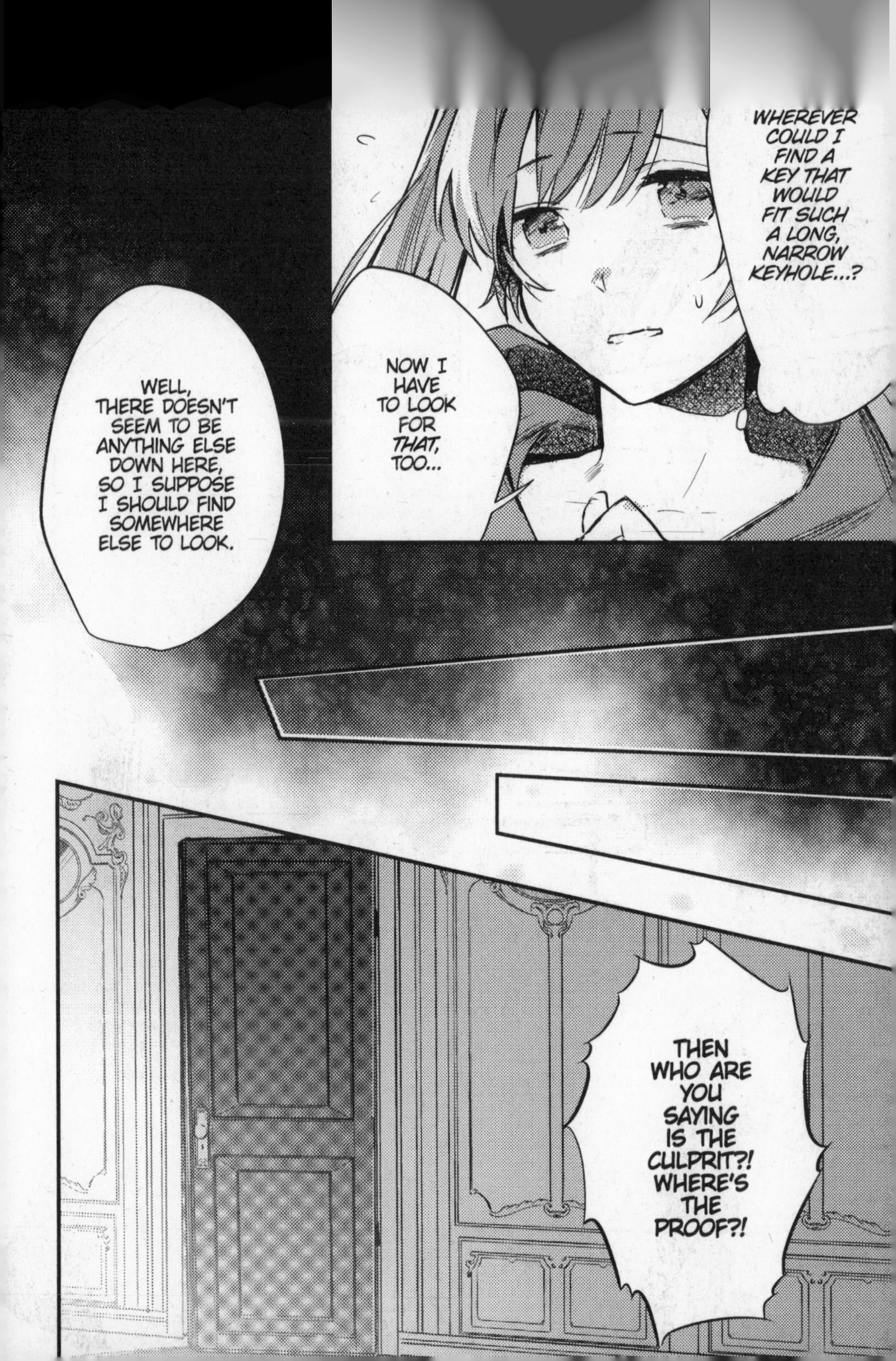
WHEREVER COULD I FIND A KEY THAT WOULD FIT SUCH A LONG, NARROW KEYHOLE...?
NOW I HAVE TO LOOK FOR THAT, TOO...
WELL, THERE DOESN'T SEEM TO BE ANYTHING ELSE DOWN HERE, SO I SUPPOSE I SHOULD FIND SOMEWHERE ELSE TO LOOK.
THEN WHO ARE YOU SAYING IS THE CULPRIT?! WHERE'S THE PROOF?!

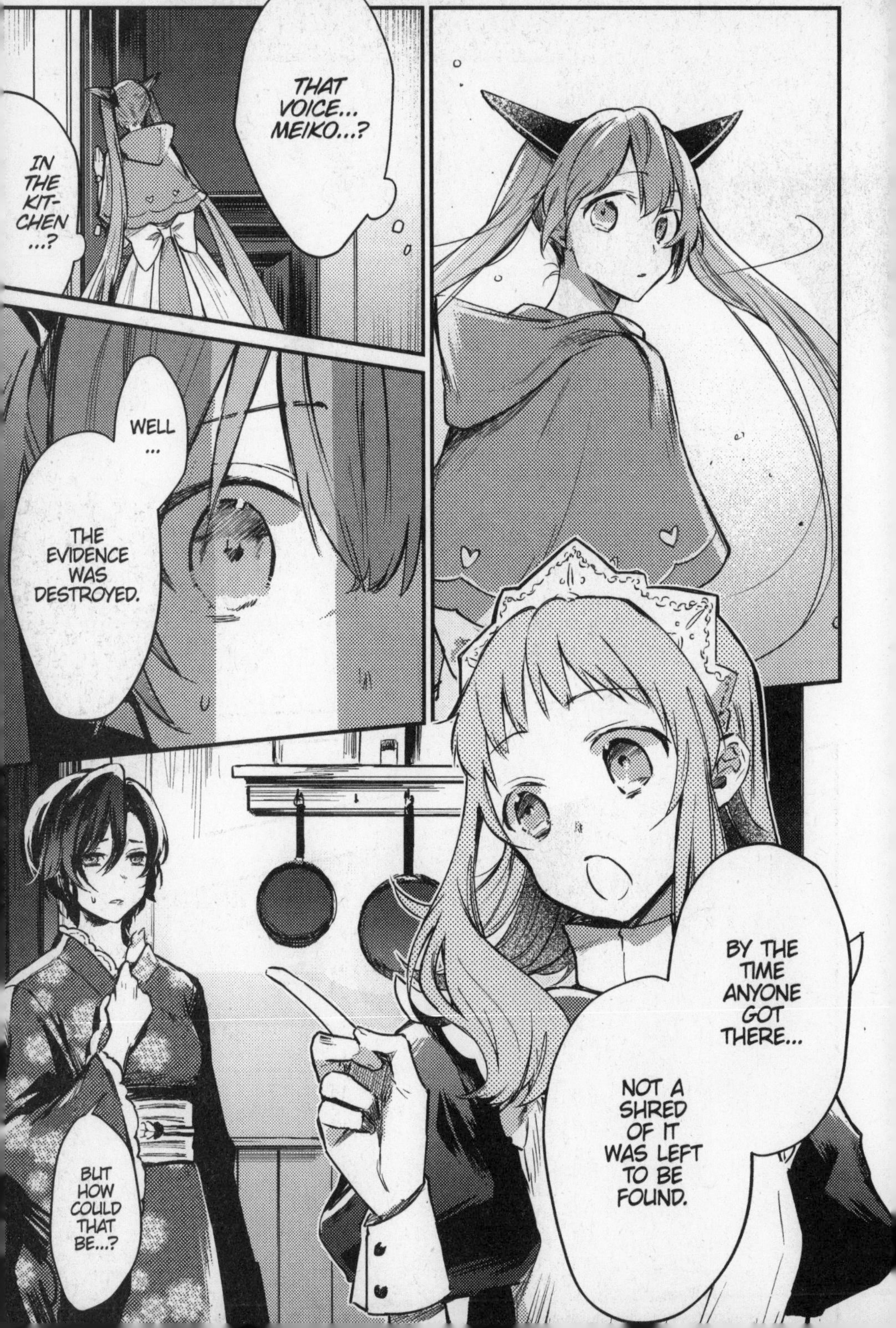
THAT VOICE... MEIKO...?
IN THE KIT-CHEN ...?
WELL ... THE EVIDENCE WAS DESTROYED.
BY THE TIME ANYONE GOT THERE...
NOT A SHRED OF IT WAS LEFT TO BE FOUND.
BUT HOW COULD THAT BE...?

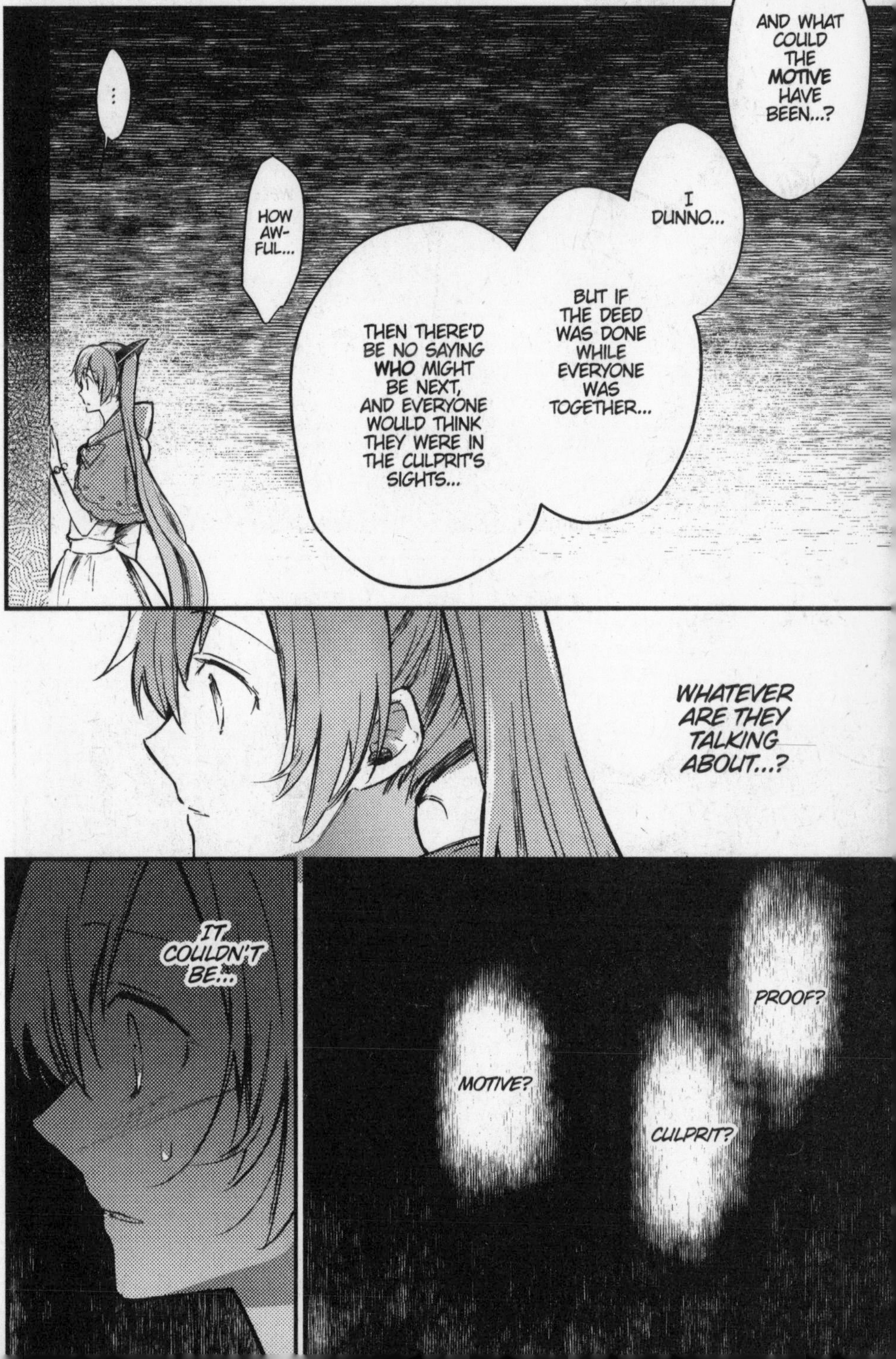
AND WHAT COULD THE MOTIVE HAVE BEEN...?
I DUNNO...
BUT IF THE DEED WAS DONE WHILE EVERYONE WAS TOGETHER...
THEN THERE'D BE NO SAYING WHO MIGHT BE NEXT, AND EVERYONE WOULD THINK THEY WERE IN THE CULPRIT'S SIGHTS...
HOW AW-FUL...
...
WHATEVER ARE THEY TALKING ABOUT...?
PROOF?
MOTIVE?
CULPRIT?
IT COULDN'T BE...

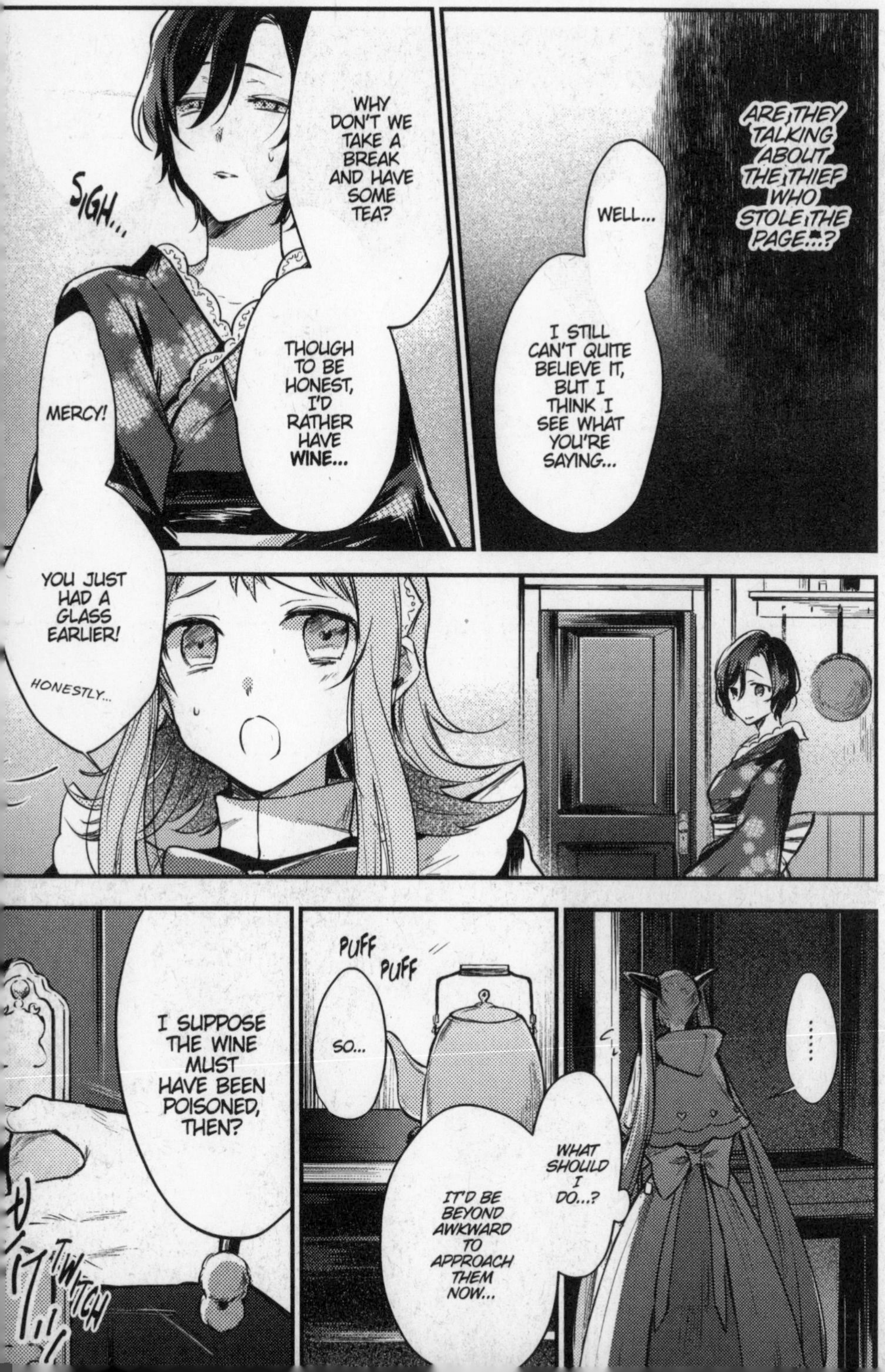
ARE THEY TALKING ABOUT THE THIEF WHO STOLE THE PAGE...?
WELL...
I STILL CAN'T QUITE BELIEVE IT, BUT I THINK I SEE WHAT YOU'RE SAYING...
WHY DON'T WE TAKE A BREAK AND HAVE SOME TEA?
THOUGH TO BE HONEST, I'D RATHER HAVE WINE...
SIGH...
MERCY!
YOU JUST HAD A GLASS EARLIER!
HONESTLY...
......
WHAT SHOULD I DO...?
IT'D BE BEYOND AWKWARD TO APPROACH THEM NOW...
PUFF
PUFF
SO...
I SUPPOSE THE WINE MUST HAVE BEEN POISONED, THEN?
TWITCH

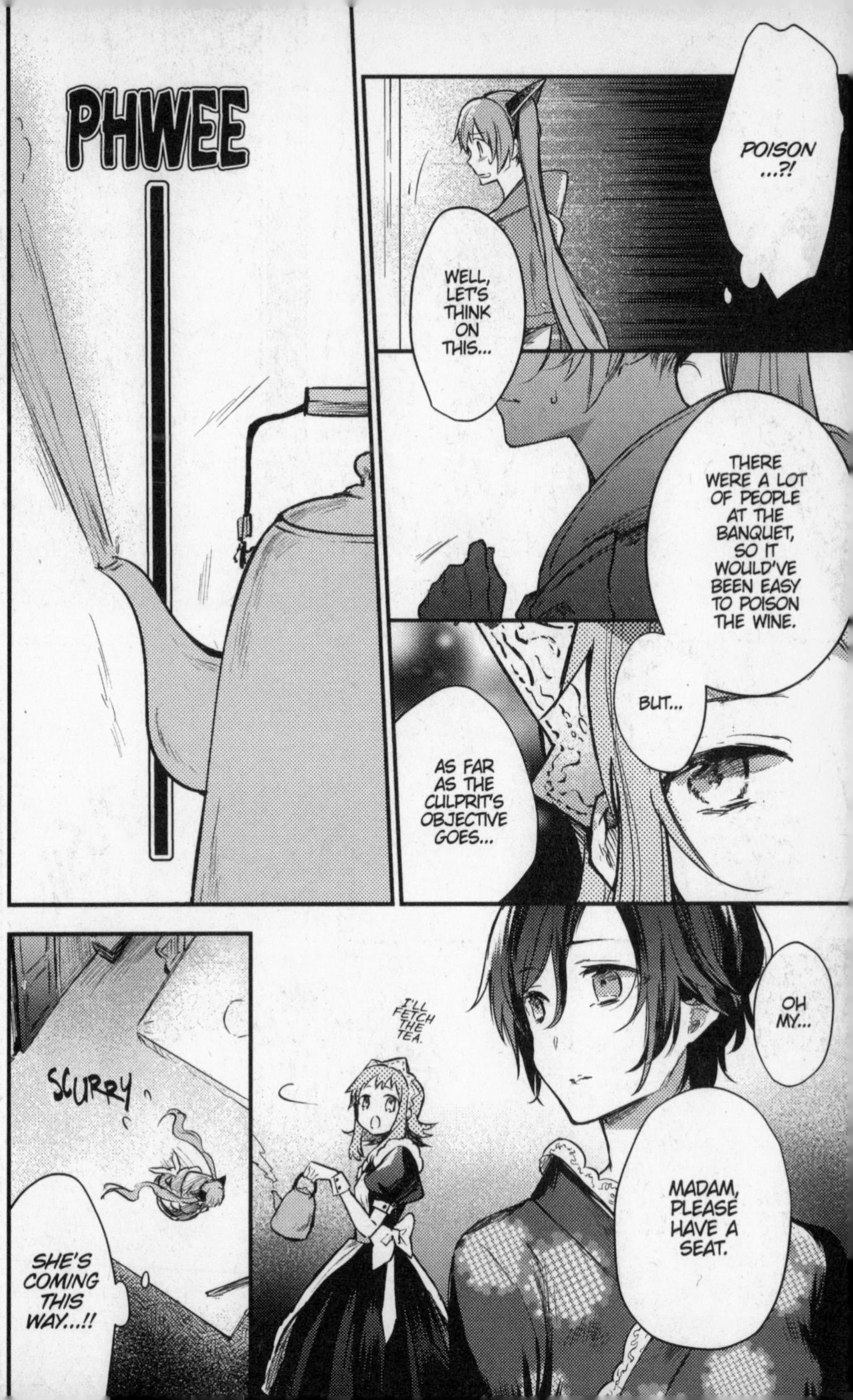
POISON ...?!
WELL, LET'S THINK ON THIS...
THERE WERE A LOT OF PEOPLE AT THE BANQUET, SO IT WOULD'VE BEEN EASY TO POISON THE WINE.
BUT...
AS FAR AS THE CULPRIT'S OBJECTIVE GOES...
PHWEE
OH MY...
MADAM, PLEASE HAVE A SEAT.
I'LL FETCH THE TEA.
SCURRY
SHE'S COMING THIS WAY...!!

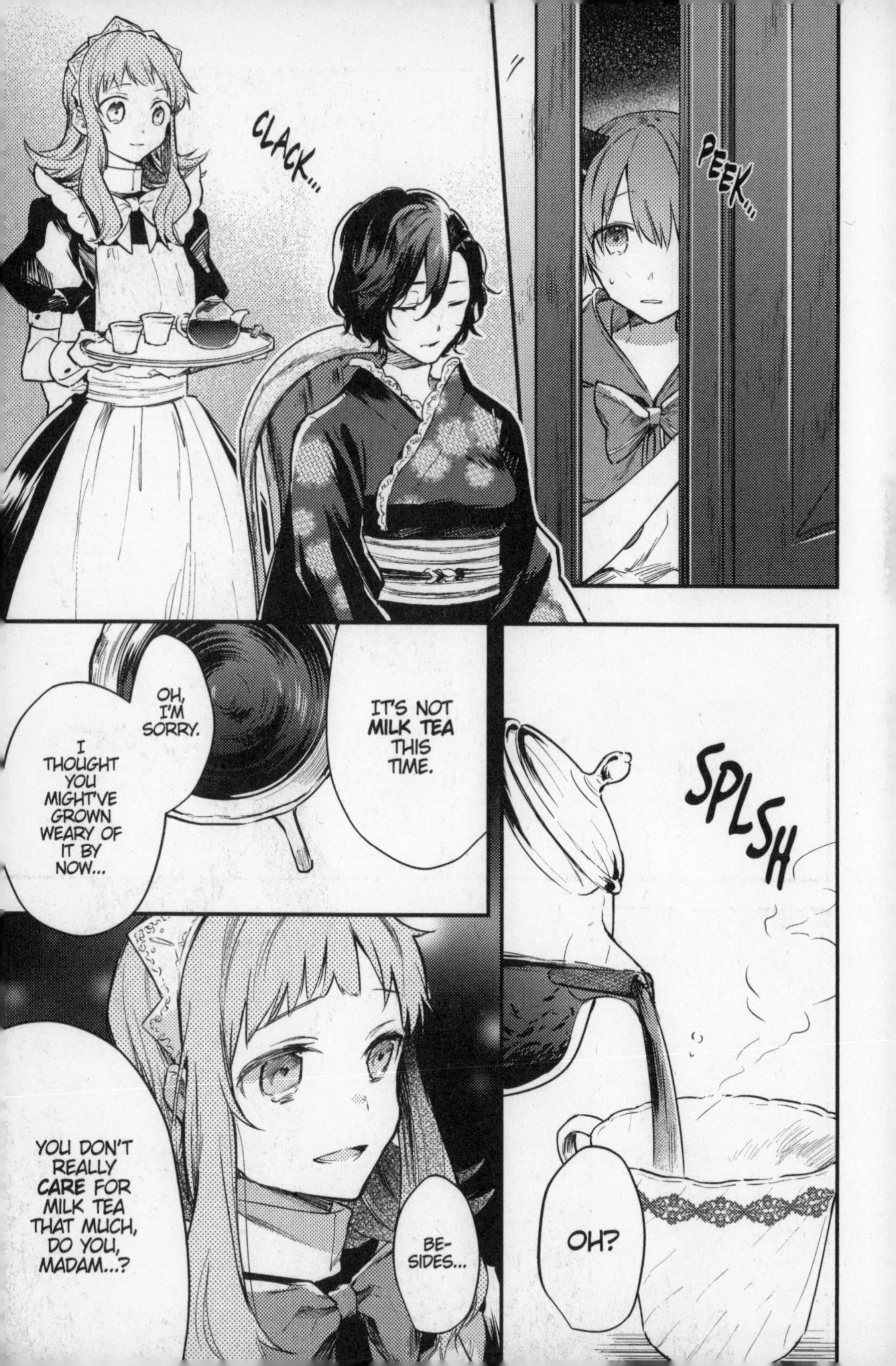
PEEK...
CLACK...
SPLSH
OH?
IT'S NOT MILK TEA THIS TIME.
OH, I'M SORRY.
I THOUGHT YOU MIGHT'VE GROWN WEARY OF IT BY NOW...
BE-SIDES...
YOU DON'T REALLY CARE FOR MILK TEA THAT MUCH, DO YOU, MADAM...?

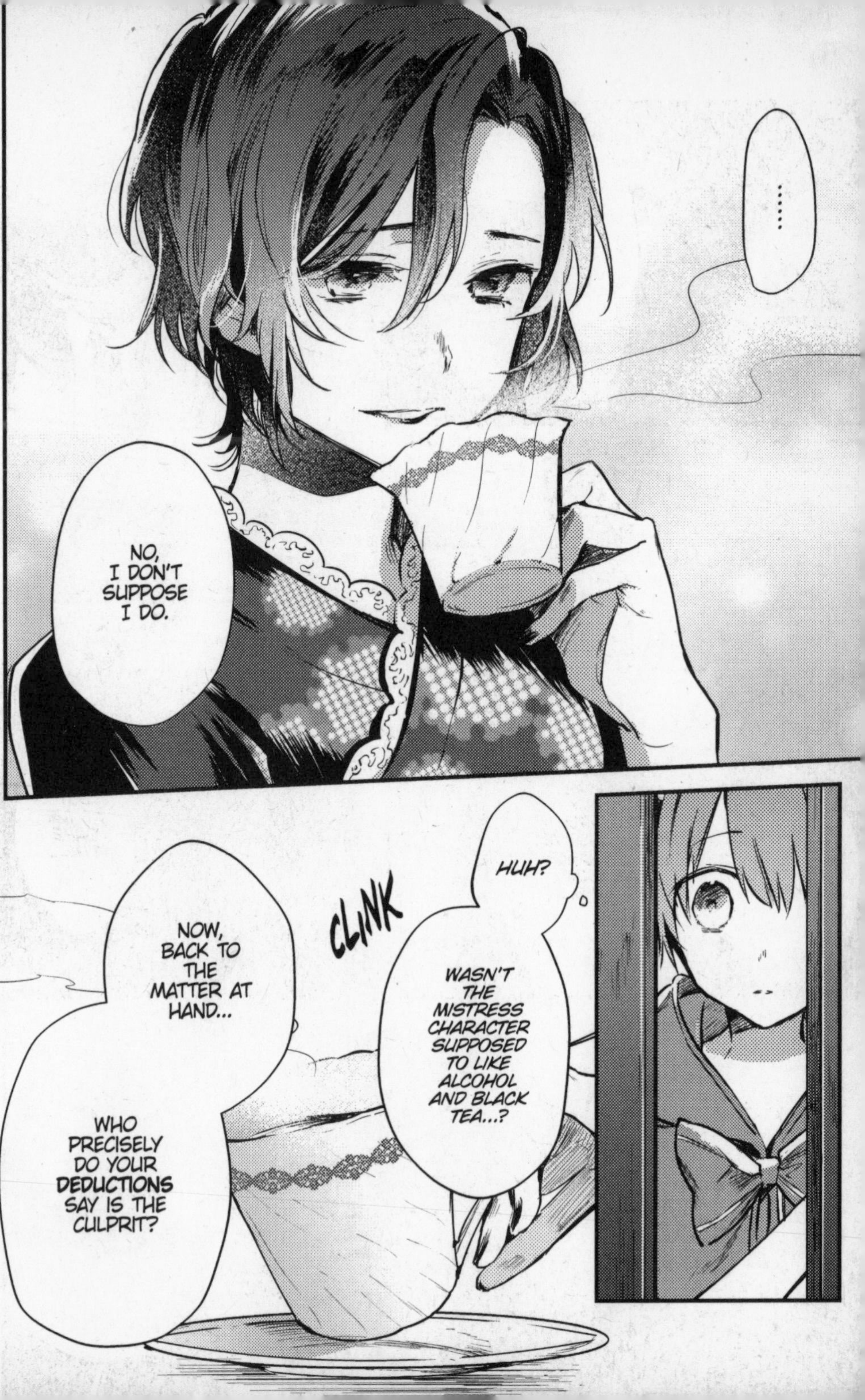
......
NO, I DON'T SUPPOSE I DO.
HUH?
WASN'T THE MISTRESS CHARACTER SUPPOSED TO LIKE ALCOHOL AND BLACK TEA...?
CLINK
NOW, BACK TO THE MATTER AT HAND...
WHO PRECISELY DO YOUR DEDUCTIONS SAY IS THE CULPRIT?

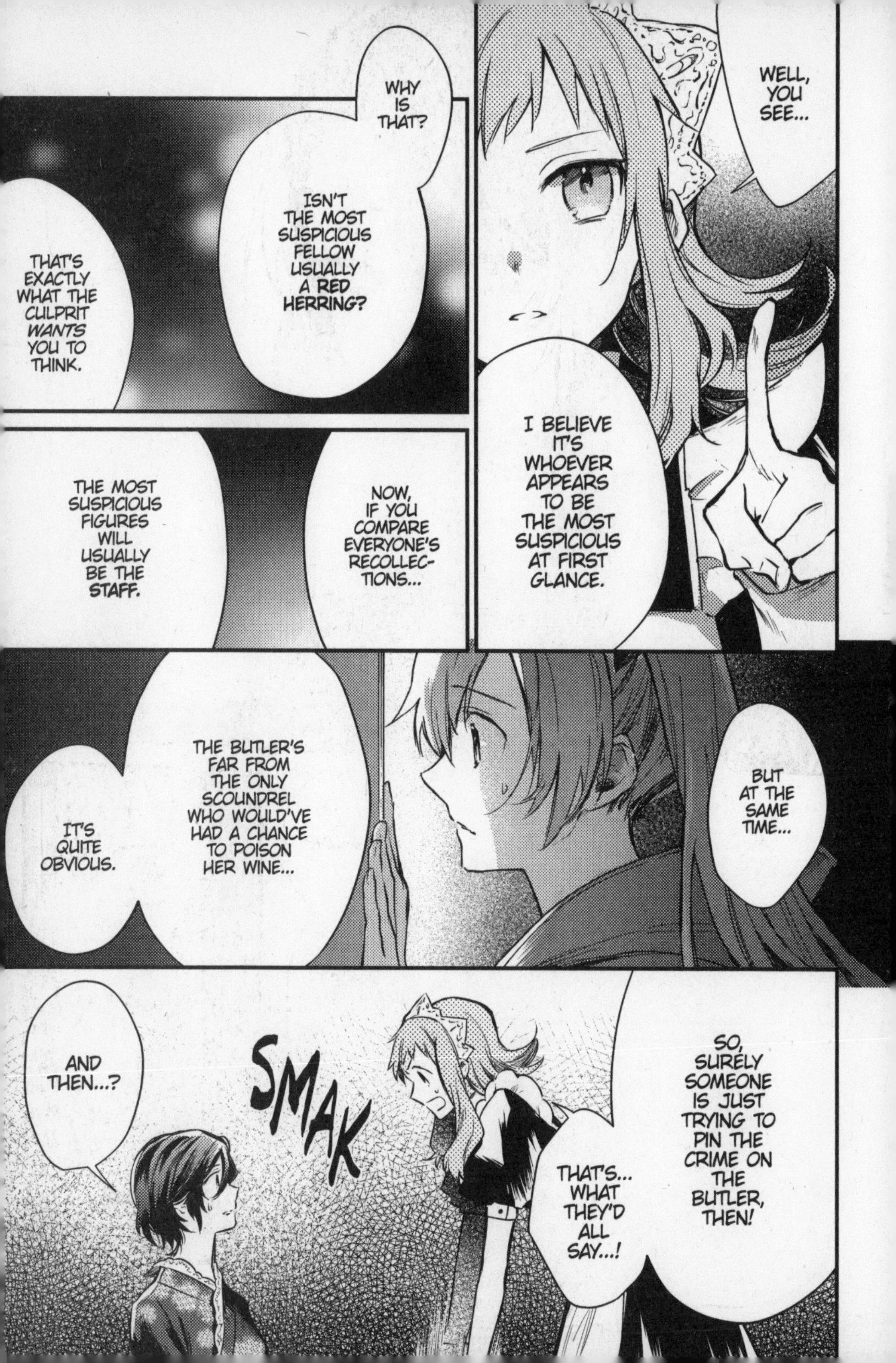

WELL, YOU SEE...
I BELIEVE IT'S WHOEVER APPEARS TO BE THE MOST SUSPICIOUS AT FIRST GLANCE.
WHY IS THAT?
ISN'T THE MOST SUSPICIOUS FELLOW USUALLY A **RED HERRING?**
THAT'S EXACTLY WHAT THE CULPRIT *WANTS* YOU TO THINK.
NOW, IF YOU COMPARE EVERYONE'S RECOLLECTIONS...
THE MOST SUSPICIOUS FIGURES WILL USUALLY BE THE **STAFF.**
BUT AT THE SAME TIME...
THE BUTLER'S FAR FROM THE ONLY SCOUNDREL WHO WOULD'VE HAD A CHANCE TO POISON HER WINE...
IT'S QUITE OBVIOUS.
SO, SURELY SOMEONE IS JUST TRYING TO PIN THE CRIME ON THE BUTLER, THEN!
THAT'S... WHAT THEY'D ALL SAY...!
SMAK
AND THEN...?

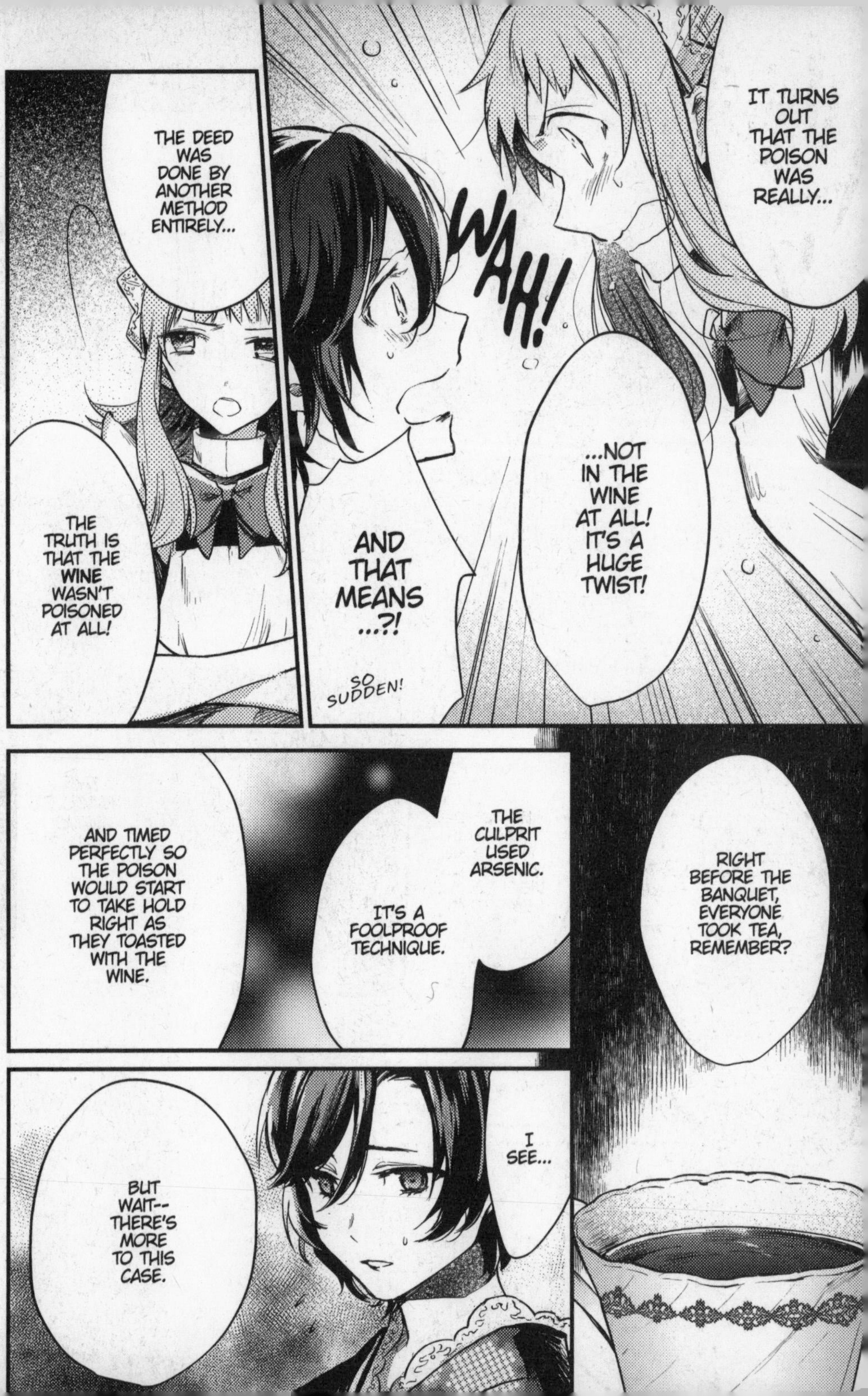
IT TURNS OUT THAT THE POISON WAS REALLY...
WAH!
...NOT IN THE WINE AT ALL! IT'S A HUGE TWIST!
AND THAT MEANS ...?!
SO SUDDEN!
THE DEED WAS DONE BY ANOTHER METHOD ENTIRELY...
THE TRUTH IS THAT THE WINE WASN'T POISONED AT ALL!
RIGHT BEFORE THE BANQUET, EVERYONE TOOK TEA, REMEMBER?
THE CULPRIT USED ARSENIC.
IT'S A FOOLPROOF TECHNIQUE.
AND TIMED PERFECTLY SO THE POISON WOULD START TO TAKE HOLD RIGHT AS THEY TOASTED WITH THE WINE.
I SEE...
BUT WAIT-- THERE'S MORE TO THIS CASE.

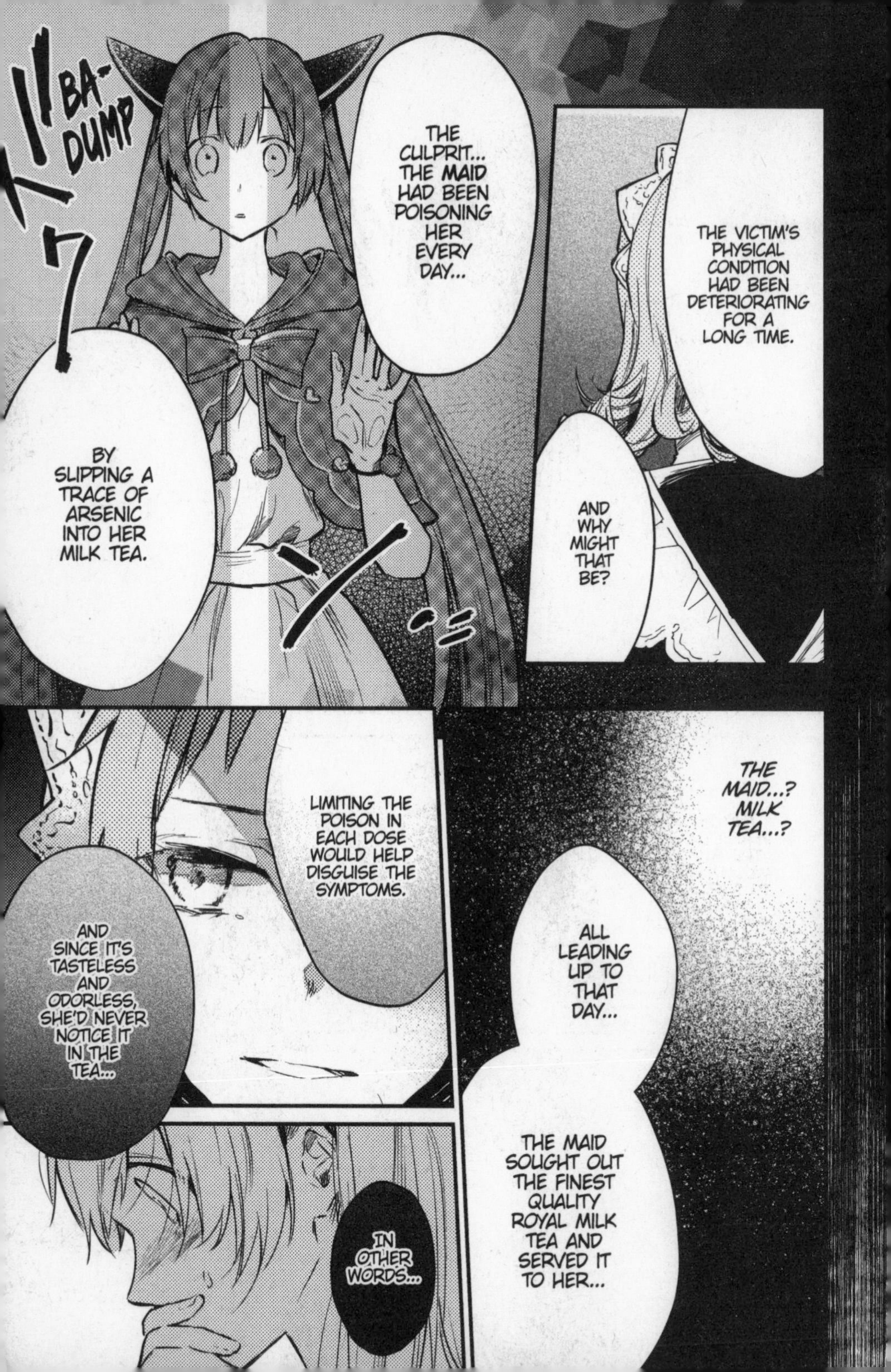
THE VICTIM'S PHYSICAL CONDITION HAD BEEN DETERIORATING FOR A LONG TIME.
AND WHY MIGHT THAT BE?
BA-DUMP
THE CULPRIT... THE MAID HAD BEEN POISONING HER EVERY DAY...
BY SLIPPING A TRACE OF ARSENIC INTO HER MILK TEA.
THE MAID...? MILK TEA...?
ALL LEADING UP TO THAT DAY...
THE MAID SOUGHT OUT THE FINEST QUALITY ROYAL MILK TEA AND SERVED IT TO HER...
LIMITING THE POISON IN EACH DOSE WOULD HELP DISGUISE THE SYMPTOMS.
AND SINCE IT'S TASTELESS AND ODORLESS, SHE'D NEVER NOTICE IT IN THE TEA...
IN OTHER WORDS...

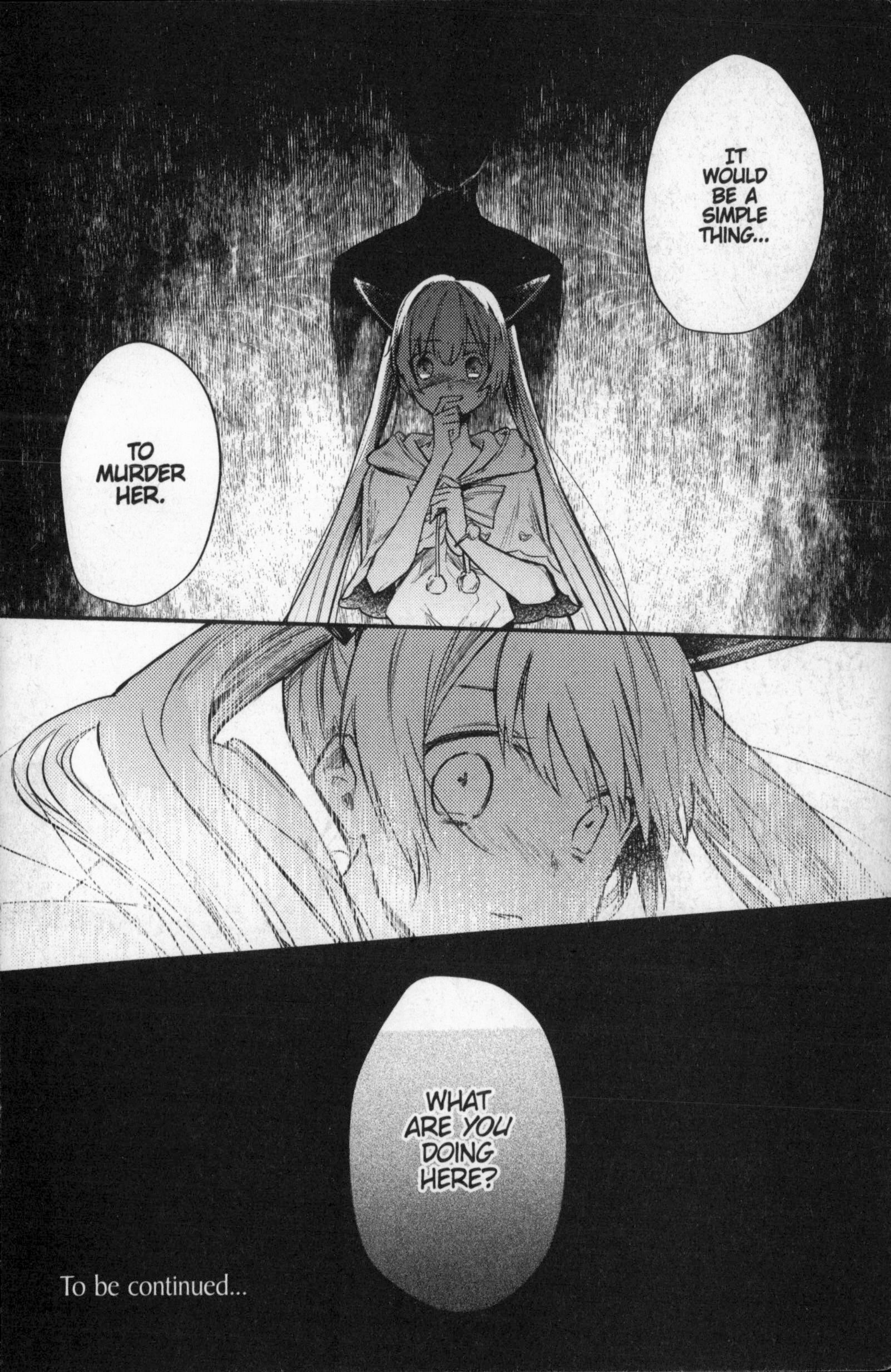
IT WOULD BE A SIMPLE THING...
TO MURDER HER.
WHAT ARE YOU DOING HERE?
To be continued...

MY FIRST SERIALIZATION,
AND MY FIRST MANGA!

IT WAS ONLY ABLE TO TAKE
SHAPE THANKS TO THE
HELP I RECEIVED FROM A
LOT OF PEOPLE.
REALLY, THANK YOU SO MUCH...!

I'VE ALWAYS LOVED THE SONG,
"BAD∞END∞NIGHT," AND
LISTENED TO IT OFTEN EVEN
BEFORE I STARTED THIS MANGA.
SO I REALLY ENJOYED DRAWING
EACH AND EVERY CHAPTER!

SO FUN!

WHEE!

I HOPE THAT I'M ABLE TO
CONVEY THE FEELINGS OF THE
SONG'S WORLD TO EVERYONE
THROUGH THIS MANGA.

WELL, SEE YOU NEXT VOLUME!

TSUBATA NOZAKI

Special Thanks

HITOSHIZUKU-P-SAN
GOTOU-SAN
SAYURI MONE-SAN
SHIN-SAN

SUSUNOSUKE-SAN
ABE-SAN
ERUBO-SAN
CHIYO ORIGAMI-SAN

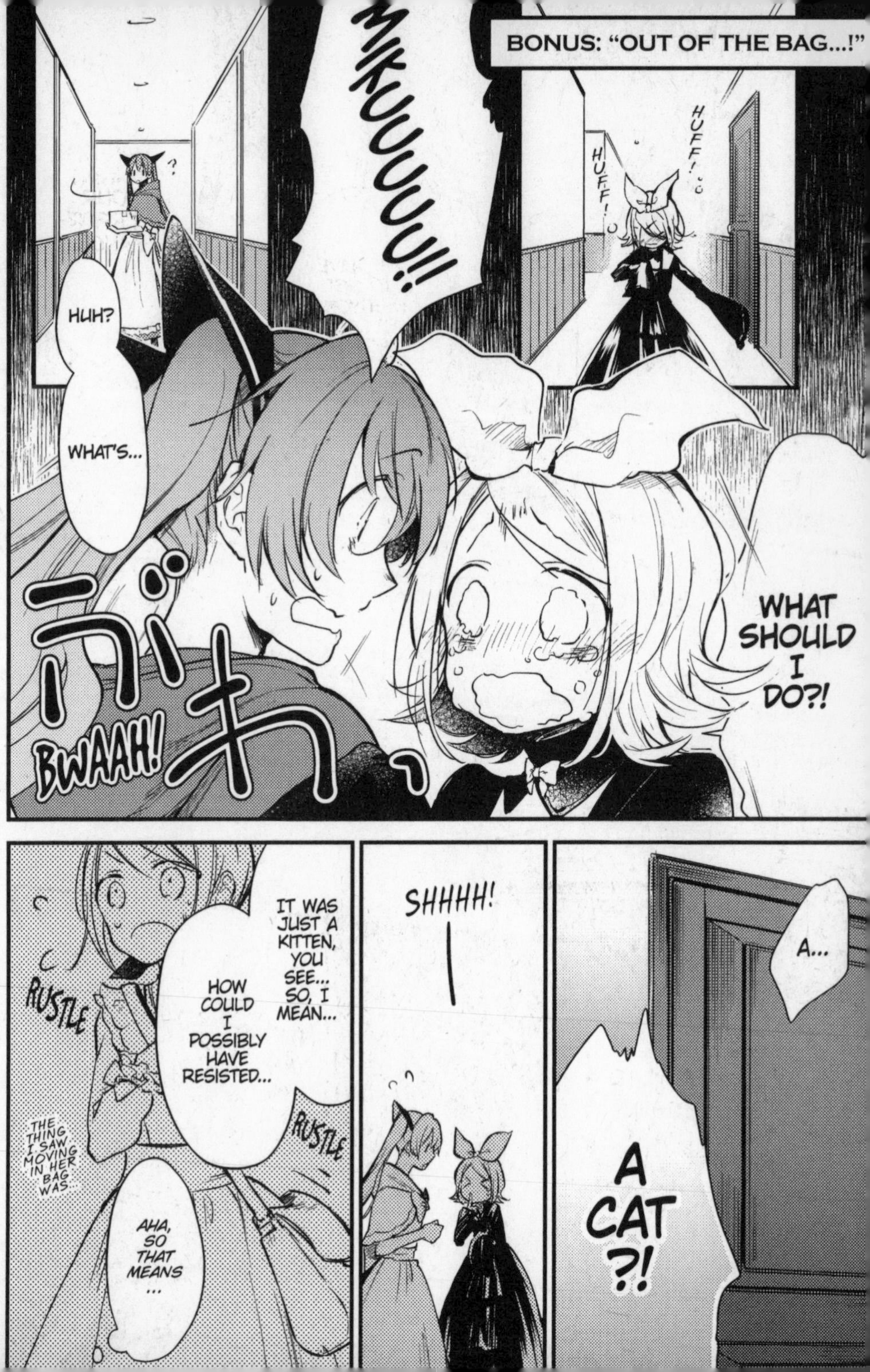
BONUS: "OUT OF THE BAG...!"
HUFF! HUFF!...
MIKUUUUUU!!!
?
HUH?
WHAT'S...
WHAT SHOULD I DO?!
ぶわっ
BWAAH!
A...
A CAT?!
SHHHH!
IT WAS JUST A KITTEN, YOU SEE... SO, I MEAN...
HOW COULD I POSSIBLY HAVE RESISTED...
RUSTLE
RUSTLE
THE THING I SAW MOVING IN HER BAG WAS...
AHA, SO THAT MEANS...

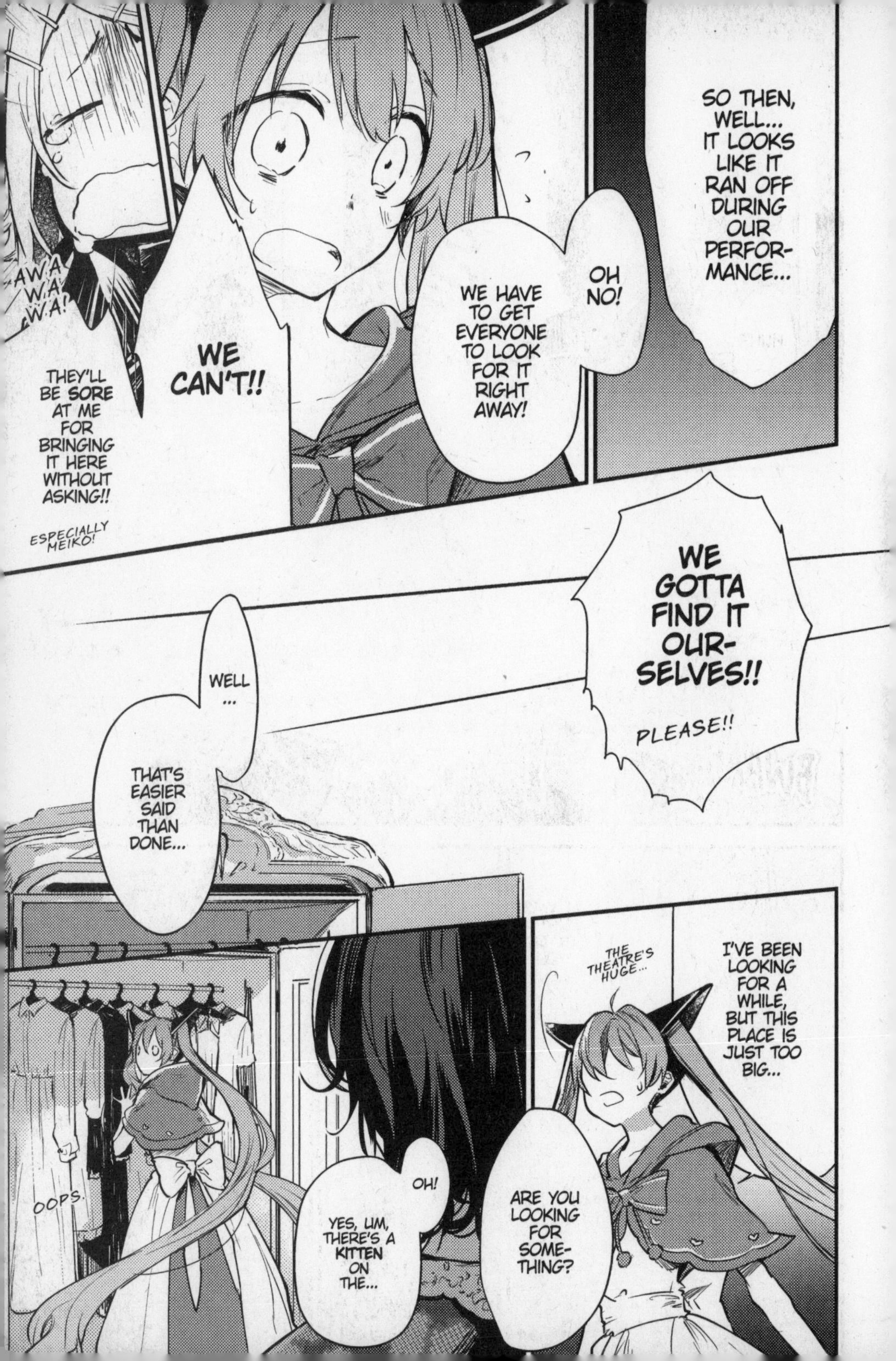
SO THEN, WELL... IT LOOKS LIKE IT RAN OFF DURING OUR PERFORMANCE...
OH NO!
WE HAVE TO GET EVERYONE TO LOOK FOR IT RIGHT AWAY!
WE CAN'T!!
AWA WA WA!
THEY'LL BE SORE AT ME FOR BRINGING IT HERE WITHOUT ASKING!!
ESPECIALLY MEIKO!
WE GOTTA FIND IT OUR-SELVES!!
PLEASE!!
WELL ...
THAT'S EASIER SAID THAN DONE...
I'VE BEEN LOOKING FOR A WHILE, BUT THIS PLACE IS JUST TOO BIG...
THE THEATRE'S HUGE...
ARE YOU LOOKING FOR SOME-THING?
OH!
YES, UM, THERE'S A KITTEN ON THE...
OOPS.

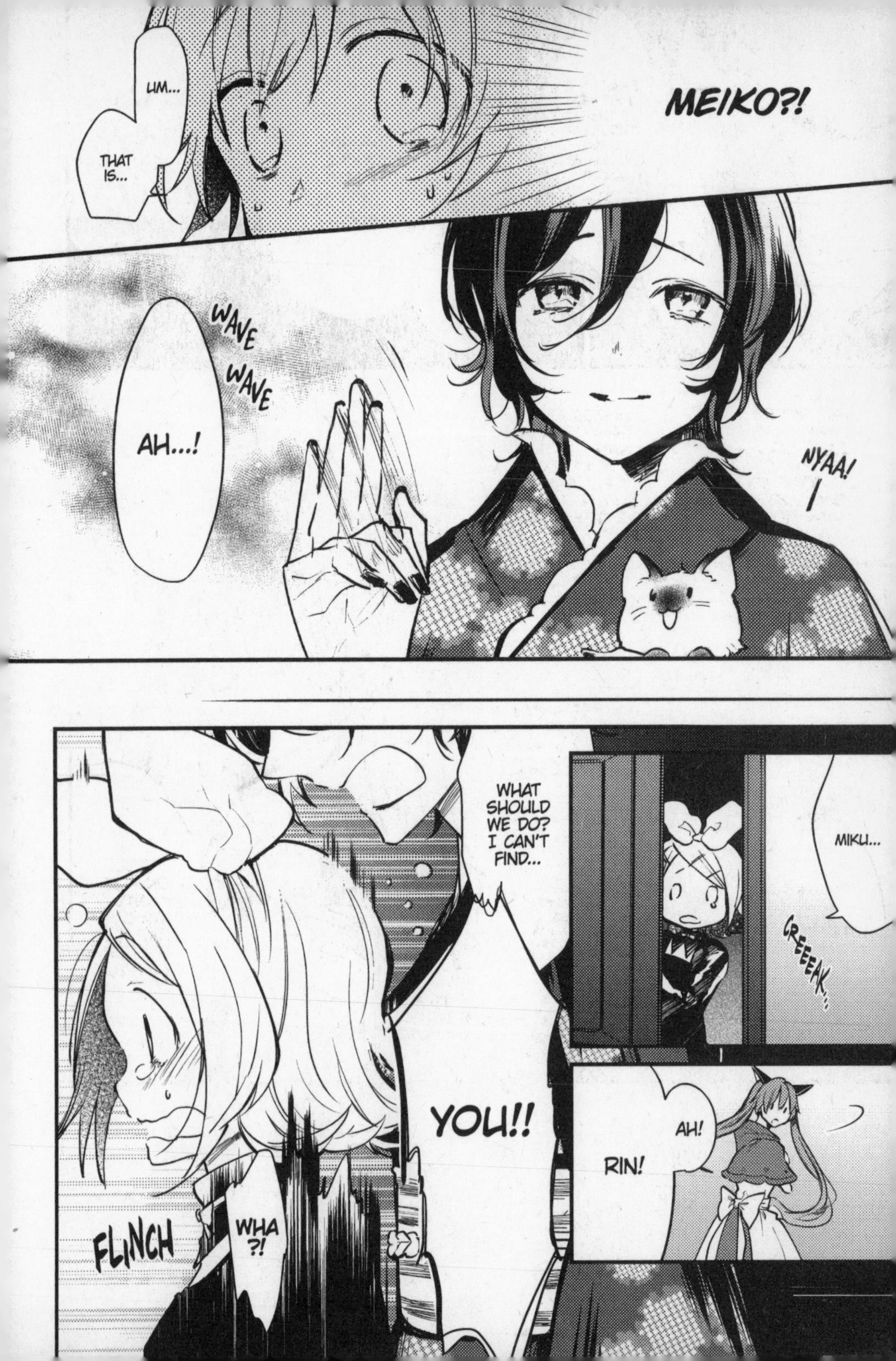
MEIKO?!
UM...
THAT IS...
NYAA!
WAVE WAVE
AH...!
MIKU...
CREEEAK...
AH!
RIN!
WHAT SHOULD WE DO? I CAN'T FIND...
YOU!!
WHA?!
FLINCH

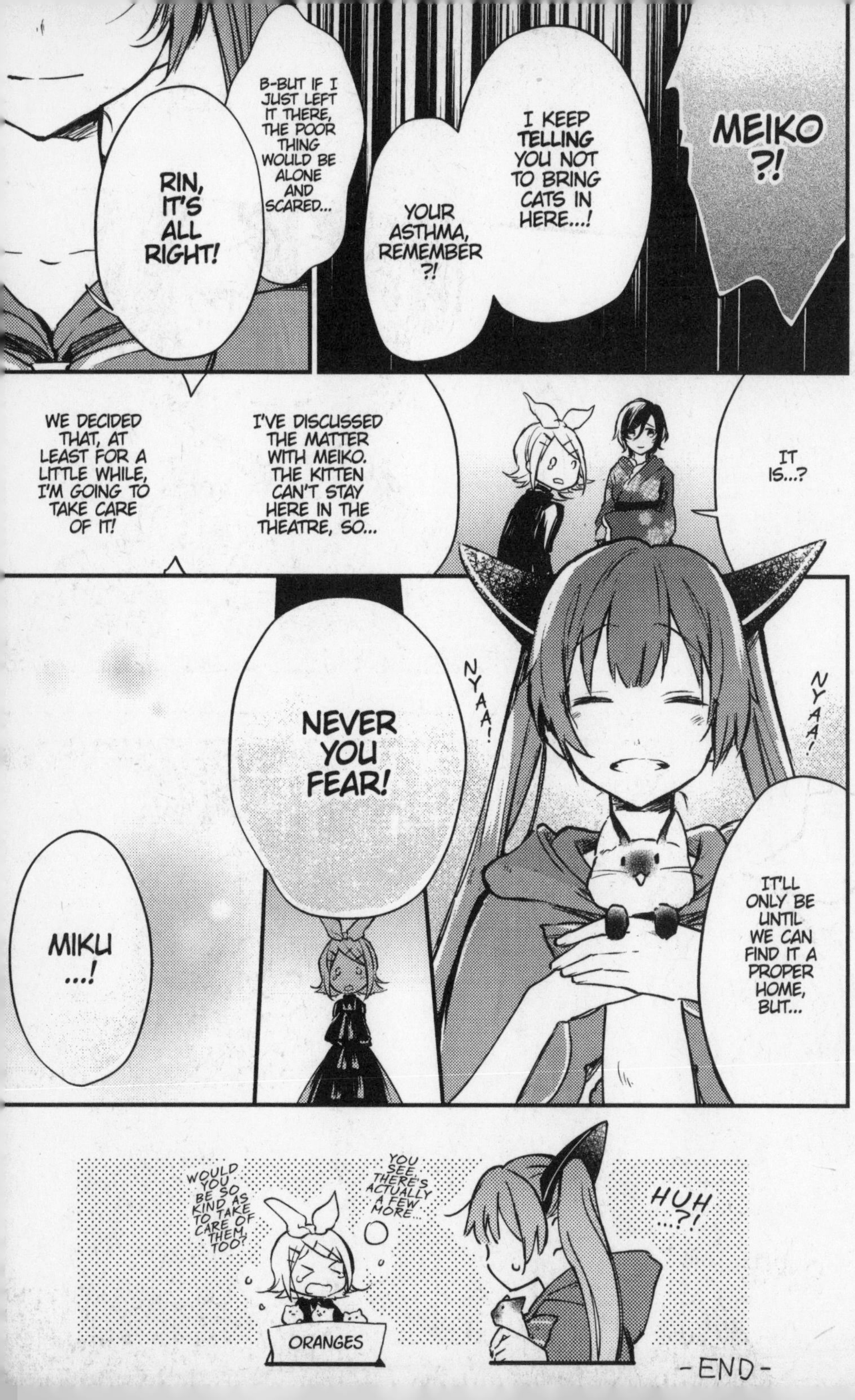
MEIKO ?!
I KEEP TELLING YOU NOT TO BRING CATS IN HERE...!
YOUR ASTHMA, REMEMBER ?!
B-BUT IF I JUST LEFT IT THERE, THE POOR THING WOULD BE ALONE AND SCARED...
RIN, IT'S ALL RIGHT!
IT IS...?
I'VE DISCUSSED THE MATTER WITH MEIKO. THE KITTEN CAN'T STAY HERE IN THE THEATRE, SO...
WE DECIDED THAT, AT LEAST FOR A LITTLE WHILE, I'M GOING TO TAKE CARE OF IT!
NYAA!
NYAA!
IT'LL ONLY BE UNTIL WE CAN FIND IT A PROPER HOME, BUT...
NEVER YOU FEAR!
MIKU ...!
HUH ...?!
YOU SEE, THERE'S ACTUALLY A FEW MORE...
WOULD YOU BE SO KIND AS TO TAKE CARE OF THEM, TOO?
ORANGES
-END-

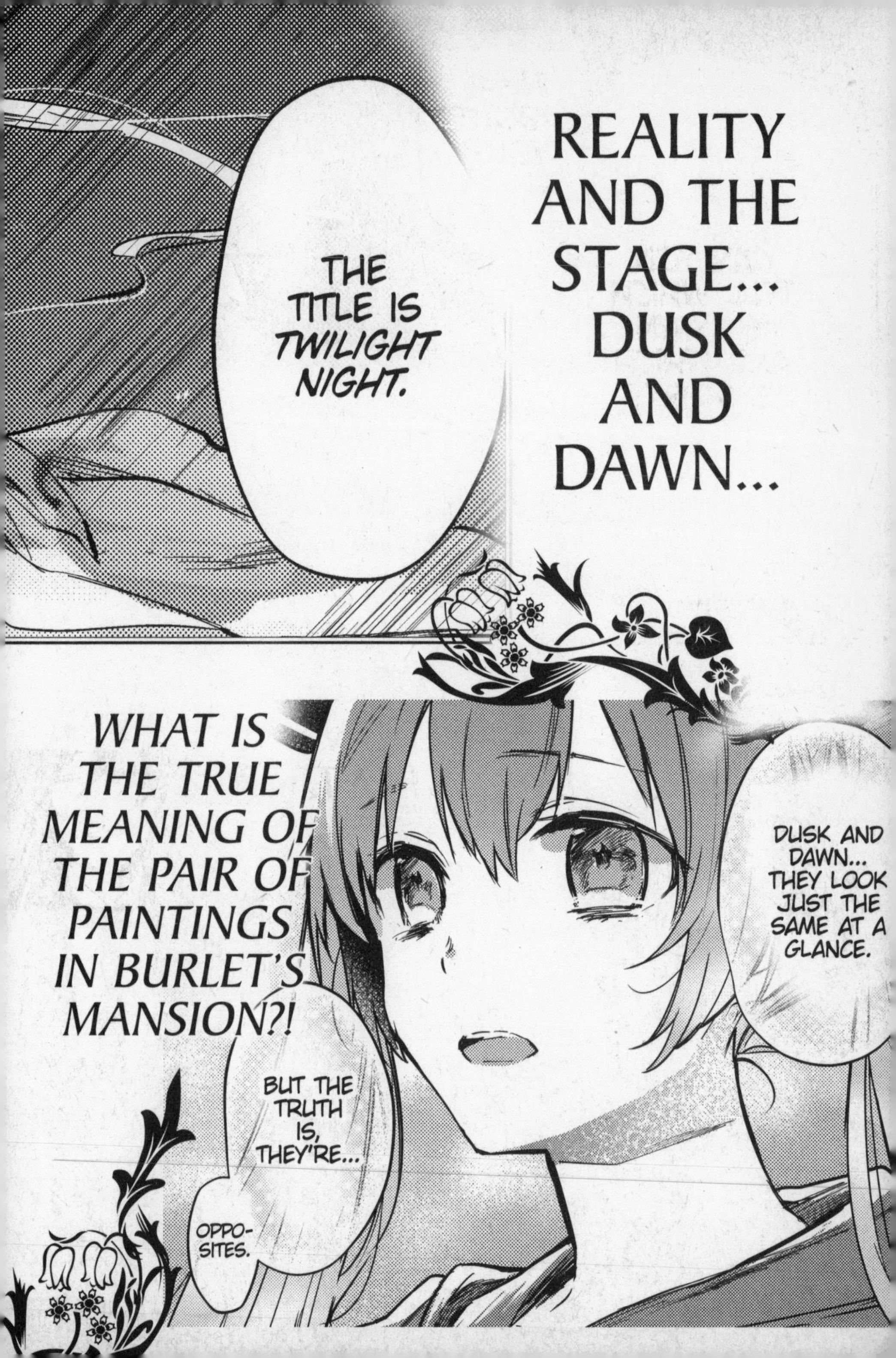
REALITY AND THE STAGE... DUSK AND DAWN...
THE TITLE IS *TWILIGHT NIGHT*.
DUSK AND DAWN... THEY LOOK JUST THE SAME AT A GLANCE.
WHAT IS THE TRUE MEANING OF THE PAIR OF PAINTINGS IN BURLET'S MANSION?!
BUT THE TRUTH IS, THEY'RE...
OPPO-SITES.

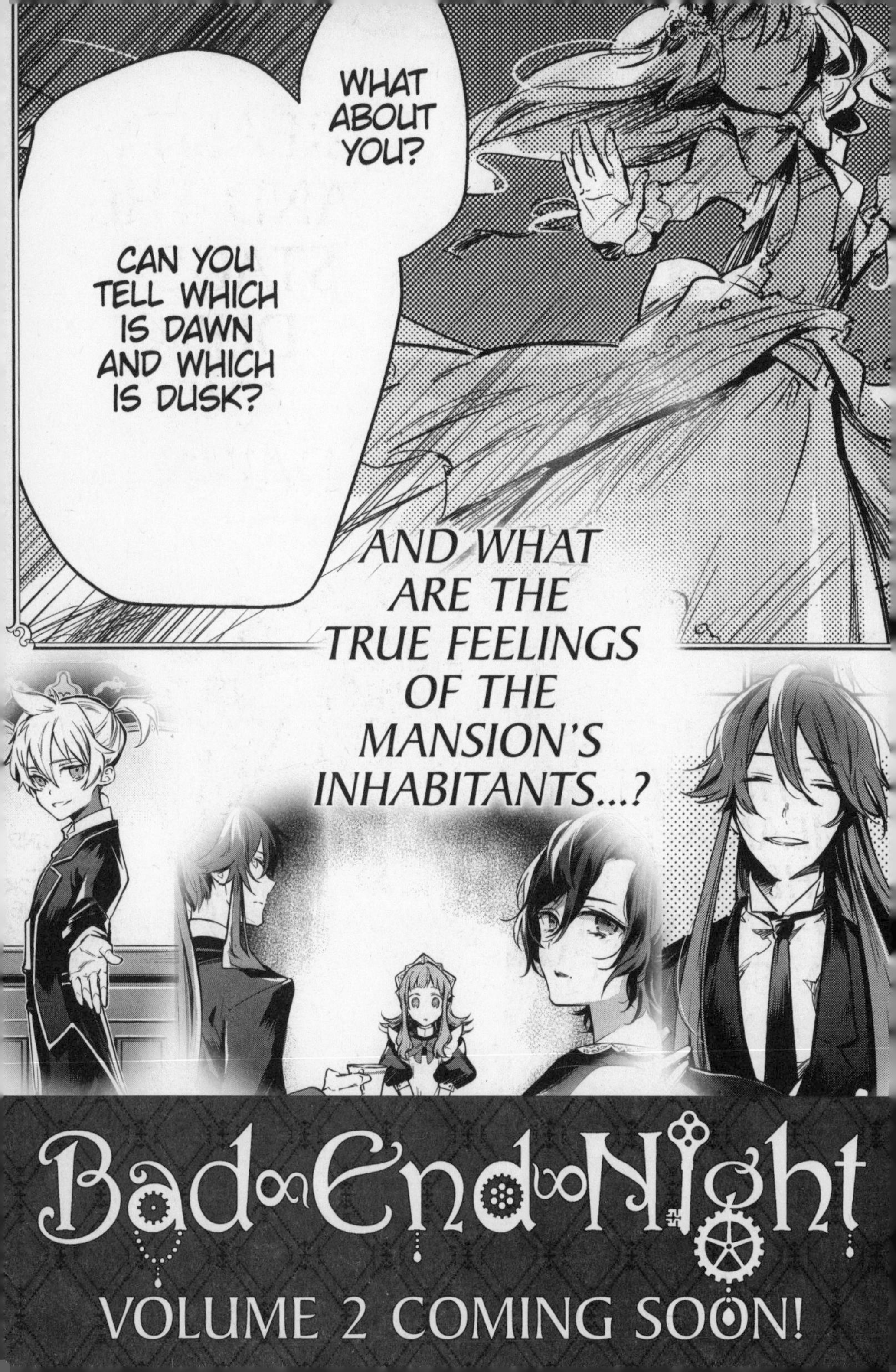
WHAT ABOUT YOU?
CAN YOU TELL WHICH IS DAWN AND WHICH IS DUSK?
AND WHAT ARE THE TRUE FEELINGS OF THE MANSION'S INHABITANTS...?
Bad∞End∞Night
VOLUME 2 COMING SOON!

SEVEN SEAS ENTERTAINMENT PRESENTS

Hatsune Miku
Bad∞End∞Night
Insane Party Vol. 1

story by HITOSHIZUKUP × YAMA △   art by TSUBATA NOZAKI

TRANSLATION
Jenny McKeon

ADAPTATION
Shanti Whitesides

LETTERING AND RETOUCH
Roland Amago
Bambi Eloriaga-Amago

COVER DESIGN
Nicky Lim

PROOFREADER
Tom Speelman

ASSISTANT EDITOR
Jenn Grunigen

PRODUCTION ASSISTANT
CK Russell

PRODUCTION MANAGER
Lissa Pattillo

EDITOR-IN-CHIEF
Adam Arnold

PUBLISHER
Jason DeAngelis

BAD∞END∞NIGHT: INSANE PARTY VOL. 1
© INTERNET Co., Ltd.
© Crypton Future Media, INC. www.piapro.net **piapro**
© HitoshizukuP, Yama · Tsubata Nozaki 2015
First published in Japan in 2015 by ICHIJINSHA Inc., Tokyo.
English translation rights arranged with ICHIJINSHA Inc., Tokyo, Japan.

Seven Seas books may be purchased in bulk for promotional, educational, or
business use. Please contact your local bookseller or the Macmillan Corporate
and Premium Sales Department at 1-800-221-7945, extension 5442, or by
e-mail at MacmillanSpecialMarkets@macmillan.com.

Seven Seas and the Seven Seas logo are trademarks of
Seven Seas Entertainment, LLC. All rights reserved.

ISBN: 978-1-626924-74-1

Printed in Canada

First Printing: May 2017

10 9 8 7 6 5 4 3 2 1

FOLLOW US ONLINE: *www.gomanga.com*

READING DIRECTIONS

This book reads from *right to left*, Japanese style. If
this is your first time reading manga, you start
reading from the top right panel on each page and
take it from there. If you get lost, just follow the
numbered diagram here. It may seem backwards at
first, but you'll get the hang of it! Have fun!!

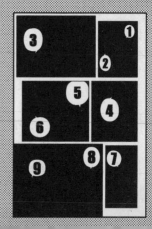